ATMANIRBHAR BHARAT

ATMANIRBHAR BHARAT

Editor

CA Sunil Vashisht

PRABHAT PRAKASHAN

Published by
PRABHAT PRAKASHAN PVT. LTD.
4/19 Asaf Ali Road,
New Delhi-110 002 (INDIA)
e-mail: prabhatbooks@gmail.com

ISBN 978-93-90366-91-0
ATMANIRBHAR BHARAT
Ed. CA Sunil Vashisht

Edition
2025

Price
₹ 1,100.00 (Rupees One Thousand One Hundred only)

Printed at
R-Tech Offset Printers, Delhi

नितिन गडकरी
NITIN GADKARI

मंत्री
सड़क परिवहन एवं राजमार्ग और
सूक्ष्म, लघु और मध्यम उद्यम
भारत सरकार
Minister
Road, Transport & Highways and
Micro, Small & Medium Enterprises
Government of India

सत्यमेव जयते

150 YEARS OF CELEBRATING THE MAHATMA

स्वच्छ भारत
एक कदम स्वच्छता की ओर

Message

It is my firm conviction that we will accomplish the mission of Atmanirbhar Bharat through our entrepreneurship, research and innovation-based scientific & technological advancement and by converting our abundant knowledge into wealth in every sphere of life.

Prime Minister Shri Narendra Modi's Mantra of Atmanirbhar Bharat is aimed at welfare of the humanity deriving inspiration from India's ancient philosophy of 'Vasudhaiv Kutumbakam' (the world is one family).

We in the ministry of Micro, Small & Medium Enterprises (MSMEs), as well as in the Ministry of Road Transport & Highways, have been striving hard to become 'vocal for local' and go 'global' reducing our dependence on imports and promoting exports.

I am glad that my esteemed friend Shri Sunil Vashisht has been vigorously promoting Prime Minister Shri Narendra Modi's vision of new India.

In the endeavour Shri Vashisht first brought out a book 'Towards New India' in 2018.

And now his new publication 'Atmanirbhar Bharat', too, highlights achievements of the Modi government to reach this goal.

I congratulate Shri Vashisht for the stupendous task of compiling such a valuable content into a remarkable book and convey my best wishes to him for great success in life.

New Delhi
20 November, 2020

(Nitin Gadkari)

168, Udyog Bhawan, Rafi Marg, New Delhi-110011, Ph. : 011-23061566, 011-23061739 Fax : 011-23063141
E-mail : min-msme@nic.in

प्रधानमंत्री जन आरोग्य योजना
आयुष्मान भारत
PM-JAY

जय विज्ञान
जय अनुसंधान

सबका साथ, सबका विकास, सबका विश्वास
Sabka Saath, Sabka Vikas, Sabka Vishwas

सत्यमेव जयते

डॉ. हर्ष वर्धन
Dr. Harsh Vardhan
स्वास्थ्य एवं परिवार कल्याण, विज्ञान और प्रौद्योगिकी
व पृथ्वी विज्ञान मंत्री, भारत सरकार
Union Minister for Health & Family Welfare,
Science & Technology and Earth Sciences
Government of India

FTS No. 1959451/2020/HFM
9th November, 2020

Dear CA Sunil Vashishtji,

I am in receipt of your letter dated 'Nil' regarding publishing of your new book 'Atmanirbhar Bharat'.

The ideas presented in the book to further the cause of Atmanirbhar Bharat are praise worthy. I am hopeful that these ideas would stimulate our youth, policy makers as well as general public to strive to fulfil the vision of Atmanirbhar Bharat as enunciated by our beloved Prime Minister. I convey my best wishes for the success of this book.

With regards,

Yours sincerely,

(Dr. Harsh Vardhan)

CA Sunil Vashisht
Editor,
Atmanirbhar Bharat,
B-3, Gulmohar Park,
New Delhi-110049

कार्यालय: 348,ए-स्कंध, निर्माण भवन, नई दिल्ली-110011 • **Office.** 348, A-Wing, Nirman Bhawan New Delhi-110011
Tele: (O) +91-11-23061661, 23063513 • **Telefax:** 23062358 • **E-mail:** hfwminister@gov.in, hfm@gov.in
निवास: 8 तीस जनवरी मार्ग, नई दिल्ली-110011 • Residence: 8, Tees January Marg, New Delhi-110011
Tele: (R) +91-11-23794649 • **Telefax:** 23794640

मंत्री
पर्यावरण, वन एवं जलवायु परिवर्तन,
सूचना एवं प्रसारण और
भारी उद्योग एवं लोक उद्यम
भारत सरकार

सत्यमेव जयते
प्रकाश जावडेकर
Prakash Javadekar

MINISTER
ENVIRONMENT, FOREST & CLIMATE CHANGE,
INFORMATION & BROADCASTING AND
HEAVY INDUSTRIES & PUBLIC ENTERPRISES
GOVERNMENT OF INDIA

Message

When India speaks of becoming self-reliant, it doesn't advocate a self-centred system. In India's self-reliance; there is a concern for the whole world's happiness, cooperation and peace, said Prime Minister Narendra Modi in one of his key addresses outlining the real spirit behind the Atmanirbhar Bharat Abhiyan. When the Prime Minister gave the call of Atmanirbhar Bharat, it was not a mere slogan but an attempt to energise the countrymen to propel themselves to do every bit to realise the goal of self-reliant New India.

In this context, it is heartening to know that one of my valued and fellow party men Suni Vashisht has decided to come up with a new book 'Atmanirbhar Bharat', which is a compilation of the articles written by sector specialists touching upon various dynamics of self-reliant India.

No doubt, this book is a big tribute to the vision of our Hon'ble Prime Minister.

My compliments to Sunil Vashisht and other authors, who have contributed their articles for the book.

With best wishes,

(Prakash Javadekar)

Date: 09.11.2020

।। प्लास्टिक नहीं, कपड़ा सही ।।

पर्यावरण भवन, जोर बाग रोड, नई दिल्ली–110003, फोन: 011–24695136, 24695132, फैक्स: 011–24695329
Paryavaran Bhawan, Jor Bagh Road, New Delhi-110003 Tel.: 011-24695136, 24695132, Fax: 011-24695329
ई–मेल/E-mail: minister-efcc@gov.in

D.O. No. 1448 /VIP/MMA/2020

मुख्तार अब्बास नक़वी
MUKHTAR ABBAS NAQVI

सत्यमेव जयते

अल्पसंख्यक कार्य मंत्री
भारत सरकार
MINISTER OF MINORITY AFFAIRS
GOVERNMENT OF INDIA

10th Nov, 2020

Dear Shri Sunil Ji

I am pleased to know that your new book 'Atmanirbhar Bharat' is going to be published.

I am confident that your book will highlight the efforts of our Hon'ble Prime Minister Shri Narendra Modi Ji towards achieving the goal of 'Atmanirbhar Bharat' (Self-reliant India).

I hope the book will contribute in strengthening our Government's endeavour to fulfil the commitment to 'Atmanirbhar Bharat'.

I wish you all the success for your new book.

With regards

Yours

(Mukhtar Abbas Naqvi)

CA Shri Sunil Vashisht
Editor, Atmanirbhar Bharat

अल्पसंख्यक कार्य मंत्रालय: प्रथम तल, पं० दीनदयाल अंत्योदय भवन, सी.जी.ओ. कम्पलेक्स, लोधी रोड, नई दिल्ली-110003 दूरभाष: 011-24360585, 24360586 फैक्स: 011-24360587
Ministry of Minority Affairs: 1st Floor, Pt. Deendayal Antyodaya Bhawan, CGO Complex, Lodhi Road, New Delhi-110003 Ph.: 011-24360585, 24360586 Fax: 011-24360587
निवास: 7, सफदरजंग रोड, नई दिल्ली - 110029 दूरभाष: 011-23011977, 23011978 **Residence** : 7, Safdarjung Road, New Delhi - 110029 Ph.: 011-23011977, 23011978

संस्थापक : नानाजी देशमुख
अध्यक्ष : वीरेन्द्रजीत सिंह

दीनदयाल शोध संस्थान
DEENDAYAL RESEARCH INSTITUTE

Founder : Nanaji Deshmukh
Chairman : Virendrajeet Singh

7-ई, स्वामी रामतीर्थ नगर, झंडेवाला एक्स., नई दिल्ली-110055
दूरभाष : 011-23526735 • टेलीफैक्स :011- 23510388

7-E, Swami Ram Tirth Nagar, Jhandewala Extn., New Delhi-110055
Phone : 011-23526735 • Telefax: 011-23510388

website : www.dri.org.in • E-mail : dridelhi1@gmail.com, dridelhi@dri.org.in

Message

I am delighted to know that Shri Sunil Vashisht, a well-known Chartered Accountant by profession and more than that, a Social and Political Activist through passion, has complied and edited a bunch of thoughtful articles, 'Atmanirbhar Bharat', contributed by very well-known and respected personalities of their field. I have gone through his first book 'Towards New India', a book dedicated to the vision of our Hon'ble Prime Minister Shri Narendra Bhai Modi. Sh. Sunil Vashisht is a great admirer of Sh. Narendra Bhai Modi, who is undoubtedly the most popular leader and statesman in the world today. I am pleased to see the evolution of Sh. Sunil Vashisht as an author and editor. I am expecting many more publications from him.

This book 'Atmanirbhar Bharat' is an ideal book to understand our Prime Minister's vision of a Self-Reliant India. The articles of the book explain various aspects of 'Atmanirbhar Bharat'. I have great admiration and respect for the contributing authors who did an excellent job of writing thoughtful and informative articles in easy to understand language.

I am happy that Sh. Sunil Vashisht was able to complete this book in spite of all the other demands on his time. I would like to congratulate and extend my best wishes to the Editor, contributing Authors and the Publisher 'Prabhat Prakashan'—the renowned publisher of nationalist publications, for their strenuous efforts in bringing out this publication.

I sincerely believe that this book shall be equally useful to the students, Research Scholars, Social and Political Activists, Policy Makers and Implementers as well as the Common Men.

(Abhay Mahajan)
(Organising Secretary)

Prof. Bhagwati Prakash Sharma
Vice Chancellor

Gautam Buddha University
(Established by UP Act No. (9) of 2002

Foreword

Atmanirbhar Bharat: A Commendable Effort

Bharat is endowed with world's largest youth population, highest area of arable land with most diverse agroclimatic zones and largest number of 63 million MSMEs, in the world. Demographically, the 135 crore population of India is equal to the aggregate populations of all the 50 European and 26 Latin American nations. Till 1500 AD Bharat accounted for more than 34% of world's GDP as stated by the British economic historian, Angus Maddison in his well researched work entitled, 'The World Economic History: A Millennium Perspective', sponsored and published by the OECD nations from their headquarters at Brussels in Belgium.

Presently as well, by optimizing use of the available water resources, India can raise its irrigation potential to 140 million hectares from the 66.7 million hectares as on date. This can enable India to feed almost two-thirds of world-population. The efforts inter alia, are already underway for making the farmers part of food system in adding value to the crop produce within the village, through Farmer Producer Organisations (FPOs) and other integrated rural development interventions being pursued for rural self-reliance.

However, self-reliance should not be misinterpreted in a narrower sense of self-contained and isolationist approach. Bharat has 200+ trade partners with 4450 items of exports and

4343 items of imports. Country has as much as 43% share of trade in GDP. Self-reliance on external front merely connotes that we should be able to meet our import costs from our exports, instead of bridging the burgeoning trade deficit from FDI and FII inflows. Unfortunately,

Greater Noida, District – Gautam Budh Nagar, Uttar Pradesh – 201312
Ph.:+ 91-0120-2344202, Fax:+ 91-0120-2344205 & 15, E-mail: vc@gbu.ac.in;
bpsharma@gbu.ac.in, Website: www.gbu.ac.in

our trade deficit has ballooned 100 fold between 1991-92 to 2018-19 from a paltry sum of $ 1.62 billion to $ 160 billion, which has led to the depreciation of the Indian Rupee from ₹ 18 to ₹ 75 per dollar. In addition to the aforesaid trade deficit, the country has also developed an investment income deficit of $ 40 billion plus, due to FDI stock being double of our Outbound Direct Investment (ODI). Though, in the post Covid-19 period the trade deficit has more than halved. Country's external borrowings are also almost equal to the available forex reserves of $ 560 billion which is also a minor cause of concern. So, a macro-economic balance in trade and current accounts, as well as in the investment incomes arising from the FDI and ODI is also of vital importance.

On having an overview of country's share in the world manufacturing too, we have just 3% share vis a vis 28% of China in the world manufacturing. Within such a small share of 3% in the world manufacturing, almost more than 70% of the manufacturing capacity in most of the sectors, and even cent percent in certain sectors in India is owned and controlled by foreign multinational corporations (MNCs). They just assemble their products in India by bringing all original equipments of the downstream value chain or even the completely knocked down kits from outside, with very little scope for domestic value addition and employment generation. Even Singapore, a city country with just 0.02 percent area 0.4% of our population has 7.5 times high technology exports than us and China has 30 times of our high technology exports. Therefore, Bharat needs to embark on a path of launching and adopting 'Made by Bharat' or 'Made By India' products and brands, instead of continuing to host for the assemble lines being run by the MNCs for most of the products ranging from mobile phones to metro trains. Japanese citizens buy only 4% foreign cars against 96% made by the Japan origin. Same is true with more or less variance for other products. Therefore, Japan has 10% of the share in world manufacturing, inspite of having just 1.6% share in global population. In India hardly 13% cars, being sold by Tata and Mahindra are made by India, rest are foreign brands largely being assembled from a large share of imported components and parts.

Another major cornerstone for self-reliance is to take care of the growing technological obsolescence of many of the 400 industry clusters spread across the country. Efforts are also needed to halt the loss of export markets by these industry clusters. India had 6.5% in world textile exports, which has more than halved. Likewise out of 525 glass manufacturing units in Firozabad, hardly 200 are surviving today and the same is true for other clusters as well. In case of most of the sunrise sectors too, like electrical vehicles, Lithium batteries and other 4IR related technology based products etc. India has not endeavoured to create requisite manufacturing eco-systems for domestic brands and home grown technologies. Manufacturing eco-system for the components and/or products, where we are dependent upon foreign supply chains, especially those located in China is also need of the hour. India has been importing 90% of the solar panels, 30% auto components, 70% active pharmaceutical intermediates, 30% of inorganic chemicals and so on from China. In the area of artificial intelligence, India is already a decade behind in product development. Even in software development as well, it is difficult to find made by India products and brands except a few like Finnacle etc. We have been doing more than two thirds of value addition for SAP-AG, Oracle, IBM and a large number of other foreign majors in software development. But, our share in the world's software product exports is less than 1% in a market of $432 billion. So, 'Made by India' products and brands is the need of hour for self-reliance in the ongoing decade of 2020.

This book entitled 'Atmanirbhar Bharat' encompasses all the facets and dimensions of self-reliance for Bharat, as well as the roadmap to embark upon the path for self-reliance. The undersigned conveys his compliments to CA Sunil Vashisht, the editor of the volume and the learned article/research paper contributors. It would prove to be a torch bearing companion for all the stakeholders and participants, desirous to embark on the way towards self-reliance of Bharat.

Greater Noida
16th November, 2020

(Prof. Bhagwati Prakash Sharma)
(Vice Chancellor)

Preface

Every citizen of India is living the dream of Atmanirbhar Bharat after the earnest call by none other than the Hon'ble Prime Minister of India Shri Narendra Modi. Such a bold invitation during the pandemic calls for contribution from every citizen in each sphere of economic activity. In order to achieve the biggest ever challenge, the nation needs a comprehensible plan to ensure overall development of each and every sector of the economy.

Agriculture remains the backbone of Indian economy accounting for 14 percent of the economy and 42 percent of total employment. Keeping the aim of doubling farmers' income in mind, there is a need to think beyond production and also in terms of value-addition, processing and marketing. Government is offering schemes in all spheres of agriculture and there is a need to make farmers aware about all such schemes for attaining greater benefits.

Ensuring better and free education to all should remain the priority but not the criteria for seeking government jobs. Therefore, the education policy in terms of skill development is a welcome step. Further, framing laws to attract private investment and greater private sector involvement is the need of the hour. Public sector banks need to prioritise lending for developing weaker and prospective sectors of the economy. With greatest ever potential for farm and religious tourism, India can emerge as one of the best tourism destinations in the world.

Bringing prosperity to the lives of thousands of poor people requires strengthening of health sector. Therefore, we need to mobilise resources for optimum utilisation of trained manpower in health sector. The determined efforts of health workers and doctors have resulted in minimising the impact of Covid-19 pandemic and showcasing our strength to manage the difficult situations. To become self-reliant, a country needs to safeguard its territorial jurisdiction which can only be possible through decisive leadership.

No doubt, the challenges in the way of attaining self-reliance are tremendous and we need to focus on diverse issues including skill development through adoption of job oriented education policy, mitigating challenges of World Trade Organisation (WTO), greater participation of private sector in economic activities, enhancing liquidity through development of banking sector, creation of environment for R&D and innovations and a greater use of information and communication technologies. Above all, we need to develop the spirit of nationalism in every citizen to achieve self-reliance at the earliest.

I feel delighted to observe the contributions made by different authors in the book which is a visionary document conceived by Shri. Sunil Vashisht. His vast experience as Director, Syndicate Bank, Chief Editor of 'Rashtriyata ke Swar', Ex Director, Bank of Maharashtra, Advisor, ICAI, District Governor, Lions Club International (2009-10), National President, Rashtriya Vichar Manch, Founder Trustee of Sadbhawna Shanti & Jagrati Mission Foundation, active member of various national level societies and BJP Cell, has made it possible to draft an inclusive plan for achieving self-reliance. I congratulate the contributors and the editor Shri Sunil Vashisht for compiling the virtual roadmap for Atmanirbhar Bharat.

—Prof. J.P. Sharma
(Vice Chancellor)
SKUAST-Jammu

Editorial

God is great. It is a truth that God Almighty is a super power and this Universe is his marvellous creation. During this Corona pandemic time, God has manifested his supreme power to make everybody realize that he is the ultimate power. He is the force who runs this whole Universe and he is the wonderful architect who has created nature to give various colours to the Universe.

During the Corona pandemic, I was confined to the four walls of my house and did not dare to go out. But, I am the kind of a person who can never sit idle. So I conceived an idea in my mind that why not do something to promote the concept of 'Atmanirbhar Bharat' which was just recently mooted by our beloved Prime Minister Shri Narendra Modi to make India a 'Self Reliant Nation'. As I sat down to write my views on it, I suddenly realized that my idea or the vision about the subject is a limited one. With God's grace, I have many friends and associates who could help me a great deal to give the concept the shape of a Book. This was yet another idea which came to my mind that why not approach those friends of mine who are mostly intellectuals and have done well in their respective fields of work, by asking them to contribute their views. I am happy to state that all of them well accepted my request and agreed to contribute to the Book. I am thankful to all of them that they made the task much easier for me by responding positively and thus showing their regard, love and affection for me.

The invaluable contributions made by so many eminent persons have made the Book kind of an 'INDRADHANUSH' by giving it various colours. Different aspects of the concept 'Atmanirbhar Bharat' are covered by them beautifully to give the Readers an idea of the capacity and capability of our Nation to manufacture almost everything indigenously and show to the world our ancient image of a 'Vishwa Guru'. The concept has been visualized in each and every piece of contribution by mentioning therein the actual facts and figures to support the idea of a 'Self Reliant India', as conceived by our PM.

Needless to mention again that the writers of various articles in the Book are experts in their line of activity and keep a high degree of eminence in their subjects. They have risen to the top level positions in their respective fields of work and possess enormous experience. I have no words to honour them. I salute them and convey my thanks for sparing their valuable time, out of their tight work schedules, towards creation of the Book.

The Book is dedicated to our worthy PM Shri Narendra Bhai Modi for his vision of 'Atmanirbhar Bharat', and who is so keen to develop India and strengthen it to the level of a Superpower in the world. I hope the Book shall be of great value to our entrepreneurs and professional who are always thinking of great ideas to take our Industries and Businesses to the next level so as to achieve the goal of all round national development, as envisaged by all great leaders of this country for all the times.

I would also, however, like to clarify that the views, contents and the writings in the Book, as contributed by various persons are of their own and they are solely responsible for them; the Editor and the Publishers have only given them a shape and are not responsible for any of the views and contents.

At the end, I pray to the Almighty that the Book serves the purpose for which it has been devised, and, apart from becoming a good and interesting reading material for the Readers, also becomes a guiding instrument in the hands of those engaged in the work of all round national development throughout the country.

—CA Sunil Vashisht
Editor

From the Desk of Editor

INDIA – TOWARDS NEW INDIA – TOWARDS SELF-RELIANT NEW INDIA is the mission and thought behind this book. Let us make our India a great India "Atmanirbhar Bharat.", where we are able to achieve our targets and goals on our own and our dependency on the world for our needs is minimised.

INDIA, BHARAT and HINDUSTAN are all synonymous for our great country. INDIA was '*sone ki chidiya*' in the past. This country was ruled by outside people and they stole, looted and did their best to weaken the country. But our spiritual strength and dedication towards our country retained its strength. We have always been a great country and now the time has come to unite ourselves in making our country self reliant.

India (1947) Towards NEW INDIA (2014) and towards Atmanirbhar Bharat (2020) was the call given by our worthy PM Shri Narendra Bhai Modiji. It was not only a call from him but it was a mission with the target and determination to take the country towards that direction. I feel it is a responsibility of every Indian to work towards achieving this mission wholeheartedly.

The policies, target and efforts have been planned toward self-reliant NEW INDIA. But so many adverse factors have had their bad effect on global economy, mainly the Corona Pandemic (Covid-19), from which the whole world is struggling till date and we also could not escape from its bad effects even after all planned measures initiated by our PM. Hopefully by the end of 2020, we understand that this bad phase shall be over and again we shall be working for "*Atmanirbhar*" Bharat. Crossing all hurdles towards economic development.

No doubt we have to struggle more to achieve our goal and mission by the planned strategy of our worthy PM Narendra Bhai Modiji who is person of a very strong will-power and very fast in taking timely decisions in the betterment of the country. We are proud of him for taking this country towards the path of progress. We should also acknowledge the efforts of earlier governments who also made a base for growth of India.

Now in this book we have taken the views of various intellectuals who are considered pillars of strength in their respective work areas and have been at helm of affairs in their organisations. The views expressed by these intellectuals are the guiding factors which can shape the country as a self-reliant India as envisaged by our PM Narendra Bhai Modi.

All plus and minus or you can say all positive and negative factors have been discussed as give a shape to the mission and how to proceed further towards self-reliant India. A critical assessment of the facts and figures and situations has been made.

The views expressed in this book are the independent views of the contributors/writer which are edited & compiled by Shri Sunil Vashisht, a Chartered Accountant by profession and Social and political activist who by his ideology and thoughts has devoted most of his life in social service for help of the poor and needy people of this country and also have earlier edited and compiled a book called 'Towards NEW INDIA' in 2018.

Hopefully this edition shall be a fantastic one and useful and shall play a great role in national development and growth of our country for Self-Reliant NEW INDIA Mission of our PM.

To conclude let us join hands in development of our country i.e. India towards NEW INDIA and ultimately towards self-reliant NEW INDIA which is voiced as *Atmanirbhar Bharat*. Let us analyse and understand that not only the government, but people or society as a whole, are also responsible for national development. Both have to play their role to achieve the mission of progress.

Let us strive hard together and make our country—*Atmanirbhar Bharat*.

A Concept of Atmanirbhar Bharat: Its Vision and Mission

The main factor for inspiration and guiding force for compilation of this book is a call given by our worthy PM Shri Narendra Bhai Modi—the call of *Atmanirbhar Bharat.* When the call of *Atmanirbhar Bharat* was made by our PM, I thought that a sincere thought and action at least was required for his mission. I conceptualised the idea and contacted my friends, well-wishers and various Intellectuals in my close circle who could contribute to this onerous task. I was overwhelmed when I received good response to my submission and was finally decided to write on the concept of '*Atmanirbhar Bharat*'. We had to discuss on various topics and various thoughts came to our mind and everyone who was willing to co-operate in this mission started writing with his love and regards towards me and confidence & faith in our PM Modiji's call. I am thankful to all contributors.

A lot has been done since 2014 by the present government led by Modiji and still a lot is yet to be done. A view and revision of thought and plan ahead is necessarily required in 2020, a year full of sorrow due to Covid-19 pandemic and other negative factors. Since 2014 a change has been observed in growth of the country and '*Ek Sunehra Bharat*' or a step Towards New India is visible. In 2019 itself, when the Govt. led by Modiji was formed with full majority, the dream of India becoming '*sone ki chidiya*' or "*Vishwaguru*" was apparent. Let us join hands in converting this dream into a reality.

This book contains various Issues and Matters which relate to Economy, Finance, Banking, Judiciary, Society, Politics and good governance etc. Let us plan for national development and for meeting such challenges undertaken by Modiji.

This book is dedicated to our worthy PM Shri Narendra Bhai Modi, who has an optimistic thought of transformation of India towards New Self-reliant India. He is not only optimistic but has also accepted a challenge of such transformation towards *Atmanirbhar* Bharat. Let us join hands to strength him. May God fulfill our dreams of *Atmanirbhar* Bharat.

—CA Sunil Vashisht
Editor

Contents

Towards Self-reliant New India

—**Sunil Vashisht**

Self-reliant India—'Atmanirbhar Bharat'

Atmanirbhar Bharat is a concept and programme to make India Self-Reliant. We have to understand the concept, mission and vision of our worthy PM Shri Narendra Bhai Modi. He has visualised a New India, a self-sufficient India who can export more and depend less on imports. We have to utilise our resources and struggle hard to achieve that mission. The government alone can't do any miracle but every citizen of this country should explore and strive hard to achieve the said mission. '*Mile sab kuch par kuch karna nahi chahte, aisa chahne waale bhi bahut hain*'

"Jo kabhi Sangharsh se prichit nhi hota,
Itihaas gawah hai wo kabhi charchit nhi hota"

The Prime Minister of India during his address to the nation on 12th May, 2020 put the high aim of '*Atmanirbhar Bharat*' or 'Self-Reliant India' before the 1.3 billion fellow citizens. This call came in the wake of global pandemic-induced lockdown when India was facing challenges to meet the domestic demand for personal protective equipment's (PPE). India quickly took steps and ramped up domestic production of the kits, as all other nations of the world were fighting with the shortage of the PPE kits with an unprecedented health emergency everywhere. There was shortage of the other basic medical equipments also which aggrevated the situation. While recognising the need of necessary goods, the government also calculated the immense possibilities of its vast human resource. It is often said that the huge population of India creates hindrance in the path or to accomplish the goal of ensuring a better life for every citizen. But, it is not at all true. The strength of this population having a great proportion of youth can be utilised as the best human resource to meet the needs of India. The PM devised ways to channelize this human strength of India and sought wholehearted participation from the people with whatever ability or skill they possess.

The 'Self-reliant India' which is in line with '*Make in India*' scheme of the government aims to produce all the essential goods and services within the boundaries of the nation so that people can access them at a cheaper cost. India has been heavily dependent on foreign countries for its everyday consumption needs. The deficit has always been a concern for policymakers as import of pharma products, engineering & machinery goods, mobile phones, computers, solar plates and other equipments etc. causes a heavy burden on the exchequer of the country. The imbalance further escalates the gravity of financial wellbeing of the nation. Prime Minister and his team after meticulous examination of the global as well as Indian trade and finance reached the much appreciable decision. The ultimate vision of the policymakers is to see India as an exporting hub.

The Clarion call of the PM clearly indicates that the government looks forward to move from command and control economy to plug-and-play. It wants to leave conservative approaches behind and build a competitive global supply chain. Along with Covid-19 pandemic, India is fighting with multiple challenges simultaneously including flood, drought, heat-wave, locust attack and earthquake. How long the government can keep waiting for normalcy? There is no certainty. So, instead of waiting for good days, the government this time moved ahead to turn crises into opportunity by making 'India self-reliant'.

The Significance of 'Self-reliant India' Program

Clear than crystal is the fact that post Covid-19 world will not be the same as the impact of pandemic and subsequent lockdown is going to stay for long. The Covid-19 has battered economies, disrupted global supply chains and affected millions of lives across the globe. Countries are trying hard to come out of the immeasurable loss to economy. India can't afford to remain silent; it needs to take constructive steps. To make Indian economy competitive in the post Covid world, utmost attention on skilling, scaling and pushing for growth is inevitable. The country has immense potential to goals and become global solution provider.

Self-reliant program would help in reviving the sectors of Indian economy in short term and in long term it will build capacities and make the country strong enough to face unprecedented situations like Covid. It will not promote protectionism in any way. Rather, it seeks to encourage the budding entrepreneurs from the rural as well as urban centers. The program emphasizes on production locally. The Prime Minister's another appeal to become 'Vocal for Local' further add wings in self-reliant India initiative.

Different places or cities of India are known for the quality production of a particular product, for instance—Mumbai for textile, Vijayawada for auto parts, Varanasi for handloom etc. India needs to create an enabling environment for these industries and promote them to enhance output. Local production of goods will be cost effective, making light on buyer's pocket. The self-reliant India program targets local traders and producers whose participation is essential for the success of the mission. There are examples of countries like China, Vietnam, South Korea and others which emphasised local production and scripted history. They are not only self-reliant but also prime exporters in global trade.

Employment generation has always been a major cancer for governments including central and state governments. It is difficult to provide adequate employment opportunities in public as well as private sectors. The government has limited seats and the educational or skill requirements of private players are high. Self-reliant India can be a boon for a young India. Besides encouraging entrepreneurship, the program will create jobs for all kinds of people-skilled or unskilled. The increased household income will push consumption that will ultimately boost production.

How the Dream Can Be Accomplished?—
A Way Towards Atmanirbhar

> *"Laut aayengi Khushiyaan abhi kuchh Gamon ka shor hai,*
> *zara sambhal kar raho doston ye Imtihaano ka daur hai"*

An aim as ambitious as Self-reliant India can be achieved by channelising all the resources of the country. To reap the benefits of resources, it is important to reach out to masses and convey them the message of the Prime Minister. The government and the ruling are making efforts to create mass awareness and turn the vision into a mass movement. The PM on the occasion of first anniversary of his government during the second term had written about establishing a communication with the people of India about the self-reliant India. The party in power is distributing the letter across the country. It is the best approach to sensitise the people. Today India has a greater proportion of educated and skilled youth. The vast human potential can make anything possible, if utilised best.

The contribution of agriculture and farming sector to GDP has though reduced over the year, but the percentage of population associated with such activities is almost the same. Around 67-68% Indians are dependent on agriculture and its income. This is the reason behind India's higher ranking in global production of various agriculture produce. If the sector is made organised and provided all the infrastructure and incentives, it will do wonders. The government is well aware of this fact and committed to realize its true potential. It is working on another ambitious aim of doubling the income by 2022. Various dedicated online portals have been launched by the government to increase the income of farming families by removing the need of middleman. These portals give farm access to market where they can get the real value of produce. Recently the Union Agriculture Minister has stressed on adopting integrated farming practices to achieve the target of new India. India can gain self-reliance in foodgrains production which are imported from foreign countries and can become the food basket for the world.

The country has witnessed the inception of Agro-Tech companies and other start-ups. The interest of entrepreneurs in agribusiness will take the government's mission ahead. These companies are expected to bring innovative ideas and approaches to boost agriculture sector. Similarly, the food companies can flourish in India. Farmers of the country produce many food grains, fruits and vegetables in greater quantity. Proper storage and processing will not only ensure food safety but also contribute to foreign trade.

Government is a key stakeholder of the program. It is focusing on all the points that need attention, making policy changes and providing financial support. Some noteworthy reforms of the government is decriminalising certain things under the Companies Act changing the definition of MSME, Insolvency and Bankruptcy Code, making coal mining more competitive amendment in Essential Commodities Act, etc. This clearly indicates the intentions of the government. The policymakers are lenient on import, but one can see the import-substitution policies in stimulus package announced during lockdown. It is aimed at boosting export. With the MUDRA loan, the government is encouraging small and medium businesses in India. It also comes up with financial packages as the need arises. It also keeps an eye on interest rates on loan and ensures availability of funds. The government is less concerned about developing required infrastructure to augment growth. It is opting for PPP model for fast completion of infrastructure projects.

The growth of a country in this century heavily depends on technological innovations and advancement. Cutting-edge technologies like Artificial Intelligence (AI), Machine Learning (ML), Robotics, Data Science, Cloud Computing have become important elements of production and service delivery. Besides, the higher penetration of internet and smartphone is equally essential. These technologies will ensure bulk production and also help in post-production activities while maintaining the standard of product. India needs investment in these technologies and the government is working closely with industry leaders, premier institutions and technocrats to create a favourable environment.

The rich demographic dividend of India can be the best companion in this journey to become self-reliant. About 65% of Indian population is below 35, which clearly states that India is young nation. They are likely to remain the major workforce for next 10 years. If these youth are guided well and their potentials are realised at all levels, there will no possibility of falling short of goal. Several MNCs are being led by Indians. It shows the capabilities of the youth in leading a movement. India has educated young population, however, the need of the hour is to help them enhance their skills as per the requirements of the time. Another important aspect of sensitising youth is to ensure equal participation of women.

Initial Success Towards Goal

"Jiska man sachcha, uska har bhav sachcha"
"Phir toh har kaam achchha – sarve bhavantu sukhina"

Since the appeal to work for a self-reliant India, all the stakeholders started looking for how they can contribute in this program. Some of them found their niche and started working. Some gained initial success while others are trying hard. As a result of their efforts, the production of PPE kits and masks reached into lakhs. The producers designed masks with local touch, depicting the rich culture of India and the region. Almost all the requirement of sanitizers have been met domestically. Automobile industry collaborated to produce ventilators and saved millions of lives. These successes have been achieved while following the lockdown norms in between the restricted business activities. So, the stride is large having possibility of meeting desired goals. We have to remember Atalji song *"Aao Phir se Diya Jalaye aur Atmanirbhar ho jaayen."*

□

Editor-in Chief. He is a qualified Chartered Accountant and has been on the board of various Nationalized Banks and PSU's. He is also a social and political activist. He was Ex National Convenor, BJP CA Cell.

Atmanirbhar Bharat as Visualised by Pt. Deendayal Upadhyaya

[Concepts of Pt. Deendayal Upadhyaya's Integral Humanism]

—Amitabh Vashisht & CA Varun Vashisht

It is said that India was once *'Sone ki Chidiya'*. What does it mean? What does it show? This shows that India was the richest country of the world and was not dependant on any other country—that it was rich and *'Atmanirbhar'* in that ancient time. Other nations of the world were acheally dependant on India for their needs.

Individual and Society

Several ideologies of the west are based on the assumption that there is an inherent conflict between the individual and society. These ideologies then take up the cause either of the one or of the other. But the fact is that there is no such inherent conflict between the two entities. The visible entity—the individual—is also the representative of the invisible society. It is through him that the society manifests itself. He is in fact the chief instrument of society, and the measure of its fulfillment. Destruction or constriction of his individuality would leave the society stunted. A flower is what it is because of its petals, and the worth of the petals lies in remaining with the flower and adding to its beauty. Developments of the individual and social good are not contradictory interests.

In the ideology of RSS it has been stressed that there should be an interrelation between individual and society and that the individual should have a commitment towards society. Deendayalji used to say that the role of RSS lies in protecting the individuality of a person and at the same time dedicating it to the good of the society. Even in the midst of individualistic politics, the selfless leadership of Deendayalji developed because of this background provided by the RSS. Hence the importance of his views in this regard. He used to say, "A man's personality is an amalgam of body, mind, intellect and soul. Happiness of the individual means happiness with reference to these constituents of his personality. If we think of only one of these attributes in exclusion of the rest then our thinking will not be perfect. We even take into consideration the previous incarnation. When we think of the happiness of an individual, we do take into consideration these four constituents of his individuality. In the same way we would include these four constituents when we think of the happiness of society. The happiness of the individual from his very birth, depends on the happiness of the society."

All Round Progress of the Individual

An individual is the aggregate of body, mind, intellect and soul. Anyone desirous of all-round progress of the individual must keep in mind all these attributes of his. All of them need to be satisfied. Only then would an individual experience real happiness. This means that both material as well as spiritual progress are to be aimed at. The wherewithal for fulfilling these four-fold wants are material means, peace, enlightenment and a feeling of *tadatmya* (identification). It is the comprehensive nature of this aim which inspires the individual to exert for social good.

The four *Purusharthas of Dharma, Artha, Kama and Moksha* have been conceived as means for the achievement of this twin objective of individual advancement and social welfare. *Dharma, Artha and Kama* sustain one another and are complimentary. To accept any one of them as the sole inspirer of human activity and to evaluate actions by that measure alone, would be to take a lop-sided view of things. However, *Dharma,* being the means for realising *Artha and Kama,* is of prime importance.

Democracy

Democracy or people's rule (*lok-tantra*) is a means for upholding *Lokadhikar* (people's rights) and promoting *Lok-Kartavya* (people's duty). Democracy has to be established not only in the political field but in the economic and social fields as well. In fact democracy is indivisible. It cannot be viewed in fragments. The absence of democracy in any one sphere is bound to affect the growth of democracy in the rest. Tolerance, dignity of the individual and a feeling of identification with the demos, the people—these are the essentials of democracy. Without these, the mere paraphernalia of democracy would be purposeless and if these essentials are there, the institutional form can vary from time to time and from country to country.

The main feature of political democracy is the right to elect representative rulers and to be elected as such. Freedom of occupation and free choice of goods are imperative for economic democracy. And social democracy arises from equality of status and opportunity. Efforts have to be made to ensure that all these rights complement one another and do not detract from the others' effect.

Democracy, equality, national independence and world peace are interrelated concepts. But in the west these concepts have often clashed with one another. The ideas of socialism and one-world government have stemmed from efforts at resolving this conflict. However, they have not only failed to do so but have weakened these concepts and created new problems. *Bharatiya Sanskriti* offers the philosophical substratum on the basis of which these concepts can be harmonised and cherished objectives realised. In the absence of such a basis, human thought and development have been stultified. The basic truths propounded by *Bharatiya Sanskriti* have validity beyond country and age. So, knowledge of these truths will provide a direction not only for our own advancement, but for the world's progress as well.

Freedom

For individuals as well as for nations, freedom is a natural urge. In bondage there is neither happiness nor peace. Along with political freedom economic and social emancipation is also necessary. Non-interference by the state in the natural interests of the individual and society constitutes political freedom. Economic freedom lies in *Artha* not proving an impediment positive or negative for man's progress. Lastly a condition in which society contributes to the individual's natural progress, rather than restricts it, is social freedom. These freedoms accrue to the individual only when the nation as such enjoys them.

Like democracy, freedom too is indivisible. Without political freedom, it is impossible to have the other two freedoms. Without economic freedom, a people cannot have social freedom, and to a great extent political freedom also. And without social freedom, economic as well as political freedom will also lose substance.

Regulation of Economy

As in the realm of politics, so in economic matters, *laissez faire* belongs only to the *Krita-yuga.* It can have relevance only in such an ideal state. Ordinarily, therefore, to ensure proper production, distribution and consumption of wealth, regulation of economy (*Arthayama*) is necessary. For this purpose a variety of institutions has taken shape. On the state too a heavy responsibility rests in this regard.

But to vest the ownership and control of all means of production in the state would lead to the centralisation of economic as well as political power. This would be wrong. It must, however, be admitted that to set the process of economic development moving, to keep the economy on an even keel and for the attainment of the nation's basic objectives the state must undertake in general to plan, direct, regulate and control economic effort and in certain specific spheres and circumstances to accept the responsibility of ownership and management too.

Ownership of Property

The issue of ownership of property is important. Some hold that an individual's right to property is absolute. There are others who consider ownership of property and particularly of means of production, as the root cause of all evil. There are thinkers who subscribe to the view that all property belongs to God and man is but a trustee for the same. As a philosophy, this concept of trusteeship is commendable. But in actual practice, the question would always remain as to what regulations and limitations should guide the trustee's conduct.

An individual or a group of individuals with which the individual is inseparably related in regard to all his needs and activities cannot live without property. With *Karma* (action) is associated the fruit thereof. From freedom to consume and use what one has earned stems the concept of property. Not to consume the entire earnings but to save therefrom is a natural tendency and a national virtue. Property gives to the individual a sense of dignity, security and satisfaction. So property cannot be done away with.

The right to property is subject to social sanction. This concept about property is a fairly complicated one and varies with time, place and object. Differences arise with the varying needs of society. Those who deny society's right to regulate property, simply wish that there should be no change in the concepts about property prevalent at a particular moment. Society has the authority and often it becomes its duty to alter property rights. There is no such thing as an absolute and immutable right of property.

The right of property however will have to be recognised subject to limitations. These limitations are determined in accordance with the needs and life-values of the society and the individual. When affluence of property renders some person indolent or parasitical and its lack deprives others of their independence, it become imperative to regulate property.

Primarily, it is the responsibility of society to provide for the rehabilitation of persons affected by changes in the prevalent concepts of property. But the principle of compensation is essential in view of the definiteness and stability it imparts.

Touchstone of a Sound Economic System

The main desideratum of a country's economic system, as of its polity, should be the all-round development of the individual. Production of wealth aims primarily at giving happiness to man. Human labour is the primary means of production. The objective of man's economic activity is to exploit natural resources in an endeavour to fulfil his requirements. That system, therefore, is the best which aids him to fulfil these requirements as also promotes his all-round welfare. A system which advances his economic good but impedes his progress in other directions cannot be considered beneficial. The focal point of interest for every economic system should be man.

The capitalist system of economy which accepts the 'economic man' as the central point of all its activities is inadequate. The selfish desire to acquire more and more profit is the motivating force in this system, with competition as its regulator. This does not conform to the *Bharatiya* philosophy. Socialism originated in reaction to the problems created by Capitalism. Its objectives are commendable but in its end-result, it has failed to profit mankind. The reason is that the analysis of society and individual by Karl Marx, the profounder of scientific socialism, is basically materialistic and so inadequate. The concept of class-conflict cannot give rise to a spirit of spontaneous and permanent cooperation.

Capitalism and socialism differ in their view of property. But both lead to its centralisation and monopolisation. So man is neglected under both.

We need a system in which man's own initiative remains unobstructed but in which, in his relation with the rest of society, human values do not suffer. This objective can be fulfilled by a decentralised economy.

Decentralised Economy

Concentration of power is repugnant to democracy and human freedom. Subject to considerations about national unity, economic power should be decentralised both horizontally as well as vertically. The process of industrialisation in the West has led to concentration of power. The institutions of public limited Company, Managing Agency, Holding Company, etc. have furthered this accumulation of wealth and power in a few hands. Most of the evils of capitalist economy owe to centralisation. Socialist system saw no evil in this centralisation. They simply sought to transfer the ownership of capital from private hands to the state. In fact under a socialist regime both economic and political powers are concentrated in the same hands, and therefore, evils due to concentration become even more accentuated. These ills can be remedied only through decentralisation. Accordingly social and economic institutions will have to be recognised. The latest inventions of science and technology favour decentralised industries. Decentralisation is highly congenial to the all-round development of human personality. Small scale mechanised industries, small trades and farms that can be run and managed under individual, family or cooperative ownership should be the basis of our economy. Large units should be exception to this rule.

Criteria of Progress

It is the responsibility of society to arrange for the upkeep of every child that is born, and to provide him with education which would enable him to develop his individuality even as he contributes to the well-being of society as a responsible member. It is the responsibility of society again to assure every able-bodied person employment and adequate leisure and every person a living. Every civilised society fulfils these obligations in some form or the other. In fact, these have become the main criteria of progress. Therefore, right to a minimum living standard, education, employment and social security and welfare will have to be accepted as fundamental rights.

The Root of our Problems—Neglect of Self

It is essential that we think about our national identity, without this identity there is no meaning of independence, nor can independence become the instrument of progress and happiness. As long as we are unaware of our national identity, we cannot recognise or develop all our potentialities. Under alien rule, this identity is suppressed. That is why nations wish to remain independent so that they can progress according to their natural bent and can experience happiness in their endeavour. Nature is powerful. An attempt to go against nature or to disregard her leads to troubles. The natural instincts cannot be disregarded but it is possible to elevate this nature to the level of culture. Modern psychology informs us how a person begins to suffer from different mental ailments when his various natural instincts are suppressed. Such a person remains restless and dejected. His abilities slowly deteriorate and become perverted. The nation too, like the individual, becomes a prey to numerous ills when its natural instincts are disregarded. The basic cause of the problems facing Bharat is the neglect of its national identity.

A majority of those who lead the nation today as well as those who take active interest in the affairs of the country are not sufficiently aware of this root cause. Consequently, opportunists with no principles reign in the politics of our country. Parties and politicians have neither principles nor aims nor a standard code of conduct. A person feels nothing wrong in leaving one party and joining another. Even alliances and mergers of parties or their bifurcations are dictated not by agreement or by differences in principles but purely by gains in elections or in positions of power. In 1939, Shri Hafiz Mohammed Ibrahim was elected on the Muslim League ticket. Later on, when he joined the Congress, he resigned in pursuance of the healthy principles of public conduct, sought re-election on the Congress ticket and was once again elected. In 1948, when Socialists left Congress and founded the Socialist Party, all those who were members of legislatures resigned and fought elections on socialist tickets. But thereafter this healthy tradition was forgotten. Now there is complete licence in politics. As a result, in the public mind there is distrust for everyone. There is hardly any person whose integrity is beyond doubt in the public mind. This situation must be changed. Otherwise unity and discipline cannot be established in the society.

Priorities of Economic Programmes

According to Deendayal, a good economy should strive for a balanced development of agriculture, industry, trade and services. However, priorities are to be fixed for a rapid economic development. Deendayal has talked of the following priorities:

- Eradication of Poverty
- Regulation of needs requirements (Standard of living)
- Surplus of Consumption Goods
- Minimum Needs
- Self-Reliance in Foodgrains
- Integral Humanism

The individual occupies a pivotal position in our system, According to the principle of *'Yatpinde tad brahmande'* (what is in microcosm is also in macrocosm), individual is the representative and chief instrument of society. Material wealth is a means to man's happiness and not an end in itself. But a system which is based on the assumption of a mass-man and fails to take into account the living man having an individuality characteristically his own is not adequate. Inadequate also is a system which looks just at one attribute of man and fails to take a comprehensive view of him as an organic being comprising of *Shareer, Mana, Buddhi* and *Atmaa* having a number of urges requiring to be fulfilled by the *Purusharthas.* Our ideal is the integral man who has the potential to share simultaneously in numerous individual and corporate entities. Integral Humanism is the corner-stone upon which our entire system needs to be built.

There have been a number of schools that have propounded humanism. But their thinking has been rooted in Western philosophies and so it is essentially materialistic. These thinkers have not been able to offer any philosophical explanation for the ethical nature or behaviour of man. If you deny spiritualism, then human relations and behaviour and the relationship between man and the Universe cannot be explained.

Happiness of an Individual

We have thought of life as integrated not only in the case of collective or social life but also in the individual life. Normally an individual is thought of in the physical bodily form. Physical comfort and luxury are considered happiness. But we know that mental worry destroys bodily happiness. Everyone desires physical comfort. But if a person is imprisoned and there he is given the finest of foods will he be happy? A person does not experience joy on getting nice food if it is also accompanied by a few abuses. There is a well-known incident in Mahabharata. When Lord Krishna went to Hastinapura as an emissary of the Pandavas, Duryodhana invited him to enjoy his hospitality. Lord Krishna declined his invitation and went instead to Vidura's home. Overjoyed by the visit of this much-revered guest, Vidura's wife served the banana skins while throwing away the kernel. But Lord Krishna enjoyed even the meal of banana skin. That is why it is said, "even a modest meal served with dignity and affection tastes better than the best delicacies served with disrespect." It is necessary, therefore, to take note of the mental happiness.

Similarly, there is an intellectual happiness which too must be considered. Even after a person gets comforts for the body, and prominence, affection etc., which please the mind, but if he is involved in some intellectual confusion he is reduced to a state almost similar to madness. And what is madness itself? A lunatic may have all physical comforts, he may be perfectly healthy and properly cared for by his relatives; but he does not possess intellectual happiness. Intellectual peace is also essential and important. We will have to take all these things into consideration.

Integral Humanism—The Only Way

Integral Humanism must necessarily make a balanced appraisal of both Bharatiya as well as Western ideologies. On the basis of this evolution it seeks to show a way which would make man progress further from his present position of thought, experience and achievement.

The western world has achieved great material progress but in the field of spiritual attainment it has not been able to make much headway. India on the other hand lags far behind in material advancement and so its spiritualism has become a hollow-sounding word. "*Nayam atma balheenana labhyah*" (The soul cannot be realised by the weak)-There can be no spiritual salvation without material prosperity. It is necessary, therefore, that we strive for strength, and material happiness, so that we may be able to build up national health and contribute to the progress of the world instead of being a burden on it.

Integral Humanism is the name we have given to the sum total of various features of *Bharatiya Sanskriti*—abiding, dynamic, synthesising and sublime. This is the ideal which determines our direction. But our idealism does not mean any doctrinaire obtuseness. An ideal has to be translated into practice. Our programme, therefore, has to be grounded in realism. Indeed realism is the forte of our programme, the measure of our achievements and the touchstone of our ideal.

□

Co-editor is a graduate in Science and a social activist. Presently working as General Manager in Deendayal Research Institute (DRI) and believes in the ideology of Bharat Ratna Rashtrarishi Nanaji Deshmukh.

Co-editor is B.Com, FCA, ACS, LLB, DISA (ICAI), CCA (ICAI) and FAFD (ICAI). He is also a qualified Insolvency professional and working as a finance consultant and auditor for various banks and corporates.

Management Challenges for Atmanirbhar Bharat

—Mrutyunjay Mahapatra

The Government of India, under the leadership of our Prime Minister, announced implementation of a slew of measures under the umbrella of *'Atmanirbhar Bharat'* or self-reliant India. The measures include financial, legal and structural liberalisation and relaxations.

The intentions of the policy makers are noble. Like everything in this world, the devil lies in the details. On the ground, implementation will be done by the managers at various levels of enterprises. The enterprises are independent of ownership and the industry or sector they operate. Question is whether the existing and traditional modes of management shall suffice? The question requires some analysis.

Let us first see what the headlines of Atmanirbhar Bharat are.

The Prime Minister announced it in two different formats. First, in his address to the nation on 12 May 2020, while announcing the large economic package, which was subsequently detailed by the FM, she made a reference of the following key thematic approaches:

1. Economy
2. Infrastructure
3. Systems and Technology
4. Demography and democracy
5. Demand, especially indigenous demand

Later, addressing the 125th anniversary of Confederation of Indian Industry on 2nd June 2020, the PM assured the Industry leaders that the growth shall be back, exhorted them on five 'I's, which are as follows:

1. Intent
2. Inclusion

3. Investments
4. Infrastructure
5. Innovation

Both these might have sounded a little different in language and articulation, but essentially pointed towards building back the economy based on India's own power of consumption and generation of economic activities. When he spoke of systems and technology, it not only meant massive computerisation for enhancing productivity, but also pointed to disrupting existing products' processes and technology to reach newer heights of excellence. So how to achieve will depend on many things; capital, plans, policy, participation and project management. However, the key shall be the management quality and involvement. This article attempts to deal with some of these challenges and suggests ways to move ahead.

The Modernisation Challenges

The first and foremost shall be the challenge of technology and modernisation. Technology brings efficiency of delivery and makes services and citizen-oriented processes predictable and transparent. So, inducting cost-efficient technologies is just one part of the whole game, but it must start with modernisation of mindsets and governance.

The first management challenge for the new India, which is self-reliant, is creating a workplace which is truly modern and different. As GE former CEO Jeff Immelt once said: "Nobody wants to work at an old-fashioned company. Nobody wants to buy products from an old-fashioned company. And nobody wants to invest in an old-fashioned company."

To understand this challenge succinctly, we must appreciate the difference between an old-world company and a modern company.

Every organisation in Atmanirbhar Bharat must begin with its people because the mindset of the people will make all the difference. In a modern company, every employee must act and feel like an entrepreneur. What does this mean? This means that rigours and disciplined execution must co-exist with the ability of extreme uncertainty in the ecosystem, which is likely to be the scenario in the next few years in our country. This will also require the ownership structures to divest and move from a single or limited hand type to a widely federated ownership of employees and other stakeholders. Decision making must be enabled to be discussed in employee forums, and not limited to the board rooms, or only a handful of the senior management functionaries.

In traditional and existing organisations of our country, the budgeting and performance management is mostly incremental. The controls and enablers are mostly short-term oriented. The Indian mindset of '*Jugaad*' has helped us in quick deliveries, but is unlikely to be a foundation of a self-reliant India. Impact analysis must come to board rooms, as well as strategy verticals of enterprises. Long-term results in modern organisations are equally important as short-term margins, because a self-reliant India is supposed to be designed and delivered as a '*Lambi race ki ghoda*'. A key ingredient of long-term is sustained and sustainable innovation. The mindset of the existing businesses and managers must go forward to embrace new things, and get beyond the comfort zones to a spirit of experimentation and degree of adventurous progress. All over the world, adventures with a benevolent objective have been the harbingers of prosperity, and the new India must anchor its progress on innovation.

In the last two or three decades, managements have been predominantly migrated to siloed functional expertise. In these, projects travel in typical waterfall fashion, at every stage hibernating for non-value and bureaucratic approvals. This must give space to collaborative and cross functional teams, which in the language of the agile are known as squads and tribes. Iteration and scientific dissection and critiquing must be integral to organisations in the new India that we are dreaming of.

Large programmes, transformational, scaled up to dazzle and impress are the hallmark of old companies. We know very well that they run into various cost and time overruns. Many times, stakeholders are wary of the ultimate delivery. In modern organisation, rapid experimentation and small projects with modular implementation as the DNA is defining the new world of impact with profit.

Technology, legal and finance functions combined with compliance, enforce processes in the old type organisations. Many times, processes overshadow and subsume time and energy of the enterprise. As compared to this, in the new India, the key aim must be serving the customers and driving the business results.

In a traditional company, accounting principles such as ROI and market shares, drive the dialogue. Many times, data and MIS is messaged to impress the supervisors. This often results in analysing things post facto and making small optical corrections. As compared to this, in the new, old & new matrices in terms of future impact and innovation quotient analysis must be incorporated into corporate and government working. For example, cash-flow, rather than post deprecation and tax profit, is to be the measure for the success of the new enterprise.

Focus with specialisation, rather than multitasking of generalists, is likely to be the big shift in the management style. Today in enterprises, non-implementers have a lot of say in project progress. As Eric Ries mentions in his book *The lean startup,* the modern company ethos have to be based on 'Think big, start small and scale fast'.

In the new age, barriers to entry via regulation and capital requirements are unlikely to be there. Competition must be encouraged to bring in quality and acceptability in the global markets. Thus, in the new age, continuous differentiation is likely to be the survival tool, rather than size and past glory. Legacy organisations must rediscover and reposition themselves, lest they face extinction.

Another thing that will bring the challenge to the old is the data use and analytics. Older organisations are semi-literate in data and are managed based on impressions and intuitive thinking anchored on past used cases. Counter-intuitive incidents and market force plays, although uncomfortable, are a must. These will require MIS to be robust and analytics as the key foundation of decision making and repositioning of strategy.

The managerial mindset also will depend on a greater acceptance of failure as the agile method of working in organisations, where innovative, small projects are taken up fast and are either taken forward or dropped based on continuous measurement of progress to customer-oriented objectives and outcomes.

The Challenges of Strategy before the Management

Strategy has always been the core concept of a business. It differentiates the organisation and makes it robust for dealing with the uncertainty. Strategy converts concepts into performance and enables organisations to exploit the opportunities.

Whether the existing strategies of Indian businesses in the context of Self-reliant India needs relook? Of course, they do. The context in which the set of initiatives have been announced, are as follows:

- Rapid change and deep uncertainty, both due to Covid and due to other factors, like technological disruptions and deep competition.

- The demographic dividend that all of us speak of also brings in rising aspirations and understanding the millennial mindset. 'Inclusion' needs to be a part of strategy and the core of the management philosophy, rather than as part of seminar themes or CSR objectives.
- The rapid shift in income generation points and the extent of urbanisation also is defining the approach to managing enterprises.
- The 'Make in India and Made for the World', if to be translated into a reality, global competitiveness must be established, end-to-end.
- Infrastructure, in the changed context, must be understood as the ecosystem, and not just the roads, airports, ports, power and telecom. Therefore, API (Application Programming Interface) middleware based on European or global standards, an optical fibre backbone and similar things must be called the systemic infrastructure. Every enterprise must build comprehensive ecosystem for collaborative contribution to the system.

The challenges of strategy will get compounded as manual workers will gradually convert into knowledge workers, and the HR factor shall attain a dynamic equilibrium.

The Challenges of re-skilling and Quicker Integration

India, in the next decade will require massive re-skilling. Entrepreneurship must be encouraged, as much as apprenticeship. One study shows that India has just 5 lac apprenticeship, whereas Germany, which is at the forefront of quality manufacturing, has 5 million (50 lac). Quality manufacturing requires top skilled workers to harness the power of industry 4.0, which is a continuous collaboration between human beings, computers and manufacturing lines, and between private and public sectors.

One of the key factors in integration is the development of templates and institutions of learning. The management in academia, industry and the government have to work synergistically to achieve this.

Project and Change Management Challenges

Systematic management, even in agile product conceptualisation and delivery methods, can never be over emphasised. Change management methods never lose relevance. However, in the context of resilient and self-reliant India, which aims at promoting and furthering the entrepreneurial mindset, what we need to do is that managerial routine must also include project management discipline. Change management, its documentation and making the communication transparent as well as participative, is likely to be a big challenge.

Conclusion

As it is said, 'The devil is in details.' Concept of Atmanirbhar Bharat is laudable. The management challenges are many, beginning from the mindset change to ecosystem change, and repositioning of strategy. Still, India has no dearth of skills and change agents, who could orchestrate innovative solutions. The key to success will be how collaboratively and quickly we act.

□

A senior Banker till recently heading one of the oldest and trusted large Banks of India as its CEO and is credited with all-round transformation of the Bank. Member of Insurance Advisory Council of India. In the past, headed global strategy, payments, transactions, and transformation programmes of SBI as its Head of Strategy and Chief Digital Officer.

Atmanirbhar Bharat: The Second Most Seminal Moment in India's Recent Economic History

—Siddharth Zarabi

It has been seven years in the making, since India under Prime Minister Narendra Modi first signalled intent to undertake a serious push, towards import substitution as part of the grand 'Make in India' strategy. The initial, tentative, steps were taken in the central government's Budget of 2015 with the then finance minister, the late Arun Jaitley, enacting an enabling provision to hike the import duty on iron and steel by as much as 50 percent. This was at a time, when steel imports had surged to nearly 8.4 million tonnes.

By 2017, the focus on using import duties as a tool to nudge foreign manufacturers to undertake manufacture in India saw hikes on items as diverse as microwaves, television sets, LED lamps and smartphones. The most recent Budget by finance minister Nirmala Sitharaman saw hikes in customs duty on over four dozen items, as part of the continuing import substitution strategy of the 'Make in India initiative'.

It is not as if earlier governments had not hiked customs duties. In 2012, Finance Minister Pranab Mukherjee doubled the import duty on gold to 4 percent, leading to a month-long protest by jewellery manufacturers in many states. Post India joining the WTO, import duty hikes have been sporadically effected, primarily as a source of revenue or for protecting domestic manufacturers, like steel companies, from Chinese imports.

There is a crucial difference in the strategy followed by the NDA government. Since coming to power in 2014, the Modi government is estimated to have hiked import duties on over 3000 goods.

This is where Prime Minister Narendra Modi's call for '*Atmanirbhar Bharat*', or a self-reliant India echoes strongly.

The forceful nature of Modi's address and the masterly linking of the self-reliance theme with the sentiment against globalisation in the post-Corona world order, could well be the second most seminal moment in India's recent economic history after Narasimha Rao allowed his finance minister Manmohan Singh to begin the process of opening up India's economy to global capital, supplies and technology.

This shift, coming as it does after three decades of that watershed moment in India's history, would have profound consequences for our industrial future.

Let us analyse the announcement through the prism of import dependence and the consequent drain on foreign exchange. A vast majority of India's import bills are on account of crude oil, gold and information, communications and technology (ICT) items.

I am purposely leaving out Gold and Crude Oil, for which there is simply not enough domestic production for any worthwhile self-reliant 'manufacturing'. This leaves us with ICT as the biggest sector to analyse the justification of the proposed move.

India imported around $ 400 billion of ICT products last year. As we fight the Coronavirus, the difficulties of supply chain disruption amidst the lockdown led to the realisation, that for each small item, whether critical or not, there is excessive dependence on China.

It is not as if Modi suddenly sprung the concept on the country. He has been dropping hints including as recently as 24 April when he, while interacting with gram panchayat members, said, "the biggest lesson the Covid-19 pandemic has taught India is to become self-reliant".

So, What is the Reality of ICT Imports?

ICT and telecom are areas where even after huge domestic potential, the goods are imported, because of faulty policies since the last 20 years. In this sector, other than mobile handsets, the balance of trade position is extremely disappointing with the ratio of imports being 10 times higher than exports, as can be seen from granular goods classification data maintained by the Department of Commerce.

Further, most imports are classified under the heading of 'others' to take advantage of the prevailing zero percent basic Duty structure under that respective heading. On careful review of the import data, it is seen that when duty was imposed on import of some of the non-ITA products, the import of the modules and parts/equipment in 'other' category increased substantially.

Despite many industry associations advocating a course correction, policies have not changed, as is evident from customs data. Given the new direction that Prime Minister Modi has set for self-reliance and import substitution, it would make sense for an immediate hike in the customs duty structure for the ICT sector to ensure self-reliance and security of India. Accordingly, all products imported under 'other category' to circumvent duty, should be brought under the 40 percent tariff structure. (There are no fears of smuggling as these goods are bulky and cannot be brought in a pocket or on the body of a person like gold.) Further, to promote design-led manufacturing in India, the Basic Customs Duty on non-ITA products should be enhanced to flat 40 percent.

Similarly, the basic customs duty on anything assembled, imported part or full, assembled printed circuit boards (PCBs), modules and sub-systems should attract 40 percent custom duty to discourage any imports in these categories of items.

To encourage the manufacturing of components ecosystem in India, customs duty on components should be gradually increased, starting from 10 percent from base year to 40 percent by the fourth year. This will promote component manufacturing in India. For fully imported products, the basic customs duty should be hiked to 75 percent in base year, and be further increased by fourth year to 100 percent, to ensure that all such importers utilise the three years to set up manufacturing units in India. The machinery for production of items should be kept at 10 percent in the base year, and then subsequently increased every year to also encourage the domestic manufacturing of the machinery that is used to produce.

Further, it is also important to immediately clarify the definition of 'importer', 'assembler' and 'manufacturer', as currently, there is no such official classification in India. The lack of a definition allows all importers, system integrators to incorrectly be portrayed as manufacturers. Thus, they falsely sell all imported products as 'Made in India'. The ICT sector is one area where despite huge domestic potential, most goods are imported. One of the reasons is that India does not have a clear definition of what is a 'manufacturer' in India.

Majority of importers or assemblers bring in the imported equipment by simply changing the sticker and declaring it as 'manufactured in India'. A similar strategy is adopted for goods in semi-knocked down (SKD) condition, where after local assembly, the product is declared as 'manufactured in India'. Such importers, system integrators, assemblers just promote foreign products and have no interest to invest in research and development (R&D) within India.

Such companies enjoy a huge advantage over those few Indian companies, who have tried to keep the flag of manufacturing alive in India all these years. These few, true Indian manufacturing companies, despite investing money in R&D and product development, lose out due to a policy and bureaucratic approach, that only promotes traders over true manufacturers.

In addition, it is essential that the authorities increase the component of preferential market access (PMA) purchase to 100 percent as per the existing Public Procurement (reference to Make in India), Order 2017 (PPP-MII Order), for all ICT products.

In 2017, the NDA government came out with a policy that specified the strategic list of items for public procurement for any project, funded wholly or partially, by the government (central or state). However, implementation in true letter and spirit remains pending. In addition, the government should also consider amending and mandate that all public procurement of domestically manufactured items be 100 percent from 1 April, 2021. This can be carried out via an amendment to 2017 Order, with time being provided for implementation.

Taken together, these changes will also ensure massive job creation and save hundreds of billions of dollars in foreign exchange and boost reserve capital accumulation in the Indian banking system.

□

A senior Indian journalist who is credited with multiple content and platform innovations in the fiercely competitive Indian news industry, and has deep knowledge and wide experience across the entire media value chain including print, television, digital and social media.

Making Indian Farmers Atmanirbhar

—Subhash Garg

India used more than 85% of its approximately 110 million hectares of cultivated area at the time of independence to produce about 50 million tons of foodgrains. More than 70% of the people employed worked in agriculture either as peasants or labourers. They worked on very small tracts of land, more often than not as unrecognised tenants. Indian farmers typically converted their labour in food. Farmers' lot was truly miserable. At the stroke of independence in 1947, India was a massively poor country. Indian agriculture was very traditional, which did not even produce enough foodgrains for feeding India's teeming millions.

First three plans (1951-1966) did not undertake any fundamental reform of agriculture system and essentially continued with the pre-independence system of agriculture production. During this first phase of Indian agriculture, India relied on three strategic interventions to realise its goal of raising annual foodgrains production to 100 million tons. First, bring in additional area under cultivation. Second, increase irrigation. Third, expand availability of fertilisers and improved seeds.

Only marginal gains were made in agriculture and food situation of India during the first 20 years, which were also more than neutralised by increase in population. On the whole, the first phase of agriculture development programmes and policy (1947-64) was quite a failure. It did not contribute much to make India atmanirbhar (self-sufficient) even for food. Actually, 1965 turned out to be the year of worst food disaster for India.

India changed the foodgrains development strategy massively in the second phase (1967-2002). The new strategy was based on three new principal planks-productivity, price and ground water irrigation. This strategy based on wide adoption of semi-dwarf varieties succeeded brilliantly.

The seeds of this spectacular performance were sown in 1963, when celebrated agriculture scientist Norman Borlaug visited India and agreed to supply seeds of Mexican semi-dwarf wheat varieties to India. Indian scientists, actively supported by the government, worked hard and successfully demonstrated the suitability of Mexican seeds for high yield wheat in India. They also bred Indian varieties, crossing Mexican seeds with Indian varieties. Semi-dwarf varieties of rice came from the east. India introduced these high yielding varieties on a big scale in 1968-69.

Foodgrain production crossed 100 million tons in 1970-71, and 200 million tons in 1998-99. Foodgrain yields, which were less than 700 kg per hectare in 1966-67, crossed 1000 kg per hectare first time in 1978-79, and 1700 kg per hectare in 1999-2000. Foodgrain yields more than tripled only in 50 years. India became atmnirbhar in food and agriculture by the end of 20th century.

Prior to 1965, Government of India undertook no price support operations in India. The MSP system got introduced in 1965 by implementing the recommendations of L.K. Jha Committee. Food Corporation of India was also established in 1965. The MSP system has got fine-tuned over the years. The Government decided in 2017-18 to provide at least 50% profit over cost of cultivation for all the MSP crops.

The foreign exchange crisis of 1991 did not have its roots in agriculture. 1991 reforms were essentially industrial sector reforms, though depreciation of rupee did benefit agriculture exports as well. The reforms of 1990s literally ignored agriculture sector.

Agriculture programmes saw considerable consolidation and diversification in the last phase of agriculture policy and programme development (2000 to continuing). However, most agriculture development programmes of today are the repackaged versions of the programmes initiated in the second phase (1965-2000).

Agriculture marketing regulatory interventions in India were started for protection of consumers' interests and streamlining supplies of agricultural raw materials to industries. The first legislation to provide for regulation of agriculture markets was the Berar Cotton and Grain Market Act 1887, which became the model for enactment of similar legislations in other parts of the country. Quite a few states enacted such legislations in the sixty years' period before independence.

APMCs, which are essentially spot wholesale marketplaces for agriculture produce, were designed to serve three broad functions-a,. to create a market place for agriculture produce, b,. to regulate the contracts, practices and intermediary payments to create a fair and low-cost trading regime for farmers and c,. to generate resources for the government to invest in agriculture infrastructure. The APMCs development in the country in the first 50 years, seemed to serve all these objectives. A big structural mistake, however, turned APMCs into a stranglehold around the farmers' neck over this period of five decades. This fundamental mistake was total monopolistic nature of APMC system.

The APMC reforms initiated in 2003, did not address the principal flaw in the agriculture produce marketing-absence of competitive markets, one-size-fits-all type of over regulation of markets implemented in a decentralised manner by organised vested interests, lack of standardisation and aggregation of farmers' produce, leasing of land not being legally permitted and exclusion of processors and wholesalers on account of storage restrictions. These APMC reforms, consequently, did not make much difference.

Farmers' Produce Trade and Commerce (Promotion and Facilitation) Ordinance, 2020 promulgated on 5th June, 2020 strikes at the root of APMCs' monopoly over wholesale agriculture produce trading. This Ordinance also virtually abolishes the system of mandi fees. The Ordinance is truly revolutionary in respect of these two fundamental deformities of agriculture produce trading system in the country. The Ordinance does not directly dismantle APMC system (the APMCs continue to exist as they are presently within the confines of their physical market yards), but has the potential of massively disrupting them indirectly.

The Ordinance-The Farmers (Empowerment and Protection) Agreement on Price Assurance and Farm Services Ordinance 2020-promulgated on 15th June builds on the Model APMC Act 2003 and Draft Model Contract Act 2018 to achieve mainstreaming of contract farming. The Ordinance excludes APMCs› jurisdiction from contract farming. The contract farming as envisaged in the Ordinance is, in essence, continuation of same artificial construct as has been the case for last 17 years. It also excessively regulates contract farming. This law is likely to meet the same fate what the contract farming provisions in the model APMC law of 2003 met with.

Essential Commodities Act 1955 (ECA-1955) was founded in 1939 as part of the Defence of India Rules. Defence of India Rules were replaced by Essential Supplies (Temporary Powers) Act, 1946. The provisions of ECA when enacted in 1955 were quite similar to the 1946 law. Continuing food-shortages provided justification of food controls in independent India and in the planned economy ushered in 1951.

Food has been the main reason ECA-1955 was sustained over several decades. Hundreds of orders were issued regulating, prohibiting, controlling prices, storage, distribution, consumption and other matters affecting foodstuffs under ECA-1955 by the time 20th century drew to a close. At some point of time, an adjunct law-Prevention of Black-marketing and Maintenance of Supplies of Essential Commodities Act, 1980-was brought in to take preventive actions against violators of control orders issued under ECA-1955.

When food position became better, instead of eliminating controls over foodstuffs, India resorted to a round-about way to defang the ECA-1955. A new Order called Removal of (Licencing requirements, Stock limits and Movement Restrictions) on Specified Foodstuffs Order 2002 was issued. This Order effectively nullified all controls on buying, stocking, selling, transporting, distributing, disposing, acquiring, using or consuming over a long list of foodstuffs-wheat, paddy/rice, coarse grains, sugar, edible oilseeds and edible oils issued under ECA-55. The 2002 Order was substantially diluted during 2006-2014. The Government reissued 2002 Order in 2016, but kept some exemptions, including on onion and pulses, for most of the time out of the scope of 2016 Liberalising Order.

The Essential Commodities (Amendment) Ordinance 2020 promulgated on 15th June does not take foodstuffs out of the scope of ECA-1955, but only modifies the regulatory and control regime in its application to foodstuffs. The Ordinance only modifies the circumstances in which the regulatory and control authority is exercised in case of foodstuffs, and, in particular, while specifying stock limits.

There is actually no need for ECA-55 to remain on statute book any longer. Not only foodstuffs, remaining 7 commodities in the ECA-55 Schedule need no control mechanism today. Like industrial goods, all the five items of agriculture, including fertiliser and hank yarn, need no protection of ECA-1955. To deal with any extraordinary situation in case of disasters, if need be, provisions of Disaster Management Act can be resorted to. Essential Commodities Act 1955 needs to be simply scrapped.

Ever since independence, India's agriculture policy and programme strategy focused on increasing production and productivity. Farmers' income was not the real goal of the policy. Only in 2014, the government specifically mentioned doubling the farmers' income by 2022, as a policy goal. It is imperative that the agriculture policies and programmes are oriented completely towards increasing farmers' income by at least five times over next ten years. This requires a multi-pronged strategy built on five critical planks of the policy and programmes:

First, an average farmer's operational land holding need to become five times than what he cultivates today, to raise his turnover to generate five times the profit/income. Second, the farmers need to get stable and predictable prices for his produce, including practically locking-in output prices before he cultivates. Third, the farmers should be able to choose right amount and quality of inputs to economise/reduce his cost of cultivation. Fourth, he should be completely free to get the best out of his land-asset. Fifth, skill-set of farmers is quite limited. There is need for a large-scale skilling required to make farmers earn income from non-farm businesses.

This would require a complete recast of today's agriculture development programmes, input subsidy regime and minimum support price regime. The expenditure governments incur under these programmes, which effectively exceeds 4 lakh crore, need to be directly delivered to farmers, freeing up the input and output markets.

□

A 1983 batch IAS officer of Rajasthan cadre. He served as Economic Affairs Secretary and Finance Secretary of India. He has also served as an Executive Director in the World Bank.

Indian Economy in the Post Covid World

—**CA Gopal Krishna Agarwal**

PM says 'India can emerge as the global nerve centre of complex modern multinational supply chains in the post Covid-19 World'.

Never Waste a Crisis

India is doing a commendable job in fighting the Corona virus pandemic. It took the epidemic seriously, unlike some other countries when it emerged on the global horizon, and has generally been ahead of the curve. Whether it's screening of international passengers, quarantine or announcing lockdown, the central government has never been found wavering or hesitant.

The first priority was to save people from this virus. The lockdown was announced when the cases were still very few. The lockdown reduced the speed of the spread of the virus and gave the Government time to set up the required health infrastructure. The government's efforts—brought good results in health care.

Covid-19 is a non-linear and uncertain event. Proper actions at the right time alone ensures that the cost of recovery is not huge. The crisis has brought in sharp focus the aspect of state capacity. Use of Big Data and Artificial Intelligence (AI) for good governance, policy formulation and welfare programmes, such as Jan Dhan Accounts, Direct Benefit Transfers and targeted delivery of social service benefits, has brought massive improvement in the state capacity.

Immediately thereafter, the health of the Indian economy became the priority of the government. The likelihood of post Covid-19 recovery being a V, U or L shaped curve will largely depend on the choice of the recovery path. Government needs to identify the areas/sectors to work on in the future. The Government action will be commensurate with the severity of the global recession. India's strengths are its Demography, Democracy and Demand, and while the first two will remain virtually unaffected by the crisis, the demand will diminish due to economic uncertainty, job losses and financial problems. Therefore, post Covid-19, government will focus on reviving demand.

Risk Diversification Strategy

The shutdown in China due to Covid-19 outbreak was a rude shock for companies as well as countries. It highlighted their vulnerability due to dependence on China. A number of multinational corporations are working on 'Risk Diversification Strategy' in reference to their huge investments in China. India can be an important player in global and regional supply chains. But, India will not automatically benefit from such a shift, and the success of Bangladesh and Vietnam is a sobering reminder.

Companies are looking for shifting their production base from China. World finds India as an attractive alternative, but the government needs to address many challenges. Rebuilding and catalysing growth has to be in an unprecedented manner. Protectionism, competition and level playing field have to be carefully balanced. It is essential for India to build on our own manufacturing facilities and make it more competitive.

There are many bottlenecks that need to be removed; the cost of acquiring land, legal and procedural delays is a big challenge. Similarly is the case with reforms in the labour sector. The cost of doing business is quite high. Our global ranking on ease of compliances, particularly tax, both direct and indirect is low. We need to rationalise expense incurred on power and logistics also.

All these challenges have the potential to be converted into opportunities, once the government embarks on the process of reforms and the industries shift their focus from demanding protectionism to an ecosystem of level playing field.

Contribution of logistics share to GDP is about 13 to 14 percent in India, whereas global benchmark is 9 to 10 percent. Industries have to bear heavy cost on transportation of goods, raw material and services. 65 percent of our transportation is by roads, which is more costly, in comparison to railways and waterways. Globally, industries dependence on road transport is 25 percent. A National Logistics Policy is in the pipeline, seeking reduction in logistics share in GDP to 10 percent by 2022. Investments into railways, roadways, waterways and airways will help in creating demand in the economy and employment, and also help in meeting the target set above.

India is moving from the regime of high interest rates to lower interest rates. RBI is continuously reducing both repo rate and reverse repo rate, but the transmission is not at the desired pace. Over the period, the risk premium in the financial institution has been reduced due to advent of IBC, NCLT etc., but again the risk has increased. Banks are unwilling to expose themselves to borrowers, particularly small and medium segment who have weak balance sheets.

Labour being one of the most crucial factors of production, has always been a contentious issue, the time is ripe for a balanced approach. Social and economic welfare of labour has been usually equated with the number of laws dealing with the subject. The net result is that labour market is characterised by extreme rigidities, while over 90 percent of the labour force is outside formal protection. Centre has consolidated labour laws into four codes and since labour is in the concurrent list, some states have unilaterally gone ahead and amended the labour laws in order to revive and attract industries. Coordinated approach is advisable.

The cost of land in India is quite high. Thus, for any green field project this cost, is a deterrent, especially if it's a small project. State governments must pool in its land holdings and make land banks available. Local authorities for cluster development and special purpose vehicle with joint participation are the road map ahead. States have a major role in land availability.

Any laxity on contract enforcement and judicial intervention on administrative decisions, is a big deterrent for businesses. India's contract enforcement ranking remains low. The Commercial Courts Act of 2015 is welcome. Setting up of commercial and district level courts will expedite mercantile dispute resolution. Also, fast tracking, New Delhi International Arbitration Centre Act in NCR will bring India to the global stage.

Reduction in compliances and transparency are a big boost for Ease Of Doing Business (EODB). A stable policy regime has a positive attribute for attracting global players. Thus, stability and predictability in laws and policies is a value to be imbibed by the Government at all times. GST with its online registration, filing of returns, assessment and refund is helping, but GST network (GSTN) remains a pain. Moving towards e-assessment and virtual taxation regime will remove harassment in due course.

India's FDI policy is quite attractive, with maximum sectors falling under automatic route and only some of them having sectoral caps. Repatriation of profits and royalties are allowed and we have current account convertibility. Section 92 of the Income Tax Act on transfer pricing, profit shifting and base erosion, has defined companies working as agencies in India for foreign companies, as permanent establishment (PE) and for Indian companies having foreign establishment, as India being place of effective management (POEM), for checking tax evasions by multinational companies (MNC).

Atmanirbhar Bharat and Global Investments

Recently, Prime Minister in his message at Indo US Business Summit, invited Global investors to invest in India; 'India offers combination of openness, opportunities and options'. He has been saying that 'India has undertaken deep structural reforms, improving domestic manufacturing and is committed to diversified international trade'. He talks about merging of domestic production and consumption with global supply chains.

Shri Narendra Modi has never shied from taking tough decisions in the interest of the nation. He has the will power and is always ready to take bold decisions; privatisation of railways, PSU disinvestments, reducing corporate tax and opening up of coal mining to private sector; may have been unpopular with certain quarters, but are necessary for the long-term health of our economy, particularly strengthening our manufacturing base. The goal is; politically and economically strong India and Atmanirbhar Bharat is the road map.

Government's Atmanirbhar Bharat Abhiyan is a 360 degree initiative to make India an economic superpower, integrating domestic manufacturing into regional and global supply chain. The focus is on five pillars of development; economy, infrastructure, technology, demography and demand. Our targets are the factors of production; land, labour, legislation and liquidity, improving their efficiency and reducing cost to make our industries, globally competitive. It is not only restricted to manufacturing, but targeted to direct benefit transfer to the needy, particularly farmers, migrant labourers, daily wagers, also resulting in the demand generation in the economy.

Atmanirbhar Bharat Abhiyan has little to do with disengagement with China alone. We saw the design of Chinese economic imperialism very early. Our disengagement with China began much earlier than many would like to believe. It began with Prime Minister opting out of (Regional Comprehensive Economic Partnership) RCEP. Chinese leadership was all out to pressurise Indian side to go for RCEP or face isolation amongst the 16 countries. But the PM stood for the interest of the Nation. In 2010, UPA II signed Free Trade Agreements (FTA) with 10 ASEAN countries, the benefits of which were being reaped by China as well. Reduced custom duties from these countries was creating inverted duty structure in domestic manufacturing sector, destroying local industries and converting manufacturers into traders. Therefore, in the last Budget in 2019, government had increased import duties in about 56 items spread across eight classification. Items like toys saw an increase of duty to 60 percent from 20 percent earlier. All these efforts were to protect domestic industries from the onslaught of dumping and competition. Without first strengthening domestic manufacturing by providing level playing field, reducing the cost and increasing the efficiency of factors of production, we cannot open the floodgates of imports.

Further, the Chinese aggression at LAC at Galwan valley, forced the government to immediately ban imports, FDI and 106 apps from China. This is being hailed as a timely move. Our government has also taken initiatives like banning FDI from bordering countries without prior approval, and other restrictions such as General financial regulations. Another 371 items have been identified for increasing import duties including non tariff barriers on some of them.

Fortunately, what we import from China are mostly where India has domestic technology, and can leverage itself for import substitution. Most of these items do not come under the essential commodities and are generaly Non-Merit Goods.

Except pharma, where China is dominating through the supply chain of API, it has not been able to penetrate into our strategic sectors. India's manufacturers need to come forward to take this golden opportunity in sectors such as toys, electrical equipments, electronics, minerals, chemicals, iron & steel, plastics, furniture, sports goods, musical instruments, fertilisers and Apps. Earlier ministry of commerce and industry had identified 12 such sectors, which now constitute 20 sectors.

If you look into the comaparative advantage theory domestically, our focus will be in areas such as agriculture, particularly food processing, automobiles, textiles, defence production, affordable housing, healthcare and education, and increase their contribution to our GDP. These sectors have ample scope, can generate large employment and are looking up, on our path to recovery.

I believe that India has a fair chance to attract global manufacturing capital and emerge as the world's factory. Facilitating setting up of manufacturing base in India falls within the jurisdiction of the Centre and the State, and the Government at all the levels will have to work collectively.

□

National Spokesperson of the Bharatiya Janata Party (Economic Affairs). He is a fellow member of the Institute of Chartered Accountants of India (ICAI). He is an Economic thinker and writes extensively for the newspapers, financial journals and delivers lectures in seminars & conferences. He is a Trustee and a Treasurer of India Policy Foundation (IPF).

Atmanirbhar Bharat Abhiyan: A Paradigm Shift

—**R.N. Dubey**

Charles E. Lindblom, an American political scientist advocated the 'Theory of Incrementalism' as a tool of public policy. The theory enunciates that the public policy-making relies heavily on past experiences and small policy steps to achieve the stated objective. The crux of this theory is that policy reforms are a continuous process and policies are revised or amended to meet the policy objectives.

There are times when such baby steps in policy efforts are not good enough to meet the demands of the situation. In such a situation, a paradigm shift in the policy effort is necessitated. The trigger for such measures may come from an economic crisis, a financial crisis, a pandemic, a change in global situation and even war or warlike situations. The announcement made by Hon'ble Prime Minister Shri Narendra Modi on 12 May, 2020, in his address to the nation, is one such paradigm shift in policy making triggered by Covid-19 Pandemic. The scope of this announcement as revealed in series of press conferences conducted by Hon'ble Finance Minister over next five days, are vast enough to be categorised as a major policy shift. The announcement targets not only matters of immediate concern due to pandemic, but also suggests sweeping reforms to address broader economic challenges. The clarion call for आत्मनिर्भर भारत अभियान or Self-Reliant India Movement with five pillars of–Economy, Infrastructure, System, Vibrant Demography and Demand is unprecedented, and is expected to be an important watershed.

1991 Reforms

In order to appreciate the Atmanirbhar Bharat Abhiyan (ABA), it may be of interest to first look at the last big economic reform which economists and policy practitioners refer to as '1991 Reforms'. India's 1991 reforms were introduced in the context of a severe balance of payment crisis. The reforms broadly comprised firstly, a macroeconomic consolidation package to address the immediate concerns of balance of payment and rising fiscal deficit and secondly, a package of structural reforms aimed to increase competitiveness of the Indian economy through increase in productivity.

The macroeconomic consolidation comprised fiscal and exchange rate policies formulated in consultation with RBI, which was to be followed through next couple of years. The Union Budget presented on 24.7.1991 announced, "elimination of structural imbalances in our fiscal system would require a reduction both in the fiscal deficit and in the revenue deficit as a proportion of GDP." Further, the system of issue of ad hoc treasury bills by the Government to RBI, which allowed replenishment of its cash balances whenever it fell below a level and hence automatic monetisation of fiscal deficit, was decided to be phased out. This reduced the dominance of the fiscal policy over monetary policy. Subsequently, the Fiscal Responsibility and Budget management Act, 2003, further enhanced the scope of monetary policy by completely disallowing RBI to purchase government securities from primary market.

The balance of payment crisis, which was the main reason for steep devaluation of rupee in 1991, necessitated significant changes in trade sector and exchange rate regime. It was decided to remove quantitative controls over imports in a phased manner and tariff rates were reduced. This signalled integration of the Indian economy with the global economy. The exchange rate system went through complete overhaul in next couple of years. It started with exim scrip scheme, which allowed exporters to import a part of their export earnings unrestricted. Further, based on the recommendations of a High Level Committee on Balance of Payments, it was decided to move from fixed exchange rate system to dual exchange rate system, and finally, to unified market determined exchange rate system.

The structural reforms primarily comprised industrial licensing, foreign investment, foreign technology agreements, public sector policy and MRTP Act, announced in the statement on Industrial Policy on 24.7.1991. Industrial licensing was abolished for all industries, irrespective of level of investment, except for certain specified industries on strategic considerations or on environmental grounds. FDI was freely allowed up to 51 percent in a large number of industries. Industries were allowed to freely enter into transfer of technology agreements as long as royalty payments were within stipulated levels. The list of industries reserved for public sector was pruned from eighteen to six. It was also decided to close loss-making public sector units deemed non-revivable. The concept of MRTP companies was abolished and MRTP Act was to be amended significantly.

The policy reforms introduced in 1991, which was followed through in subsequent years, did have significant impact in integrating Indian economy with the global economy and creating new opportunities for a large section of the population. India's per capita GDP had grown by 3.2 % between 1960 and 1991. This increased to 5.3 percent between 1996 and 2016. Further, India has been largely able to adhere to prudent fiscal norms and sagacious balance of payment situation.

Atmanirbhar Bharat Abhiyan

Though the trigger for 'Atmanirbhar Bharat Abhiyan (ABA) or Self-Reliant India Movement' can be said to be Covid-19, various other domestic and global developments were laying the seeds for this major announcement. Last thirty years have been a period of rapid globalisation. Countries which started early have taken lead by following a focused policy approach on international trade. The global market place and supply chains have not only become extremely competitive, but globalisation has become part of the institutions' psyche. This has enabled unprecedented quickness to satisfy global demands. Further, just in time inventory norms ensures that resources flow to the most competitive areas. However, these developments throw-up huge challenges to even developed economies because of their relatively rising costs and inability to match the competitiveness thrown by economies with ability to supply goods and services at relatively lower costs. Further, the slowing global economy and rising protectionism is throwing up new global challenges. The world trade growth, which had plummeted in the wake of global financial crisis in 2008, rebounded strongly in 2010 and 2011 but again nosedived in 2012. Since then, except for 2007, it has not crossed 3 percent mark. The average global merchandise trade growth during

2000-2018 has been less than 4 percent and average global GDP growth rate during the same period was less than 3 percent. The WTO Director-General, Roberto Azevêdo, in a press release on 2.4.2019 summarised the trade scenario, "Trade cannot play its full role in driving growth, when we see such high levels of uncertainty. It is increasingly urgent that we resolve tensions and focus on charting a positive path forward for global trade, which responds to the real challenges in today's economy–such as the technological revolution and the imperative of creating jobs and boosting development. WTO members are working to do this, and are discussing ways to strengthen and safeguard the trading system. This is vital. If we forget the fundamental importance of the rules-based trading system we would risk weakening it, which would be an historic mistake with repercussions for jobs, growth and stability around the world."

The slowing of global growth and trade had its impact on Indian economy. The weak environment for global manufacturing, trade and demand has contributed to slowing down of India's GDP growth, moderating from 7.1 percent in first quarter of 2018-19 to 3.1 percent in fourth quarter of 2019-20. This period has also witnessed decline in credit growth, attributed to growing risk aversion of banks that continue to apprehend the build-up of Non-Performing Assets (NPAs). The developments in financial sector have impacted the real estate sector. The relative share of industrial sector in the economy has registered a decline. Under such global and domestic economic situation, the country witnessed the Covid-19 pandemic.

Basic Ingredients of ABA

The Basic ingredients of Atmanirbhar Bharat Abhiyan (ABA) are:

a. Measures to meet immediate challenges faced by poor, labourers, migrants, farmers, industries, service sector and even state governments. This includes monetary policy measures announced by RBI to address the liquidity issue.

b. Policy reforms to resurrect the economy and to meet global challenges. The focus is on credit/equity, insurance, guarantee and ease of doing business.

Important announcements with far reaching consequences and some of the important measures to provide immediate relief due to pandemic are summarised below.

Measures to Meet Immediate Challenges Faced by Poor, Labourers, Migrants, Farmers, Industries, Service Sector and even State Governments

First and foremost, the state governments have been empowered to face the challenge posed by pandemic by raising their borrowing limits from 3% to 5% of Gross State Domestic Product (GSDP) for the year 2020-21. Commitment has been made to provide collateral free loans to all business including MSMEs, subject to certain conditions upto ₹ 3 lakh crore. Interest on loans is capped and guarantee on principle and interest will be provided to banks and NBFCs.

Employee Provident Fund (EPF): Under the PM Garib Kalyan Yojana, the government to pay 12% of employer and 12% of employee contribution into the EPF accounts of eligible establishments for the months of March to August.

Statutory PF contribution: Statutory PF contribution of both the employer and employee reduced from 12% to 10% each for all establishments covered by EPFO for next three months, except for Central Public Sector Enterprises (CPSEs) and State Public Sector Units (PSUs).

Street vendors: A special scheme launched to facilitate easy access to credit for street vendors. Under this scheme, bank credit will be provided to each vendor for an initial working capital of up to ₹ 10,000.

Migrant Workers: Under the 'One Nation One Card' scheme, migrant workers will be able to access the Public Distribution System (Ration) from any Fair Price Shop in India. Migrant workers, who are not beneficiaries under the National Food Security Act ration card or state card, will be provided 5 kg of grains per person and 1 kg of chana per family per month for two months, for free. Further, migrant labour/urban poor will be provided living facilities at affordable rent under 'Affordable Rental Housing Complexes (ARHC)' of Pradhan Mantri Awas Yojana (PMAY). This will be achieved by: (i) converting government funded housing in the cities into ARHCs through PPPs, and (ii) incentivising manufacturing units, industries, institutions, associations to develop ARHCs on their private land and operate them.

Policy Reforms to Resurrect the Economy and Meet Global Challenges

Privatisation of Public Sector Enterprise (PSEs): A new PSE policy has been announced with plans to privatise PSEs except the ones functioning in certain strategic sector. In strategic sectors, at least one PSE will remain, but private sector will also be allowed. To minimise wasteful administrative costs, number of enterprises in strategic sectors will ordinarily be only one to four; others will be privatised/ merged/ brought under holding companies.

Legal framework: The cornerstone for business to flourish and to attract global investors is to have a robust legal framework related to property rights, including registration of property, laws of contracts, dispute resolution, bankruptcy which are not very intrusive and work efficiently in time-bound manner. ABA will aim to work on a mission mode on the next phase of Ease of Doing Business Reforms relating to easy registration of property, fast disposal of commercial disputes and simpler tax regime for making India one of the easiest places to do business. Decriminalisation of 16 compoundable offences under the Companies Act, 2013 have already been shifted to an in-house adjudication and penalty mechanism. Further, majority of compoundable sections in Companies Law are proposed to be shifted to internal adjudication mechanism. Government is also working on special insolvency framework for MSMEs under Section 240A of IBC, 2018. Further threshold to initiate insolvency proceedings raised from ₹ 1 lakh to ₹ 1 crore. These measures will also decalogue National Company Law Tribunal.

State level reforms: State level reforms will be in four areas: Universalisation of 'One Nation One Rationcard', Ease of Doing Business, Power distribution and Urban local body revenues. Under One Nation One Card scheme, migrant workers will be able to access the Public Distribution System (Ration) from any Fair Price Shop anywhere in India. The scheme will introduce inter-state portability of access to ration for migrant labourers. All states/union territories are required to complete full automation of fair price shops by March 2021, for achieving 100% national portability.

Sectoral reforms:

a. Coal mining-In order to introduce competition, transparency, and private sector participation, complete opening of commercial mining in coal sector is proposed. Any party would be allowed to bid and sell in open market compared to existing regime, where only captive consumers with end-use ownership could bid.

b. Mineral Sector-Distinction between captive and non-captive mines removed to allow transfer of mining leases and sale of surplus unused minerals, leading to better efficiency in mining and production.
c. Defence-FDI limit in the defence manufacturing under automatic route will be raised from 49% to 74%. It is proposed to notify a list of weapons/platforms for ban on import with year-wise timelines. This will encourage indigenous development and production of weapons and platforms not only for domestic use, but also for export.
d. Civil Aviation-Only 60% of the Indian airspace is freely available. Restrictions on utilisation of the Indian Air Space will be eased so that civilian flying becomes more efficient.
e. Agriculture-Stock limits set under Essential Commodities Act have proved to be a major stumbling block in India becoming an active partner in global food supply chain. Government proposes to amend the Essential Commodities Act, 1955 to ensure better price realisation for farmers by attracting investments and making agriculture sector competitive. Stock limit to be imposed only under very exceptional circumstances like national calamities, famine with surge in prices. No such stock limit shall apply to processors or value chain participants, subject to their installed capacity or to any exporter, subject to the export demand. Similarly, Agricultural Produce Market Committee Act has been a hindrance in free flow of agricultural produce and fragmentation of market and supply chain, leading to suboptimal price realisation by the farmers. Farmers are bound to sell agriculture produce only to licensees in APMCs. Government has proposed to bring a Central law to provide adequate choices to farmer to sell produce at attractive price and remove barrier to free Inter-State Trade in agriculture.

Except for the policy initiatives to meet the immediate challenges due to pandemic, the real impact of the Atmanirbhar Bharat Abhiyan will become more profound and visible in times to come.

References

1. Charles E. Lindblom, The Science of 'Muddling Through'.
2. Rakesh Mohan, India Transformed, 25 Years of Economic Reforms.
3. Report of the High Level Advisor Group set up by Ministry of Commerce and Industry.
4. PIB releases on Atmanirbhar Bharat Abhiyan.

□

Senior officer of Indian Economic Service, retired as Senior Advisor (Additional Secretary) in Ministry of Finance. He has wide experience in public policy formulation and implementation.

Skill Development: The Cornerstone of Atmanirbhar Bharat

—Vandana Jena

Introduction

The vision of a 'Self-Reliant India,' was first enunciated by Mahatma Gandhi, who envisioned Gram Swaraj and gave a clarion call for 'Swadeshi,' during India's freedom struggle. The Panchayati Raj system prevalent in India is an offshoot of Gandhiji's vision of Gram Swaraj. However, after globalisation and liberalisation, the world is being perceived as a global village with thrust on interdependence among nations. It was Prime Minister Shri Narendra Modi, who revived the idea of Swadeshi by promoting the idea of `Make in India.' Today, it is one of the major planks of Atmanirbhar Bharat or `Self-Reliant India.' As the Prime Minister unfurled the tricolor at the ramparts of the Red Fort on 15 August, 2020, and enunciated his vision of Atmanirbhar Bharat, he transformed his vision from 'Make in India,' to 'Make for the World'. When the world is in the midst of a Covid-19 Pandemic, the wisdom of his vision deserves to be applauded. When countries in the West were grappling with the shortages of masks, in India, many organisations including self-help groups and skill development institutions jumped into the fray to meet this demand. Starting with a shortage of PPE kits, N 95 masks and Ventilators, at the outset of the Covid-19 Pandemic, India increased its capacity manifold to meet this demand.

While the Hon'ble Prime Minister in his address highlighted skill development, his vision expanded the boundaries even further, as he spoke of a number of new schemes like the *National Infrastructure Pipeline Project, the Jal Jeevan Mission etc.* it is evident that a new skill set will be required to deliver these schemes. Skill Development or 'Kaushal Vikas,' is the key plank on which the vision of `Self-Reliant India,' would rest.

Skill Development-Opportunities and Constraints

India is fortunate, that it is in a position to meet the challenge of skilling, as it is set to reap the demographic dividend. The National Policy for Skill Development and Entrepreneurship 2015 stated, "Today, India is one of the youngest nations in the world, with more than 62% of its population in the working age group (15-59 years) and more than 54% of its total population below 25 years of age. Its population pyramid is expected to bulge across the 15-59 age group over the next decade. It is further estimated that the average age of the population in India by 2020 will be 29 years, as against 40 years in USA, 46 years in Europe and 47 years in Japan."[1]

In fact, during the next two decades, the labour force in the West is expected to decline by 4%, while in India, it is estimated to increase by 32%. This would be both a challenge as well as an opportunity for India. To reap the demographic dividend, Indian workforce must be provided with employable skills and knowledge, so that they can contribute to India's economic growth.

There are, of course, a number of challenges with regard to skill development in India. The first, of course, is that only 4.69%of the total workforce in India has undergone formal skill training as compared to 68% in UK, 75% in Germany, 52% in USA, 80% in Japan and 96% in South Korea.[2]

On demand side, a skill gap study has been conducted by NSDC over 2010-2014, which indicates that there is an additional net incremental requirement of 109.73 million skilled manpower by 2022, in twenty four key sectors.[3]

According to the Periodic Labour Force Survey (PLFS) 2017-18, only 13.53 percent of the workforce in the productive age-group of 15-59 years has received training (2.26 percent formal vocational/technical training and 11.27 percent informal training). A large section among informally trained workers, about 55.9 percent received it either through self-learning (28.66 percent) or hereditary (27.24 percent) and about 38.51 percent have received it on-the-job.[4]

1. National Policy for Skill Development and Entrepreneurship 2015. Page 2.
2. National Policy for Skill Development and Entrepreneurship 2015-page 6.
3. National Policy for Skill Development and Entrepreneurship 2015-page 6.
4. Economic Survey Volume II Page 281.

Another key constraint is the fact that in the public perception, specifically the perception of the parents, vocational education is considered the last option for those who have not been able to get a foothold into the formal academic system. This mindset is unfortunately held worldwide.

The problem is further aggravated by the fact that the vocational education programmes in India are not really aligned to the requirements of the industry. In the past, instead of being concentrated in one Ministry, skill development programmes were spread across a large number of Ministries, with little coordination between them. Furthermore, there is paucity of good quality Trainers.

Another pertinent issue is that India has a large number of skilled artisans, artists and workers, who have the requisite expertise and skills but no certification, as they have not undergone formal skill training. Furthermore, most of the workforce is in the informal sector, where it is difficult to gauge its growth.

Women constitute half of the popultion, but according to the Census data, there has been a continuing fall in labour force participation rate of women from 33.3% to 26.5% in rural areas, and from 17.8% to 15.5% in urban areas between 2004 and 2011.

Job creation for skilled youth is also a major challenge before the nation. Entrepreneurship has tremendous growth potential, but the number of entrepreneurs in India is very low. Accelerating entrepreneurship is essential for employment generation in India. The National Policy for Skill Development and Entrepreneurship 2015, addresses many of these issues.

Initiatives Under Skill Development

The Government has given a new impetus to Skill Development by creating the Ministry of Skill Development and Entrepreneurship and by initiating new schemes, some of which are mentioned below. The thrust of these schemes is on placement as well as entrepreneurship and innovation which is the need of the hour.

Pradhan Mantri Kaushal Vikas Yojana

The Pradhan Mantri Kaushal Vikas Yojana (PMKVY) is a flagship programme of the Ministry of Skill Development and Entrepreneurship which enables a large number of prospective youth to take up Short

Term Training (STT) and Recognition of Prior Learning (RPL) through empanelled Training Centers /Training Providers throughout the country. The trainings under PMKVY include, among others, trades like housekeeping, apparel, refrigeration, welding, security, construction, masonry, plumbings, hospitality, beauty, wellness, healthcare and retail.

Under the Recognition of Prior Learning component of PMKVY, individuals with prior learning experience or skills are assessed and certified in any of the three Projects i.e., RPL Camps, RPL at Employers Premises and RPL centres. Institutions like the National Skill Development Corporation, Sector Skill Council, Assessment Agencies and Training Partners implement the PMKVY scheme, which is aligned to other Missions of the Government such as Make in India, Digital India, Swachh Bharat and Smart Cities.

Under PMKVY, approximately 69.03 lakh candidates, (38.01 lakh through Short Term Training and 31.02 lakh through Recognition of Prior Learning) have been trained throughout the country by November 2019. [5]

Jan Shikshan Sansthan

The Scheme of Jan Shikshan Sansthan (Institutes of Polyvalent Education) is another Scheme under the Ministry of Skill Development and Entrepreneurship, which caters to the target group of 18-45 and provides training at the doorstep of the people, which is a boon especially for women. A range of trainings is provided to the trainees, from bee-keeping and dairying to plumbing, masonry and tv repairs. The Jan Shikshan Sansthans also facilitate the trainees to form self-help groups and help them to access credit from institutions like NABARD etc.

Deen Dayal Upadhyaya Gramin Kaushalya Yojana

Another major scheme for skilling is the Deen Dayal Upadhyaya Gramin Kaushalya Yojana,(DDU-GKY), which is the skilling and placement initiative of the Ministry of Rural Development (MoRD), Government of India. The scheme focusses on addressing the occupational aspirations of rural youth and enhancing their skills for wage employment. The scheme aims to support programmes like Make in India, Digital India, Smart Cities and Start Up India. The DDU-GKY projects are market linked and implemented in the PPP mode. Curriculum framing and Assessment Support is done through

5. Economic Survey Volume II Page 281

the National Council on Vocational Training, Sector Skill Councils etc. In addition to domain skills, there are dedicated training hours for soft skills, spoken English and basic computers, as it has been recognised that these skills are as important as domain skills for employability.

Garib Kalyan Rojgar Abhiyan

To resolve the issue of the employability of migrant labour, who returned to States like Bihar, Jharkhand and UP from States like Maharashtra and Gujarat amidst the Covid-19 Pandemic, the Government has launched the Garib Kalyan Rojgar Abhiyan. The Scheme aims to enable the migrant workers to generate employment in their own villages. The scheme, launched on 20 June, 2020 with an initial funding of ₹ 50,000 crore, aims to give 125 days of employment to 670,000 migrant workers across six states of Bihar, Uttar Pradesh, Madhya Pradesh, Rajasthan, Odisha and Jharkhand.

The Road Ahead

As the nation gears itself to 'Make for the World,' and give shape to the Prime Minister's call for 'Vocal for Local,' India will continue to strengthen its skilling initiative. It will also strive to strengthen entrepreneurship in the country.

In his Independence day speech on 15 August, 2014, the Hon'ble Prime Minister had said, "Today, the world and India need a skilled workforce. If we have to promote the development of our country, then our mission has to be 'Skill Development' and 'Skilled India'. Millions and Millions of Indian youth should acquire the skills, which could contribute towards making India a modern country.... I also want to create a pool of young people who are able to create jobs and the ones who are not capable of creating jobs and do not have the opportunities, they must be in a position to face their counterparts in any corner of the world, while keeping their heads high by virtue of their hard work and their dexterity of hands and win the hearts of people around the world through their skills." His words are as relevant today, as they were then. Skill Development will be the cornerstone of Atmanirbhar Bharat.

□

An IAS officer belonging to the 1979 batch (Odisha cadre) served as Secretary, Government of India, Department of Land Resources, Ministry of Rural Development prior to her retirement. Subsequently, she served as a part-time Non-Official Director on the Board of Syndicate Bank. She is a writer and poet, and has published two novels, three short story collections and a collection of middles.

Resolve for Self-reliance is No Protectionism

—Ashwani Mahajan

During the last three decades of globalisation, the protection of domestic industry was considered like a crime. It was being said that free trade is the panacea of all economic problems. The rationale was that hindrance to the free trade would make our industries inefficient, as lack of competition will hinder efficiency and would affect competitiveness. During the Corona period, there has been a big change in the thinking of policy makers in India and the world. Prime Minister Narendra Modi has said that the biggest lesson the country has learnt in this corona crisis is that we have to become self-reliant. The Prime Minister says that we have to be vocal for the local (indigenous), and be reverent for the local and promote the same. To make the village self-reliant, we would need to make requisite efforts. For this, all the people's representatives, technocrats, leaders of industry and trade, social activists; all will have to make concerted efforts. We know that India has been a country of diversities. Every province, every district of our country, and even every village has its own speciality. We know that each district is known for one or more types of skills, agricultural product(s) or one or more industrial clusters. Generally, more than one type of characteristics exists in the same district. In the absence of incentives over the years, districts have been losing their distinct identities with regard to their industries, skills and agriculture produce. In fact, every district of our country produces a variety of excellent agricultural products but due to lack of appropriate system of incentives, storage and marketing, many of these products are facing the danger of extinction. Sometimes, despite having domestic capabilities in the efficient production of these products, the country has to even import them. On the other hand, so far as manufacturing is concerned, various districts of the country are known for modern and traditional industries. There are places like Ludhiana, which is famous for woollen hosiery and bicycle industry, Tirupur for hosiery, Agra for shoes and iron forging, Bhadohi for carpets, Banaras and Kanjipuram for sarees, and many others, which are world famous. Chinese dumping and neglect of the government, red tape, inspector raj, lack of finance, lack of access to new technology, etc. are some of the reasons that have led to the decline of these clusters. In the past, due to the obsession with globalisation and the domination of multinational companies, these industries witnessed a significant decline. Today, when we are talking about self-reliance, efforts are also needed to be made to preserve and enhance their local products, according to their specialisation. Along with the efforts of the Central and State Governments towards protection and promotion of local industries, if the people's representatives, industry and trade leaders, social activists, etc. make efforts, then these enterprises will naturally get a new life. Learning lesson from pandemic, if the country revives and promotes its manufacturing, which has deteriorated due to perverted policy framework and unfair competition from China, then it will increase employment and income in the country and improve the standard of living of the people.

Self-reliance will not Come Overnight

Some people believe that in this era of globalisation, we are so much connected with the rest of the world that our efforts to become self-reliant can prove to be regressive and suicidal. They say that if the import of components coming from China is stopped, then our industries will come to standstill. Such people fail to appreciate that resolve to self-reliance is not about stopping imports from China altogether, but to gradually reduce dependence on China. Due to apathy of governments in the past towards dumping of Chinese goods, our industries got destroyed. However, we have to rebuild our industry and we need to ready ourselves to find alternatives. We must not forget that most of the imports from China are those which are either produced or could be produced in the country. These include steel, chemicals, machinery, vehicles, fertilizers, pesticides etc. There are many imports which do not even require high technology. Such zero technology products can easily be produced in the country in a short span of time. In such a situation, a lot of imports from China can be stopped. In the past 90 percent of APIs (Active Pharmaceutical Ingredients required for our pharmaceutical industry were produced in the country. This industry can also be revived in India, with efforts from the government. For their revival, the government has already implemented an incentive scheme of more than ₹ 11000 crore. Apart from this, we can try to increase production of electronics, telecom, mobile phones, other consumer goods etc. in India. The government has already rolled out a plan to revive electronic and mobile phone industry.

Self-reliance is not Protectionism

Policy of self-reliance by increasing production in the country cannot be equated with protectionism. It is of course true that for new industries to flourish, the import duty on goods coming from abroad will have to be increased a bit; to discourage dumping, anti-dumping duties, in some cases safeguard duties, may also be needed. Standards are also needed to prevent inferior foreign goods and alongside a host of non-tariff barriers may need to be imposed. Those who call these measures as protectionist, must understand that US imposes more than 6500 non-tariff barriers, China imposes more than 3,500 such barriers, while India imposes only nearly 350 such barriers.

Using of WTO Provisions is also no Protectionism

It has to be understood that the protectionism before the new economic policy of 1991 led to inefficient industrialisation because during that period, heavy import duties (100 percent to 600 percent) were levied in India, which can actually said to be a hindrance to efficiency. The era of high import tariffs has already ended after the WTO came into existence. India is already bound by WTO rules. But there are provisions and flexibilities in the WTO as well, through which we can promote our industries and protect them from unequal competition. The globalisation of the last three decades and the obsession of our policy makers with free trade have led to lowering of import tariffs well below the WTO-bound rates. Whereas WTO rules allow India to have an average import duty of upto 40 percent, our average import duty is less than even 10 percent. Under these provisions, the Government of India increased import duties on some items including electronics, mobile phones, consumer goods, etc. from 10 percent to 20 percent and this helped reducing imports significantly. In the last 2 years between 2017-18 and 2019-20, India's trade deficit with China has come down from $ 63.2 billion to $ 48.6 billion. Apart from anti-dumping duties and countervailing duties, we can also impose non-tariff barriers and encourage Indian industries by implementing standards. Such actions cannot be equated with pre-1991 protectionism. Almost all countries impose tariff and non-tariff barriers for the protection and promotion of their industries, so why can't India do the same? India's unilateral free trade will prove suicidal when other countries are increasing import duties in the name of trade war. Therefore, critics have to understand that the continuous decline of industries due to cheap Chinese imports is not in the country's interest. Why a steadily increasing trade deficit does not distract critics, is beyond comprehension. The need of the hour is that efforts should be made to stop imports primarily with incentives to our industries. And after that, by making products of international standards, we can not only fulfil the requirements of the country, but can export also to foreign countries. It has to be understood that every country is protecting its industries, so we cannot equate measures adopted under the WTO provisions with protectionism. In fact, this effort of self-sufficiency of the country can play an important role in raising income and employment in the country.

□

National Co-Convener of Swadeshi Jagaran Manch (SJM), an Indian political and cultural organisation. He worked as an author and columnist. He is an associate professor at PGDAV College, Delhi. He is Chief Editor of Journal of Contemporary Indian Polity and Economy, since 2011.

Challenges Towards Atmanirbhar Bharat

—**Sheshadri Chari**

Never before has the global economy been under extreme stress as it is now, as a result of the Covid-19 pandemic that has affected the whole world. The extent of spread of the affliction, the fatality rate and the degree of containment seem to have no correlation to the economic indices or the nature of governance of the countries. Truly, the pandemic has revealed a somewhat strange but realistic side of globalisation.

After the end of World War-II, a number of institutions were set up by the West, especially the US, to revive the economies of the allies and work towards peace and prosperity. These institutions have withstood the global challenges, economic crisis and the Cold War. Probably for the first time in the last about seventy years, the world is witnessing a global lockdown, total shutdown of international travel, closure of manufacturing facilities and trade and commerce grinding to a halt. Has the Coronavirus shown us a trailer of the apocalypse?

India was probably one of those few countries which went into lockdown mode at the very early stage of the pandemic. But this had a devastating effect on our economy, which was already experiencing a recessionary trend during the last quarter of 2019. According to government sources, the combined Index of Industrial Production (IIP) of Eight Core Industries stood at 131.4 in June 2019, which was merely 0.2 percent higher, as compared to the index of June 2018. Automobile sector recorded negative growth and the real estate sector was facing huge problems in debt repayment as inventories piled up.

It was in such a challenging situation that the Covid-19 originating from Wuhan province in China hit India and the world pushing Indian and global economies faster and closer to recession.

According to the report by UNCTAD, the world economy will go into recession this year (or whatever is left of it) with a predicted loss of trillions of dollars of global income due to the Coronavirus pandemic spelling serious trouble for developing countries with the likely exception of India and China, according to a latest UN trade report. Many governments have announced stimulus packages but the economic dent is estimated to be so large that it has become difficult to assess the impact until now.

In a quick and decisive move, Prime Minister Narendra Modi in his address to the nation on 12 May 2020, pledged a total spending of ₹ 20 lakh crore to weather the fallout of the corona virus pandemic. This was among the largest economic stimulus packages announced by nations around the world. As mentioned by the Prime Minister, Atmanirbhar Bharat Abhiyan or Self-reliant India Mission was estimated to be about 10 percent of India's GDP. But unlike the most relief packages announced globally, India's INR Twenty Lakh Crore package was not entirely in new spending but included the ₹ 1.7 lakh crore package the government had announced in March under the PM Garib Kalyan Yojana as well as the steps taken by the Reserve Bank of India (RBI) such as liquidity enhancing measures and interest rate cuts amounting to ₹ 8 lakh crore. The package was announced in 5 phases.

The first one included 6 measures for micro, small and medium enterprises (MSMEs), two for Employee Provident Fund (EPF), two for HFCs / MFIs / NBFCs, one for power sector, one for real estate, one for contractors and two as direct tax measures. The central Govt. announced that it will be providing collateral- free loans amounting to ₹ 3 lakh crore to facilitate MSMEs whilst also changing the definition of MSMEs. There has been a change in EPF rates from 12% to 10%. The government will also be providing an emergency liquidity infusion of ₹ 90,000 crore to DISCOMS. TCS/ TDS rates were reduced by 25% for all purposes leading to a ₹ 50,000 crore liquidity.

In the second phase, the main focus was on migrant workers, street vendors, small traders, small farmers and self-employed persons. Around 8 crore migrants were expected to benefit from the free food supply scheme for non-ration cardholders with an outlay of ₹ 3500 crore. The government aims to cover 100% beneficiaries under the 'One Nation One Ration Card' scheme by 31st May, 2021. A ₹ 50,000 crore special credit facility was announced for street vendors. Around 2.5 crore farmers were to be benefitted by the ₹ 2 lakh concessional credit extended towards Kisan Credit Card. Furthermore, central government issued directions to state governments to provide enrolment and provide employment under MGNREGA to workers in their own states.

The 3rd economic dose of Atmanirbhar Bharat Abhiyan focused on agriculture and allied activities, government and administrative reforms. The government allocated ₹ 1 lakh crore for farm-based infrastructure. The government also announced ₹ 10,000 crore for micro food enterprises, ₹ 20,000 crore under the PM Matsya Sampada Yojna, ₹ 13,000 crore under the FMD Livestock Disease Control Scheme, ₹ 4000 crore for promotion of herbal cultivation, ₹ 500 crore for promotion of bee-keeping and an additional ₹ 500 crore for Operation Greens apart from establishing a thorough support system for farmers. The central government proposed to allocate an additional amount of ₹ 40,000 crore under the MGNREGS Scheme as well.

In the 4th tranche of Atmanirbhar Bharat Abhiyan, the central Govt. focused on structural reforms in 8 sectors. These were Coal, Minerals mining, Defence production, Civil Aviation (airspace management, PPP and airports, MRO Hubs), Power distribution sector, Social Infrastructure, Space and Atomic energy sectors. Around ₹ 8100 crore will be used for Viability Gap Funding which will boost private investment in Health and Education sectors. Moreover, the coal sector, defence production, power distribution and space sector will now be privatised as well. In the atomic energy sector, the Research Reactor will be established in Public Private Partnership (PPP) mode for production of medical isotopes for cancer.

The 5th dose of these reforms focused mainly on the Health and Education sectors. Till date, the government had already announced help worth ₹ 15,000 crore for Covid-19 containment. In order to leverage IT, the government has rolled out e-Sanjeevani tele-consultation services. To ensure capacity building, iGOT platform has been launched.

Other measures cover Ease of Doing Business for corporates, Public Sector Enterprise Policy for a New and Self-reliant India, supporting state governments and promoting state level reforms and further enhancement of Ease of Doing business through IBC related measures.

The emphasis on controlling the pandemic through lockdown and restrictions on the movement of people and goods could have resulted, to some extent, in preventing the virus attack from becoming a mass killer like the deadly plague. But the crippling effect these restrictions have had on the economy is far too serious to be repaired in a few weeks or even months. The task of reviving the collapsed economy seems to be even more difficult than handling the pandemic, that was responsible for it or dealing with the country where the Coronavirus pandemic originated.

The lockdown, loss of work, disruptions in normal activities and above all the fear of the killer pandemic kept people indoors for more than five months, as of now. While the pandemic does not appear to have become any less virulent, people have accepted the reality that one will have to live with the situation as a result of Covid-19. There is no post-Covid-19 plan; it is rather planning for future, while living with Covid-19.

With production facilities closed and business centres on a lockdown mode, the fundamentals of trade have gone into a tailspin. The central government seems to have left the decision of opening commercial establishments to the states' discretion. As shops and establishments open, the owners will discover the horrors of the closed shops.

The initial announcements by the Prime Minister and the Ministry of Finance extending financial packages to business, corporate houses as well as the general public, will take time to produce the desired results. In the given circumstances, the government will have to do much more to fuel demand in addition to announcing reforms in instalments. The central and state governments will have to coordinate to plan and prepare a strategy document comprising of minimum of seven broad heads including suggestions on various sectors by technical experts, industrial associations, private sector companies and think-tanks. The subjects identified could be as mentioned below:

Destination India

Considering the scenario where companies across the globe are uprooting their base from China and relocating to other parts of the world, it presents a window of opportunity for India which may serve as a lucrative alternative market for the world to invest. Therefore, it becomes crucial for the country to re-examine its investment and FDI policies to attract more foreign investors which will ultimately boost economic growth.

Make in India

In order to strengthen the initiative by the Government of India, there is a need to enhance skill-development, foster innovation and support local businesses through the means of local production and consumption thereby reducing the reliance on foreign and imported products. India's manufacturing sector has been stagnant over a long period of time. There is a dire need to push for implementable and feasible policy solutions which will expand our production capacities thereby bridging the gap in the disrupted supply chains and making India the manufacturing hub for not only domestic consumption but also for exports.

MSME Sector

MSMEs, which presently contribute 30% of our GDP and serve as the backbone of our economy have been deeply affected by the ongoing unprecedented Covid-19 crises leading to an increase in the level of unemployment, pay-cuts and high level of uncertainty. Given the limited resources available and liquidity crunch in the market, this sector needs full-fledged attention to revive the Indian economy to avoid any closure of business units and insolvencies.

Ease of Doing Businesses

With a number of parameters ranging from the registration process to getting electricity to business compliances, it is essential to ease the restrictions imposed for businesses, simplify laws and allow the businesses to grow further. We need to policy-induce higher EDB to promote entrepreneurship nationally. This will further lead to an increase in the employment opportunities, higher tax revenues and also an increase in the purchasing power of the public. In order to strengthen economic growth initiatives, there is a need to enhance skill-development, foster innovation and support local businesses through the means of local production and consumption thereby reducing the reliance on foreign and imported products.

More importantly, very little has been done so far on the technology and innovation aspects of economy in general and defence, IT and Artificial Intelligence sectors in particular.

Youth in R&D and Innovation

The power to reform and change the nation with a fresher and an innovative approach lies with the youth of the country. For the youth to prosper and design out-of-the-box solutions in multi-faceted sectors, there is a need to push for an evolved research and development, further leading to innovative models and solutions. We need policies which incentivise the youth to conduct high-quality research and make intelligent decisions.

Tax and Regulatory Reforms

In the current scenario, companies and industries facing uncertainty need significant tax measures and regulatory reforms on a sectoral basis which can have a positive impact on their businesses and promote trade. Considering restricting plans PE risks, work-home solutions are to name a few.

The Central Board of Direct Taxes (CBDT) is introducing faceless scrutiny assessment and communication through e-mail with tax payers. This will avoid frequent visits to tax office and is expected to bring down possible harassment and tax terrorism. The regressive tax system has less to do with the political dispensation and is more of a legacy issue. The government can either accept its inability to reign in errant officers and correct the aberrations, or bite the bullet and introduce structural tax reforms. A regressive tax regime will neither help ease of business nor fuel demand among the consumers which is extremely important at this stage of low demand.

Speaking at the India-US Business Forum, the Prime Minister has appealed for increased investments in India, invited the US companies to partner with Indian industry and lauded the general atmosphere of transparency in India. But for a speedy economic recovery, the government will have to do much more than what it is attempting at present.

Agro-Industry and Food Security

In times of the ongoing pandemic and accompanying economic crises, food crisis is the major concern for the Indian government. The main challenge is to ensure that enough food is available to the lower strata. Knowing the size of the population and the difficulties in the logistics involved to expand outreach, various social protection and welfare programmes have failed to produce the expected outcomes when it comes to reaching the targeted audience. There is a need to streamline the procurement, storage and supply chain management systems and ensure that the food commodities are available at all locations. Refining the delivery and distribution systems and allocating cash transfers are other means through which the government may overcome the current issue of food shortage.

As the Covid-19 situation improves and normalcy returns, there will be a quantum jump in demand, domestic as well as export. There could be a race for relocation of manufacturing facilities in China. India will be a natural choice for the world to come and invest, given the vibrant democratic dispensation, strong institutional framework, transparent and free judiciary and above all, a buoyant and optimistic population. Nothing can keep us away from a bright and prosperous future.

□

An Indian politician, journalist, author and strategic and foreign policy analyst. He formerly served as head of the Foreign Affairs Cell at BJP headquarters. He is a commentator on security and strategic affairs and was former editor of English weekly 'Organiser'.

Financing of Private Infrastructure Projects in India

—CA K.S. Oberoi

The infrastructure requirements of India are very large, and are increasing rapidly because of strong economic growth. The Government recognises that the public sector is unlikely to mobilise the required resources and that the private sector must be brought in to participate in the opportunity.

Private sector participation in infrastructure will not only ensure a larger flow of resources but also will introduce greater efficiency in the supply of these services. The explosion of global capital markets and the resultant expansion of private capital flows to emerging market economies have provided opportunities to finance infrastructure projects in these countries provided the projects are commercially viable. Several experienced international companies are interested in investing in infrastructure development in India provided the overall investment climate is perceived as attractive and many domestic entrepreneurs are also keen to enter these sectors.

Despite these apparently favourable circumstances, the experience in introducing private investment into infrastructure development has been mixed. The pace of implementation has been much slower than was initially expected. The slow pace does not reflect the lack of private capital. Although the resources available are probably inadequate to meet all of the infrastructure needs of the country, which are indeed enormous, fewer private sector projects are currently being financed than are feasible with current levels of resource availability. The constraint is not the availability of resource but to structure the projects in a manner which attracts private financing.

The reasons pertain to difficulties in implementing private sector infrastructure projects. The problems are associated with the fact that infrastructure projects are usually subject to tariff regulation; the nature of the risks associated with such infrastructure projects is such that there is a need to address the risks to ensure interest of the private financers to enable a suitable mix of long-term finance.

Tariffs on all infrastructure projects are regulated; private operators are not free to fix or adjust tariffs at will. The tariff is generally fixed in advance and adjustable over time only in accordance with contractual terms. Private investment can be attracted into a tariff-regulated sector only if investors are convinced that tariffs will be set and periodically adjusted in a manner that ensures an adequate rate of return to investors. Equally important, the public utility character of infrastructure projects requires that the tariff be perceived as 'fair' to consumers. This balance is not always easy to strike, and disputes over tariffs can delay project implementation.

An alternative to fixing tariffs is competitive bidding. This approach is a transparent way of determining the lowest tariff at which the project can be implemented. Existing public sector suppliers can participate competitively which will establish a level playing field for the private and public sectors.

Debt Financing

Infrastructure projects in India are perceived as unusually vulnerable to risks which constrains financing. Risks are perceived as high, partly because projects are typically undertaken not by established utility companies with strong balance sheets but by special purpose companies executing individual projects on a build-operate-transfer or build-own-operate basis. Equity investors may be willing to accept higher levels of risk in return for higher expected returns on their equity but lenders typically have a lower tolerance for risk and a greater need for risk mitigation mechanisms. Although governments conduct project negotiations with the sponsors, it is the lenders behind the scenes who set risk mitigation standards and determine whether projects are financeable.

Once suitable tariff fixing mechanisms and risk mitigation structures are in place, private sector projects become financeable in principle. At this stage, project implementation depends on the ability to develop a financing package with a mix of finance suitable for the project. This mix varies from sector to sector. Sectors which face relatively high market risks, may require a relatively low debt component, with debt-to-equity ratios close to 1:1. Power projects with assured power purchase arrangements may be financeable with debt-to-equity ratios of 2.5:1 or even 3:1. The maturity requirements of debt will also vary across sectors. Power and roads, which have longer payoff periods, typically require long maturities, while telecommunication projects can manage with shorter maturities. The mix between domestic and external financing also requires careful consideration. Even if external financing is available from well-managed developing countries, foreign exchange risk management considerations may argue in favour of keeping the amount of foreign financing within reasonable limits. There are limitations and constraints associated with each source of debt and equity financing which should be kept in mind when devising financing packages for individual projects.

Equity Financing

Private sector infrastructure projects require substantial equity financing with higher equity requirements required for projects with higher levels of perceived risk. Project sponsors are an important source of equity but they contribute only part of the total equity in most cases. Although preconstruction or developmental costs represent only a small fraction of total cost in infrastructure projects, they can nevertheless run into several millions of dollars, all of which must be financed by equity provided by project sponsors.

Well-structured projects can expect to mobilise equity from international infrastructure funds specialising in investment in infrastructure projects. The amounts available through these funds remain modest relative to the total requirement but the pool of global capital they can tap is very large and the flow of equity from this source could increase substantially if bankable projects become available and the track record of implementation improves. An important aspect of these funds is that they allow international investors to pool risks by investing in a mix of projects. They also enable institutional investors who are relatively risk-averse, to invest in infrastructure projects after the construction stage when project risks are much lower. This provides valuable opportunities for 'take-out' financing, enabling projects to be financed through the earlier and riskier stage by much larger involvement of equity from the sponsors or by high-cost debt with a subsequent restructuring through attraction of equity from infrastructure funds through sale of sponsors' equity or refinancing of debt with equity.

A limited amount of equity support for private sector infrastructure is also available from multilateral organisations such as the International Finance Corporation and the private sector window of the Asian Development Bank. Although these funds can provide only a small amount of capital, their participation in a project provides comfort to other investors. The scope for raising equity from domestic capital markets is limited.

Innovative Instruments with Which to Promote Debt Financing

Innovative financing instruments such as the use of mezzanine debt, can sometimes attract domestic financing to infrastructure projects. Mezzanine debt refers to hybrid instruments that are somewhere between debt and equity (subordinated to secured debt but senior to equity in the hierarchy of creditors). A variety of such instruments including simple subordinated debt, convertible debt, debt with stock warrants, and debt with an additional interest payment above the coupon rate contingent upon financial performance, exist. These instruments appeal to investors looking for higher returns than secured debt provides or for a share in the 'upside' risk of the project. Introduction of mezzanine debt in project financing for a given level of equity helps to improve the quality of senior debt and therefore its marketability.

Conclusion

Despite active pursuit of private investment in infrastructure by most developing countries and a growing number of success stories, the pace of such investment remains slower than initially expected.

Major reason for problem is because infrastructure sector is invariably subject to tariff regulation, and it is difficult to strike a balance between ensuring that tariffs are sufficiently remunerative to private investors and ensuring that they are seen as fair to consumers. Consumer acceptance is especially a problem where consumers have grown accustomed to unrealistically low tariffs charged by public sector systems, reflecting large explicit or implicit subsidies.

Risks associated with infrastructure projects also pose special problems in implementation. Many of the risks are common to any commercial venture and can be handled in proven ways. But other risks are unique to infrastructure, for example, those arising from interface with regulatory authorities and with other government-dominated agencies.

Independent regulatory authorities with a clear mandate to ensure fair treatment for private sector suppliers help to reduce perceptions of risk, as does an efficient legal system that provides quick redress especially in matters relating to contract enforcement. Few countries have all these institutions in place, however, and deficiencies in this area explain some of the delay in project implementation.

Once remunerative tariff structures and acceptable risk mitigation arrangements are in place, projects have to achieve financial closure. This requires mobilising an appropriate mix of financing in terms of equity and debt. Infrastructure projects require long debt maturities reflecting the long payback period. In the absence of long-term debt, they need reasonable assurance of refinancing or 'take-out' financing.

Availability of domestic finance is perhaps the most serious constraint on infrastructure financing. Infrastructure projects cannot be financed exclusively or even primarily through external capital, if only because tariffs are usually fixed in domestic currency and a large share of foreign currency financing implies a correspondingly high foreign exchange risk. A substantial share of project costs must, therefore, be domestically financed.

The biggest challenge is accessing long-term debt. International bond markets are the logical source for such capital, but access to these markets remains limited especially for new companies implementing projects.

Despite these problems, an increasing number of private sector projects are being implemented in the country. Greater clarity in policy and proactive efforts by governments to create the conditions necessary to attract private investment in infrastructure will result in successful implementation of more and more projects.

□

Chartered Accountant who has served as Independent director on the board of various nationalised banks. He is a global consultant in finance and banking.

Evolution of Banking Industry in India

—CA S. Ravi

The banking industry in India forms the base for the economic growth and development of the country. Major changes in the banking system and management have been seen over the years with the advancement in technology and the dynamic changes in the needs and wants of the people. The Indian Banking industry is currently worth ₹ 81 trillion (US $ 1.31 trillion).The Indian banking sector consists of 12 public sector banks, 22 private sector banks and 43 foreign banks along with 61 regional rural banks (RRBs) and more than 90,000 credit cooperatives, in addition to 6 currently active payment banks. Roughly, the contribution of the banking sector to GDP is about 7.7% of GDP. Banking sector has generated employment in the economy for about 1.5 million people.

The first bank of India was the Bank of Hindustan. It was established in 1770 and located in the then Indian capital of Calcutta. Following the path of Bank of Hindustan, various other banks were established in India. They were: The General Bank of India (1786-1791), Oudh Commercial Bank (1881-1958), Bank of Bengal (1809), Bank of Bombay (1840) and Bank of Madras (1843). Some other banks were launched later too, such as Allahabad Bank (1865), Punjab National Bank (1894), Bank of India (1906) and Bank of Baroda (1908).The East India Company had established three banks: Bank of Bengal, Bank of Bombay and Bank of Madras and called them the Presidential Banks. These three banks were later merged into one single bank in 1921, which was called the "Imperial Bank of India. This bank was later nationalised in 1955 and was named The State Bank of India, which is currently the largest Public sector Bank.

When India got independence in 1947, all the major banks of the country were led privately, which was a cause for concern as the people living in the rural areas were still dependent on informal sources i.e. money lenders for financial assistance. To solve this problem, the Government decided to nationalise the Banks. The Regional Rural Banks in India were also established in the year 1975 for the development of rural areas in India. These banks were nationalised under the Banking Regulation Act, 1949 and the Reserve Bank of India was nationalised in 1949.14 banks were nationalised in 1969. These banks had deposits worth more than 50 crore. These were Allahabad Bank, Bank of India, Bank of Baroda, Bank of Maharashtra, Central Bank of India, Canara Bank, Dena Bank, Indian Overseas Bank, Indian Bank, Punjab National Bank, Syndicate Bank, Union Bank of India, United Bank and UCO Bank. In the year 1980, another 6 banks were nationalised taking the number of nationalised banks to 20. These banks included Andhra Bank, Corporation Bank, New Bank of India, Oriental Bank of Commerce, Punjab & Sind Bank and Vijaya Bank.

Apart from the above mentioned 20 banks, there were seven subsidiaries of SBI which were nationalised in 1959. These were State Banks of Patiala, Hyderabad, Bikaner & Jaipur, Mysore, Travancore, Saurashtra and Indore. All these banks were later merged with the State Bank of India by 2017.Once the banks were established in the country, regular monitoring and regulations need to be followed to continue the profits provided by the banking sector.

The next big development was the introduction of Private sector banks in India. RBI gave license to 10 Private sector banks to establish themselves in the country. These banks included Global Trust Bank, ICICI Bank, HDFC Bank, Axis Bank, Bank of Punjab, IndusInd Bank, Centurion Bank, IDBI Bank, Times Bank and Development Credit Bank.

Specialized developmental financial institutions created support for industry and industrialisation. These institutions were set up as they could support many enterprises. The relevance of these institutions was lost in the early 90s as they became Non-viable due to lowering of interest rates. IDBI got converted into a bank, ICICI merged with ICICI bank to become a universal bank and IFCI became an NBFC. IDBI Bank was privatised in 2018 as per the plan by Government of India.

Government of India in the last few years has taken a lot of measures to transform Indian banks so as to make them relevant and also to strengthen them, so that the confidence of depositors is restored.

Some other key developments took place:

- Foreign Banks could now start joint ventures with Indian Banks.
- Payments banks were introduced with the development in the field of banking and technology.
- Small Finance Banks were allowed to set up their branches across India

Under the Budget 2019-20, Government proposed ₹ 70,000 crore (US$ 10.2 billion) to the public sector banks.

In April 2020, the Government decided to consolidate operations of 10 public sector banks (PSBs) into four 'mega banks'. Oriental Bank of Commerce (OBC) and United Bank of India merged with Punjab National Bank (PNB). After the merger, these together formed the second-largest public sector bank in the country after State Bank of India (SBI). Syndicate Bank merged with Canara Bank, making it the fourth-largest public sector lender. Allahabad Bank merged with Indian Bank. Andhra Bank and Corporation Bank both were merged with Union Bank of India. Post the merger, now there are 12 PSU banks-six merged banks and six independent public sector banks.

The 6 banks in which other Banks were merged are SBI, Bank of Baroda, Punjab National Bank, Canara Bank, Union Bank of India and Indian Bank while the 6 independent banks are Indian Overseas Bank, UCO Bank, Bank of Maharashtra, Punjab and Sind Bank, Bank of India and Central Bank of India.

Digitalisation means the adoption of technology. Digital India is the Indian government's flagship programme with a vision to convert India into a digitally empowered country. Faceless, paperless, cashless is the requirement of Indian government. Registration, Invoicing, Payment selection, Payment confirmation are the important phases of digital payment system. This generally includes three electronic payment instruments like cash, cheque and card. Digital banking provides solutions to bankers for their short-term and long-term business and technological requirements. In the present scenario, factors like enhancing of customer satisfaction, unified customer experience, faster output, infinite banking volumes, financial inclusion, operational efficiencies, scale of economy etc. are being sought by leveraging digital banking technologies. Digitalisation is not an option for banking industry, rather it is inevitable. The implementation of demonetisation led the government onto the path towards digital transactions. The main objective of the government of India is make 25 billion digital transactions through multiple facilities, thus creating a cashless economy. Digitalisation of banking requires platforms like Unified Payment Interface (UPI), Aadhaar Pay, Debit Cards and Immediate Payment Service (IMPS). Payment banks were introduced to boost digital banking. The currently active payment banks include Airtel Payments Bank, India Post Payments Bank, Fino Payments Bank, Jio Payments Bank, Paytm Payments Bank and NSDL Payments Bank.

A number of factors brought about the mechanisation and digitisation in banking industry in India. The setting up of standard cheque encoders was the first step forward in digital transformation in banking. Magnetic Ink Character Recognition (MICR) helps in the sorting and processing of cheques with each bank branch having a MICR code. To minimise errors and speed up the process, banks began using computer technology with standard personal computers, and then setting up their own local area networks (LAN). As the networks grew and banks began to connect, Core banking came into being. Centralised Online Real time Exchange (CORE) banking thus allowed customers to perform financial transactions and access their account from any of the participating banks branches. These services made it easier for customers to operate their accounts and slowly led to the coining of the phrase: Anytime, Anywhere Banking. Then Automated Teller Machines (ATMs) arrived on the scene and electronic fund transfers were made possible. Online banking and Tele banking made their appearance in the 2000s and different modes of online fund transfers were instituted like Real Time Gross Settlement (RTGS), Immediate Payment System (IMPS). National Electronics Fund Transfer (NEFT) and National Electronic Clearing Service (NECS). Recent years have seen the growth in mobile banking services and other innovative services online. The role of digitisation of banking in India that began in the 1980s has certainly come a long way.

A major part of Indian banking moved online with internet banking and apps available for fund transfer. In March 2019, India's eleven largest banks–ICICI Bank, Kotak Mahindra Bank, HDFC Bank, Yes Bank, Standard Chartered Bank, RBL Bank, South Indian Bank, Axis Bank, IndusInd Bank, State Bank of India and Bank of Baroda launched the first ever blockchain-linked loan system in the country.

The Volume of Transactions in Digital Banking (Volume in Million)

Year	RTGS	Retail Electronic Clearing (ECS, NEFT, IMPS)	Prepaid Payment Instruments (M-Wallets, Paper Vouchers, PPI Cards)
2011-12	55.1	512.4	30.6
2012-13	68.5	694.1	66.9
2013-14	81.1	1108.3	133.6
2014-15	92.8	1687.4	314.5
2015-16	98.4	3141.5	748.0
2016-17	107.8	4222.9	1963.7
2017-18	124.4	6382.4	3459.0

Source: RBI Bulletin

With the increasing usage of smart phones, digitalisation of banking sector is inevitable to catch up with the increasing expectations of the world. It indeed reduced human errors and increased convenience. With the help of digital banking, most businesses do not have to rely on the bank operation timings. Now the transactions can be made even in the odd hours. There are some transactions like paying bills or making regular payments that can be automated on the digital banking platform. As a result, the businesses are able to save a lot of time on the manual processes and this has a great impact on their productivity. The number of customer base has also increased because of the convenience in 'Anywhere Banking'. Digitisation has reduced human error. It is possible to access and analyze the data anytime enabling a strong reporting system. Digital banking is converting the brick and mortar banks into more green and efficient places to operate. There are a plethora of options that people can opt for when it comes to banking. In the present scenario, people can check their bank account details, pay their bills online, transfer money to other accounts, and all these can be done very comfortably at their residence. For this, the only requirement is the internet connection. India's banking system has come a long way and it needs to keep evolving and adjusting to modern capabilities and technologies.

Prime Minister Shri Narendra Modi in 2015 had desired what banks become through process of digitalisation. He gave these memorable lines-

"I dream for digital India, where mobile and E banking ensures financial inclusion that has turned into a reality. Indian banking will continue to grow so as to become big and increase its global footsteps."

References

1. http://www.iosrjournals.org/iosr-jef/papers/Vol10-Issue3/SEries-2/A1003020105.pdf
2. https://byjus.com/bank-exam/history-banking-india/
3. IBEF-Banking Report May 2020

□

A Chartered Accountant (CA) and is the former Chairman of Bombay Stock Exchange (BSE). He also serves as an Independent Director of Tourism Finance Corporation of India. In 2019, Ravi also joined SBI Payments Services Pvt. Ltd as one of the Board Directors. Before joining BSE, Ravi served on boards of various companies such as UTI Company Pvt Ltd., SMERA Ratings, SBI-SG Global Securities, STCI Finance, and BOI Merchant Bankers.

'Atmavishwas' in Atmanirbhar Bharat

—CA Jayant Gokhale

Atmanirbhar Bharat! Prime Minister Shri Narendra Modi has rightly given this call as India faced the Covid-19 crisis along with the rest of the world. When faced with this unforeseen pandemic, which has the world in its clutches, various nations have reacted differently. While some have taken aggressive measures to curb the spread of virus notwithstanding the cost to the economy; others have taken a more passive approach preferring to put economic interests above that of general well-being. Each country has paid and shall continue to pay the cost for what decision its leaders chose to take. That is where leadership is well and truly tested. Thankfully, the leadership that Modiji has provided has ensured that although the impact of Covid continues to spread, India's death rate (taken as a percentage of population) is amongst the lowest. This is because some courageous and hard decisions were taken early on. It is rightly said that—**when the going gets tough-the tough get going**. The government headed by Shri Modi-took the tough decision to impose an almost total lockdown in less than three weeks from the time that the first case was detected in India. Given the size and magnitude of the country and the poor level of medical infrastructure available to large segments of the population, this was essential and can be considered to be the factor underlying the relatively sound performance in responding to the Covid-19 pandemic.

However, the response of a nation can never be a purely defensive and reactive one. A dynamic leadership always looks at every crisis as an opportunity. Arising out of this need for restricting international commerce, Modiji gave the call for Atmanirbhar Bharat. A very quick reference to the statistics which are available on the web will show that in response to these calls, India is one of the few countries that has swiftly reacted to the crisis by ensuring that supplies of all critical items such as masks, PPE sets, testing kits, ventilators and other ancillary hospital equipment were all made available domestically in the shortest duration. This was done by numerous methods such as government requisition, private innovation, diversion of existing manufacturing capabilities, creating or developing indigenously the necessary machinery and processes and identification of appropriate material supplies for enabling such production. The fact that a country so large was able to make the necessary resources in terms of material and manpower available at numerous production centres across the country, and thereafter, to package and transmit the essential finished goods to the most affected cities, towns and other agglomerations that were most affected, shows our capability not just for manufacturing technology but also the indigenous skills in logistics.

That these capabilities of Atmanirbhar Bharat existed (though not recognised universally) has been proved beyond doubt-notwithstanding what critics might say. However, rather than analyse the excellent response that the public and private sector has been able to provide in this time of crisis, I would prefer to focus on what I consider to be a more significant and long-lasting development. Various critics have argued that Atmanirbhar Bharat Abhiyan is nothing but old wine in new bottles. The concept of relying upon Indian goods can be traced back to the swadeshi movement. However, that was on a different scale and spoke more about reliance on basic goods such as khadi, village produce and to certain extent, industrial raw materials such as steel etc. In the 70 years since independence, our economy has advanced tremendously and we are on the threshold of becoming a global economic power. Under these circumstances, it would have been easy to simply impose a ban on certain imports or despite the WTO / GATT agreements, invoke the health safeguards and for that reason, create tariff barriers or erect invisible trade obstacles which would ensure that foreign goods and services would be blocked during the period of Covid-19.

However, creation of such trade barriers or import bans reflects a basically defensive mindset. It is important to understand that Modiji has reflected the growing confidence that every Indian feels in our ability to compete fairly and on equal terms with the rest of the world. This according to me is the main highlight of the Atmanirbhar Bharat Abhiyan. This sort of program is one born out of a sense of quiet confidence in oneself and in one's capability and capacity. In today's world we are truly living up to the thoughts expressed by Rabindranath Thakur in his classical work *Chitto Jetha Bhayshunyo [Where the Mind Is Without Fear]* [6]which says in his own words

Where the mind is without fear and the head is held high;
Where knowledge is free;
Where the mind is led forward by thee
Into ever-widening thought and action—
Into that heaven of freedom, my Father, let my country awake.

When the country came under the heel of the British, one underlying concept which was continually embedded in the minds of our countrymen was that Indians and Orientals were inferior in thought and intellect; that the British were bringing order and civilisation, for which the 'natives' had no capacity. This became a fundamental belief which made many Indians who received the education/patronage of the British, remain subservient to their European Masters. The imprint of this brainwashing has taken a long time to wipe out from the collective memory of Indians. There were, of course, notable exceptions such as Tilak, Gokhale, Bose and Savarkar, who sought to establish the richness of our culture, and intellectual abilities, but these were partially counterbalanced by the westernised Nehruvian ideology which still embraced the Westminster culture and refrained from an all-out assertion of Indian equality on all planes. Post-independence events such as the 1971 war, the Pokhran blast and numerous other high points gradually eroded the subservient mindset. However, the fact that India was not fully economically independent (leading to requirements for food aid, PL 480, financial bailouts and loans from the Aid India Consortium, IMF etc.) led to the continued perpetration of the psyche, that kept Indians hesitant and unwilling to call the shots.

Narendra Modi, the first Prime Minister to be born in independent India inherited none of this baggage. As a grass roots leader who worked his way to the top by sheer grit and determination, he embodied the belief that India has enormous untapped potential and is subservient to none.

6. Poem 35 out of the Collection Gitanjali–mentioned in his Nobel Prize citation

This confidence is a matter of mindset. It is amply reflected in Modiji's bold leadership repeatedly tackling the bull by its horns. India's recent conduct under the leadership of Modiji in various spheres underlines the shift from a cautious/defensive approach to a confident/aggressive mindset. A series of events such as the decisive cross-border response to the Pulwama attack, the launch of 103 ancillary satellites with a single launch of the PSLV-C37 and the swift diplomatic and military moves to counter China at the LAC are illustrative of this confidence that flows from the top and is fully reflected in the minds of his many admirers and citizenry at large.

In today's world, there are two important universally accepted truths:

a. That economic power, rather than military conquests will define the future of the next few centuries, (and that it is expected that the economic power will shift to Asia within this century).
b. The battles of dominance are won in the mind before they have even started on the ground.

It is in this context that one needs to see the very astute and timely move towards Atmanirbhar Bharat. India has adequately demonstrated that it has

- the men (highly educated and skilled manpower),
- materials (virtually all the essential minerals, metals including rare earths)
- technology (treading in uncharted territory of atomic power, space, pharmaceuticals and vaccines etc.) &
- the manufacturing and logistics capability that has been amply demonstrated in the recent past.

What is needed is to bring this all together in a well thought out cohesive manner. That is the essential role of leadership. That is the role that Modiji has instinctively identified and the path on which he has consciously embarked. There are those who feel that Atmanirbhar Bharat is nothing but a different slogan for the 'Make-in-India' campaign or a reincarnation of the swadeshi movement. But in response I would only say that it requires vision to see the grand design. A lesser mind would see the stone column at the Kailasa Temple at Ellora and admire its intricate carving. It would, however, require a mind capable of a much broader grasp and vision to appreciate the grandeur and the near impossibility of visualising the entire Kailasa Temple top-down, carving it in such manner to give shape to such vision, and to thus create a wonder that has endured for centuries. It, therefore, depends upon your mental capability, whether you see only the carving or the grand design. I would compare the Atmanirbhar Bharat Abhiyan to such a master plan for the India of tomorrow. Looked at in isolation, it is undoubtedly the need of the hour and which will definitely benefit the nation in the short run. However; looked at with greater vision and clarity, you will discern the trademark stamp of a nation coming out from the shadows of domination to the confident mindset (Atmavishwas) of an emerging world power as per the blueprint of its architect, Shri Narendra Modi, the visionary of Atmanirbhar Bharat. This visionary (Modiji) truly believes that this dream of Atmanirbhar Bharat will certainly come true with our collective Atmavishwas. □

B.Com, FCA, LLB. Has been a member of the Central Council of ICAI for 4 consecutive terms. He has been Independent Director (ID) and Chairman of Audit Committee in Syndicate Bank.

Atmanirbhar Bharat Abhiyan

—Mukesh Sharma

Just around a year ago who had imagined that a deadly pandemic originating from Wuhan city in China, termed as COVID-19, will trap the entire would gradually in its grip and put a question mark on the life and livelihood across economies throughout the world. Although a bit late, the pandemic entered India in early March this year and put us into a different phase of life altogether. On the one hand, it brought the necessity of containing its infectious spread in view of the limited availability of health services and infrastructure in our country and on the other, it inflicted a severe blow on the economy of the nation as a whole. The continuous lockdown imposed for months together was followed by closure of a majority of manufacturing, service units and trade activities and a good number of agriculture and allied activities were also critically affected throughout the nation.

Another threat was given by China to the nation's security in the form of a deep encroachment in **Ladakh** area in Indian Territory. It is pertinent to mention here that from China, India is having the highest domestic imports causing a huge trade deficit. Despite all such challenges, the stable government of B.J.P., led by a strong leader **Mr. Narendra Modi**, accepted it as a challenge and strategically attempted to convert this crisis situation into an opportunity, to make India self-reliant i.e. Atmanirbhar Bharat. In his address to the nation on 12 May, 2020, the Prime Minister, Mr. Narendra Modi, termed this campaign as **'Atmanirbhar Bharat Abhiyan** (Self-Reliant India Campaign)' which is going to provide a big opportunity in the crises time to make the country **'A 21st Century India'**. The campaign will also focus on land, labour, liquidity and laws. The financial package declared under it will cater to various sections including cottage industry, MSMEs, labourers, middle class and industries, among others.

The entire campaign is planned to be based on the following **5 pillars:**

Economy: is the main pillar of the campaign which will bring result as a reflection on the economy in quantum jump rather than on incremental basis.

Infrastructure: is another important pillar of the campaign for overall growth in all the sectors, discussed as under in detail.

System: to cope up with the quantum rise in the economy, the system should be based on ultimate modern Information technology-driven arrangements.

Vibrant Demography: is the strongest pillar of the campaign which will lead to us to success. The percentage of youth in Indian population of both the genders which is quite high, is our source of energy for a self-reliant India, Atmanirbhar Bharat.

Demand: Demand factor in our Economy has to be kept high whereby the strength of our demand and supply chain should be utilised to the full capacity, otherwise the foremost objective will be forfeited.

The prime objectives of the ANBA are**: First**: Interim measures such as liquidity infusion and direct cash transfers for the poor in high stress. **Second**: Long-term reforms in growth stimulus sectors in order to make our products & services more aligned with customers' expectations and to make these competitive also, in the global market.

He specifically emphasised and motivated all the Indians to become **vocal for our local products in order to make them global** i.e. not only to purchase and encourage self-use of the local products, but also to motivate others to do so. **The ultimate message of Hon'ble PM behind this gamut is "*Dunia se jude rahate hue aarthik vikas ke sath logon ke jeevan ki gunvatta ko behtar karna*"**

For this very purpose, a **special economic package worth more than ₹ 20 lakh crore** (which is about 10 percent of the India›s total GDP) was unveiled by the Hon'ble PM on behalf of the government, which will in turn support the various sectors of the economy as under:

Primary Sector: Agriculture & allied activities: The agriculture package of ₹ **1.63 lakh crore** included farm-gate and aggregation point infrastructure, fisheries, animal husbandries, and others like animal vaccination and micro food enterprises. The migrant and farmer package of ₹ **3.16 lakh crore** included concessional credit via Kisan Credit Card, farm working capital, affordable housing etc.

Secondary Sector: Micro, Small and Medium Enterprises (MSMEs): The non-bank liquidity package of ₹ **5.94 lakh crore** includes MSMEs, NBFCs, MFIs, housing finance companies etc. MSMEs are the largest employment generating sector of Indian economy.

To support MSME sector, another significant change is in the definition of MSME by raising the investment limit in the plant & machinery and an additional criterion of turnover has since been introduced. Service sector will also be brought under MSME. The necessary changes in the law will be introduced accordingly.

Revised MSME Classification			
Composite Criteria: Investment on plant & machinery and Annual Turnover			
Classification	**Micro**	**Small**	**Medium**
Manufacturing & Services	Investment in P&M < ₹ 1.00 crore and Turnover < ₹ 5.00 crore	Investment in P&M < ₹ 10.00 crore and Turnover < ₹ 50.00 crore	Investment P&M < ₹ 20.00 crore and Turnover < ₹ 100.00 crore

A few government decisions are worth mentioning: No global tender will be allowed in Government procurement tenders up to ₹ 200 crore. **Emergency working capital of ₹ 3 lakh crore for MSMEs has been created.** Additional working capital finance of 20 percent of the outstanding credit will be provided in the form of term loan at a concessional rate of interest without collateral, as the amount will be 100 percent guaranteed by the government. A provision of ₹ 20,000 crore is made for stressed MSMEs. Fund of Funds (FoF) with an amount of ₹ 10,000 crore will provide equity funding support for MSMEs.

Other Sectors: The welfare and health package of ₹ **1.85 lakh crore** included women and pensioner benefits, MNREGA, emergency health response, and others like food and financial security. Pradhan Mantri Garib Kalyan Package (PMGK) was introduced in April 2020 in order to provide relief to the underprivileged and help them fight the battle against Covid-19. The budget allocated to the scheme was ₹ 1.70 lakh crore to support through various ways and means.

RBI's liquidity measures: ₹ **5.24 lakh crore** included two phases of targeted long-term repo operations, CRR cut, marginal standing facility limit increase, refinancing facilities, and mutual fund special liquidity facility. The above rough estimate suggests that the RBI's decisions have provided this additional liquidity since the start of the Covid-19 crisis. Add this to the ₹ 1.7 lakh crore of the first fiscal relief package announced by the Centre. Together, the two already account for 40 percent of the ₹ 20-lakh crore package. That leaves an effective amount of ₹ 12 lakh crore. However, if the government is including RBI's liquidity decisions in the calculation, then the actual fresh spending by the government could be considerably lower than ₹ 12 lakh crore. That's because RBI has been coming out with long-term bond-buying operations (long-term repo operation or LTRO, to infuse liquidity into the banking system) worth ₹ 1 lakh crore at a time. If for argument sake, RBI comes out with another LTRO of ₹ 1 lakh crore, then the overall fiscal help falls by the same amount. Direct expenditure by a government, either by way of wage subsidy or direct benefit transfer or any other measure immediately and necessarily stimulates the economy; in other words, that money necessarily reaches the people, either as someone's salary or someone's purchase, but the credit ease in broader sense prompts the economy.

New Horizon of Growth in **Atmanirbhar Bharat Abhiyan** (Self-Reliant India Campaign)

Coal Sector

Government plans to introduce competition, transparency and private sector participation in the Coal Sector through: Revenue sharing mechanism, instead of regime of fixed Rupee/tonne Entry norms' will be liberalised. Government also plans to invest a total of ₹ 50,000 crore in infrastructure development in the coal sector. This will be focused on evaluation of enhanced Coal India Limited's (CIL) target of 1 billion tons coal production by 2023-24, plus coal production from private blocks. This will include ₹ 18,000 crore worth of investment in mechanised transfer of coal.

Mineral Sector

In order to enhance private investments in the mineral sector, 500 mining blocks would be offered through an open and transparent auction process. Government also plans to introduce few policy reforms in order to increase efficiency in mining and production.

Defence Sector

Government has increased the Foreign Direct Investment in Defence manufacturing under automatic route, from 49 percent to 74 percent.

'Make in India' for Self-Reliance in Defence Production will be promoted by notifying a list of weapons/platforms for ban on import with year-wise timelines, indigenisation of imported spares, and separate budget provisioning for domestic capital procurement. This will help reduce huge Defence import bill.

Aviation Sector

Government plans to ease the Indian Airspace so that civilian flying becomes more efficient. It is estimated to bring a total benefit of about ₹ 1,000 crore per year for the aviation sector. India also plans to become a global hub for Aircraft repair & maintenance. Major engine manufacturers in the world are also expected to increase their engine repair facilities in India in the coming year.

Power Sector

Government plans to introduce tariff policy reform in order to conserve consumer rights as well as promote industry. It also plans to privatise the sector in UTs, in order to improve services to consumers and enhance operational and financial efficiency in distribution.

Social Infrastructure Sector

In order to enhance the quantum of Viability Gap Funding (VGF) up to 30 percent each of total project cost, government has allocated ₹ 8,100 crore.

Space Sector

The government plans to provide opportunity to private companies in satellite launches and space-based services. Policies will be reformed accordingly. Liberal geo-spatial data policy will provide remote-sensing data to tech-entrepreneurs.

Atomic Energy Related Reforms

In order to provide affordable treatment for cancer and other diseases with the help of medical isotopes and research reactor, these will be developed under PPP model. Nuclear sector will be linked with India's robust start-up ecosystem and for this, Technology Development-cum-Incubation Centres will be set up for nurturing synergy between research facilities and tech-entrepreneurs.

Education Sector

Government has launched PM eVIDYA, a programme for multi-mode access to digital/online education. Other initiatives to be launched include Manodarpan, New National Curriculum and Pedagogical framework, National Foundational Literacy and Numeracy Mission **PM eVidya,** DIKSHA for school education across States/UTs: e-content and QR coded energised textbooks to be provided for all grades (one class, one channel), one earmarked TV channel for each grade from 1 to 12, extensive use of radio, community radio and podcasts, special e-content for visually and hearing-impaired people. **Manodarpan**: to be launched on an immediate basis to provide psychological support for students, teachers and families on mental health and well-being. **New National Curriculum and Pedagogical framework** for early childhood, school and teachers will be launched, integrated with global and 21st century skill requirements. **National Foundational Literacy and Numeracy Mission**–to be launched by December 2020 to ensure that every child attains learning levels and outcomes in grade 5.

Ease of Doing Business for Corporates & PSU Policy for Self-reliant India

Direct listing of securities by Indian public companies in permissible foreign jurisdictions. Private companies which list NCDs on stock exchanges will not be considered as listed companies. Provisions of Par IXA (Producer Companies) of Companies Act, 1956 to be included in Companies Act, 2013. Provision to create additional/ specialised benches for NCLAT. Lower penalties for all defaults for Small Companies, One-person Companies, Producer Companies and Start-ups. As per plan for PSU, Policy under this campaign includes notification of strategic sectors to be covered by state & central government, and on the contrary, privatisation of certain required public sector.

Support to State Governments

Central government has extended its support to State government from 3 percent to 5 percent for 2020-21 only, providing states extra resource of ₹ 4.28 lakh crore.

All this is in expectation to strengthen and give a renewed boost to the various sections of the economy towards a firm and planned developmental journey of the nation in the coming future. In order to prove the determination of **a self-reliant India** '4Ls', Land, Labour, Liquidity and Laws, been emphasised in this package.

The Atmanirbhar Bharat Abhiyan-2

Specifically includes certain critical reforms, which have an ample degree of bearing on attainment of the desired level of results, pre dominantly are civil service reforms, government reform, financial reforms, urban reforms, education reform, skill reforms, and labour reforms etc., a time-taking cumbersome process to take over for a brighter tomorrow.

While concluding the note, we find that a big lesson has been taught to us by this global pandemic—**'Be Indian and Buy Indian'**. We have now become critically aware of our own supply chain, and since realised that our over dependence on import from other countries for various critical items will ultimately put us at their mercy. In order to avoid such adversity, self-reliance is the only option left with us to go for local manufacturing, local market and local supply chain to move forward for all about **'Made in India'**. Obviously, **the Atmanirbhar Bharat Abhiyan** (Self-reliant India Campaign) and relief package puts bold reforms and momentum at the heart of Government's plan to make India a self-sustaining economy so that any other crisis that may emerge in future could be effectively tackled.

The author: Mukesh Sharma is a senior operational banker, recently superannuated as Corporate General Manager from Bank of Baroda, He also headed Nainital Bank (a local area scheduled commercial bank) as Chairman & CEO (2016 to 2019). Presently, a practicing Advocate under Bar Council of Delhi & working as a socio-legal activist perusing certain important PILs in significant social areas of importance. He is going to submit his Ph.D. research work on 'NPA Management in Private Sector Banks'.

□

Retired as General Manager from Bank of Baroda. He also served as Chairman of Nainital Bank and is credited with the growth of the bank during his tenure as Chairman.

Cillages:
Cities Enveloped by Villages

—Tulsi Tawari

"Progress does not mean trampling on the weak. Everyone needs a fair chance to grow, to be master of their own destiny. Strong individuals, without losing the culture of collectivism is the Third-Way that India can offer to the world. By designing cities with an envelope of enriching villages as the Earth is covered by Life-sustaining Atmosphere."

Should India of the 21st century not offer a new way of living-option—where the landscape evolves into "optimally-populated cities, surrounded by envelope of enriching villages"? OR Would it simply continue to repeat mistakes from the past with concentration of money in a few over-populated slum-breeding unhealthy cities (ie, 10% of nation's space), while villages stay as object of desertion (ie, 90% of the nation's space), meant only for those who could not make it to cities.

Economic value computation is fraught with errors, by ignoring the worth of precious yet non-tradable wealth (such as, social fabric of a vital community-life, growing-up in vicinity of nature, farms, rivers and forests, etc).

Shifting from a smaller place to a metro city like Mumbai or Delhi, has become the sign of progress for individuals in India. This mindset, prevalent all over the nation, has resulted in massive migration to metro cities over seven decades after independence in 1947. No wonder, these cities are collapsing today under the pressure where 80,000 people are crushed together into one square mile whereas, a few miles away from these cities, you may hardly find 600 people living within a square mile. (see Exhibit-1)

Exhibit-1... State of affairs in Cities and Villages in India

Opportunities remain centred in large metro cities, such as Mumbai, Delhi, etc.

Cities have become increasingly uninhabitable due to pathetic living conditions due to over-crowded space, high cost of good living, over burdened infrastructure, all forms of pollution, lack of personal time and social time due to long travels from home to work. On the whole, nation's surplus resources are being grossly wasted for survival needs of those who live in or continue to migrate to cities.

Villages are deprived...

of access to superior human-growth avenues such as quality education, knowledge-creating institutions, exposure to modern technologies, high-calibre expertise from multi-disciplines, global linkages, high-income jobs, etc. Villages therefore remain grossly under-utilised. One-way migration of the young working population from villages to cities continues. On the whole, villages of India represent the wasted potential of a major portion of land, material and human resources of the country.

Lately, since about 30 years ago, software export revolution took off in a big way from Bangalore. A new dollar-economy ($ 25 billion per year today), attracted 5 million new people, doubling the population density from around 12000 persons per square mile to 30000, a strategic blunder. Crushed under the burden, even lakes are burning with unmanageable garbage. Instead, Bangalore could have remained the beautiful city of gardens, while a few new wealth-creative townships could have been created in a 100-200 miles periphery with the fresh dollar wealth. Quality of life for everyone (old and new population) would have been far better, with no crunch of space, time, travel, affordability and cleaner air while bringing new growth to lacs of villagers in their native places. Due to lack of a strategic vision, we have been destroying our good cities one after another through linear expansions stretching over 50 kms from end to end, while wasting away the identities of villages around, as well.

Why is it necessary to follow a model of growth already proven futile? There can be another way: India can achieve abundance of prosperity through combining the strengths of cities and enriched villages as a seamless entity, in tune with the futuristic internet-empowered knowledge-driven era.

Here are a few pointers for new policies....

1. **Knowledge-driven enterprises** that lead to technological innovations and new wealth-creation opportunities. Sectors may include local crops, natural resources, traditional skills as strengths such as, orange, cotton, textile fabrics, minerals etc.
2. **City's population-density restrained** within optimal limits, to avoid congestion and increase in travel-time. Facilitate new population growth in rural regions, through new expanding wealth-creation opportunities.
3. **Villages act as rural-growth clusters** by facilitating local entrepreneurships and appropriate technologies to develop and nurture agriculture, manufacturing and other services, based on local resources and market needs. For instance, city dwellers need fresh food, vegetables and fruits grown naturally within distance. Villagers need opportunity to add income through making value-added products such as nutritional food, furniture, etc.
4. **New business-clusters away from cities** are developed in well-defined areas between existing city and villages with provisions for work-n-living in same campuses. With internet connectivity, exclusivity of geographical location has become irrelevant for several types of businesses and industries such as IT, professional consulting, residential schools, residential colleges, doctor-owned hospitals, etc. This would enhance the quality of knowledge-presence in and around villages, while the quality of life would become a superior option for many who could balance their life between cities and villages.
5. **Construction and FSI** (floor-space-index) policy to be defined in such a manner that speculative investors are minimal, while actual home and office-users are encouraged. Low prices of land and housing should be a stated goal to ensure that economic growth is achieved through value-addition activities and not easy-money through shortage-led speculations. Isn't high-price of house or land an **illusion of success** ? Everyone may feel happy to see their house price rising, without realising that how expensive it would be to add one extra room when children grow? Can their real earnings support speculative cost increase?
6. **Redesign Big-picture of Harmonious coexistence,** where Gram-Panchayats and villagers are not victimised and continue

to retain their own culture and identities. **Pre-sanctioned zones** for various forms of activities can make spaces for all forms of activities in harmony with each other. Agriculture and industry (from cottage to heavy) can easily be made to co-exist, with prior planning with inputs from multi-disciplinary experts. Land-acquisition need not be an issue, in view of pre-sanctioned areas for heavy industry.

7. **Easy money vs Earned value-added wealth**: Villagers are better off with value-added wealth-creation activities, as compared to selling their lands at speculative high prices, without knowing what to do with too large a sum available at one shot. Experience from across the nation during the past two decades is that such riches end up wasting their newfound wealth in luxurious cars, mansions, drinks and drugs, etc. over a few years and may not be fit for any meaningful work at later times. New generation not equipped suitably with skills or vision, benefitted with such easy money go off-track, is a general observation. Women in such houses end up being the greatest losers as they need to work in menial jobs to take care of their families, eventually.

Cities enveloped by villages can become a role model of new development philosophy, where:

- We harness the existing knowledge strengths of the city in the creation of several 'Decentralised Entrepreneurial Towns' (let us call them Ci-llages, ie, city-like villages) by turning talented local youth as new breed entrepreneurs. Thus, creating greater employment for future generations, near their homes and families.
- We ensure that a cluster of 4-6 villages prosper with value-added wealth created from local agricultural crops, such as cotton, spices, bamboos, frozen-food etc. Appropriate technologies already exist all around us awaiting a well-organised integrated coordination.
- We ensure that a meagre population of 500-1000 in villages grow to become 5000-10,000 over a period of few years, through resource-based planned local economy, with integral development having residential schools, residential colleges, smaller and yet specialised hospitals set up by young and talented practitioners, entertainment and sports centres, etc. Thus, providing future generation with greater possibility in fulfilling their own dreams

and leading their lesser-talented brethren for better lives. New created wealth would bring about both prosperity and happiness through collective growth of society.

- With internet affordability being widespread, these new townships could also attract high-end technological talents from India and abroad, who live and work in these smaller towns, while doing business with clients all over the world. India can thus evolve her own model of progress, where larger cities and decentralised villages-turned-towns co-exist, and grow to their optimal size. This would also reduce the urban-rural divide that currently exists in the system. These decentralised towns would provide ample opportunities to the future generations and reduce the excessive charm of living only in a metro city.

Reversal-of-Migration can be the new theme for next 50-60 years, when India is recreated through her own new breed of young entrepreneurs, willing to take plunge in pride of rebuilding the nation from bottoms-up. Existing cities also become unburdened and find greater space and breeze of fresh air. In fact, India can be redesigned through evolving a 'Cillage-Masterplan', that has a city not exceeding 10 kms, surrounded by 100-200 villages around; thus a vision of 5000 Cillages in the next 50 years!!

Advantages in creating Decentralised-Entrepreneurial Towns of Future

- **Greater Opportunity to Live own Dreams:** Youth finds greater opportunities to set up own enterprises, thus fulfilling their dreams rather than becoming an un-noticed entity in larger corporations.
- **The 21st century Challenge for Youth of India:** New township creations become the pride and motto of young India. Indian youth needs a purposeful challenge that inspires them-Rebuilding the Nation through wealth-creating towns is quite a challenge requiring millions of youth engaged for the next 50-60 years. Imagine how neat Indian landscape would look everywhere, should this become true!
- **Value-added Wealth-creative Independent Regions:** India creates wealth from within, thus strengthening domestic economy without dependence on large capital infusion from

larger corporations from outside the country. With strong internal domestic economy built over value-addition of own local resources, would provide sustained and economic-independence to every region and nation as a whole. Export and foreign investments can bring recognition and further prosperity and growth, but it need not become a necessity for an independent nation.

- **Easy Skill Upgrade for Masses:** Majority of people (not necessarily equipped with high-end skills required in larger cities), can easily be retrained for building these simpler and smaller townships, and find well-paying employment near their homes without moving to metro-cities. This would solve the slum issues in larger cities and thus unburden them from over-population.
- **Retired Knowledge-Bank Utilisation:** Lacs of Senior knowledge people of India, healthy yet retired, would find a new meaning and purpose in guiding the youth in terms of training in science, technology, enterprises, management, economics, arts & culture, sports, etc.
- **Alternate Lifestyle, Renewable Energy & Recycling of waste:** At today's level of fuel and mineral consumption by the prosperous city-people, the rest of the society could never ever be able to enjoy similar benefits. Smaller decentralised towns would facilitate alternate lifestyles to people, which would allow for lesser consumption of energy. As a result, alternate technologies based on renewable resources, could help achieve sustainable growth without damaging nature. Furthermore, new lifestyles would provide easier recycling of waste through converting them into useful wealth and energy for local population. Handling of massive tonnages of waste in larger cities is polluting land, air and water bodies alike.
- **Family-Values & Social Fabric:** For centuries, India's major strength has been her culture of family values, extending to larger community beyond own family even. Large and complex cities have been attracting talented youth away from their families and communities, living in nuclear families. Future youth can recreate the concept of joint families in smaller towns, as one has greater control over one's time. Strengthening of family and social fabric would naturally enhance overall happiness and develop greater resilience in society to cope up with difficulties too.

- **Equity of Wealth as against Widening Disparity in Large cities:** In all large cities, people can be seen living in two vividly different worlds. One, gated residential complexes, where more prosperous ones live whereas masses live in filthy slums, next door. Such gross disparity eventually leads to social unrest, crimes, more policing, unclean cities, and eventually insensitivity towards disadvantaged ones. This can hardly be called growth in a civilised society. Decentralised towns would lead to greater equity among the masses with possibility to own a simple yet spacious home in smaller towns.
- **Intellectual Corruption & Speculative Siphoning of wealth abated:** Larger cities become complex systems and easier hideouts for people who manipulate and exploit masses through scheming and speculative ploys with money. This is one of the reasons that add to concentration of capital in fewer hands. In smaller townships where social fabrics are very strong, such negative overtures are not only easily visible but are discouraged, as the society looks down upon such practices.
- **Harnessing of age-old Traditional Knowledge & Artisan Skills:** India has history of thousand years. As such, traditional knowledge and skills in various forms still exist such as in healthcare, nutrition, organic farming, herbs, vegetable dyes, arts & culture etc. For want of purchasing power in villages, these expertise are losing relevance. New wealth-creating and prosperous decentralised smaller towns could provide big boost to such traditional abilities and offer nature-compatible solutions and opportunities.
- **Greater Time for Children affects their Emotional Skills:** In larger cities, one is always pressed for time as everyone ends up wasting 2-4 hours in travel alone. People are unable to find time to communicate with their own children on daily basis. This naturally diminishes emotional side of the child, who has more focus on self only. On the contrary, a smaller town and community life provides more balanced environment for children's growth, who experience greater affection and care from people around.
- **Surplus Time for Creative Pursuits:** In a nation well-organised in decentralised manner, each region has greater chances to establish unique identity through creative efforts. This becomes

possible, as people have greater control of their time and could invest their surplus time (saved from unnecessary travel in larger cities) in nurturing their creative pursuits.

- **Balanced Growth of larger Cities as well:** With vibrant smaller townships around, larger cities are unburdened from over-population and have greater ability to develop larger ideas and innovations with help from within and around its borders. In fact, smaller towns can act as centres of new research and experiments for knowledge people staying in larger cities.
- **Easier Governance:** With gram-panchayat equipped with modern tools and practices in terms of society's growth prospective and empowered by wealth-creative local population, the governance becomes direct, grass-rooted, simpler and easier as against the complex and distant, as of now.
- **Optimal utilisation of Public Funds & Lower taxations:** An entrepreneurial society, living largely in smaller towns, could lead to major savings in public fund requirements, both in townships and cities as infrastructure costs in decentralised societies would naturally be gradual and wealth-creative too.

A strong, healthy and wealthy rural India is the key to overall national prosperity, peace and harmony among its myriad communities. No leader in the past 70 years has tapped the unbound wealth-creation potential of rural India.

Reversal of Migration can be the theme for the future of New India! The idea is to 'unlock' the inherent potential of rural India and create a new role-model for economic growth during 21st century which is fair to each citizen of any background living in any part of the country (*rural/urban*) and nature-friendly too.

Time will tell... whether New India will show a new way of life to the nation and the world.

□

Former Co-chairperson of Screening Committee of Niti Aayog, member BOC-IIT Bhilai and an eminent author.

A Self-reliant India: A Strategic Vision and a Practical Mission

—CA Vinod Jain

The Indian economy has been passing through testing time for last about two years. There have been several economic and political factors impacting India's Growth story. The challenges have surmounted with the latest advent of Covid-19, an epidemic which had brought major economic activity to a grinding halt for several weeks and months. The lockdown followed by phased unlock process has been very painful. India has realised that it could survive one of the worst challenges in the history of mankind only because Indian economy has been self-reliant in respect of most of the necessities.

The Prime Minister has called upon the nation to be self-reliant in all the economic and business sectors. This matter is important for India. We, as a nation, have to prepare all-industrial sector, service sector and agriculture sector to be self-reliant in respect of all inputs and outputs. The commitment for self-reliance requires that the economic climate needs to be geared up to enable wealth creators to garner their entrepreneurial skills and resources so that the dream of a self-reliant India can be achieved.

The present Article will concentrate on certain specific economic and business sectors so that a deeper-to-the-point suggestions can be brought out for strategic thinking and action.

Banking and Financial Services Sector

1. **₹ 3 Lakh Crore Scheme:** The Government announced a highly effective scheme to support mid-size and small size borrowers wherein the loans are Guaranteed by Government of India. The following suggestions need consideration:

- To cover the businesses upto ₹ 250 crore turnover (in place of ₹ 100 crore announced), as the limit of MSME has also been increased to ₹ 250 crore.
- The upper limit of existing borrowing was fixed at ₹ 25 crore. This may also be proportionately increased.
- Interest amount is required to be excluded for determining eligibility of funding.
- In certain cases, the interest debited on 29th February end of the day and serviced by borrower next day or a separate deposit is kept with the lender is also included in the amount outstanding as on 29th February.
- The Government is required to consider giving such facility even to those businesses, which were not having borrowings as on 29th Feb, 2020, or their actual borrowing was vey less. The maximum limit can be based on: Working Capital Borrowing: 20% of credit entitlement/ maximum permissible bank finance (MPBF) to be determined based on turnover (25% to 30% of projected turnover as MPBF)
- Rate of interest: maximum rate of interest can be 3 percent above Repo rate for banks and NBFCs. NBFC actual lending can be refinanced by a bank at Repo plus 200 basis point.

2. **Moratorium amount repayment along with interest**

   This amount is currently payable immediately after completion of 6 months' period. The Government may consider spreading this amount over 2 to 3 years.
3. **10 percent additional limit:** In many cases, this facility has been denied. Private sector banks have refused in 90 percent plus cases. Even the cases where the facility has been extended by the bank concerned, the limit could not be availed, as Drawing power may not be available due to bank's fixed norms, although borrower has good security cover. The Government may consider providing this amount as **working capital term loan, repayable in over 2 years.**
4. **Growth of bank Credit:**

   The following actions may be necessary to ensure growth of non-food bank credit:

- **Fear factor in lenders:** Hon'ble FM has already assured that the CVC, CBI and banks disciplinary cells will not take any adverse view of lending and other business decisions taken by bank officers in good faith. It is important to issue a formal circular in this regard **to firmly convey** that once a decision is approved by a Committee, and is recorded transparently in internal information system, no authority will be able to question the judgement of officers at any level unless malafide is clear. The onus to prove *malafide* beyond doubt with *mens rea* will be of the authority before initiating any action.

- **Fear factor in Entrepreneur:** The risk is inherent in business and NPA cannot be considered as an ugly word. If greenfield investment is to be made, there could be genuine circumstances in which cash flow may take longer to stabilise, or even COD of project may get delayed due to reasons beyond control or comprehension of businesses. In case of default, the wealth creator Entrepreneurs need not be subjected to SFIO, ED or DRI and other investigative authorities. PMLA, Benami law need to be activated only in cases of anti-national crimes like drug trafficking, illegal Arms, terrorism and the like heinous crimes. The Criminal and penal provisions in tax statue also need to be only exercised in exceptional circumstances where highly material public interest is getting adversely impacted. It may be important to de- criminalise tax statue and economic non-compliance.
- **Invocation of Insolvency and Bankruptcy code (IBC)** should be restricted. In case of a genuine default or delay, an opportunity of restructuring and Reschedulement and additional resources should be provided in case of need. The fear of losing even the existing business in case of an expansion or diversification going wrong, has negatively impacted the risk-taking ability of Entrepreneurs. The resolution professional needs to only monitor the finances and operational control of the entity under resolution process. The existing management should be free to take all day-to-day decisions in the interest of the Company. The Role of Committee of Creditors is very important and it can review RP report and approve all policy decisions as proposed by the Board.
- **Personal Guarantee:** The lenders have started insisting on personal guarantee of Entrepreneurs irrespective of size of the project. This further dampens the risk-taking ability of

Entrepreneurs. It may be noted that developed countries like USA have no such concept of a personal liability in case of borrowing and the lenders restrict their charge only to primary security created from the lending. The RBI Master Circular mandates a personal guarantee in all cases, except large listed Companies. This is a growth dampener. In USA or Europe, no personal guarantee is required and security of assets created by the business are relied upon for lending.

- **Collateral Security**: This is a related point and insistence by banks and other lenders on providing collateral security outside the business also impact the investment climate negatively, as even a very good project will not find favour unless secured by additional collateral security from promoters' personal assets. There is no such international practice in developed countries like USA, Europe or China.
- **Development Financial Institutions:** A significant growth in India was led by DFIs set up in early 1960s, like IDBI, IFCI, ICICI and state level SFCs and SIDCs. There is a dire need for a mega large DFI specialised in industrial development and with ability to provide long-term funding with low rate of interest. Alternatively, the mega 4 PSBs can play similar developmental role.

5. **Interest rates**: The major reason for large NPAs has been high interest rates and penal rates charged by lenders during 2004-2014.The banks need to keep their Net Interest Margin (NIM) in control, and ensure that Indian economy is able to offer internationally competitive rate of interest. The regulator may consider maximum NIM for all lenders. An interest subvention to banks for lending to manufacturing and construction may also be worth considering.
6. **Development of Industry clusters:** The Government needs to identify appropriate location in every block and district, so that industry cluster of select industries can be developed. This needs to include:

- An industrial estate with fully developed land, power stations, water treatment plant, pollution treatment plant,
- large, mid-size and small flatted factories with plug and play facilities. This is to be provided at highly concessional rent so that

all factories can start within 15 days of conceptual decision by Entrepreneur.

- Research centre funded by Government with teams of scientists to support private researchers to undertake research and development of new products, design, prototype and to undertake all kinds of experiments and trials.
- Roads and street lighting and common facilities required in the industrial cluster.
- Hospitals and nursing homes.
- Entertainment joints, cinema halls, clubs and facilities.
- Sports and physical fitness centre.
- Residential Flats and apartments for different categories of workforce.
- Schools and colleges
- Religious places
- Logistic centres for transportation of goods-Railhead, Roads, bus terminus and related facilities
- Shops and Markets

7. **Registrations and approvals:** The KYC, business registration, license, permit, environment clearance, ESI, PF, GST, PAN, TAN, MSME, land or factory allotment and all other registrations can be combined in one single form to be submitted online with reference to Standard operating guidelines and all approvals and clearances can be provided within 7 days.
8. **Compliance by a single Electronic form on a single national portal:** In respect of all returns and compliances, a single form can be developed in which all necessary inputs can be filled by business organisation in respect of all necessary returns and filings. This master form may be updated monthly by large concerns, and quarterly by MSME units and small mid-size businesses. This will include all compliances under income tax law, GST, Companies Act, PF, ESI, FEMA, labour laws and environment law. The unorganised sector, micro and other specified sectors can be exempted from most of the sections of the form.
9. **Demand push:** To push the demand in the economy, the Government may consider

- substantial relief in direct tax-including Corporate Tax for 2 years (Rebate of X % of tax payable across board), to enable a larger income remaining in the hand of individuals and corporates.
- Deficit financing of budget by issuance of long-term bond in favour of RBI with nominal interest, to enable funding of huge infra and budgetary spend. This will bring down inflation and result in demand push, besides ensuring growth in the economy.

10. **Employment Push:** The above actions will in any case bring growth and employment in the economy. The employment-oriented trade, services and manufacturing sector can be promoted by an appropriate tax incentive for every additional employee. The scheme of funding employers' contribution to PF and ESI by the state for initial 3 years of first employment for all employees in MSME sector, will be a long-term booster. MSME manufacturing sector can be considered for refund of 25% output GST paid in cash.

Other Key Tasks of the Industry from the Government in the Current Perspective of Covid

11. **Cash Flow:** To permit manufacturing sector and services to bring in capital to invest in their business. No source for this money to be asked and money brought in can be taxed at normal rates/ concessional rates. Money has to be used for business with at least 5year lock in and can be used for expansion, new industry, repayment to lenders and for working capital. Section 115BBE of Income Tax Act, 1961 may be withdrawn/amended. (To Ensure free flow of informal funds into mainstream).
12. **Misuse of Section 68**: Section 68 read with Section 115BB is being misused during assessments and tax administration. A very heavy rate of tax and high penalty is being used as a criminal punishment measure. Restoration of pre 2016 period may be considered here.
13. **Applicability of PMLA and Benami law**: currently being prone to severe misuse against genuine business transaction, even where no non-compliance of tax laws or other economic laws is involved. A high-level committee of Chief Commissioners with Chamber representatives to examine prima facie and give prior

approval before initiation of cases. All existing cases should also be reviewed on the same basis, and all tax evasion and other civil cases to be dealt with in respective law. Not to consider businessmen as criminals. This will help alleviate investment climate.

14. **No GST on output on Real Estate**. Also, entire input credit of such developer to be refunded for supply in next twelve months. **Stamp duty** on such supply may also be exempted for 24 Months.
15. **Automobile (50%), Textile** and other high employment sectors can also be given similar substantial benefits of subvention on output GST for 12 months-Automobile (50%), Textile (75%).
16. **GST–Input credit should not be disallowed** under any of the circumstances to ensure seamless credit. Unused Input credit to be refunded in all cases including in case of Goods and Services which are exempt from taxation.
17. **GST-Reverse charge** payment in all cases may be exempted in all Business to business supply. The Government will not have any revenue loss in the process as entire reverse charge is immediately claimed as input credit.
18. GST law, Income Tax law as well as other economic laws also need decriminalisation. To restrict penalty and prosecution only to large material frauds and manipulations.
19. GST subvention to all MSME–Micro and small manufacturing units up to 20% of GST on output to enable growth of this sector including large-scale employment and deep-routed economic activity.
20. **GST and Income Tax discretionary powers in terms of law** with officers are required to be eradicated to near zero level.

The faith and trust on wealth creators has to be brought in the entire system, as per dream of PM Narendra Modiji.

□

Has about 38 years of experience in the field of Taxation, Audit, Accounting, Finance, Banking Law, Education and strategic planning and business management. Presently, Shri Jain is a Member, High Powered Committee appointed by Finance Ministry to simplify Income Tax Laws. He has been appointed as a Government Nominee Director on the Board of Directors of Coal India Limited.

Creating Liquidity for Revival of Economy

—Dr. Raj K. Agarwal
—Dr. Rakesh Gupta

Due to the countrywide lockdown announced to tackle the menace of Covid-19, economic activities have been paralysed. Except for the essential items, all manufacturing activities have come to a halt. Industry is under pressure to meet out fixed costs such as salary and wages, rent, interest, power expenses etc. which are required to be paid even during the lockdown period. There are hardly any revenue being realised as the entire flow of funds is stuck at every end. After opening of the lockdown, when manufacturing activity is expected to be resumed, industry is going to face acute shortage of liquidity. We would have to prepare in advance for creating enough liquidity in the system so that economic activities may be revived in a smooth and quick manner. All-round steps are required to be taken by the industry, banks and the government alike, for this purpose.

Actions to be Taken by Industry

At this critical time, promoters should not hesitate to infuse further equity in the business by liquidating their surplus personal assets to the extent feasible. Due to fear of recurrence of Covid-19, it is difficult to estimate the longevity of the problem and the pace with which the economic activity may be revived. Therefore, it is significant to observe that one should not fall into debt trap by over leveraging.

Mother units should defer their expansion plans and extend support to the vendors by making timely payments of outstanding dues. Wherever necessary, even some advance payments may be required to be released so that entire chain of products is activated.

Industry should defer the Capex plans and instead, working capital management should be the priority. Focus should be on increasing efficiency, cutting cost and controlling all non-essential expenses. Fixed expenses relating to salary, wages, rent, etc. may be re-negotiated linking them with the productivity or turnover.

Actions on Part of the Banks

This is the time when public and private banks are also expected to play constructive & proactive role in revival of economy. They should extend support to the industry along with the exercise of close monitoring. Banks would have to think as businessmen and not merely as a lender. Additional working capital limits may be sanctioned to the industry to meet out essential expenses. It has been expressed by the government and RBI that there is enough liquidity available with the banks, but it has to be passed on to the industry in judicious manner.

Further, banks are expected to pass on the cut in interest rates announced by RBI, to the borrowers which would provide requisite impetus to the demand particularly in the real estate and auto sector.

Actions on Part of the Government

One can appreciate that Government is not having sufficient fiscal space to provide financial incentives or stimulus package to the industry. The priority of the government is to provide relief package to 800 million people by providing them food and other necessary items of livelihood. But, the government can certainly help the industry by providing business-friendly environment, taking measures to create ease of doing business, remaining soft on rigorous investigation of past defaults and strengthening mutual trust and confidence with the business community. This is the time when entire energy should be deployed to revive the economy.

This is high time when idle assets stacked in the form of cash or gold should be brought into the system. Bonds in the nature of 'Special Bearer Bonds' as issued in the year 1991 may be introduced. Second option may be to issue 'Console Bonds', where interest is paid periodically but there is no commitment of fixed period of repayment of the principal amount.

Under the Income Tax Act, any income/investment, source of which is not satisfactorily explained by the assessee, is taxed as deemed income under sections 68 to 69D of the Income Tax Act, 1961. Prior to the amendment by Taxation Laws (Second Amendment) Act 2016 made with effect from AY 2017-18, rate of income tax applicable on such income was maximum marginal rate i.e. 30% plus surcharge, cess, etc. In November 2016, when demonetisation of currency took place, effective rate of tax on such incomes was increased upto 75% plus cess, by making amendment under section 115BBE of the Act by the above Amendment Act brought on 15.12.2016, but making the new tax rate effective from A.Y. 2017-18 on income earned from 1st April, 2016. It was so done, so that unaccounted cash deposited in old currency after demonetisation attract higher rate of tax which includes the element of 'penalty' also. It was done in this manner because as per legal position, penalty provision could not be introduced retrospectively and government wanted such unaccounted money to suffer element of penalty also along with the tax, particularly when just six months back during April-May 2016, Income disclosure scheme, 2016 was announced imposing tax, surcharges and penalty aggregating to 45% of unaccounted income.

It needs to be appreciated that the situation has changed and the priority of the government is to bring back economy on the right path and infuse liquidity in the system. The objective with which rate of tax under the said section 115BBE was increased, is no more relevant and therefore, such high rate of tax is not desirable. In case rate of tax under section 115BBE is brought down to the maximum marginal rate, it may provide an opportunity to introduce unaccounted cash into the system by paying the tax at maximum marginal rate and declaring the same as current year's income. This position of law existed prior to amendment made by the Taxation Laws (Second Amendment) Act 2016.

It may further be appreciated that such amendment in section 115BBE or declaration of unaccounted cash by paying tax at maximum marginal rate would not be in the nature of any immunity scheme. In such cases, tax-payers cannot claim telescoping of any other undisclosed income evidences of which are found in the course of any kind of inquiry, assessment or investigation by the tax department against such income. In case evidences of any undisclosed income are detected, tax payers may be separately taxed and penalised for such undisclosed income.

Another provision of the Income Tax Act 1961, which may be amended at this critical juncture is the taxability of anonymous donations received by the charitable organisations registered under section 12AA of the Income Tax Act, 1961. Section 115BBC was introduced by the Finance Act 2006 w.e.f.1.04.2007, providing that anonymous donations received by the charitable trusts or institutions are taxable in excess of 5% of the total donations received. Prior to introduction of section 115BBC, such anonymous donations were not taxable in the case of charitable institutions. It was so done so as to ensure that unaccounted cash, source of which is not explained, is taxed and does not become eligible for tax exemption under section 11 of the Income Tax Act, if utilised for charitable purpose. In case section 115BBC taxing the anonymous donations is withdrawn, it would pave the way to utilise such unaccounted cash for the much-needed charitable activities, relief to the poor etc. which is most urgently required at this moment. Instead of controlling the source of the funds, such charitable institutions can be regulated and investigated by scrutinising the application of the funds.

The above two amendments under the Income Tax Act, 1961 may go a long way to bring requisite liquidity in the system, payment of taxes to the government and utilisation of the funds for revival of socio-economic activities.

Further, post lockdown period, say, for at least six months, payment of GST may be permitted to be made on quarterly basis or with a deferment of 2-3 months, so that some initial working capital remains in the hands of the businessmen. All pending governments' dues or tax refunds too may be released immediately by all government departments.

Idle gold accumulated by the individuals or trusts is another huge idle asset and some scheme in the nature of Gold monetisation scheme may be introduced so as to bring such idle assets in productive use.

We all would have to appreciate that the present situation is an extraordinary situation and government is also expected to take extraordinary steps and out-of-the-box measures. The priority of the government is to ensure that economic activities are resumed at the earliest and there is no loss of jobs. Even unorganised sector or informal economy may be helpful in preventing loss of jobs and maintaining much needed demand & purchasing power in the system.

□

An FCA, FCS, AICWA, MBA, LLM and Ph.D. and is an eminent professional.

An FCA, FCS, AICWA, MBA, LLM and Ph.D. He is an Ex-Member of Income Tax Appellate Tribunal and is expert on taxation.

National Education Policy 2020

—Dr. Ashok Kumar Gadiya

Introduction

The present education system of our country is producing millions of graduates, post-graduates and thousands of Ph.D. every year. The degree holders are coming out from Universities and colleges with high hopes of getting employment either in Government sector or in private sector. Some of them are aspiring to go abroad, 99% of the pass out students are looking for employment or looking for to start new business for their livelihood and to serve their parents and close relatives.

But looking at the present situation, we found that very few out of millions of pass out students are able to fulfil their dreams, the majority pass out students are unemployed and feeling helpless.

We all are aware that this unfortunate position is because of the fact that 95% of our pass out students are unemployable because they do not have that much of skill and capability which is required by employers.

In order to bridge this gap, major reforms that can bring high quality and integrity into education system so that it can produce confident, self-reliant, capable and professional youth, who are either employable or can become entrepreneurs. The National Education Policy 2020 has been placed before the public by Hon'ble Education Minister, Sh. Ramesh Pokhrial 'Nishank' under the leadership of Hon'ble Prime Minister Sh. Narendra Modi Ji.

Now, we discuss the National Education Policy 2020 in brief:

Part–I–School Education

School Education (5 + 3 + 3 + 4) = 15

A. Foundation Stage

B. Preparatory Stage

C. Middle Stage

D. Secondary Stage

A. Foundation Stage:

Age–3 Class–F1

Age–4 Class–F2

Age–5 Class–F3

Features:

i. Learning through playing
ii. No formal teaching
iii. No School Bag
iv. No Uniform
v. No Homework
vi. Teacher will play with children
vii. No language bar
viii. Communication with any language
ix. Development of logical and emotional mind of child
x. Puzzle game
xi. Multitasking game
xii. Personality development
xiii. Knowledge of hygiene
xiv. Mannerism
xv. Rhymes
xvi. Entire focus on natural mental development of child
xvii. Knowing colours, shapes and numbers
xviii. Ethical and moral development through storytelling and role play etc.

Age–6 Class–1

Age–7 Class–2

Features:

i. Learning through books
ii. Regional Languages/Hindi/English Language
iii. No Exam–No Pressure

B. Preparatory Stage:

Age–8 Class–3

Age–9 Class–4

Age–10 Class–5

Features:

i. Books and subjects,

ii. Learning through activities

iii. Regional language/Hindi/English

iv. Exams monthly, quarterly, half-yearly & annually.

v. No pressure on students.

C. Middle Stage:

Age–11 Class–6

Age–12 Class–7

Age–13 Class–8

Features:

vi. Subjects may be 4 or 5

vi. Computer Education

vii. One Indian language may be Sanskrit, Urdu, Marathi, or any language, Vocational, Educational, Teaching in regional/ English/Hindi language.

i. Exams monthly, quarterly, half-yearly & annually.

D. Secondary Stage:

Age–14 Class–9

Age–15 Class–10

Age–16 Class–11

Age–17 Class–12

Features:

i. Multidisciplinary selection of subjects, Semester Exam, Question will be asked to test critical thinking, Foreign Language.

ii. Vocational Education, No Stream, No cramming.

iii. All schools will be accredited and grading will be given only on the basis of periodic audit.

iv. School Fee may be Regulated.

Part–II–Higher Education

1. Vision of Future Higher Education:

i. Establishment of Multidisciplinary University in every District of Country.

ii. Establishment of Colleges and Higher Education Institutions across India those offer medium of instruction or programmes in Local/Indian languages.

iii. Multidisciplinary Undergraduate Education.

iv. Earning of Gradual autonomy through graded development of Institutions.

v. Changing curriculum, pedagogy, assessment and examination.

vi. Appointment of faculties strictly on merits, on the basis of teaching, research and services in the field of education.

vii. Establishment of National Research Foundation to fund research projects of Universities and Colleges.

viii. Universities, Colleges and Higher Education Institutions will be Governed by qualified independent board and will have required autonomy.

ix. 'Light & Tight' regulations to Universities, Colleges and Higher Education Institutions by a single regulator of higher education.

x. Providing academic learning material, easily accessible to learners through online and distance learning mode.

2. Under New Education Policy:

University means a Multidisciplinary institution of higher learning that offers Undergraduate and Post Graduate programmes with high quality research and community engagement.

Through this definition, there will be two types of Universities:

A. Research Intensive Universities:

Those universities will emphasise on research and teaching both.

B. Teaching Intensive Universities:

Where a greater emphasis will be on teaching, but they will conduct significant research also.

C. There would be widespread spread of Autonomous Degree Granting Colleges which will be multidisciplinary and will be teaching intensive and will grant Undergraduate degrees, they will be generally upgraded through Graded development to Universities.

As soon as a College is accredited by a National agency of accreditation and obtain a required benchmark, it will be granted autonomous status and that college will be able to award Undergraduate degrees in Multidisciplinary Courses.

D. Each degree awarding College will have at least 3000 or more than 3000 students doing undergraduate courses in various subjects under Multidisciplinary options.

E. It is planned that by 2040, all Higher Education Institutions will become Multidisciplinary and their strength will be not less than 3000 each.

F. It is also planned that by doing so, the gross enrolment ratio (GER) number will be 50% by 2035.

G. Emphasis will be on developing large number of outstanding public institutions through public funding. However, equal opportunities will be given to the promoters who wanted to establish private institutions but they will not be funded by public funds. Those institutions which are fully accredited, will be motivated to expand their capacity.

H. The institutions who are accredited for O.D.L. will be encouraged and supported to develop high quality online and distance learning courses.

I. Gradually, Single-Stream HEI will be phased out and will be converted into Multidisciplinary Higher Education Institutions.

J. Over a period of 15 years, the concept of affiliated colleges will be phased out and affiliating Universities will also be phased out.
The colleges will become Multidisciplinary degree awarding institutions.

K. Under the National Education Policy, it is envisaged that the HEI will be an integrated institution which will include academic, professional and vocational education.

L. University, worldwide, means a multidisciplinary institution of higher learning that offers undergraduate, graduate and Ph.D. programmes and engages in High-quality teaching and research. The present complex nomenclature of HEIs in the country such as 'deemed to be university' 'affiliating university', 'affiliating technical university, 'unitary university' shall be replaced simply by 'university' on fulfilling the criteria, as per norms.

3. Outcome of Higher Education:

A. In the new Education Policy, it is aimed that the student who is doing undergraduate course, he or she should be able to study, understand and develop critical thinking in the areas of Science, Technology,

Engineering & Mathematics, Commerce, Humanities and Vocational education as per his/her choice. After completion of his/her studies, one should have developed critical thinking, problem-solving ability, teamwork and communication skill.

Teaching should increase social, moral and innovational awareness of the student and the student should step forward for some research work.

Above all, the New Education System will ensure that the student is developed all round i.e. mentally, physically and ethically. At the end, the student should be converted into confident, self-reliant, responsible, professional youth of the country.

B. The Course Curriculum will be flexible, multiple entry and exit facility will be designed in accordance to requirement of Society, Government and Industry. It would be comprehensive, regularly updated and will be supported by high quality pedagogy. The assessment will be scientific to know the real learning outcome of the study.

Appropriate teaching methodology will be designed in accordance to requirement of the students and course concerned.

The examination system will be credit-based.

C. The undergraduate degree programme will be of either 3 or 4-year duration with multiple exit options. In this period of 3 or 4 years, after completion of one year, a certificate will be issued, after completion of 2 years, a diploma will be issued, after completion of 3 years, degree will be awarded subject to the condition that to minimum marks required to pass a course have been obtained by the student concerned.

3-Years degree course will be sufficient for appearing in any competitive exam, it will be a full-fledged graduate degree. If opted to complete 4 years then it will be a research degree. In this year, major area of study will be research on a particular project.

The P.G. (Master Degree Programme) will be of 2 years for students who have completed graduation course in 3 years, and P.G. programme will be of 1 (one) year for students who had completed 4 years graduate research programme. There will be no M. Phil programme in any University.

For doing Ph.D. programme, one should either have Master Degree or 4-year Bachelor's degree programme.

The institutions may start integrated programme of 5 years which will be known as Bachelor and Master Degree programme.

D. Under New Education Policy, it is planned that Model Public Universities will be established that would be known as Multidisciplinary Education and Research University which will be aimed to attain the Highest Global Standards in quality education.

E. All HEIs will focus on research and innovation by setting up start-ups, incubation centers, technology development centers, establish industry-academic linkages, Interdisciplinary Research in the area of social issues and public health along with Production, Agriculture, Law, Social Science, Humanities and Services.

4. Support for Students:

A. The teachers will be fully trained to act as mentors and guides of the students. The counselling of students will be an integral part of day-to-day teaching by the teachers.

B. The students from socio-economically background will be encouraged to complete higher education of their choice. Appropriate financial, moral, emotional support will be given.

C. In order to successfully run ODL and online education programmes, the quality, courses, teaching modules, study materials and online lectures will be prepared and it will be ensured that the quality of ODL and online educational programme is nowhere compromised.

D. All educational programmes either offline, online or in ODL mode will be students-friendly and will achieve global standards of quality.

5. Internationalization:

A. All HEIs will make efforts to attract international students in the area of studies like Engineering, Health Sciences, Computer & IT and other Indian courses like Astrology, Yoga, Ayush, Arts, Music, History, Culture etc.

B. India will be promoted as Global study destination providing premium education at affordable cost thereby helping to restore its role as 'Vishwaguru'.

C. Every HEIs will have separate International students' office, in order to welcome them, support them and encourage them to pursue their studies and research in India.

D. The collaboration with International Universities in the areas of training and research, student exchange, faculties exchange and joint research will be promoted.

E. The top 100 Universities of world will be invited to open their campuses in India. Similarly, the top higher institutions of India will be allowed to open their campuses overseas.

6. Motivated, Energized and Capable Faculty:

A. The teachers will be fully trained to act as mentors and guides of the student. The counseling of students will be integral part of day-to-day teaching by the teachers.

B. Regular training, counseling and updating knowledge of faculties.

C. All HEIs will be equipped with the basic infrastructure and facilities including clean drinking water, clean working toilets blackboards, offices, libraries, labs and pleasant classroom spaces and campuses. Every classroom shall have access to the latest educational technology that enables better learning experiences.

D. Teaching, Counselling and Research will be integral part of duties of a teacher.

E. There will be an adequate student-teacher ratio, so that no excessive work load is imposed on teachers.

F. Practice of two-way teaching theory and student-centric teaching methodology.

G. Excellence in teaching, counseling and research will be properly awarded.

7. Teacher Education:

A. Teacher Education System in our country will be completely changed.

B. The present structure and working of NCTE will be closed.

C. In order to improve and reach the levels of integrity and credibility required to restore the prestige of the teaching profession, the Regulatory System shall be empowered to take stringent action against substandard and dysfunctional teacher education institutions (TEIs), that do not meet basic educational criteria after giving one year for remedy of the breaches. By 2030, only educationally sound, multidisciplinary and integrated teacher education programmes shall be allowed and rest will have to be closed.

D. The 4-year integrated B.Ed. offered by such multidisciplinary HEIs will, by 2030, become the minimal degree qualification for school teachers. The 4-year integrated B.Ed. will be a dual–major holistic Bachelor's degree in Education, as well as specialised subject such as a language, history, music, mathematics, computer science, chemistry, economics, art, physical education, etc. Beyond the teaching of cutting-edge pedagogy, the teacher education will include grounding in sociology, history, science, psychology, early childhood care and education, foundational literacy and numeracy, knowledge of India and its values/ethos/art/traditions, and more. The HEI offering the 4-year integrated B.Ed. may also run a 2-year B.Ed. for students, who have already received a Bachelor's degree in a specialised subject. 1-year B.Ed. may also be offered for candidates, who have received a 4-year undergraduate degree in a specialised subject. Scholarships for meritorious students will be established for the purpose of attracting outstanding candidates to the 4-year, 2-year and 1-year B.Ed. programmes.

E. In order to maintain uniform standards for teacher education, the admission to pre-service teacher preparation programmes shall be through suitable subject and aptitude tests, conducted by the National Testing Agency and shall be standardized, keeping in view the linguistic and cultural diversity of the country.

F. All fresh Ph.D. entrants, irrespective of discipline, will be required to take credit-based courses in teaching/education/pedagogy/writing related to their chosen Ph.D. subject during their doctoral training period. Exposure to pedagogical practices, designing curriculum, credible evaluation systems, communication, and so on will be ensured, since many research scholars will go on to become faculty or public representatives/communicators of their chosen disciplines, Ph.D. students will also have a minimum number of hours of actual teaching experience gathered through teaching assistantships and other means. Ph.D. programmes at universities around the country will be re-oriented for this purpose.

8. Vocational Education:

A. The 12th Five–year plan (2012-2017) estimated that only a very small percentage of the Indian workforce in the age group of 19-24 (less than 5%) received formal vocational education, whereas in countries such as the USA, the number is 52%, in Germany 75% and in South Korea it is as high as 96%. These numbers only underline the urgency of the need to hasten the spread of vocational education in India.

B. This policy aims to overcome the social status hierarchy associated with vocational education and requires integration of vocational education programmes into mainstream education in all education institutions in a phased manner. Beginning with vocational exposure at early ages in middle and secondary school, quality vocational education will be integrated smoothly into higher education. It will ensure that every child learns at least one vocation and is exposed to several more. This could lead to emphasising the dignity of labour and importance of various vocations involving Indian arts and artisanship.

C. By 2025, at least 50% of learners through the school and higher education system shall have exposure to vocational education for which a clear action plan with targets and timelines will be developed.

9. Research:

In order to promote and regulate research, National Research Foundation will be established.

A. The Primary activities of the NRF will be to:

a. Fund competitive, peer-reviewed grant proposals of all types and across all disciplines;
b. Seed, grow, and facilitate research at academic institutions, particularly at universities and colleges where research is currently in a nascent stage, through mentoring of such institutions;
c. Act as a liaison between researchers and relevant branches of government as well as industry, so that research scholars are constantly made aware of the most urgent national research issues, and so that policymakers are constantly made aware of the latest research breakthroughs so as to allow breakthroughs to the options brought into policy and/or implementation; and
d. Recognise outstanding research and progress.

10. Regulatory System of Higher Education:

In order to regulate the entire Higher Education System except Law and Medicine, one Supreme Authority will be constituted, which will be known as Higher Education Commission of India.

Under this Commission, there will be Four Councils:

1. **National Higher Education Regulatory Council (NHERC):**
    a. This Council will regulate Higher Education Sector including teacher education and excluding Legal and Medical Education.
    b. This Council will work on the principal of 'light but tight' regulations and compliances.
    c. Good governance will be ensured through online and offline public disclosures of all finances, audit, procedures, infrastructure, faculties, non-teaching staff, number of students, courses and placements of the students by all HEIs.
    d. All above information will have to be placed on public website maintained by NHERC.
    e. Complaint and grievances from stakeholders and others arising out of such disclosures will be monitored by NHERC in coordination with concerned HEIs.
2. **National Accreditation Council (NAC):**
    a. This Council will grant accreditation to HEIs on the basis of their infrastructure, courses, curriculum, teaching pedagogy, number of teachers appointed and their qualifications and research work of the teacher and institutions etc.
    b. The promotion of HEIs will be through grading of NAC, it would be a continuous process of upgrading of HEIs till attainment of to accepted benchmarks.
3. **Higher Education Grants Council (HEGC):**
    a. The Higher Education Grants Council (HEGC) will carry out funding and financing of higher education based on transparent criteria including the IDPs prepared by the institutions and the progress made on their implementation. HEGC will be entrusted with the disbursement of scholarship and development funds for launching new focus areas and expanding quality programme offering at HEIs across disciplines and fields.
4. **General Education Council (GEC):**
    a. General Education Council (GEC) which will frame expected learning outcomes for higher education programmes, also referred to as 'graduate attributes'. A National Higher Education Qualification Framework (NHEQF) will be formulated by the GEC and it shall be in sync with the National Skills Qualifications

Framework (NSQF) to ease the integration of vocational education into higher education. Higher education qualifications leading to a degree/diploma/certificate shall be described by the NHEQF in terms of such learning outcomes. In addition, the GEC shall set up facilitative norms for issues such as credit transfer, equivalence etc., through the NHEQF. The GEC will be mandated to identify specific skills that students must acquire during their academic programmes with the aim of preparing well-rounded learners with 21st Century Skills.

b. The professional councils, such as the Indian Council of Agricultural Research (ICAR), Veterinary Council of India (VCI), National Council for Teaching Education (NCTE), Council of Architecture (CoA), National Council for Vocational Education and Training (NCVET) etc. will act as Professional Standard Setting Bodies (PSSBs). They will play a key role in the higher education system and will be invited to be members of the GEC. These bodies, after restricting as PSSBs, will continue to draw the curricula, lay down academic standards and coordinate between teaching, research and extension of their domain/discipline, as members of the GEC. As members of the GEC, they would help in specifying the curriculum framework within which HEIs may prepare their own curricula. Thus, PSSBs would also set the standards or expectations in particular fields of learning and practice, while having no regulatory role. All HEIs will decide how their educational programmes respond to these standards, among other consideration, and would also be able to reach out for support from these standard-setting bodies or PSSBs, if needed.

11. Conclusion:

The National Education Policy 2020 is a vast document ranging from page 1 to 200, it is very difficult to conclude such a detailed document. However, the main points can be summarised in the following manner:

a. Under this policy, the aim is India must have an education system by 2040 that is second to none, with equitable access to the highest-quality education for all learners, regardless of their social or economic background.

b. The fundamental principles that will guide both the education system at large as well as the individual institutions within it are:

i. recognising, identifying, and fostering the unique capabilities of each student by sensitising teachers as well as parents to promote each student's holistic development in both academic and non-academic spheres.

ii. according the highest priority to achieving Foundational Literacy and Numeracy by all students by Grade 3;

iii. flexibility, so that learners have the ability to choose their learning subject and programmes and thereby choose their own paths in life according to their talents and interests;

iv. no hard separations between arts and sciences, between curricular and extra-curricular activities, between vocational and academic streams etc.

v. multidisciplinary and a holistic education across the sciences, social sciences, arts, humanities and sports for a multidisciplinary world, in order to ensure the unity and integrity of all knowledge;

vi. emphasis on conceptual understanding rather than rote learning and learning-for-exams.;

vii. creativity and critical thinking to encourage logical decision-making and innovation;

viii. ethics and human & constitutional values like empathy, respect for others, cleanliness, courtesy, democratic spirit, spirit of service, respect for public property, scientific temper, liberty, responsibility, pluralism, equality and justice;

ix. promoting multilingualism and the power of language in teaching and learning;

x. life skills such as communication, cooperation, teamwork and resilience;

xi. focus on regular formative assessment for learning rather than the summative assessment that encourages today's coaching culture;

xii. extensive use of technology in teaching and learning, removing language barriers, increasing access for Divyang students and educational planning and management;

xiii. respect for diversity and respect for the local context in all curriculum, pedagogy and policy, always keeping in mind that education is a concurrent subject;

xiv. full equity and inclusion as the cornerstone of all educational decisions to ensure that all students are able to thrive in the education system;

xv. synergy in curriculum across all levels of education from early childhood care and education to school education and to higher education;

xvi. teachers and faculty as the heart of the learning process–their recruitment, continuous professional development, positive working environments and service conditions;

xvii. a 'light but tight' regulatory framework to ensure integrity, transparency and resource efficiency of the educational system through audit and public disclosure while encouraging innovation and out-of-the-box ideas through autonomy, good governance and empowerment;

xviii. outstanding research as a corequisite for outstanding education and development;

xix. continuous review of progress based on sustained research and regular assessment by educational experts;

xx. a rootedness and pride in India and its rich, diverse, ancient and modern culture and knowledge systems and traditions;

xxi. education is a public service; access to quality education must be considered a basic right of every child;

xxii. substantial investment in a strong, vibrant public education system as well as the encouragement and facilitation of true philanthropic private and community participation.

c. The Vision of this Policy: This National Educational Policy envisions an education system rooted in Indian ethos that contributes directly to transforming India, that is Bharat, sustainably into an equitable and vibrant knowledge society by providing high-quality education to all and thereby making India a global knowledge superpower. This Policy envisages that the curriculum and pedagogy of our institutions must develop among the students a deep sense of respect towards the fundamental duties and Constitutional values, bonding with one's country, and a conscious awareness of one's roles and responsibilities in a changing world. The vision of the Policy is to instil among the learners a deep-rooted pride in being Indian, not only in thoughts but also in spirit, intellect, and deeds, as well as to develop knowledge skills, values and dispositions, that support responsible commitment to human rights, sustainable development and living, and global well-being, thereby reflecting a truly global citizen.

d. This policy envisages that the extant 10+2 structure in school education will be modified with a new pedagogical and curricular restricting of 5+3+3+4 covering ages 3-18.

e. This policy envisions a complete overhaul and re-energising of the highest education system to overcome these challenges and thereby deliver high-quality higher education with equity and inclusion. This policy's vision includes the following key changes to the current system:

i. Moving towards a higher educational system consisting of large, multidisciplinary universities and colleges with at least one in or near every district, and with more HEIs across India that offer medium of instruction or programmes in local/Indian languages.

ii. moving towards a more multidisciplinary undergraduate education;

iii. moving towards faculty and institutional autonomy;

iv. revamping curriculum, pedagogy, assessment and student support for enhanced student experiences;

v. reaffirming the integrity of faculty and institutional leadership positions through merit-appointments and career progression based on teaching, research and services;

vi. establishment of National Research Foundation to fund outstanding peer-reviewed research and to actively seed research in universities and colleges.

vii. governance of HEIs by highly qualified independent board having academic and administrative autonomy;

viii. 'light but tight' regulation by a single regulator for higher education;

ix. increased access, equity and inclusion through a range of measures including greater opportunities for outstanding public education; scholarships by private/philanthropic universities for disadvantaged and underprivileged students; online education, and Open Distance Learning (ODL); and all infrastructure and learning materials accessible and available to learners with disabilities.

f. In order to govern and control the entire higher education, the Higher Education Commission of India will be constituted:
Higher Education Commission of India (HECI) will have four limbs:

NHERC	NAC	HEGC	GEC

Suggestions

A. After completing 12th class, every student should go for compulsory military training and serve nation for 2 years without any remuneration either in Army or in Armed forces like BSF, ITBP, CRPF, NDRF etc.

B. There should be compulsory moral education paper upto graduation level which should teach morality, ethics, Nationalism, Freedom Movement of India, National Heroes, Saints, Educationists and Scientists etc.

C. Government of India should establish National Education Finance Corporation, which should grant loans to Higher Education Institutions long-term and short-term on concessional rate of interest for creation of necessary infrastructure. Loans should be given to public and private institutions without any discrimination, it should also grant loans to needy students on very nominal rate of interest. Repayment of loans should be ensured through convenient instalments. All grants and scholarships should be stopped; by doing so, there will be equal playing field for public and private institutions.

□

Chairman of Mewar group of Institutions. An eminent professional, educationist and nationalist, CA (Dr.) Ashok Kumar Gadia has gained a prominent position in society due to the exemplary work he has done in his career. His rise to prominence in such a short span can be attributed to his strong will-power, calibre, conviction, dedication and leadership quality.

Innovations in Agriculture Sector to Make India Self-reliant

—**Prabhat Kumar & P.K. Ghosh**

India is one of the agriculturally important countries in the world and has strong net-work of agriculture education, research and expansion. As per the historical record, India is committed to thrive and excel independently. During 1965-66, India imported food grains from the US under PL-480 scheme and the situation was 'ship-to-mouth'. This condition was also exacerbated with the growing population, which compelled India to increase its food production as a topmost priority with commitment. With the introduction of high-yielding semi-dwarf varieties of rice from IRRI, Philippines and wheat from Mexico, which, combined with right policies of government to provide essential inputs and market facilities, credit etc., revolutionised Indian agriculture. In addition to these innovative ideas and policies, the food production reached the level of self-sufficiency until today. For instance, the food production during 1950-51 was 54 million tonnes and reached 285 million tonnes during 2018-19. After the fourth five-year plan, India made its stand of self-sufficiency after being affected by a year of worst drought. Later, the focus had been given on agricultural research and education in the country, for sustaining self-sufficiency in agriculture sector at all times of change of conditions within the country and also globally. Although more than 65 percent of rural population is depending on agriculture sector, the average monthly income is about ₹ 6500. It reveals under employment and large population in India dependent on agriculture, which is unsustainable. Therefore, there is a need to boost rural economy, create new infrastructure and other innovations in this sector. India has been emphasising for innovative techniques. The main advantage for India is its richest natural resources and needs only planning and execution on innovation front.

Self-reliant living means learning to grow your own, make your own, sell your own and bake your own in the rural homestead farming and urban homestead or mini-farms. Self-reliance is the way forward. There is no better time to do this especially with the presence of climate change, food shortage and the gloom of economic uncertainty. In the context to make India atmanirbhar, for achieving self-reliance and self-sustainability in agriculture is easier and more cost-efficient compared with other sectors of the economy. Presently, Gross Value Add of agriculture sector is about 18 trillion rupees with the growth rate of approximately 2 percent on year-on-year basis. A key economic driver, the sector needs to adapt to the challenges that it is facing today. India has three greatest challenges ahead of the 21st century and they are (i) sustaining food and nutritional security (ii) adaptation and mitigation to climate change and (iii) sustainable use of critical resources like water, land and energy. By the year 2050, annual foodgrain production would need to grow to 333 million tonnes. Even then, the contribution of key foodgrains in acreage terms in India is 15 percent and the production contribution is mere 8.7 percent. It clearly shows that the use of innovative technology is necessary to meet the forecasted demand in a sustainable manner and move Indian agriculture along the growth path and make India atmanirbhar. India needs to rapidly move towards **'innovation-led agricultural growth'**. This has to be achieved with speed, scale and sustainability. On the basis of current situation, it is foreseen that India have to adopt advanced methods for agriculture. India's achievements in agriculture sector are unevenly distributed and have remained lower than the potential. Agriculture is not to be compared with achievements made in space, IT, telecom, services, automobiles, medical science, transport etc. though we achieved a bigger jump compared to the situation in 1960s.

The decade of 2010-20 was declared as the **Indian Decade of Innovation**. We have benefited a lot from our established **'Indian Agriculture Research System'**. However, we need to understand that any National Agricultural Research System (NARS) is **activity**-based. Agricultural Knowledge and Information Systems (AKIS) are **output**-based, and National **agricultural innovation systems** (NAIS), however, are **outcome**-based. We are being benefitted in this system available in India. Technological and institutional innovations are needed throughout the production, marketing, policy research and enterprise domains as our Hon'ble Prime Minster and Krishi Mantri ji have emphasised on many platforms.First and the most powerful way of getting 'more from less', is by using the **power of new technology**, such as information and communication technology, nanotechnology, space technology, modern biotechnology etc. However, a robust policy level innovation is a must to achieve this.

Several innovative options for agriculture to make India self-reliant are available and discussed in many platforms, but what is needed is that to implement and push these innovations to end-users, there is a need of strong networking system involving Research Institution, Central and State Government, Private sectors, NGOs and Other local bodies, and their dedication towards upliftment of livelihood of the farming community. Some of these Innovations are highlighted here:

- **Sustainable use of natural resource base**: Balanced nutrient use, INM, residue management, efficient crops and water management, enhancing NUE, WUE, WP etc.
- **Crop Diversification**: Diversification of rice, wheat, maize and cotton-based system to reduce farmers' risks and enhance income and employment.

Of late, enabling technology and policy support helped pulse production to reach near self-sufficiency. On the contrary, oilseed sector is still lagging behind, and the current import is 67% of the requirement costing >70,000 crore INR annually. To reduce it to about 15% by 2022, area expansion (4.5mha), yield enhancement (0.33t/ha) and yield gap reduction, need to be pursued. **Rice fallows and half of the upland rice area** measuring around 12-14 mha should be used for oilseeds and pulses

- **Establishment of Zone-specific seed Hubs**: Seed is the basic requirement for a secure and sustainable farming. Non-availability or poor-quality seed is the basic constraint to most farmers, which affect their farming every year. Good quality seedling materials (propagules) for fruits and vegetables are also not available at the time of planting season; the start-up is also possible for the rural youths and farmers. Thus, there is an urgent need to strengthen existing seed production programmes and extend it to field and fodder crops, livestock and even fisheries for being self-reliant. This is an integral part of the Self-reliant farming. Interlinking of hubs can be established in a particular region in the country.

- **Development of multiple stress-tolerant crops and animals & their variety/breeds**: Flood and droughts occur in same place in areas in a single cropping season. Again, multiple diseases, insects cause huge loss to agriculture. 'CR Dhan 801 & 802' are the example of multiple stress tolerance, which can tolerate both flood and drought to a great extent.
- **Target-based programme on climate resilient nutri-cereals and biofortified crops**: Millets are much more climate resilient (requires less water, thrives under harsh environment), and enriched in nutritional properties and minerals than the cereals. To overcome protein energy malnutrition and also Zn and Fe deficiency, there is urgent need to develop and promote biofortified crops
- **Promotion of self-reliant and climate resilient Integrated Farming System (IFS) for small holder:**
  About 85% farmers in India are small and marginal. Also, climatic anomalies like drought, flood, frosts, cyclones are a recurrent phenomenon in India. Thus, IFS is the de-risking mechanism not only to enhance productivity, nutrition and employment but also to reduce farmers' risks due to climatic aberrations and provide assured income under all circumstances. Therefore, **Promotion of specialised farming for high income is the need of the hour.** Poultry farming, Commercial fish farming, ornamental fish, Dairying etc., should be sub-commponet of IFS. Each region of the country should come out with some IFS model for replication in farmers' fields.
- **Promoting Secondary and Specialty agriculture**: Scented/aromatic products/products with GI Tags, Niche items etc. must be promoted for higher income.
- **Promoting alternative source of income**: Each farmer must have at least one alternative source of income either through a shop, processing unit, custom hiring or any other service sectors.
- **Promote organic farming:** Productivity of all crops in India is much less than the world average productivity. Organic system of cultivation increases productivity in the long run. It also improves the quality of produce and economic returns apart from ensuring sustainability of agriculture. Thus, organic system of cultivation needs to be encouraged.

- **Group farming approach:** can be a viable option for marginal (<1 ha) and small landholders (1-2 ha). These categories of landholders share about 86% of total 145.73 million operational landholding with average holding size of 1.08 ha, and about 40% workers of total population in India. Pooling of cultivable land, investible funds and labour force would be required. This approach could provide small and marginal farmers, distressed farmers an opportunity for developing multi-enterprise-based farming and cluster-based promotion of agro-commodities for higher economic returns, for example group farming outperformed individual farming in Kerala, South Goa, Odisha, and in many places. This may be promoted to other states as well. This will empower farm women also.
- **Integrated aquaculture farming:** This would be effective for resource-poor farmers as well as unemployed youths and migrants, to produce additional fishes from marine and inland aquaculture. Shrimp polyculture with brackish water fish and crab-fish polyculture in coastal belt of India have been found to be very lucrative and promising. This will open up huge export earnings in aquaculture products.
- **Branding of local farm products** to be sold globally, the branding helping to tide over price spirals and making farmers quality-conscious
- **Technology-enabled supply chain** through the use of RFID, advanced GIS/GPS, tracing and traceability systems.
- **Precision agriculture** could be achieved with the use of advanced GIS/GPS and sensors can guide planting/irrigation, monitor yields, fine-tune inputs and by improving yields as well as reducing the use of water and fertilizer.
- **Promotion of high-tech automated precision farming:** Target: educated youths with IT knowledge. Moderately skilled agricultural workers with access to smart apps using smartphones or tablets also benefitted
- **Developing water harvesting capacity and irrigation infrastructure**: RWH and its efficient use must be promoted to reduce pressure on ground water and increase irrigated area.
- **Wasteland Utilisation:** States like Gujarat have more than 25 lakh hectares of wasteland. This is non-cultivable. It is highly saline and underground water is also saline. Such land has remained

uncultivated for 1000 years. But modern technology now provides solution to this problem. Salinity- resistant crops like Baval, date palm, Jatropha etc. can be developed. There is technology available for harvesting every drop of water, that is received by rainfall. Micro irrigation is for efficient and economical use of water resources. The challenge is to develop these land resources. The constraint is its cost. One-hectare land would need approximately ₹ 2.0 lakh. This is not within the means of a farmer. This is an area where participation by industry is essential. Private and public relationship can go a long way in utilisation of such land resources and provide more employment and income.

- **Achieving Land Degradation Neutrality**: India has about 120.8 m ha of degraded land, which is not only contributing to low productivity and poverty but also to greenhouse gas emission and huge economic loss. UN General Assembly 2015 has called for achieving a LDN world by 2030, and India has committed to rehabilitate 26 m ha. This needs a special attention of all sectors.
- **Agro-forestry and carbon farming:** Integrated farming system incorporating agro-forestry may help meet the future requirements of agriculture diversification. Inclusion of small farmers in 'Green India Mission' by adopting agro-forestry in CDM projects through community and grid approach will be helpful to get extra income through carbon credits. At national level, a simple carbon credit system should be developed especially for small and marginal farmers, so that financial benefits can reach them at the time of payments for irrigation, electricity, purchase of farm equipment and machinery etc. Tree-based integrated farming system (agroforestry) should be promoted (a minimum 5-10% land of small and marginal farmers and 20-25% land of large farmers) to ameliorate the effect of climate change on agriculture. Accelerated Fodder Development Plan (AFDP) and the proposed Fodder Mission need to include agroforestry for silvi-pasture and tree fodder production in all areas, and especially, in arid and semi-arid areas.

Vertical Farming-Vertical farming is a concept of commercial farming whereby plants, animals, fungi and other life forms are cultivated for food, fuel, fibre or other products or services by artificially stacking them vertically above each other. Vertical farming is a popular method of agriculture in urban areas which needs immediate attention. The idea defines the production of fruits, vegetables, medicinal producing plants and other plant products in the cities.

- **Solar and wind energy utilisation in farming:** India should set priority towards harvesting non-renewable energy as this sector is very weak as compared to other countries and large number of rural population is still using domestic fuel for cooking.
- **Location-specific farm mechanisation strategy:** To attract and retain youth in agriculture, special emphasis should be given on AI technology like use of drone for pest management. Custom hiring centre, formation of FPO, Farmers Community centre, Farmers Association group are some other options.
- **Creating-sufficient cold storage facilities:** by capacity enhancement of existing cold storages, and creating new infrastructures for storage of vegetables and fruits for year-round supply to market, and also to consumers.
- **Strengthening food processing micro-industries at the village or suburban areas:** Target in our country is to process about 25% of produce, which is presently less than 3%. In USA, as high as 65% farm produce are processed. Promotion of this particular enterprise will provide employment to farmers and rural youths. Scientific back-up is not lacking. Food processing is important in India because the country is leading in production of pulses, jute and milk, ranked second in production of vegetables and fruits, third in cereals in the world. There are about 39,748 food-processing industries under organised sector in India. Processing of several agri-and animal-based products can be developed at the rural level and also for huge export earnings. The government schemes would be effectively utilised to initiate micro level industries by the farmers and rural migrant workers. The industrial expansion team should give it priority. It can develop young entrepreneurs form farmers. These projects require low investment. With proper bank-credit linkages, the rural scene can change rapidly. Along with this, there is a need to pay attention to the growing demand of services especially in rural areas and more rural youth to seize it. **Similarly, strengthening quarantine system** needs special attention to protect genetic materials and not allow spurious materials inside.

- **Strong survey and surveillance** for transboundary pests and diseases using modern tools, preferably remote sensing, drones, etc.
- **Seed Export and regulatory system:** India can emerge as an important seed producer and a large exporter of seeds to many developing countries in South and South-east Asia as well as Africa. The country can produce very competitively-priced seeds for hybrid rice, hybrid corn, hybrid Bt HT cotton, and several vegetables including tomato, potato and okra provided we set our regulatory system right. To stop illegal spread of some GM crops, our regulatory system should be very effective and simple. The issues related to the bottlenecks holding India back from becoming the seed capital of the developing world should be solved at government level. As livestock is also equally important component, quality seed production for fodders and forage crops need to be taken up with R& D.
- **Robust extension system with public-private partnership**
  Strengthening village level group organisations viz. Farmer Producer Organisations (FPOs) and Self-Help Groups (SHGs) by providing more financial support and liberalised governance. **Micro-enterprise development in agriculture and allied sector** is a very good option. It has ample potential to provide employment and generating a stable income farmer. This can be achieved by formalising FPOs and SHGs in India. Farmers may form cluster-based cooperatives for crops and commodities viz. rice, jute, potato, mango, bamboo, chilli etc., which will create more employment, boost production, marketing and better livelihood to returnees and the famers. **Skill development and vocational training for farmers and youths** will accelerate agri-based business by the rural people in India. Youths should be encouraged to join the '**Make in India**' programme of the Government of India. For skill development, technical support should be obtained from National Skill Development Council and Agricultural Skills Council of India, National Institute of Food Technology, Entrepreneurship and Management and the Indian Institute of Food Processing Technology. As penetration of the mobile services and other digital infrastructure has increased, India has significant advantages, thus, mobile-based extension approaches (**digital advisory services**) to be scaled-up to connect with small and marginal farmers, to provide real time solutions for their agri-needs, weather advisories, and also information about

the input providers such as soil-testing labs, seeds, agro-chemicals and fertilizer suppliers etc.

- **Efficient utilisation of Government schemes:** By developing efficient mechanism to transfer funds to farmers under the existing Government schemes and new allocation of funds for agriculture and allied sectors towards self-reliant mission India announced by the Government in the pandemic era. The Government's financial package is very attractive and should be utilised for promotion of herbal plants cultivation, integrated beekeeping and value addition. The schemes should be implemented effectively such as *'Agri Infrastructure Fund', emergency working capital, Pradhan Mantri Matsya Sampada Yojana, Animal Husbandry infrastructure development, Employment push through the Compensatory Afforestation Management and Planning.*
- **Stronger linkages with international organisations:** The suggestions and policy recommendations of international organisation (FAO, WHO, IFPRI, IMF, World Bank, UNDP, CGIAR institutes, IFAD, WFP etc.) should be considered for implementation of different schemes at the country level. This will strengthen Indian agriculture and revive the battered economy, and make India self-reliant.
- **On-farm processing of agricultural products** using solar energy applications, **compost preparation** using agricultural wastes and residues, **biopesticide from locally available plant resources, android based solutions** for soil, water and nutrient management, **sensor based grading and packaging of produces, drudgery reducing tools** and implements for marginal and small farmers, **cold chain transportation of agricultural produces**, replications of cooperative model of AMUL dairy at the village level are some of the priorities for the country for becoming self-resilient.
- **Real time market information** by using mobile communications, voice-based call centers and expert systems for real time price discovery, weather information and cultivation trends needs immediate attention.
- Technology enabled **crop insurance**, where use of **real time data from weather stations** could be used to predict the rainfall.
- The **'collective intelligence'** of the innovators must be used in enhancing the productivity of the workers in agriculture, while reducing or removing the drudgery in their fields.

- **Market infrastructure:** Israel has shown a way to the world that even on a desert land, with low rainfall, a prosperous agriculture and agro processing industry can be built up. In fact, geographical and agro-climatic situation in Gujarat, Rajasthan and Israel are similar. States like Gujarat can provide 100% requirement of country in crops like oil seeds and pulses where today major imports are taking place. Israel technique, as it is known, is high-tech. It is based on soil and moisture conservation and continuous soil analyses to apply required nutrients. But crucial to success is the market strategy. Daily planeloads of products are sent to important capitals of Europe. The government provided great support in developing common brand for export of agricultural products and helped market efforts by setting up link centers. This is not difficult to replicate. It is necessary to develop an independent market identity for export of horticulture produce. This has been done for milk products under AMUL brand–but it did not extend to other agriculture produce. At present, there is under-cutting between the producers themselves which is taken advantage of by importers.
- **Contract farming:** Contract farming is actually a contract to purchase agri produce at a predetermined price before the season commences. It is not a contract for taking over the farm. Farmers are to be provided a supply of quality raw material and a better price. The processor in turn stands to gain, as he has a steady supply for processing ensured. Gujarat policy for contract farming provides for (i) tripartite agreement between the farmer, contract sponsor and APMC; (ii) A facilitator role for APMC; and (iii) A provision in the agreement to encompass all the details / specifications of contract.
- **Government interventions and support:** Indian agriculture needs diversification, innovation and adoption of practices for its sustainability. Indian farmers are also facing problems of high indebtedness due to low income which is not enough to repay loans and feed family or live honourably. The high indebtedness needs to be reduced by increasing the production and productivity of all crops and by creating opportunities of additional income from allied sector activities through better integration and bringing out change in agricultural marketing practices and laws. It may be necessary to assure farmers with farm income and help them in their individual

crisis and individual crop failures apart from supportive general crop insurance. India being a country of small farmers, it is necessary that they get the benefits of trade within the production and productivity of their small land holdings.

- **Assure income to small farmers:** A farm income assurance scheme should be introduced either by way of remunerative price mechanism for all crops with procurement facilities at farm gate, or through private market mechanism with subsidies payable directly to farmer. Some areas need attention like **Rescue small farmers from individual crisis, ensure farmers the infrastructure and other facilities, Facilitate agro-processing for small farmer's produce.**
- **Role of private sector***:* The **private sector** has a greater role to play in the advancement of the agro-technologies in India. With the vision of **'Make In India',** government involvement and government adhered innovation and investment is increasing. Now, it is the modern agricultural implements and machine manufacturers that need to bring innovation and new agro-techniques to Modernised Farmlands of India. In the seed sector, the growing need for R&D along with developments in **agrochemicals** such as increasing use of **bio-fertilizers** and bio-release **smart fertilizers**, has been developed. The farm implements sector, however, is yet to become a major market segment and tractors remain a major sector of investment. **The irrigation sub-sector** also needs to evolve for Indian farming with large investments.
- **Smart agriculture:** Smart farming and precision agriculture play a crucial part in sustainable agriculture, using big data and new technologies as IoT, drone imagery and smartphone apps to harvest as much matter and products as possible, while consuming less energy and inputs (fertilizers, phytosanitary products and water. Popularisation of soilless cultivation and incentives for small scale industries to produce vegetables hydroponically.
- **Digiculture:** Application of modern digital tools in agriculture for making more profitable farming needs immediate attention for promoting agricultural growth in 21st century. These are Artificial intelligence in agriculture precisely in crop forewarning systems and plant protection systems, Crop and Soil Monitoring, Predictive Agricultural Analytics, Supply Chain Efficiencies and Agricultural Product Grading.

Development of digital tools for precision agriculture for timely management of farm activities, App based field monitoring systems, App based mechanisation in agriculture, Computer operated drones for input delivery, application of ROBOTICS in field of agriculture-for big data recording and management digitally and transfer to computers. **Unmanned Aerial Vehicles (UAV)** can be used to monitor and observe important data and resolution of up to 1 cm/pixel and air pressure. This data can help the farmer to make an informed decision.

- **Data Science**-Collecting data for soil health, fertilizers, drones, seed quality, amount of rain will help to assess the quality and predict the quantity of crop yield. Data science will highlight the improvement necessary in agriculture and motivate people to research and escalate to new technology.

Conclusion

The agri-innovation has been taken up on the right path in India to achieve its goal and we need more commitment for achieving the challenges ahead to feed the growing population. Top five trends of innovations expected to shape Indian agriculture industry are digital **innovation, climate risk management strategy, developing the start-up ecosystem, Farmer Producer Organisations (FPOs) and water management initiatives.** The new vision for agriculture innovation must be focussed on Growth to efficiency, Employment Generation, Food, Security to Nutrition and Health, Shortage Management to Surplus Management, Input Intensive to Knowledge Intensive Agriculture, Climate Change and Sustainability, Production and Producers, Policy Interventions, Regulations and Reforms. There is a need to draw area production plans for animal husbandry and to grow crops to meet India's nutritional requirement considering agroecological zones and the changing climate. The aim should be to figure out a suitable basket of crops for each area. Integrating the efforts of these organisations to identify niche areas viz, value addition, rural infrastructure, logistics, warehousing, quality certification, etc. can provide livelihood opportunities for migrant workers bearing the brunt of the Covid-19 lockdown. The effective utilisation of MGNREGA can also create adequate work days, with a thrust on rural infrastructure. The Cabinet's decision to allow farmers to sell directly through e-trading platforms to entities of their choice instead of being confined to state mandis, is another game changer. This will enable contract farming and inter-state trade. However, breakthroughs are needed in areas of transportation, logistics, and digital access and payments, to enable widespread prosperity. Thus, focus must be on production, distribution, and management of food i.e., the complete agricultural value chain.

□

A renowned agriculturist presently serving as National Coordinator, National Agriculture Higher education project, ICAR. He has contributed immensely in teaching, research and extension.

An Agriculture Scientist with diverse experience who is currently Founder, Director and Vice Chancellor, ICAR-National Institute of Biotic Stress Management, Baronda, Raipur.

From Self-reliant Villages to Self-reliant India

—Naresh Sirohi

Due to Covid-19 outbreak, the whole world is going through a historical event. From one side, this disease has caused a serious crisis in existence of the human beings and on another side, it has caused severe downslide in economy and given a deep shock to economically powerful nations of the world. The lockdowns of a few days have caused to wind up all economic activities everywhere in the world. It has, now, posed an unprecedented challenge before the Economists and the political Leaders of the world.

The current situation is entirely different from those circumstances in which all the laws, which determine economic policies and all the isms, viz. Capitalism, Socialism, Maoism were born and flourished.

The three worldwide economic slowdowns in the last hundred years have caused severe crises to the world' economy but the economic crisis caused by the Covid-19 is entirely different because in the present crisis, all the people who run the economy such as merchants and traders, entrepreneurs, industrialists, managers, Government officials, transporters and the people working in the financial and other institutions are also under lockdown at home. Only farmers and the farm labourers are working in the field to safeguard 'Food Security Mission' and run the wheels of economy.

Given all these circumstances, it is being noticed that the western world, which had been moving ahead by adopting and implementing development model, based on latest economic mechanism and Science & technology for the last two and half centuries, but now, due to Covid-19 situation, a big change in the mindset of those supporters of globalisation and liberalisation has been felt.

While keeping in view the situation which emerged due to Covid-19, the people of the western world are adopting Swadeshi (indigenous) and moving forward to establish an economy which is based on the policy of Self-reliance whereas Indian traditional economy is already based on the policy of Swadeshi and Self-dependence and India has been following such economy based on self-reliance for many centuries.

Now, Prime Minister Shri Narendra Modi has taken a resolution to make India 'a Self-reliant Nation' in all sectors including agriculture, manufacturing and service sector.

In the last few months, three major ordinances, in view of agricultural reforms, have been issued by the Government of India. By amending 'Agricultural Produce Market Committee (APMC) Act', second provisions of 'Contract Farming' and third Essential Commodity Act, now the Government has initiated a process of connecting farmers directly with the industries.

Recently, while launching an 'Agriculture Fund' worth Rupees one lakh crore, the Prime Minister has said that the government is committed to free marginal farmers from the clutches of 'middle men' and 'commission agents'.

This is not only the resolution of the Prime Minister but all of us are also fully committed to make 'Self-reliant India'.

But at present, there is a need to improve the system that implements and executes such resolutions. First of all, by accurate assessment and analysis of our nation's history, geography and current situation, and by correcting the mistakes committed in the past, we need to move forward by making plans and policies as per our capabilities.

In terms of natural resources, India is a very rich country in the field of agriculture and animal husbandry in the world. India's total geographical area is approximately 328.7 million hectares, that is only 2.4 percent of the world's total geographical area, but eighteen percent of the world's population resides here.

Soil, water, biological resources and climate are very important for cultivation. If we assess and analyse these factors in the context of India, we can easily understand how much our country is rich in physical resources.

Our Natural Wealth

Only 11% of the total land of the world is suitable for agriculture, whereas 56% of the total land of our country is cultivable.

Around 64 types of soil are found in the world, whereas altogether, 46 types of soil are found in India.

When we assess the availability of rainwater, surface and groundwater in the country, we are very rich.

On an average, there are four thousand billion square metres precipitation (rain), which takes place annually in the country. But this is another thing that we are able to use only ten to fifteen percent of it.

The total area of the country is 328.7 million hectares, out of which, approximately 300 million hectares is under catchment area.

In terms of rivers, there are around 445 rivers in the country whose total length is around 2 lakh kilometres.

In 1947, according to an estimate, there were around 2.8 million lakes and ponds in the country to conserve rainwater, whose numbers have now sharply gone down. India has been a rich country in terms of groundwater too but because of Green Revolution, excessive water exploitation took place due to which around 264 districts of the country had gone into Dark Zone. At present, Groundwater level is decreasing at the rate of 0.3 metres annually.

There are 15 types of Climatic Regions in the world and as per agricultural climatic zones, the number goes up to 127 types of climatic zones. All of these are found in India.

In terms of seasons, all the six seasons of the world are found in India.

In the perspective of Biological diversity, there are 48 thousand types of plants and trees which are found here in which, 15 hundreds are edible plants and there are 811 breeds of domestic and wild animals found in the country which are 11 percent and 10 percent of the world's total biological wealth respectively.

Around 375 varieties of fruits, 280 varieties of vegetables, 80 varieties of roots or tubers and 60 varieties of edible flowers, seeds and dry fruits are found in the country.

We have, approximately 75 hundred kilometres long Coastal lines and 20 lakh square kilometres of Exclusive Economic Zone, which not only help in increasing fisheries but also enhance the scope of extraction of crude oil, minerals and gases as well as electricity generation.

History of Agriculture in India

History of Indian agriculture is as old as India. According to Royal Commission on Agriculture formed in 1936, cultivation of crops is being practised for the last 11 thousand years. In ancient and medieval India, in the form of foodgrains, rice, wheat, millets and pulses were cultivated and it has been found in the records that ancient India was not only self-sufficient in production of foodgrains but it also used to export various agricultural products such as spices, rice, cotton, and silk to many countries of the world.

Though India was a densely populated country but adequate rainfall, adequate sources of irrigation, favourable climatic condition for cultivation and fertility of soil made it possible to cultivate twice in an year which ultimately helped in large-scale production of crops in that period.

In the assessments done by various historians, Indian Farmers have always been skilled, hardworking, independent and self-respecting and the village industries have been rich and prosperous due to their prosperity. 25 percent of Indian population was engaged in industries. The prosperity of our farmers began to eclipse during the medieval period especially after the era of Mughal King Akbar. Indian agriculture was ruined which also caused reduction in availability of foodgrains. The problem, which arose due to decreased production of foodgrains in the medieval period, grew further when the British Empire was founded in India because the cultivation of commercial crops such as Tea, Coffee, Indigo, Cannabis, Jute, Cotton, Silk and sugarcane was given prominence over food crops and cultivation of foodgrains was not given much importance by the British. For example-from year 1901 to 1947, there was a sharp downfall in production of foodgrains, whereas, during the same period, population of Indiagrew by 38 percent and the cultivable area increased by 18 percent only.

After Independence, agricultural was going through a difficult phase in India. Import of food grains became mandatory to meet the domestic demand which grew up rapidly. Import of food grains grew from 1.5 million tonnes in 1946 to 4.8 million tonnes in 1950 and it reached the highest level of 10.4 million tonnes in 1966.

All reforms, so far, in the agriculture sector in the last 70 years need to be analysed by dividing them into seven phases

First phase: After Independence, the first round was from 1947 to 1968 in which expansion in sowing area, growth in irrigation facilities and laws related to land reforms have played main role.

Second phase: It was a period from 1968 to 1980, in which high-yielding variety (HYV) seeds, fertilizers, insecticides and new technology were used which is also called as the period of emergence of Green Revolution.

Third phase: It was a period between 1981 and 1991 during which a policy of minimum support price (MSP) for agricultural products, procurement of crops by the government and a nationwide system for storage and distribution of foodgrains, was launched.

Fourth phase: It was a period from 1991 to 1998 which was an era of liberalisation and globalisation in which World Trade Organisation was formed. A big change began when industries, service sector and Intellectual Properties were included in the world trade along with agriculture sector with certain rules and regulations.

Fifth phase: It was a period from 1999 to 2004. In this phase, National Commission on Farmers was constituted on 18 November, 2004 under the chairmanship of Dr. M.S. Swaminathan to promote organic farming, rural basic infrastructure construction, viz. roads, electricity, education and health etc. as well as to remove discrepancies in agriculture. The Commission submitted its last report to the Union Government on 4 October, 2006.

Sixth Phase: from 2014 to 2019, it was started by Modi Government with objectives of enhancing production and doubling farmers' income. To fulfil this resolution, various schemes and programmes such as-Soil Health Card, Drip Irrigation Scheme, Per Drop More Crop Scheme, Direct Benefit Transfer Programme, New Crop Insurance Scheme etc. along with Value Addition Programme and Connecting farmers directly with Agriculture Markets have been started.

Seventh Phase: It has been started in 2020, keeping in view the circumstances which emerged due to Covid-19 pandemic, the main focus of this phase is to expand programmes and assignments to fulfil the resolution of Self-reliant India by making self-reliant villages.

After Independence, the governments of that period took many initiatives for agricultural reforms including Green Revolution, as a consequence of which, it is logical to mention that during 1950-51, the total production of foodgrains was 50.8 million tonnes, fruits and vegetables

25 million tonnes, milk 17 million tonnes, eggs 1.8 billion and fresh fish 0.75 million tonnes only whereas in 2019-2020, the total production has gone up manifolds. India has produced 284 million tonnes of food grains, 281.8 million tonnes of fruits and vegetables,185 million tonnes milk, 87 billions eggs and 13.8 million tonnes of fresh fish. Since 1950-51, there has been 5.6 times increase in foodgrains production, 13.8 times increase in vegetables and fruits, 100 times increase in production of eggs, 9.6 times in milk and 14.4 times increase in fish production.

During Green Revolution, use of fertilizers had a very important role, along with irrigation, in the increment of foodgrain production. In 1950-51, per hectare consumption of fertilizer was less than 1 kilogram, which increased to 74 kilogram per hectare in 1995-96 and further increased to 131.6 kilogram in 2014-15, and it has reached up to 137 kilogram per hectare in 2018-19.

Subsidy given by the government on chemical fertilizers was ₹60 crore in 1976-77 which has increased up to ₹40338 crore in 2007-08 and further increased up to ₹90000 crore in 2019-20.

The point to be noted here is that in spite of bringing in enormous changes over the years to increase foodgrains production through a series of agricultural reforms and green revolution but due to unfavourable 'Terms of Trade' practices in agriculture, farmers' income could not grow relatively compared to the people who are engaged in non-farm jobs; rather the difference in income between these two classes has increased day by day. So, we can simply say that whatever wealth has been generated due to growth in the country's total economy, the same has not been equally distributed among all sections of the society especially the rural community did not get its proper share. Secondly, it projected new challenges before the nation, i.e., declining productivity, inadequate and unbalanced use of nutrients-especially Nitrogen, reduced usage efficiency of water & nutrients, degradation of natural resources, lack of proper quantity of water for irrigation, very high increase in input cost of agriculture and equipment, growing diseases in plants due to insects, and along with the increased concern for nutritional quality and food security, challenges such as adverse effects of climate change are also there.

It would not be wrong to say that Green Revolution has become a boon for Agriculture and Food Security, but on the other side, it has also become a bane for soil, water, biological diversity, human health, and cultivation based on the principle of co-existence with nature has been severely affected. Today, it has become a well-known fact.

Keeping in view the circumstances which emerged due to Covid-19 pandemic, there is a need for such a system of farming which is based on principle of co-existence with nature in which there should be a provision for sustainable use of natural resources such as land, water and biological wealth etc. To accomplish the resolution of Self-reliant India by building self-sufficient villages, there is a need to adopt integrated system of agriculture which is based on the principle of co-existence-given by nature so that farmers could get rid of their humiliating life-burdened with debt & unnecessary dependence on markets so that they could live with their self-respect and make their villages self-reliant.

Concept of Self-sufficient Village

India is a country that resides in its villages and without making villages fully Self-sufficient, the dream of Self-reliant India cannot be fulfilled.

Therefore, the government is required to focus on the policy, i.e. 'From self-sufficient villages to self-reliant India'. keeping in view the situation of the country, that emerged due to crisis of Covid-19 pandemic, some more agricultural reforms are due so that the condition of the villages could be improved.

First of all, we shall have to make a road map to reduce dependence of the villages on markets in view of building 'self-sufficient Villages'.

For safeguarding food security of the villages, we shall have to revamp the agricultural system based on Integrated Farming Techniques so that proper food for the villagers, adequate fodder for the cattle and seed & grains for birds could be arranged. Through this farming technique, along with all the essential consumable items such as cereals, pulses, oilseeds, vegetables for all the villagers, it will require to produce cotton, jute and sugarcane for making sugar, jaggery, candies, vinegar, etc.

Apart from agriculture, farmers and landless workers get extra income from animal husbandry. Therefore, farmers have to make provisions of fodder for cattle in their crop circle. Adoption of crop circle will lessen people's dependence on markets for food articles and hence the villages will become self-contained and self-reliant.

Around 60 percent population of the villages are directly dependent on farms. Apart from this, around 40 percent of village population comprises of landless workers. They are dependent on small scale industries for their livelihood and as an alternative, they also help in farming.

India is a land of different types of agriculture climatic zones. Hence, according to agricultural climatic zone, there can be many different formats for Integrated Farming System. I, myself, have been an eyewitness of such methods of farming in the decade of 1970s.

Similarly, there is also a need to develop 'Gram Bazaar Haat (Village Markets)' at Nyay Panchayat level, to provide markets for additional production held in the village.

Many people from the villages left for the cities in hope of having better lifestyles, now they have returned to their villages. Therefore, additional employment will have to be arranged for them in the village itself. For this, along with agriculture, for food processing, value addition service and to reach the customer directly, we shall have to make network of streamlined marketing. The Prime Minister has also mentioned 'Farm to Fork' process.

This process will help farmers to get profitable price of their farm products. Proper marketing and value addition done by smaller units will be able to provide respectable jobs to the additional population living in the villages.

Therefore, it is important to keep three things in mind, while making plans for Self-reliance. First is to know the population density of that area, second is to know about the types and the quantity of crop production of the area and third is to know about the framework of water conservation. Keeping these three things in mind, the plan needs to be structured.

The first basic need of a person is food and water. Therefore, while strengthening Food Security, it is necessary to conserve and store food items in adequate quantity, at least, for a period of one year. During rainy season, we should work for water conservation, i.e. the quantity of water which we use after extracting from the ground all round the year, the same quantity of water should be returned or refilled to the ground during rainy season.

The village's food and water should be available in the village, block's food and water in the block and district's food and water in the district.

Despite Covid-19 pandemic, our country is rich in food grains today, which has become possible because of our farmers.

Every year, unnecessary freight movements of thousands of tonnes of food grains and wastage, will be stopped. Many shortcomings in supply chain have been exposed during this crisis from which we need to take lessons.

We need to wipe out the shortcomings found in the supply chains of intra-district, inter-district and metropolitan area transport systems respectively.

It has been predicted that India with a population of 170 crore (1.7 billion) will become the most populous country of the world by 2050.

Then, we shall have to produce 457 million tonnes of foodgrains (including 50 million tonnes of pulses). In the same way, we need to enhance production of other food items such as 45.2 million tonnes of edible oils, 438.6 million tonnes of vegetables, 183.4 million tonnes of fruits, 483 million tonnes of milk, 58.2 million tonnes of sugar, 18.1 million tonnes of meat, 27.2 million tonnes of fish and 202.5 billion eggs.

For this, the productivity of land and water will need to be increased four times and three times respectively. Energy consumption efficiency will require to be doubled and labour productivity will need a 6-fold-increase.

The country will have to adopt a sustainable policy of all-round development to supply foodgrains to the fast growing population because the scope for growth in cultivable area is almost next to nothing. Apart from it, due to continuous and extensive farming, the soil is gradually losing its fertility. Therefore, it needs to improve and enhance soil fertility and recharge it with macro and micro nutrients. The country cannot compromise with supply of proper Nutrition with essential nutrients for tackling invisible starvation and malnutrition. As of current situation, keeping in view soil health and its productivity as well as farmers' income, other than chemical fertilizers, use of sufficient organic manure (fertilizer) is required.

Keeping in mind the small holding of farmers, there is a need to develop such an agricultural system that should not only increase farmers' income, but should remain favourable for the environment also.

□

A political and social activist. He has been National Vice President, BJP Kisan Morcha and Founder Advisor of DD Kisan Channel.

Transforming India Through 'The Digital India Campaign'

—CA K. Raghu

India is one of the fastest growing economies in the world and is running and progressing with lightning speed. Technology plays the key role in the development of any country and to ensure steady and fast growth of the nation, the government has to embrace technology and 'Digital India Campaign' has been launched by the Government to usher in the Digital revolution.

One of the major achievements of the Government post 2014 Lok Sabha elections was the launch of 'The Digital India Campaign'. The ambitious 'Digital India Campaign' was inaugurated by the Prime Minister of India, Shri Narendra Modi on 1st July, 2015. The Digital India initiative is the direct result of the government's thrust upon utilising digitised instruments for complete realisation of various socio-economic and welfare schemes.

E-governance was introduced way back in the mid-1990s in order to computerise various government departments and streamline procedural matters. Back in the 1990s when computer languages and capacity were at their nascent stage, the e-governance schemes designed for mainly public utility purpose, could not achieve their full potential. There was a constant lag between the accessibility of citizens to various people-centric services. The aim of e-governance was to mitigate this issue and establish a decentralised accessibility of welfare schemes through digital networks. Thus, under the broader framework of National e-governance plan of 2006, the Digital India Campaign was launched in order to provide digitisation across every single rural area, enhance digital connectivity between rural and urban networks for both governance as well as infrastructural purpose and to ensure technology is used in its highest utilitarian function.

Objectives and Goals of Digital India Campaign

The three primary objectives for the Digital India Campaign are as follows:

- **'Digital infrastructure as a core utility to every citizen'**
- **'Governance and services on demand'**
- **'Digital empowerment of citizens'.**

With the above goals being discussed, it is clear that the government is keen on taking India at par with core developed digitised economies like the US and UK where digitisation has enabled to bridge the gap between areas on the basis of uniform digital access. As pointed out by several experts, utilising digital infrastructure in the best of citizens' interests without making exceptions, will help further in decentralising public welfare schemes which were otherwise being underutilised so far.

With people becoming wary about the risks and frauds related to Digitalisation, the Government has designed this Digital Campaign to suit the needs of the entire population keeping the futuristic vision of India in mind. The Government seeks to unify rural areas by bringing them under the ambit of the broadband facility.

The chief concept governing the Digital India campaign was the focus on recognising the power that digital technology can harness when disbursed among people in a way that uses technology to empower and not just entertain. '**Bharat Net Programme**' was, thus, launched with the objective of using optical fiber in order to connect all the rural villages and gram panchayats under the rural broadband network. The Bharat Broadband Network Limited, which currently oversees the Bharat Net Programme was assigned the custody of Digital India campaign.

Another dynamic idea linked to the initiation of the Digital India campaign was to create a **digital locker** facility, that would keep digitised versions of every document issued to citizens by the government, which can be accessible to citizens through an e-signature facility as well as synchronising accounts with **Aadhaar**. The idea was to reduce dependency upon paper and bureaucratic procedures to a bare minimum. Also, a digital signature for various processes was designed to address the growing complexity of modern life that permitted fewer people to be physically present in order to complete official procedures. The government recognised the power which the current telecom industry wields with respect to data connectivity through mobile and smart phone network. Digital India has also been visualised by Shri Narendra Modi as the foundation stone of 'M-governance' which stands for 'Mobile Governance'. The mobile portal is conceptualised to bring every aspect of governance under a centralised portal, bridging the gap between mobile and computer users with similar facilities available to both.

Digitalisation in the Global Scenario

Digitalisation is the cause of large-scale and sweeping transformations across multiple aspects of business providing unparalleled opportunities for value creation and capture, as well as being a source of major risk. Digital platforms are recasting the relationships between customers, workers, and employers as the silicon chip's reach permeates almost everything we do—from buying groceries online to finding a partner on a matrimony website. As computing power improves dramatically and more and more people around the world participate in the digital economy, we should think carefully about how to devise policies that will allow us to fully exploit the digital revolution's benefits while minimising job dislocation.

The question of whether this is a new trend or rather an existing one adapting to different conditions, raises questions. There is no doubt, however, that the complexity of these transformations, the impact they have cross-industry, and the pace at which they are occurring is truly unprecedented. Rapid and continuous technology developments are transforming the skills required for most existing jobs, creating completely new types of roles, and also rendering obsolete entire sets of current job functions. According to a US Department of Labor report, 65 percent of today's school children will eventually be employed in jobs that have yet to be invented. This not only has significant implications on how these children have to be educated and trained, but also implies that the current workforce may have to question the longevity of their existing employment and how they can ensure they are earning a living in the mid-term, given the changing nature of the labour market and the jobs available.

Uber, the world's largest taxi company, owns no vehicles. **Facebook**, the world's most popular media owner, creates no content. **Alibaba**, the most valuable retailer, has no inventory and **Airbnb**, the world's largest accommodation provider, owns no real estate. This shows that people have found a way to adapt to digitalisation and cater to the needs of people in such a way that it is convenient to the public as well as profitable to them.

Since the concept of Digitalisation is new to India, to meet these Global standards is going to be difficult in the beginning. However, under the Governance of Shri Narendra Modi, the concept of Digital India has already found its way onto becoming a successful campaign in our nation.

Impact of Digital India on Indian lives—The Indian Scenario

Training & Education: A lot of projects are launched by the government to empower people, as the programme is aimed at ameliorating urban-rural connect. As per the sources, the government is looking for qualified trainers to train approximately 3 lakh service delivery agents. These agents can further run a business related to IT services. In rural areas, training programmes are required for millennia to become job-fit for IT and telecom industries. Many start-ups such as BYJUs have already made digitalised academic training classes a tremendous success which has paved the way for convenient computerised education for Indians during this unprecedented Covid-19 situation.

Healthcare: According to Arvind Gupta, Digital India Foundation Head, eHealth is an essential project of the Digital India initiative to tackle the deficit of more than 1.5 million doctors. Under this project, people can avail online services like getting diagnostic reports, checking the status of blood banks, making payments for health care and much more. Many digital platforms such as NetMeds and CureFit have already become successful in this area of business by enabling remote consultancy services especially during this pandemic.

Start-ups: Budding entrepreneurs have ample opportunities to receive information and advertise their business on **'Start-up India',** a government platform. Startups such as Swiggy, Vogo, Dream 11, Dunzo, Ola and many more, using Digital India as their base, have already become a huge success among the masses and have also managed to generate employment which is a great sign for the Digital India campaign.

Infrastructural growth: To support digitalisation, infrastructure is being built and this has resulted in burgeoning employment opportunities. Even freelancers are needed to digitalise all the official documents for the government. This can be done by any person who has an Aadhaar Card number and can type on a computer or a mobile device. Under the Digital India initiative, rural and semi-rural areas have better connectivity to the cities and this has led to the growth of e-commerce space. This has resulted in better opportunities for postal services, BPOs and more.

Payments: Almost everyone in the urban parts of India and most people belonging to rural India have already started adapting to digitalised payments such as Net banking, Credit and Debit cards, e-wallets, UPI, etc. Even small shopkeepers use digital means of receiving payments through e-wallets and UPI. Most organisations even use digitalised methods of making payments to vendors as well as employees, completely replacing the traditional method of payments through cheques, cash etc.

Impact of Covid-19 on Digital India Campaign

Digitalisation is emerging as a potent medium for all business transactions during this Covid-19 crisis and it is here to stay. The Digital India movement is a giant technological leap, which is lubricating the wheels of India's economy during this crisis.

The RBI, National Payments Corporation of India (NPCI), along with government bodies, banks, financial institutions, regulatory authorities, are already teaming up to promote the faster adoption of digital payment methods. The emphasis is on using NEFT, IMPS, and UPI. Though different economies are at different stages across the world, Covid-19 has definitely cleared the road for digital payment methods in India. However, the cyber security of these platforms becomes crucial at this time. As cash flow is halted for many during this time, cyber criminals are using emerging techniques like EMI Moratorium scams as bait. Attackers are stealing personal data and banking details, among others, and are committing fraud. In India, RBI already has put in place the 'Central Payment Fraud Registry' (CPFR), to ensure quick and systemic responses in cases of financial frauds.

The pandemic has given us a chance to re-evaluate and push businesses everywhere into an accelerated state of digitalisation. Covid-19 has increased the adoption of digital payment solutions significantly. E-payment options are making it possible for people to sit at home and order essentials online from Flipkart or Amazon or any other such e-commerce platforms. The use of digital payments was already growing, but we have now seen it grow even more exponentially, owing to the current situation.

Furthermore, Banking and Personal finance institutions are trying to limit customer walk-ins by augmenting their digital capabilities and extending new online services. We see exacerbated use of hybrid cloud and hyper-converged platforms, as people have realised the importance of cloud-based communication-enabled business processing. This has also led to the strengthening of cyber security systems to safeguard sensitive data and protect assets from malicious data breaches.

The Way Forward

The Government has the following views regarding the successful development of Digital India campaign:

- **Artificial Intelligence:** NITI Aayog or the National Institution for Transforming India will be starting a national program for spearheading efforts in the domain of artificial intelligence including research and development of its applications and The Department of Science and Technology will launch a mission on Cyber Physical Systems to support establishment of centres of excellence. It will focus on research, training and skilling in robotics, artificial intelligence, digital manufacturing, big data analysis, quantum communication and internet of things.
- **Aadhaar like unique ID for enterprises:** Stating that the Aadhaar system has made easy access of public services to citizens, the government has proposed that every individual enterprise in India will be assigned a unique ID in a new scheme.
- **Rural Connectivity:** The Finance Minister said that one lakh gram panchayats have been connected through high-speed optical fiber network under Phase I of the BharatNet project. The mission of broadband access to over 20 crore rural Indians in about two lakh fifty thousand villages has been realised successfully. Five lakh Wi-Fi hotspots will be established to offer broadband access to five crore rural citizens.
- **Telecom infrastructure:** Funds worth ₹ 1.33 lakh crore in 2019-20 for creation and augmentation of Telecom infrastructure have been allocated, for a country with over 1 billion mobile phone users. To tap the benefits of 'Fifth Generation' (5G) technologies and its adoption,

the Department of Telecom has supported establishment of an indigenous 5G Test Bed at IIT, Chennai.

- **Digital toll payments:** To facilitate smooth road travel, toll payments have been digitalised as the government plans to replace the system of physical payment of cash with Fastags and other electronic payment systems. The number of Fastags have gone up from about 60,000 in December, 2016 to over 70 lakh now in 2020.
- **Education:** The government proposed to bolster digital intensity in education through the transformation from "black- board" to 'digital board'. The recently launched digital portal 'DIKSHA' aims at skill enhancement of teachers.

Conclusion

The Indian government is taking right steps towards ensuring and delivering better and transparent government services to the citizens. They are using the latest technologies, re-engineering the processes that will assure that citizens get better services than the previous attempts. We hope this crusade goes on and we get all the services online at our fingertips. As all these services, payments, data transfers, data storage will be online, Government needs to ensure the better cyber security.

Coronavirus has broken the supply chain while rupturing the demand and market trends. As we're forced to work remotely and use technologies for the first time, we're realising the benefits they deliver. Organisations are getting deeper into digital transformation. There is a paradigm shift to remote banking, digital payments, and direct financial aid, which is further pushing the financial industry to become digital. This transformation will inevitably promote India's Digital Mission. Policymakers need to support the ways people and organisations are using the internet to come together and deal with new pressures, as our lives shift abruptly online.

□

A practising Chartered Accountant from Bangalore and Former President of the Institute of Chartered Accountants of India for 2013-14. He is a specialist in Taxation and Business Consulting.

Need for Quality Higher Education and Skill Development

—Prof. Bupinder Zutshi

The appeal of Prime Minister, Shri Narendra Modi, for self-reliant India, (*Atmanirbhar Bharat*) aims at a serious reflection on whether we are making the best use of our natural, human and technological resources. Prime Minister emphasised that self-reliance was essential for India's global competitiveness. He said that reforms over the past 6 years have to be taken forward to build a self-reliant India. He further said that the corona outbreak had shown us the importance of local markets and local supply chains. He said that we needed to adopt the mantra of 'local' and work towards its progress. The world is now looking towards humanity-centric globalisation. In this respect, the Prime Minister expressed confidence that India could lead the way. He praised India's ancient culture saying that the wisdom of age-old principles such as *Vasudaiva Kutumbakam* and harmony with nature ensure that world progress is central to India's conception of progress. India should plan to convert this crisis into an opportunity and strengthen its fight by becoming *Atmanirbhar* or self-reliant.

As India has opened up after four phases of lockdown, it is seeking to find new doors and windows of opportunity to galvanise our unused and hidden potential. It is aiming to discover possibilities for spurring inclusive, equitable growth to discover new value chains that would create wealth, to harness the untapped human potential and optimally utilise the natural resources. It is embarking on a mission that would make the country self-reliant. The Atmanirbhar Bharat Abhiyan, as it is called, is a mission to galvanise the forces of growth across the country in various sectors of the economy. It's a launch pad for fostering entrepreneurship, nurturing innovation and creation of an ecosystem for rural-urban symbiotic development.

India is blessed with a vast array of natural resources, a huge demographic advantage with over two-thirds of our population under the age of 35 years, a large farming community that indefatigably ensures food security for all of us, dynamic captains of industry who are creating world-class institutions and a set of young, aspirational and entrepreneurial path-breakers. But, what we lack is to make the connection between these strands to weave the fabric of a new India that not only meets its domestic demand for goods and services but also builds global brands that the world will recognise as uniquely Indian.

In the Indian context, self-reliance should not mean divorcing international trade. India will have to seriously engage with the neighbouring region and the world but at the same time, we require strengthen our domestic industry by streamlining the governance system and go far beyond mere amendments and announcements.

After all, the Covid-19 pandemic economic crisis is of a much larger nature compared to 1991 or even the 2008-2009 economic meltdowns. Question is how to convert five pillars of '*Atmanirbhar Bharat*' Abhiyan, so eloquently enumerated by Prime Minister Modi as economy, infrastructure, technology, vibrant demography and demand, to hold up India's collapsing economic edifice?

The call for 'vocal for local' by Prime Minister, is in the real sense of the term, the recognition and promotion of the intrinsic strength of Indian entrepreneurship waiting to be freed from the shackles of inextricable tangles of land, labour, liquidity and laws, as PM Modi pointed out. Several steps have been taken in this direction by the Government of India to amend the archaic laws and make laws in tune with current realities.

The 'Vocal For Local' campaign coming from the most popular, Prime Minister is bound to make positive results, as this very articulation of intent had many a multinational brand and their many avatars scurrying into strategy huddles, to think up an appropriate plan. But it requires necessary conducive conditions, especially quality higher education and skill development of human resources. India is navigating this complex odyssey with great agility, flexibility, sensitivity and tenacity. The challenge has engendered a spirit of solidarity and unity. It has shown yet again how resilient we can collectively be.

Pradhan Mantri Garib Kalyan Package (PMGK) was introduced in April 2020 in order to provide relief to the underprivileged and help them fight the battle against Covid-19. The budget allocated to the scheme was ₹ 1.70 lakh crore (US$ 24.12 billion). This package was followed by a special economic package which intends to benefit various segments including cottage industry, Micro, Small and Medium Enterprises (MSMEs), labourers, middle class and industries, among others. The economic package that was announced by the Prime Minister along with various packages released during the lockdown period comes to around ₹ 20 lakh crore (US$ 283.73 billion) which is about 10 percent of India's GDP. It is expected to provide support and strength to various sections of the country and give a renewed boost to the development journey of the country from 2020 onwards. In order to prove the determination of a self-reliant India, review of existing policies related to Land, Labour, Liquidity and Laws have all been emphasised in this package.

Shri Venkaiah Naidu, Vice-President of India, reflected that the decisions taken by the government of India in June 2020 will "have a far-reaching impact on the farm and non-farm sectors in rural areas as well as on the development and sustainability of medium, small and micro-enterprises. It tends to turn the current challenge into an opportunity. If the sound policy intent can be effectively translated into practice, it is bound to have a profound impact on our country's economy, especially in rural areas"

Minister of Finance & Corporate Affairs, Ms Nirmala Sitharaman made all the announcements related to various sectors on different days, split under five tranches, giving detailed information about the steps being carried out by the government.

Role of Quality Higher Education

Providing quality higher education and optimal skills to the youth is the key to galvanise our unused and hidden potential. It only underlines the need to be on our own with respect to basic and core necessities, based on our ability to meet them with our known available resources and technologies.

Education is a key enabler for inclusive growth, sustainable development and participation in a democracy. It stimulates economic growth and empowers citizens to make informed decisions. Quality higher education is the key for creating knowledge societies which can innovate and empower people with right skills and knowledge (to enable them to make value addition) to allow them to take wise decisions for human welfare and sustainable development which is crucial for national development and a Self-reliant India.

The role of education to meet the basic learning needs of every person-child, youth and adult in shaping human development has been emphasised through several cross-cultural studies. Development economists have shown that more educated and literate educated parents have higher income levels, healthier lives, lower fertility and less disease-prone children. The significant positive effect of the quantity and quality of education (measured in terms of enrolment ratios, average years of schooling and transition rates) on aggregate economic growth has been established in the studies, discussing the relationship between education and national development. The learning needs generally comprise of both essential learning outcomes such as literacy, oral expression, numeracy, and problem solving and the basic learning outcomes such as knowledge, skills, values, and attitudes which are required by human beings to be able to survive, to develop their full capacities, to live and work in dignity, to participate fully in development, to improve the quality of their lives, to make informed decisions and to continue lifelong learning. The scope of the basic learning needs and how they should be met varies with individual countries and cultures, and inevitably, changes with the passage of time. (Chabbott and Ramirez, 2000); (Topel, 1999), (Weiner, 1991), (Hannum and Buchmann, 2004).

However, education and health have been the most neglected sectors in the public policy framework in India. The education sector needs a paradigm shift in its development strategy for generating a mass movement to take the process of universalisation of quality education forward, as poverty and deprivation remains India's biggest challenges in ensuring equitable and inclusive educational opportunities. India needs to improve access to quality of education services especially for girls and marginalised communities like the Scheduled Castes, Scheduled Tribes, other socio-economically backward communities and children living in difficult circumstances.

A knowledge-based society needs to develop human and intellectual capital, as such capital is the source of ideas and innovation. The strategies toward human resource development must be comprehensive, from nurturing the skills, creativity and talent of the students and the workforce, to the development of entrepreneurship. Schools and colleges have traditionally strived to provide a strong foundation in mathematics and science. In the knowledge society, schools and universities need to develop the students' ability to think, assimilate and evaluate information and knowledge and apply this knowledge continually on their own. Schools and universities need to develop a more holistic curriculum to instil, not only technical skills but skills that are needed for their students to operate effectively in the information economy also.

Research, innovation and information does not necessarily lead to knowledge societies unless innovation and information provides problem solving solutions towards challenges of acquiring, absorbing and communicating the innovation and information by concerned implementers. Empowering each Indian with right skills and knowledge (to enable him/her to create value addition) is crucial for national development. If people are poor, it is because they have not been empowered with right skills which can provide value addition in the competitive world of market economics.

There is an urgent need to provide technical assistance to improve access, quality of education, skills' development through policy interventions, capacity and institution building, programme management, design and implementation, monitoring and evaluation, learning assessments and research. All our services and solutions should be tailored to the specific needs of end-users in view of distinct local circumstances, customs, expectations and cultures. There is urgent requirement to work with diverse stakeholders in order to deliver sustainable solutions for the global human capital conundrum to compete with global giants.

Most observers of higher education in India feel that performance of higher education institutions has been less than satisfactory in terms of access, equity and quality. Now, there is an urgent need to work for the development of the educational sector to meet the needs of the emerging opportunities. Apart from concerns relating to deteriorating standards, there is reported exploitation of students by many private providers. Ensuring equitable access to quality higher education for students coming from poor families is a major challenge. Students from poor background are put to further disadvantage since they are not academically prepared to crack highly competitive entrance examinations that have bias towards urban elite and rich students having access to private tuitions and coaching. Education in basic sciences and subjects that are not market-friendly has suffered.

Research in higher education institutions is at its lowest ebb. There is an inadequate and diminishing financial support for higher education from the government and from society. Many colleges established in rural areas are non-viable, are under-enrolled and have extremely poor infrastructure and facilities with just a few teachers.

Some of the leading challenges before the higher education system are continuous upgradation of curriculum to keep in pace with rapid growth of science and technology; globalisation and the resultant challenges from the international universities; grooming of many private institutions without any method of ensuring maintenance of quality and standard; need for adequate funding to meet the demands of various novel innovative programmes; developing a meaningful and purposeful interface between the universities, National Research Laboratories, industries, government and society etc. ICT in higher education policy may not be able to completely overcome all these challenges though it may play a role in information and resource sharing. Although India aims to attain a Higher education GER of 30% by 2020, it's still much behind countries like China, which, currently, boasts an enrolment ratio of 43.39%. USA's GER is 85.8%.

Currently, India spends around 2.7% of its gross domestic product (GDP) on school education and 3.9% of its GDP on overall education (CBGA–CRY 2016). This is much lower than the benchmark of at least 6% of GDP as recommended by the Kothari Commission in 1966 and subsequently reiterated by Kasturirangan Committee and many other committees over time. As there is a consistent decline in the union government's percentage share in the country's budgetary spending on education and a shift of responsibility progressively towards states, the onus of allocating more resources for the implementation of the action agenda will be more on states and private sector.

Many IIT graduates, well-trained in technology, have chosen not to contribute their skills to the burgeoning technology sector in India; perhaps a significant proportion of them leave the country immediately upon graduation to pursue advanced studies abroad, and most do not return. A stunning 86 percent of Indian students in the fields of science and technology who obtain degrees in the United States, do not return home immediately following their graduation. A body of dedicated and able teachers work at the IITs and IIMs but the lure of jobs abroad and in the private sector makes it increasingly difficult to lure the best and brightest to the academic profession in Indian universities and other reputed colleges. We must make conditions conducive for their return to India so that their contribution can be utilised to propel skill development among youth which is urgently required to prepare Self-reliant India.

Consequently, the road map for a three-tiered education system with a varying regulatory mechanism and skewed distribution of resources towards institutions in the top tiers, fuels the fear of withdrawal of the financial responsibility of the government towards universities in the lowest tiers which serve the largest number of students.

Skill Development Education in India

The country presently faces a dual challenge of severe paucity of highly-trained, quality skilled labour as well as non-employability of large sections of the educated workforce that possess little or no job skills. The skill development issue in India is thus pertinent both at the demand and supply level. Making Self-reliant India (*Atmanirbhar Bhara*t) a reality, requires to infuse demand side challenge like expansion of economic activities that requires large number of skilled workers. On the supply side, a simple look at the projected youth population provides a fair reason to believe that India has the strength to cater to this demand. However, the employability quotient is questionable and remains a major area of concern in states with manufacturing hubs and industrial units. Already huge gaps exist between the industry requirements and the level of skills of workers due to varied reasons including inadequate training infrastructures, inappropriate mix of skills and education, outdated curricula, limited industry interfaces, limited quality standards of skills imparted to youth etc. Moreover, there is a disconnect between the formal education system and work requirements compounding the challenges related to the skill gap. A concerted action is thus required on the supply side to ensure sustained employability of the Indian youth.

Today, as India treads on the path of becoming a knowledge economy, we face a paradox of intensifying skill shortages coupled with unemployment or underemployment among highly educated workers. While a shortage of skills (or under-education) is definitely a cause of concern, surplus education (or over-education) has also led to underutilisation of skills and further lower demand for low-skill workers. There is persistent skill mismatch that has an adverse impact on most industries. It becomes more pronounced in case of a labour-intensive industry like software, manufacturing of textiles and clothing and construction sector industries which is one of the largest sectors, not only in terms of size, but also in terms of providing employment in India.

The NITI Aayog has acknowledged that the skill development initiative by the Government of India has failed to achieve the desired outcome. Thus, for continuity of education, the action agenda has also designed a series of strategies to strengthen skill education. The agenda includes proposals like setting up a Skill Assessment Board and a national-level Overseas Employment Promotion Agency under the Ministry of External Affairs for better management and regulation of initiatives for skill education.

The story of entrepreneurship in India over the years has been far from satisfactory. According to economist Ejaz Ghani, contrary to what many believe, 'India produces too few entrepreneurs for its stage of development,' and the industry is characterised by a sluggish pace of creation of new businesses and start-ups as compared to the other competing countries. In a World Bank report, Ghani et al. note that self-employment is virtually either very low or non-existent in the Indian formal manufacturing sector.

There have been major challenges to skills' development in India. First is less collaboration with industry and private sector. Creating avenues for private sector engagement has been a crucial strategic pillar for India. Skill development faces several forms of market failures including information asymmetries–a skilled person knows his or her skills, but a potential employer does not; if employers had all the information, their willingness to pay for a skilled person would rise. Recognition of Prior Learning (RPL) is an example of an intervention to address information asymmetry. The study for Centre for Monitoring Indian Economy (CMIE) suggests there are more than 390 million individuals who have acquired skills informally–through self-learning, on-the-job learning, inherited skills or other sources. But majority of them lack appropriate quality skills for the jobs. Of these, a majority (384 million) are working, showing the scope for RPL and apprenticeship-related interventions, but their productivity is much below their potential due to lack of appropriate skill capacities. Both of these interventions typically involve collaboration with industry and the private sector even when they are part of publicly funded programmes or schemes.

Another issue is skill development in externalities. For example, when a firm spends resources on developing the skills of an employee, he or she can quit and join another firm thus benefitting the latter firm and not the firm that incurred the training cost. In India, there are a variety of skill development models–government-funded programmes that fully or partially subsidise training/apprenticeships, market-led trainings (where trainees pay for the course), market-led apprenticeships and industry-led/on-the-job training. The not-for-profit National Skill Development Corporation (NSDC) was set up as a public-private partnership (PPP) to stimulate private sector participation in the Indian skill development sector. A core role of the NSDC is, therefore, providing long-term development finance to organisations to build for-profit vocational training initiatives. Ministry of Skill Development and Entrepreneurship (MSDE) implements government grant-based vocational training programmes where infrastructure is set up by private providers and training costs are subsidised by the government.

Issues, Challenges and Way Forward

Resources Mobilisation: Bulk of the enrolment in higher education is handled by state universities and their affiliated colleges. However, these state universities receive very small amounts of grants in comparison to Central Universities funded by University Grants Commission (UGC), Government of India. Nearly 65% of the University Grants Commission (UGC) budget is utilised by the central universities and their colleges, while state universities and their affiliated colleges get only the remaining 35%. It is, therefore, recommended that the mobilisation of funds in state universities should be explored through other means such as endowments, contributions from industry, alumni, etc.

Faculty Induction: According to UGC, the total number of sanctioned teaching posts in various Central Universities are 16,699 for professors, 4,731 for associate professors and 9,585 for assistant professors as in 2018. Out of the total sanctioned teaching posts, 5,925 (35%) professor posts, 2,183 (46%) associate professor posts and 2,459 (26%) assistant professor posts are vacant. The Committee reasoned that this could be due to two reasons: (i) young students don't find the teaching profession attractive; or (ii) the recruitment process is long and involves too many procedural formalities. The recruitment process should start well before a post is vacated. In addition, to make the profession of teaching more lucrative, faculty should be encouraged to undertake consultancy projects and be provided financial support for start-ups.

Accountability and Performance of Teachers: At present, there is no mechanism for ensuring the accountability and performance of professors in universities and colleges. This is unlike foreign universities where the performance of college faculty is evaluated by their peers and students. In this context, a system of performance audit of professors based on the feedback given by their students and colleagues should be set up. Other inputs like research papers, publications by teachers should be added in the performance audit in due course of time.

Induction of Employable Skills: Lack of employable skills in students of technical education has been observed. Identification of skill gaps in different sectors and offering courses for enhancing employability in them has been recommended by several committees. Some strategies in this regard can include: (i) Industry Institute Student Training Support, (ii) Industrial Challenge Open Forum, (iii) Long Term Student Industry Placement Scheme and (iv) Industrial Finishing Schools.

Accreditation of Institutions: Accreditation of skills taught in higher educational institutions needs to be at the core of the regulatory arrangement in higher education. Further, quality assurance agencies should guarantee basic minimum standards of technical education to meet the industry demand for quality manpower. The National Board of Accreditation should act as a catalyst towards quality enhancement and quality assurance of higher technical education. Reputed industry associations, media houses and professional bodies should be encouraged to carry forward the process of rating of skills taught in Indian universities and institutions. A robust rating system will give rise to healthy competition amongst universities and help improve their performance.

Industry and Academia Collaboration: Industry and Academia connect is necessary to ensure curriculum and skills in line with requirements by the industry. Skill building is really very crucial to ensure employability of academia to understand and make sure good jobs (keeping in view knowledge, skills, global professional skill etc.).

Incentives to Teachers and Researchers: Industry and students are expecting specialised courses to be offered so that they get the latest and best in education and they are also industry ready and employable. Vocational and Diploma courses need to be made more attractive to facilitate specialised programs being offered to students. Incentives should be provided to teachers and researchers to make these professions more attractive for the younger generation.

Promoting Innovative Practices: The new technologies offer vast opportunities for progress in all walks of life. It offers opportunities for economic growth, improved health, better service delivery, improved learning and socio-cultural advances. Though efforts are required to improve the country's innovative capacity, yet the efforts should be to build on the existing strengths in light of new understanding of the research innovation-growth linkage.

Utilising Information Age: The world is entering into an Information Age and developments in communication, information and technology will open up new and cost-effective approaches for providing the reach of higher education to the youth as well as to those who need continuing education for meeting the demands of explosion of information, fast-changing nature of occupations, and lifelong education.

Student-Centred Education and Dynamic Methods: Methods of higher education also have to be appropriate to the needs of learning to learn, learning to do, learning to be and learning to become. Student-centred education and employment of dynamic methods of education will require from teachers new attitudes and new skills. Methods of teaching through lectures will have to subordinate to the methods that will lay stress on self-study, personal consultation between teachers and pupils, and dynamic sessions of seminars and workshops. Methods of distance education will have to be employed on a vast scale.

□

M.A., M.Phil, Ph.D. Senior Fellow ICSSR and former Professor, Centre for the Study of Regional Development, Jawaharlal Nehru University, New Delhi. He has more than 43 years of teaching and research experience at post-graduate and research level.

A Mission Towards Making India Self-reliant

—CA C.L. Shah

Atmanirbhar Bharat is the vision of the Prime Minister of India, Narendra Modi of making India a self-reliant nation.While the idea was first proposed by Prime Minister Narendra Modi, some of its features are similar to the Swadeshi movement launched on 7 August, 1905, to take on the British regime of the time.

Since independence, we have not really trusted our people or their expertise, our resources, our home-grown industries or our brilliant entrepreneurs. In the early years after independence, we trusted public sector units with overseeing development works in various fields, but when that failed, we took to globalisation in 1991. Globalisation opened us to foreign direct investments, MNCs and foreigners, in turn leading to a capital-based growth system which brought with it, its own set of problems. Thereafter, we allowed the imports of subsidised Chinese goods which put several industries out of business as the Chinese imports reduced the demand for indigenous products. This made people subsist on government doles rather than being valuable contributors to the economy.

The Covid-19 pandemic has brought global economic activity to a virtual halt. While the world was long expecting a recession, the pandemic has surely pulled the trigger. The International Monetary Fund estimates global economy to contract by 3% this year and expects the clout to further deepen should the virus not recede in the latter half of 2020. With global lockdowns imposed to check spread of Covid-19 causing economic turmoil that is touted to be worst since the 1930s, nations around the world have announced what came to be known as 'Coronavirus Stimulus

Packages.' The US has committed to the largest rescue package by any country in pure dollar terms of US$ 2.7 trillion but as percentage of GDP, it works out to 13% of GDP. Japan has announced a package equivalent to 21.1 percent of its GDP. It has outlined USD 1.1 trillion recovery package and plans for further spending.

Covid-19 Stimulus package in terms of GDP

Country	Package in terms of GDP (%)
Japan	21.1
Luxemburg	20.7
Belgium	19.2
USA	13.0
Sweden	12.0
Australia	10.8
Germany	10.7
India	10.0
France	9.3
Spain	7.3
Italy	5.7

As for the Indian economy, growth has been decelerating for the past eight quarters, and indications by Reserve Bank of India suggest growth contracting for the first time in four decades this year.

On 12 May, 2020, Prime Minister Narendra Modi in his address to the nation announced a mega economic stimulus package amounting to ₹ 20.97 lakh crore under the 'Atmanirbhar Bharat Abhiyan'. The focus of the package aimed at making India self-reliant in the post Covid-19 economic reconstruction. Prime Minister Modi spoke about achieving self-reliance by giving thrust on two themes: **'Vocal for Local'** and **'Local to Global'**. He said the economic package would play an important role in making India 'self-reliant' and that it would benefit labourers, farmers, honest taxpayers, MSMEs and the cottage industry. He said making the country self-reliant was the only way to make 21st century belong to India. The Prime Minister also highlighted that India's self-reliance would be based on five pillars.

The Five pillars of Atmanirbhar Bharat are:

1. **Economy:** An economy that takes quantum jumps and not incremental change.
2. **Infrastructure:** Infrastructure that should be world-class and becomes the identity of India, which is synonymous with a modern India.
3. **System:** A system that is based on the technology-driven arrangement fulfilling the dreams of 21st century, not the policy of the past century.
4. **Demography:** A vibrant demography of the largest democracy, which is the source of energy for a self-reliant India.
5. **Demand:** Demand, whereby the strength of our demand and supply chain should be utilised to full capacity. Lay emphasis on the importance of strengthening all stakeholders in the supply chain to increase, as well as fulfil, the demand.

Later, both Finance Ministry as well as Reserve Bank of India unveiled slew of schemes announced under the ₹ 20.97 lakh crore Atmanirbhar Bharat Abhiyan package which is going to have a multiplier effect on the Indian economy. The Atmanirbhar Bharat Abhiyan package is solely focused on survival of business and sets a road map for the revival of the economy. As far as the Indian economy is concerned, growth has been decelerating for the past eight quarters, and indications by Reserve Bank of India suggest growth contracting for the first time in four decades this year.

Stimulus Package Under Atmanirbhar Bharat

Sl. No.	Tranche	Amount (₹ Crore)
1.	Pradhan Mantri Garib Kalyan Yojana	**1,92,800**
2.	Other packages announced by FM	
	I	5,94,550
	II	3,10,000
	III	1,50,000
	IV	8,100
	V	40,000
	Total (I to V)	**11,02,650**
3.	Liquidity injection by RBI	**8,01,603**
	TOTAL (1+2+3)	**20,97,053**

1. Pradhan Mantri Garib Kalyan Yojana: ₹ 1,92,800/- crore

Soon after the announcement of lockdown on 24 March 2020, Modi Government under the Pradhan Mantri Garib Kalyan Yojana unveiled relief package worth ₹ 1,92,800/- crore which includes ₹ 15,000/- crore towards anti-Covid health facilities and ₹ 7,800/- crore loss of revenue. The main aim of the package is to help organised sectors, farmers, and the poor to battle the economic disruption that has been caused by the Covid-19 outbreak. The said relief package which initially lapsed on 30th June, 2020 was further extended till November 2020.

Key highlights of this package are:

- Cash transfer via DBT will be provided by the government to households, women, women under Jan Dhan Yojana, Divyang, poor pensioners, widows, Mahatma Gandhi National Rural Employment Guarantee Act (MNREGA) workers, and farmers.
- Individuals working on the frontlines, ASHA workers, nurses, and paramedics will receive a medical insurance cover worth ₹ 50 lakh. This will benefit around 20 lakh individuals.
- ₹ 500 will be provided per month as an ex-gratia amount to women Jan Dhan Yojana account holders. The amount will be provided up to November 2020 to help the poor to run their households. This will help about 20 crore women.
- The welfare fund can be used by state governments to help construction and building labourers. The ₹ 31,000 crore that is available in the District Mineral Foundation Funds can be used to help individuals who are facing financial difficulties due to the lockdown.
- Amendments will be made to the Employees' Provident Fund Organisation (EPFO) Scheme so that organised sector workers can withdraw the non-refundable advance. Up to five months' salary or 75% of the amount available, whichever is lower, can be withdrawn. This move will benefit around 4.8 crore workers who are part of the Employees' Provident Fund (EPF) Scheme.
- For the next five months, the employee's and the employer's contribution towards the EPF scheme will be paid by the government. However, this benefit will be provided to organisations that have up to 100 employees (90% of them must earn less than ₹ 15,000).

- LPG cylinders will be provided for free to around 8.3 crore families that come under the below poverty line. Cylinders will be provided for the next three months. However, the families must come under the Ujjwala Scheme.
- For the upcoming five months, widows, poor senior citizens, and Divyang will be given ₹ 1,000. The move will help around 3 crore individuals.
- An increase in wages will be provided for MNREGA workers. According to the government, this move will help 5 crore families. An increase in wage will lead to an additional income of ₹ 2,000 for every worker.
- Via the PM-KISAN scheme, an up-front amount of ₹ 2,000 will be provided to farmers. Under the scheme, farmers receive ₹ 6,000 every year. The move will benefit around 8.69 crore farmers.
- Women Self-Help Groups (SHGs) that come under the National Rural Livelihood Mission (NRLM) will be provided collateral-free loans of up to ₹ 20 lakhs.
- Under the food scheme, Pradhan Mantri Garib Kalyan Anna Yojana, benefits will be provided to about 80 crore individuals. Under the scheme, 5 kilograms (kg) of rice/wheat will be provided for free. For the next five months, 1 kg of pulse (one choice) will be provided for every household.

2. Other Packages Announced by Finance Minister

I. The part-I package: ₹ 5,94,550/- Crore

The part-I package announced by the Finance Minister, Nirmala Sitharaman on 13th May, 2020 has predominantly eyed MSMEs which account for 35% of the GDP and contribute to one third of the exports. With these measures, combined with the slogans of **'Vocal for Local'** and **'Local to Global'** for our domestically manufactured products, purchase of MSME products in government procurement, benefits of new definition, market linkage and TDS measures, the MSME sector can see steady revival in demand.

Key highlights of this package are:

- Collateral-free loans for businesses and MSMEs worth ₹ 3 lakh crore. Apart from that, a package of ₹ 20,000 crore was announced for stressed MSMEs. The government is infusing an equity of ₹ 50,000 crore in MSMEs which have potential for growth.

- For Revival of NBFCs, the FM announced a liquidity scheme of ₹ 30,000 crore. Further, a ₹ 45,000 crore of partial credit guarantee scheme 2.0 was announced, which will help them to provide loans to individual MSMEs.
- For both employers and employees, provident fund rates were reduced from 12 percent to 10 percent. The reduction will lead to saving of ₹ 6,750 crore and further EPF support provided for business and workers, will provide a relief of ₹ 2,800 crore.
- Further, liquidity injection was announced for DISCOMs to the tune of ₹ 90,000 crore.
- A reduction in tax deducted at source (TDS) amounts to a relief of ₹ 50,000 crore.

II. The part-II package: ₹ 3,10,000/- crore

The part-II package included free foodgrain to stranded migrant workers for two months and credit to farmers, totalling ₹ 3.10 lakh crore.

Key highlights of this package are:

- The package of ₹ 3,500 crore was set aside for free foodgrain supply to migrant labourers for the next two months.
- In the second tranche, FM also announced interest subvention for Micro Units Development and Refinance Agency Bank (MUDRA) Shishu loans of ₹ 1,500 crore.
- Special credit facility of ₹ 5,000 crore was announced for street vendors.
- An amount of ₹ 70,000 crore was set aside for housing through which the government aims to provide affordable renting facilities to migrants.
- Besides, through NABARD, additional re-finance support of ₹ 30,000 crore will be provided for crop loans.
- Through Kisan Credit Cards, farmers will be provided an additional credit of ₹ 2 lakh crore.

III. The part-III package: ₹ 1,50,000/- crore

The part-III package set aside ₹ 1,50,000/- crore for agriculture and allied sectors.

Key highlights of this package are:

- The government has taken up ₹ 10,000 crore projects to formalise Micro Food Enterprises (MFEs).
- ₹ 15000 crore to set up dairy cooperatives at a 2% annual interest rate. Additional 2% interest subsidy on instant payment/interest servicing.
- The government has come up with ₹ 20,000 crore projects for fishermen called Fisheries Resources Scheme (PM Matsya Sampada Yojana).
- To promote herbal farming, 10,000,000 hectares of land will be used in the next 2 years with an investment of ₹ 4,000 crore.
- ₹ 1 lac crore provided for aggregators, FPOs, primary agriculture societies for strengthening farm gate infrastructure, for cold chains especially for private and start-ups.
- An amount of ₹ 15,000 crore was allocated as Animal Husbandry Infrastructure Development Fund. 100% vaccination of all cattle (about 53 crore animals) to eradicate foot and mouth disease.
- ₹ 500 crore for Bee-keeping to benefit 2 lakh beekeepers.
- ₹ 500 crore for Operation Greens. This scheme will be extended to all fruits and vegetables starting with tomatoes, onions and potatoes.
- A central law will be enacted to provide adequate choice for farmers to sell products at attractive prices, provide an adequate barrier-free international trade and provide an E-trading structure for agricultural products.
- All Agricultural products including cereals, edible oils, oilseeds, pulses, onions, and potatoes should be regulated by amending the Essential Commodities Act, 1955.

IV. The part-IV package-₹ 8,100/- Crore

The part-IV package announced as 'New Horizons of Growth' is the phrase that epitomises FM's fourth tranche of Atmanirbhar Bharat Abhiyan. Some significant sectoral reforms announced cover eight major sectors in India namely, Coal, Minerals, Defence, Civil Aviation, Space, Power, Social Infrastructure and Atomic Energy. Most of the measures relate to privatisation to attract more investments, making policy reforms, providing for specific production-linked incentives and subsidies through DBT.

These structural reforms can stir the Indian economy towards a self-reliant economy and increase its competitiveness globally. Although these measures do not seem to have an immediate impact, it may still help in job creation during the long run. One of the announcements that caught all eyes was the increase in FDI limit for defence production from the present 49% to 74%.

Key highlights of this package are:

Coal Sector:

- Private sector participation has been allowed. Now, private players in the coal sector can bid for a coal block and sell in the open market. Earlier, only the captive consumers who did not supply the coal further, could participate. The entry norms are liberalised with no strict eligibility criteria. Still, the interested players must make an upfront payment with a threshold limit. The revenue will be shared between the government and the private participant replacing the fixed rupee per tonne revenue regime. About 50 blocks will be offered to begin with.
- Further exploration of the partially explored coal mines will be allowed through the auction system giving opportunities to the private players to participate in the process. They can earn incentives by rebate in revenue sharing if the production schedules are achieved.
- ₹ 50,000 crore to be invested for coal infrastructure development. The investment will cover for the evacuation of an estimated 1 billion tons of coal production by Coal India Limited (CIL) together with that of the private counterparts. It will also cover for the cost of transporting coal using the conveyor belts from mines to railway sidings through a mechanised system thereby reducing the environmental side effects.
- Incentives for coal gasification/liquefaction, giving rebate while sharing revenue.
- Auction of Coal Bed Methane (CBM) will be organised from the coal mines of CIL.
- Simplification of the mining plan will promote an automatic 40% increase in annual production.
- ₹ 5,000 crore relief is offered by way of concessions in commercial terms by CIL to its consumers.

Mineral Sector:

- A composite exploration-cum-mining-cum-production system to be introduced that allows seamless integration of multiple processes in the mineral industry. About 500 blocks will be auctioned through a transparent process to begin with.
- Joint auction of bauxite and coal mineral blocks to be launched. The initiative will boost the aluminium industry and reduce electricity costs.
- Captive and non-captive mines will no longer be differentiated, since it will encourage a smooth transfer of mining leases and allow the sale of surplus minerals.
- Mining Index to be fixed for different minerals by the Ministry of Mining.
- The stamp duty payable will be rationalised for the purchase of the mining lease.

Defence Sector:

- The Foreign Direct Investment (FDI) limit in defence production has been increased to 74%. It was raised from the earlier limit of 49% to promote self-reliance through domestic defence manufacturing and 'Make in India' initiatives. Further, a list of weapons/platforms shall be banned from imports, while the spares will be indigenised to reduce a huge import bill. A separate budget shall be provisioned for domestic capital procurement.
- Union FM has announced the corporatisation of Ordnance Factory Board, allowing it to be soon listed on the stock exchange while still maintaining a 100% Government of India stake.
- The defence procurement process to be henceforth time-bound through several initiatives such as setting up of Project Management Units (PMU) to manage contracts, framing a General Staff Qualitative Requirements (GSQRs) of weapons or platforms and undertaking trials and testing procedures.

Civil Aviation Sector:

- Annual flying cost savings estimated is ₹ 1,000 crore by removing the restrictions on Indian airspace utilisation which currently stands at 60% only. The new changes in airspace management, in turn, reduces the fuel use, saves time and induces a positive impact on the environment.

- Public-Private Partnerships (PPP) for the development of Indian airports. On recognising the revenue opportunity by its first round of bids for PPP mode for operation and maintaining airports, second and third rounds are proposed. The second round of bidding shall commence shortly for six airports identified by the Airports Authority of India (AAI). At the same time, the third round shall also offer six more. The revenue expected through additional investment in 12 airports via the first two rounds stands at ₹ 13,000 crore.
- India to soon be globally accepted as the Maintenance, Repair and Overhaul (MRO) hub. While recently the GST Council reduced the GST rate on MRO activities to 5%, the government plans to merge the MRO of both the defence and civil aviation sectors. It will foster economies of scale by reducing the maintenance costs of airlines. Foreign engine manufacturers popular across the globe will set up engine repair facilities in India within a year, as the cost of repairs will rise by 1.5 times in the next three years.

Power Sector:

- A new Tariff Policy will soon be released. DISCOM inefficiencies will be addressed at length. It included standardisation of services across the board and the levy of penalty on DISCOM for load-shedding. It will ensure timely payments to power generation companies (GENCOs). A Direct Benefit Transfer (DBT) is being proposed for releasing subsidy. At the same time, the installation of smart prepaid meters is a part of the reform.
- Power distribution in Union Territories to be privatised. The government is checking the feasibility of privatising the power distribution and supply on a pilot basis by starting with the UTs. The power departments and utilities will be privatised that is considered to lead to better customer service and financial efficiency in the distribution.

Social Infrastructure (Hospital & Healthcare) Sector:

- ₹ 8,100 crore to be invested by increasing the Viability Gap Funding limit. The government enhanced the quantum of VG up to 30% from the present 20% of the total project cost in the social infrastructure projects in each investment by centre, state and statutory bodies. The projects will be proposed by the central or state governments including statutory entities and help such healthcare institutions financially sustain its business. The VGF limit to remain 20% in other sectors.

Space Sector:

- Private participation to be allowed in the space sector for the first time. The activities to be privatised in the future will cover satellite launches and space-based services, planetary exploration, outer space travel etc. The government will frame a policy, pass legislation and set up a suitable regulatory environment to govern these activities. Union FM, Nirmala Sitharaman also announced that such private participants could utilise the assets, facilities and capacities of ISRO. It allows level-playing opportunity while exploring new space prospects for the country.
- Liberal geospatial data policy is being framed to provide remote-sensing data to tech-entrepreneurs.

Atomic Energy Sector:

- A PPP model to be adopted for establishing research reactors and irradiation facilities. Atomic energy will be used for encouraging better facilities for medical treatments for cancer patients and food preservation by farmers.

Start-ups:

- Technology-cum-incubation centres to be set up across India to allow start-ups for developing innovative and cost-effective technologies.

Industrial parks:

- 3,376 industrial parks/estates/SEZs in 5 lakh hectares have been mapped on IIS.

V. The part-V package-₹ 40,000/- crore

In the part-V package, the Finance Minister highlighted measures for doing ease of doing business, promotion of e-learning, help provided to states, support to public & private sectors and highlighted the seven most important areas under which the stimulus package is distributed which includes-Mahatma Gandhi National Rural Employment Act, Health (rural and urban) and education, Businesses and Covid, Decriminalisation of business, Ease of doing business, PSU related matters, State government and resources. To boost employment in the country, an additional

₹ 40,000 crore was allocated to Mahatma Gandhi National Rural Employment Guarantee Act (MGNREGA).

3. Liquidity Injection by RBI-₹ 8,01,603/- crore

The RBI's main focus is to ensure that there is enough money with financial institutions of all shapes and sizes to lend to customers. The Reserve Bank of India on 17 March, 2020 and 17 April, 2020 announced a host of emergency measures to help banking and non banking finance companies (NBFCs) with cash infusions and persuading banks to lend funds rather than parking them by lowering the reverse repo rate. The central bank has also sought to open the funding tap for stretched microfinance institutions (MFIs), ease bad-loan recognition norms, help states borrow more as they seek to cope with Covid-19 containment.

Key highlights of the package are:

- **Repo Rate:** RBI reduced Repo Rate to 4%.
- **Reverse Repo:** The Reverse Repo rate was further cut to 3.35% from 3.75%.
- **Loan Moratorium:** In a massive relief for the middle class, the RBI Governor also announced that lenders could give a moratorium of 6 months on term loans outstanding as on 1 March, 2020. This is applicable to All Commercial Banks including Regional, Rural, Small Finance, Co-Op Banks, All India Financial Institutions and NBFCs including Housing Finance and Microfinance.
- **CRR:** The RBI also announced that the Cash Reserve Ratio (CRR) would be reduced by 100 bps, or 1%, to 3%. This would be applicable from March 28 and would inject ₹ 1,37,000 crore.
- **LTRO:** The RBI will also undertake Long Term Repo Operations (LTRO) thus allowing further liquidity with the banks. The banks, however, are specified that this liquidity will be deployed in commercial papers, investment grade corporate bonds and non-convertible debentures. Targeted amount ₹ 50,000/- crore.
- **Ease of Working Capital financing:** Borrowers were allowed lending on recalculated drawing power by reducing margins and/ or by reassessing the working capital cycle for the borrowers. The RBI also specified that such a move would not result in asset classification downgrade.

- **Refinance**-₹ 50,000/-crore allocated for refinance to SIDBI, NABARD and NHB.
- **Dividend**-Banks were directed to skip dividend for financial year 2020-21 to conserve its resources for further lending.
- **Working Capital Interest:** Interest moratorium shall also be permitted to all lending institutions up to 30.09.2020.

The recent pattern of migrants returning to their states will shift the demand-supply curves substantially. Economic growth which previously came with massive urbanisation, will now be seen in a different way. If we can make all the basic necessities like food, water, shelter, internet connectivity and some employment opportunities available within rural areas, a good number of migrants might just stay back and it will indeed reduce the pressure on our larger cities. The state governments can establish clusters and manufacturing hubs within small villages which will undeniably put the economy back on track without relying upon cities as much as in the past. This would also avoid over-crowding in cities.

The ₹ 20.97 lakh crore economic package declared by the central government will surely be a great boost to the nation since the money circulation that slowed down, will again gain momentum. New dynamics of demand-supply cycle will emerge. Disruptive, innovative and collaborative consumption will shift the lines of the economy. We have to wait and watch whether new forms of localisation rather than globalisation will emerge that will determine the demand-supply curves.

Modiji's vision of Atmanirbhar Bharat is not about isolation or anti-globalisation. The objective is to become competitive and, therefore, the focus is to make India simple in doing business. Atmanirbhar Bharat is not meant to promote protectionism or isolationism by erecting trade barriers. Rather, it seeks to make the Indian economy robust in the long run by scaling up manufacturing, accelerating infrastructure development, attracting investments and promoting a consumption-led growth.

□

B.Sc., FCA, FCS, FCMA and is a financial and corporate consultant.

Reimagining the Possible: Embracing the Power of Digital

—CA Sidheshwar Bhalla

'It is not the strongest of the species that survives, nor the most intelligent that survives. It is the one that is the most adaptable to change.'

—Charles Darwin

The world is changing at a breakneck speed and **Digital** is a major game-changer driving business transformation across the globe. Disruptions ranging from hyperautomation to human augmentation are taking the world by storm and redefining the way companies operate. Instead of resisting this digital evolution, companies need to embrace it, thus making way for optimising the benefits of disruption.

Disruption is more than a technology story and can be turned from a threat to an opportunity. It is a cycle where technology innovation spawns changes in the market and competitive dynamics and vice versa. Digital Transformation is a key theme in helping this journey of disruption into growth opportunity. Digital Transformation Global Spending is spiralling upwards and will double by 2022 (*Source: Global Digital Pulse Survey 2017)*. IT spending in India continues to be driven by digital business transformation initiatives from both private and public organisations.

To set the context, let's talk about some of the commonly used terms in the Digital era:

- **Digitisation:** It is a process through which information in physical format is converted into its digital/electronic counterparts. It enables to create value out of meaningful data in some computer based systems or automated processes.

- **Digitalisation:** It's the process of leveraging Digitisation to aid in the efficiency/improvement of business processes, obviously using computer-aided software.
- **Digital Transformation:** It's a process through which organisations use Digitisation and or various emerging technologies to transform the business processes to make them more efficient. However, when it comes to a digital transformation, it's much more than IT and it largely involves processes, people and strategy. The key attribute of digital is ADOPTION and that is what makes the 'people' attribute so important. Essentially, it's a combination of **Mindset**, **Culture**, **Clear Strategy** and **Technology** enablement which leads to the desired results for transformation.

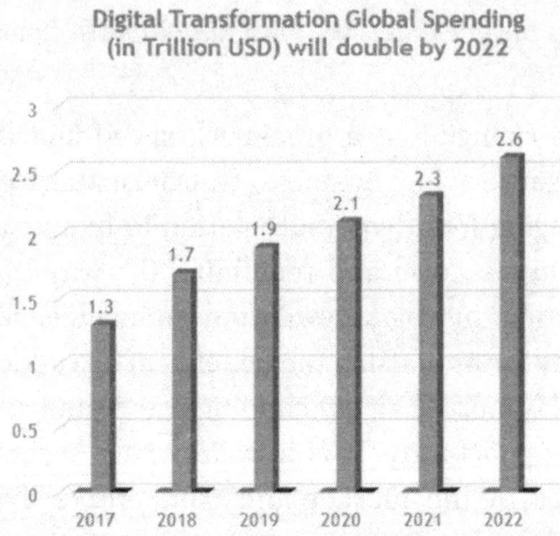

Source: Global Digital Pulse Survey

Based on some of the recent statistics, the global spending in digital transformation is going to double by 2022.

With the exponential increase in opportunities, the challenges are skyrocketing as well. To cope with and carve a strong foothold in this emerging digital environment, businesses need to think and do things differently–which essentially means...

Reinventing yourself: Regardless of the industry, many organisations are looking to harness technology to drive business growth and transformation. While new organisations are born digital, many CIOs in organisations that are digital non-natives, struggle to close the gap between traditional technology stocks and emerging digital capabilities—

cloud, mobile, social, automation, cognitive, and more—that can enable streamlined processes, increase employee and customer engagement and drive new business models.

As a very empirical **approach** to this transformation journey, is defined a 10-step Guide to Digital Transformation. This, however, varies across industries and based on the current digital maturity level of the organisation, will need to be tailored while doing the digital strategy and road map.

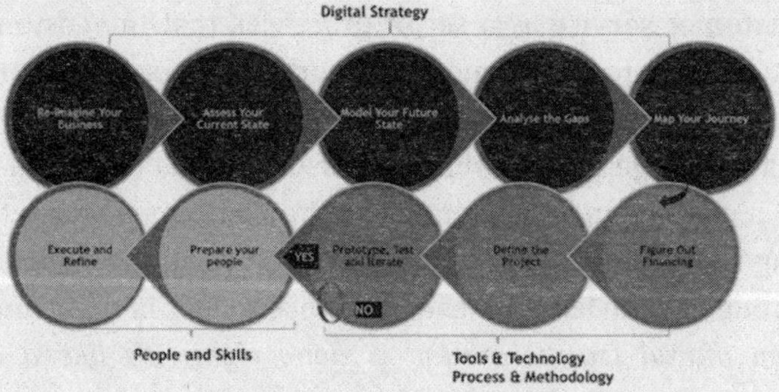

Following are the seven **key measurable benefits** that organisations can expect from their digital investments:

- Improved decision making
- Enhanced customer/ client experience
- Improved efficiencies
- Increased agility and innovation in work culture
- Provides data-driven insights
- Provides accurate market segmentation
- Last but not the least, fosters a digital culture which allows the workforce to remain productive and engaged in the transformation without feeling overwhelmed or disconnected from the process.

Organisations that view digital transformation as mainly a technology difference from traditional transformation through business process re-engineering will end up missing the power of digital transformation. How is digital transformation different from business process re-engineering? A digital transformation journey moves an organisation from a process-defined world to a data-driven world.

In our current world, businesses are set up along processes and they try to develop world-class processes. Six Sigma and other tools are designed to refine and improve those processes to create efficiency, focus and improvement in quality. In contrast, digital transformation shrinks down processes that a business currently does or could do, automates work people were doing and turns the process into software. What's left is data.

The Power of Digital Transformation is a Data-driven World. This allows organisations to look at their business through the lens of data instead of the lens of process. Suddenly, the data make clear that people matter, the customer experience matters. For instance, instead of seeing customer service as a set of processes that the customer or the organisation initiates, customer data forces the organisation to think about the customer experience.

As data emerge and the ability to associate that data with indicators or issues, it enables an organisation to not only become more efficient but also change what it does. The business impact resulting from viewing the world through a data lens, instead of a process lens, is super-powerful.

'When digital transformation is done right, it's like a caterpillar turning into a butterfly, but when done wrong, all you have is a really fast caterpillar.'-George Westerman, Principal Research Scientist with the MIT Sloan Initiative on the Digital Economy.

□

Has 17+ years of professional experience as a Chartered Accountant and Company Secretary. He is Secretary and member of India Board of The Institute of Internal Auditors (IIA) and holds the position of President for IIA, Delhi Chapter. He is a Partner & National Leader–Governance Risk & Compliance with Mazars in India. Prior to this, he was associated with KPMG, GE, EY, Deloitte, BDO.

Blueprint for Atmanirbhar Bharat

—**Dr. Rashmi Tripathi**

Prime Minister Narendra Modi, in his address to the nation on 12th May, 2020 said Covid-19 crisis had 'explained to us the importance of local manufacturing, local market and local supply chain', and had called for increased 'self-reliance' on domestic goods and services.

Here self-reliance does not at all means producing all the kinds of goods and services or challenging the established theory of comparative advantage which improves overall well-being of the world, but it simply means having capability to generate goods and services which are basics for survival of the people to minimise pains induced by externalities like pandemic or war like situation. Countries should continue to trade and manufacture as per competitive advantage, but revisit to build basic capabilities to face global disruptions, which countries faced in the recent past, which was unprecedented and take learnings from it.

When any country plans to become self-reliant it has to think beyond Covid. Today, one is facing Covid, tomorrow we may face some other type of calamity which may cause disruption in important necessities which are basic for mere survival.

Obviously, all the countries are reworking their manufacturing policies. Every country needs to revisit its import and export list and carve out strategy to reduce dependence on important items/services and try to build up onshore capabilities at least to a level which ensures survival.

Learning from Japan's post-war success, countries like South Korea, Taiwan, Singapore and Hong Kong took huge technological and industrial strides in the 1970s and 80s. South Korea, in particular, climbed determinedly up the technology ladder and value chains in electronic goods, consumer durables, automobiles, micro-processors, personal computers and heavy machinery. It emerged as a global powerhouse not only in manufacturing, but also in indigenously developed technologies. Taiwan developed technologies and manufacturing capacities in robotics and micro-processors, while Singapore and Hong Kong adapted advanced technologies in niche areas. These self-reliant capabilities were enabled, among other factors, by planned state investments in R&D including basic research (3-5% of GDP), technology and policy support to private corporations, infrastructure and, importantly, education and skill development (4-6% of GDP).

China is, of course, unique in scale and in its determination to become a superpower not just geopolitically but also in self-reliant S&T and industrial capability. China advanced purposefully from low-end mass manufacturing to a dominant role in global supply chains. It has now decided on shifting to advanced manufacturing and has set itself a target of becoming a world leader by 2035 in 5G, supercomputing, Internet of Things, artificial intelligence (AI), autonomous vehicles, biotech/pharma and other technologies of the 'fourth industrial revolution'.

Recalibration of priorities will go a long way in creating a self-reliant economy. As resources are limited, it is necessary to channelise resources in such a manner which goes a long-way in making India self-reliant and also provides platform for long-term growth. There is also need to understand that self-reliance is not possible without a good GDP growth as resources are required by government, which it would be deploying to make India *Atmanirbhar*.

At this juncture, the major problem which the economy is facing is lack of demand, which is caused by increase in joblessness, accentuated by lockdown and decrease in sources of income of people. With the reverse migration of workers to their villages, the pressure on the rural economy is increasing while the source of income has dried, which was there in the pre-covid period. Having said this, various ways have to be explored to increase the income of rural inhabitants. One of the ways is to put cash in the hands of rural population in the form of NREGA program or through the recently launched 'Garib Kalyan Rojgar Abhiyan'. The rozgar programs will help in two ways; first, it will increase income of rural population due to receiving of wages, thereby supporting rural consumption and another, by creating rural infrastructure which will give fillip to rural economy and thus help in creating resources for increasing future income of rural populace. The rural infrastructure may be like creating roads, deepening of ponds, construction of schools, hospitals, etc. in rural areas under these rojgar creation programs.

Another major problem is of the farmers who are not getting the right price for their produce. The price which farmers get for their produce and the actual price at which these products are available in the city, there is huge difference. This difference amount is either going in the pockets of middleman or corporates. In order to address this problem, there is need to study the models adopted in other countries to ensure reasonable price for farmers' produce, be it cereals, fruits, vegetables or milk. One model followed in US is of farmers market.

The US food security programme entitles beneficiaries to spend cash transfers to buy from markets where only farmers are allowed to sell. Promoting such a model will also shift some of the profits in the food economy currently going to middleman or to corporate players, towards farmers. It could be rolled out on a pilot basis and then expanded gradually. Additional focus be also given on horticulture and dairy to ensure its procurement from production place and delivery at demand place as these produces are highly perishable. This will help in addressing two issues, first, producers will get reasonable price for their produce and second, it will help in checking inflation in these products.

Another way of increasing income of farmers and making India self-reliant in agri-products is by increasing farm productivity. Increasing investment in agricultural infrastructure and implementing reforms to improve market access, rationalise price supports, improving farmer access to new technologies, seeds, land or finance, and streamlining agricultural administration and extension services can help to achieve annual yield growth of 5.5 percent. Eco-system should support greater leasing of land and cooperative sharing of resources like tractors and other agri-equipments. They should effect greater connectivity, both virtual and through logistic networks, of the farmer to warehouses, rural industry and final consumers. This would bring India's yields into line with those in other emerging Asian countries by 2022. This will help India to further become self-reliant on foodgrains, fruits, vegetables, fodder for animals etc. The broader intent should be to enable some farmers to move out of agriculture allowing the remaining farmers to enjoy economies of scale.

Government may also consider lowering GST rates especially on consumer goods or two-wheelers or any other products which govt identifies necessary, to boost its sales and contain joblessness at least for a year or so.

Another major step should be to increase public expenditure on education, skill development and public health system. No country has achieved self-reliance without mass quality in these areas. This is the first and foremost step taken by all the developed countries. They invested heavily in these two areas and brought up the literacy and life expectancy rate.

As per the 2011 India census, India's national literacy is only 74.04%. Literacy in India is not homogeneous, some states in India have higher literacy rates than others. India still has a literacy rate of what China had in 1991. And it is a very known fact that we have underinvested in these two areas, even after knowing that they are the solution to 70% of our country's problems. When we invest on educational system, then only we can imagine creating a mass force of professionals and thereafter, establishing oneself in research and development to support various sectors in their growth.

India's health scenario is dismal with diseases and malnutrition constantly affecting the poorest quarter of the populace. Mortality is still relatively high.

To improve the situation, there is a need for building hospital chains with all medical facilities which matches global standards. In few places, public hospitals are there and are also having latest medical equipments but they lack doctors and staff to operate these equipments. If we improve and do investment in this segment, it will help to serve the Indians and also help in earning foreign currency in the form of medical tourism. India's doctors and hospitals could treat more of its own people as well as the world if India facilitated the opening of more medical colleges and hospitals.

In 1991, when India adopted liberalisation, privatisation and globalisation (LPG), it was believed that advanced technologies could simply be bought from anywhere at lower costs without realisation that it has its own challenges. There is a need for technology policy which strikes a difficult balance between providing a certain amount of protection to allow the country's own technological developments to come to light on the one hand and making sure there are enough competitive impulses to prevent losing track of international developments on the other.

State-funded R&D, including in basic research, by PSUs and research institutions and universities needs to be scaled up significantly well above the dismal 1% of GDP currently. We invest around one-tenth of what China is investing in high-end technologies.

Upgraded and reoriented PSUs would also be crucial given their distinctive place in the ecosystem. Even today, most R&D in India is conducted by PSUs, and much of the smaller but rising proportion of private sector R&D is by foreign corporations in information technology and biotechnology/pharma. Given the disinclination of most of the private sector towards R&D and high-tech manufacturing, significant government reinvestment in PSUs and R&D is essential for self-reliance. India is not as attentive as required to the advancements in AI, IoT, Data Sciences, Life Sciences, New energy resources, materials etc. In the future, a country's strength/destiny will be determined by its level of Science & Technology.

Similarly, though we have the second-largest army, fourth largest Air Force and the seventh-largest navy, but, the equipments which we use is not the latest or of the best technology. Moreover, we import 99% of our defence equipment. The countries which have made high-end technology equipments are also hesitant to sell it to other countries as they perceive it risky to part with these technologies. India should also try to bring down its dependence on other countries for its defence. This area also requires a lot of investment and research.

Along with scaling up investment in research and development, Govt should also give greater thrust on basic infrastructure.

Basic infrastructure in India such as roads, power grid, water, communications, infrastructure, housing and education are often below standards and not catching up with the tune of its economic progress. Continued poor infrastructure might serve as a bottleneck to further economic development. The government is, however, improving the infrastructure such as expanding the freeway and highway system and bringing it up to global standards.

Further reforms and public infrastructure investments could make it easier for all types of manufacturing businesses—foreign and Indian alike—to achieve scale and efficiency.

Land acquisition today is extremely difficult which then impedes construction, not just of highways and railroads, but also of industrial plants, office parks and affordable housing. India needs to accelerate the mapping of land and the process of establishing ownership title especially in the poorest states. It also needs to establish a more transparent process of determining and altering land zoning as well as registering changes in ownership, recognising that some agricultural land will inevitably have to be used for development. Finally, while forcible land acquisition should be used extremely rarely, the Centre should draw on the best practices in states to modify the legislation on land acquisition so that it becomes easier to implement while protecting the interests of the seller.

Similar attention should be paid to reviving stalled infrastructure projects with delays ranging from a few months to more than ten years. To revive power sector, best practices across states should be shared and also past contracts are adhered to so that producers have confidence they will be compensated. There should be more competition within state-owned distribution companies especially among units facing customers-for instance, by breaking up that function and possibly privatising some of it. Competition could also be encouraged from other out-of-state distribution companies—including allowing producers to sell to the highest bidder on the national grid. The telecom sector deserves special mention which is heading towards a monopoly or duopoly which will cost to the nation in the form of high tariffs. India should re-examine its regulatory process and ensure a level playing field within the sector.

The road and other infrastructure projects can spur economic activity, boost construction and create jobs. Even to invite foreign direct investment and manufacturing by foreign majors and to leverage its benefit, the investment in the above sectors is required. The countries which do not develop capabilities in skill development are unable to leverage benefits of technologies.

All the issues discussed above, if addressed, will help India only if it identifies which products it wants to exclusively manufacture in the country in which it has competitive advantage and other products which it wants to manufacture to become self-reliant.

Exports as a percentage of GDP rose constantly in India until the global financial crisis hit in 2008. There was a brief recovery after the crisis, but since then, there has been a sharp fall in share of exports in India's total GDP. After having reached a peak of 17% in 2013-14, exports accounted for just 12.1% of India's GDP in 2018-19. Deepening trade wars and the current slowdown in the global economy does not bode well for future export growth. But, India needs to work in the direction of identifying products which it could produce for exporting and also the items from import basket which it could produce to reduce dependence on the world, with a blueprint for short-term, mid-term and long-term production. There may be a few things which India may produce immediately but there may be many which will require long-term commitments to establish capabilities.

Indian-made products are hardly used by other countries, they are unable to compete globally and are used by Indians only. We need to become producers rather than just being consumers.

India completely missed out on the 'third industrial revolution' comprising electronic goods, micro-processors, personal computers, mobile phones and decentralised manufacturing and global value chains during the so-called lost decade(s). Today, India is the world's second largest smartphone market. However, it does not make any of these phones itself and manufactures only a small fraction of solar photovoltaic cells and modules currently used, with ambitious future targets.

The government should ideally identify sectors where it wants to reduce imports and then provide attractive incentives to both foreign and domestic entrepreneurs who are willing to invest in these sectors within a reasonable but short window. This should ideally be the beginning of the making of a long-term trade and industrial policy for India. The Government should also renegotiate with its trading countries on imports as well as exports and try to clear some roadblocks which would not have been easy earlier.

All this can be achieved if supported by robust infrastructure which supports all these segments by developing skills as per industry requirement, highways, transport systems, railways, logistics, warehouses, SEZ near ports to reduce transport cost etc., as discussed earlier.

Last but not the least, India heavily depends on foreign oil-a phenomenon likely to continue until non-fossil/renewable energy technology becomes economically viable in the country. To avert an energy crisis, India is desperately seeking alternate means of energy. As for now, India is energetically expensive since India has to import over 80% of its energy. Considering India's limited ability to increase domestic supply right now, oil imports are likely to reach new highs over the coming years—something detrimental to India's long-term growth.

India's spend on oil imports directly affect various macroeconomic factors including its current account deficits, oil subsidies, and foreign exchange reserves, a butterfly effect that could trickle down and swell inflation, raise food prices and so on. Every country has to find its own solutions for energy transition and bringing down its dependence on fossil fuels, and India is no different.

Central government along with RBI immediately resorted to several measures sensing the impact of Covid, spanning in various dimensions to provide support to the poor, sustain critical services, give relief to daily wage earners, and give forbearance to banks and businesses and infuse liquidity in the system.

Within a month of announcement of 'Atmanirbhar Bharat' pledge by Center, Department of Commerce, Department for Promotion of Industry and Internal Trade (DPIIT), the Ministry of Civil Aviation, alongside utilities such as BSNL and some state electricity boards, have either issued policy directives or are working to tweak rules to push domestic manufacturing and services. This is just the beginning of the journey which leads to self-reliant India. If, Indian Govt takes measures as discussed above, definitely we will become a self-reliant and developed economy in mid-term.

□

An economist and writes on various economic issues. She was an Economist with Syndicate Bank. Presently she is serving as DGM with Canara Bank.

Healthcare

—Dr. Neeraj Ashri

There was this old photograph of future PM of India, Mr. Narendra Modi, standing outside the White house like a tourist that caught my attention. What was he thinking, I wondered? Was he comparing American and Indian systems like myself or many others would frequently do on arriving here?

Comparing the life in two countries is the major topic for discussion among friends during social gatherings. After more than 2 decades in united states, my mind no longer converts dollars to rupees while making a purchase, similarly conversations about India and USA get less frequent with passing time, however, it does come up during crisis such as Covid-19.

I am not an expert in Indian or US healthcare system but few things are quite noticeable. I think both India and America can learn from each other, there are several good things on both sides.

Health Insurance

Money plays a big role in healthcare. One of the frequent complaints against doctors in India is that they order unnecessary imaging, tests and procedures. Probably, one of the reasons for violence against doctors is mistrust over cost of healthcare. I myself would be reluctant to practice medicine in India if every test or procedure ordered would be scrutinised by lay public and looked at with suspicion. Fact is that modern medicine can not be practiced without proper tests and imaging.

Majority of patients in America have health insurance. With healthcare insurance paying the bills, I have never been accused of cheating by the patients. Of course, we are not free to order things without oversight and there is lot of burn-out among physicians due to paperwork and time it takes to get approval from insurance companies. Universal insurance of the population with proper but not overburdening oversight would ensure cost-effective use of diagnostic and therapeutic tools in a physician's armamentarium.

To prevent excessive paperwork, doctors should be allowed to order tests as necessary without questions, some tests should be automatically approved for a given condition based on best scientific evidence and cost effectiveness. Also, physicians can be randomly asked to submit justification for some of the tests they have ordered. Possibly like tax audits. Punishment could be reprimanding them for minor errors and monetary fines for repeated deliberate offences. This would avoid unnecessary burden on physicians like in America and cut down the bureaucracy and possibly corruption.

Bread for All But Please Bring Your Own Butter

We must be cognizant of the fact that resources have limits. In America, people without insurance can not afford to have a simplest of doctor visit and their health deteriorates significantly due to lack of cheap and effective medications. Ultimately, taxpayer foots the bill when these productive members of society become disabled from their conditions and end up on social welfare. Now their healthcare cost is borne by government, same government that could have fixed the problem much cheaper, if acted sooner.

On the other hand, countless people with insurance including government insurance get ridiculously expensive medications and procedures with minimal cost, many of them are not even lifesaving.

If resources were to be limitless, everyone should get the best care regardless of cost but that is not the case. Therefore, Government should provide insurance of primary care services and set of medications and procedures that proves to be most cost-effective for population health. For more expensive medications and procedures, people must be encouraged to self-pay or have secondary insurance of their own. When countless children die from malnutrition, why should government provide for heart bypass surgery to few?

'Ayushman Bharat Pradhan Mantri Jan Arogya Yojana' is a particularly good start in this regard. I hope it continues to improve with time and allocates resources to get the maximum benefit for the greatest number of people. It is truly fortunate for India that it also has a very robust privately run health care system which can supplement need for more expensive and specialised care, if needed.

A Stitch in Time Saves Nine

Politically, it is a hard sell to tell people that without money, they cannot get highly specialised and expensive care which could have prolonged their life. Only possible way to tackle that is to decrease the demand for such services. Emphasis should be on prevention and not treatment. In America, doctors treat diseases not patients and that is the reason for Health care spending making up 17 percent of the GDP. Spending money on nutrition, vaccination, education, sanitation and annual free check-ups would avert major health care problems later. Preventive and social medicine spending should increase as also money spent on building playgrounds and parks. Screening for communicable and chronic diseases like Diabetes and high blood pressure should be free and so should vaccination. In 1980, we used to have a period during school for Yoga classes and it was mandatory for us to attend such classes. I hope that tradition has been carried forward.

Conflict of Interest

I believe other major reason for violence and mistrust against physician in India is conflict of interest. In USA, it is illegal for physician to make money by ordering tests or imaging. In fact, doing labs in-house requires special licensing and only few of the tests can be done in-house.

Similarly, opening and running a pharmacy requires licensing and regulations. We should encourage such policies in India.

Over my time practicing in USA, laws have been passed to regulate the interactions between pharmaceutical companies and medical professionals. For example, all meals and reimbursements to physicians are now reported online and general public can access that information. Gifts to physicians are no longer allowed. Similarly, common sense measures can also be introduced in India. It is difficult for Government to watch each physician but making pharmaceutical companies and device makers publish this information online, is a highly practical solution to the problem.

At the same time, government must recognise that becoming a doctor and practicing medicine is one of the most challenging endeavour. It takes many years of intense hard work and sacrifices to become a doctor. They should be rewarded well for their services so that their families are taken care of and they would be less tempted to look for additional revenue sources. It is heartening to see salary increases for physicians in government services over the years and this tradition should continue. It may be good idea to reward physicians monetarily for extra and better work. At present, everyone gets paid the same regardless of work they do, based on my understanding. However, criterion selected for such extra compensation should be very objective. Patient satisfaction surveys should not be a sole criterion. It encourages physicians to please the patient instead of providing their best opinion. It eventually leads to medical services becoming hospitality services. America has erred in this regard and I believe opioid epidemic has a lot to do with doctors unwilling to hurt their reputation by denying pain medications to demanding patients. These surveys also have a bias as most motivated patients participating in these are the ones that are not happy. No one criterion would be perfect, maybe number of criteria after thorough discussions among medical professionals.

Maybe we can even incentivise doctors in rural areas by paying them extra.

Computerised Records

I think government-run clinics should be paperless. Computerised records have been introduced during my time practicing medicine in USA. I see the benefits in terms of efficiency and waste reduction. It is not uncommon for physician to find that test or imaging they are about to order, has already been done at another healthcare facility. This leads to better care and savings. Ultimately, private clinics should also be incentivised to use electronic health records. One mistake US Government made was to allow thousands of vendors to provide various platforms for Electronic Health Records (EHR). Unfortunately, these proprietary programs do not talk to each other. That defeats the purpose of efficiency and waste reduction. I wish that India should allow only few vendors to provide electronic health record programs and it should be easy to link them for better integration of information.

All the records even in doctor's offices should be computerised, and physicians should maintain records in secure and confidential manner. The system of patient bringing their own medical records at each visit seems antiquated.

Advanced Health Care Practitioners

America has far greater number of physicians per unit of population, despite that physician shortages are expected to grow with ageing population.

India, despite younger demographics also face challenge. Unfortunately, this void is filled by quacks and people who have no medical education.

We must recognise that physicians are not the solution for every problem. It takes much more time and resources to train a physician. We should be able be create a workforce of professionals with less time-consuming and rigorous education for most primary care services. On the lines of trained dai program, we can provide additional training to nurses and pharmacists so that they can diagnose and treat common minor ailments.

Similarly, not every doctor needs the services of fully trained nurse. Young people can be offered shortened nursing training after high school, to assist doctors in their day-to-day practice. Such courses in US lead to degree of medical assistant or Licensed practical nurse.

It is a rampant and dangerous practice in India for people to self-diagnose and treat medical conditions. Such practitioners can save the public from going to quacks or buying prescription medications over the counter from pharmacies. Once general public has access to reasonably cheap and proper care, pharmacists who provide medications without proper prescriptions, should be heavily fined.

On the same token, ambulance services should improve. Paramedics on board should have advance training. I am sure law provides ambulances right of the way but it does not get followed frequently. Ambulances should be accorded same privileges as VIP vehicles.

Protocol and Best Practices

For advance health care practitioners to integrate and unburden physician, some care could be protocol based. For example, care for heart attacks, stroke, pneumonia treatment during hospitalisation can be largely protocol driven. However, protocol should be designed, based on best scientific evidence and should be revised periodically. These protocols may serve as guidelines only and physicians should be allowed some leeway.

Physician practice model: Most medical practices in USA are group practices where a group of physicians join hands and provide care to patients. In these settings, physicians take calls by turn to cater to the after-office hours needs of the patients. In India, physicians like to practice solo mostly. This may lead to substandard care as doctors need time off work to rejuvenate, spend time with families and travel. Time when they are not responsible for patient care. May be government can encourage group practices by giving them tax benefits. For practices to serve patients on government schemes, they may be made to provide 24/7 care.

Medical Malpractice

Malpractice drives cost of healthcare as physicians fear getting sued and practice defensive medicine. India on the other hand used to have no accountability whatsoever. I think a middle path would be best. One reason for so many lawsuits in America is that most states have no cap on monetary compensation for malpractice. Also, Attorney keeps the exceptionally large chunk of malpractice awards. There should be maximum percent of money that can be charged by attorneys and law firms out of any award for winning a case; this should avoid frivolous lawsuits. Additionally, there should be a cap on monetary compensation. Otherwise India is going to face the same challenges and no amount of money would be enough to pay for defensive medicine. I remember a study from Harvard that showed that care provided at Safdarjung hospital at New Delhi was fraction of the cost of similar treatment in USA. During my residency days at this hospital, I recall that we treated patients and not their attorney. Such joy of practicing without fear is missing in United states.

Alternative Medicines

I am not much knowledgeable in the field of Ayurveda or Homoeopathy but I believe we should conduct rigorous scientific studies. Also, these practitioners should be held to same standards as rest of their peers in medical profession. I think we have a huge potential to market proven alternative medicine treatments to rest of the world. It may not be a bad idea to provide medical students in allopathic medicine some introduction to alternative medicine and vice versa.

□

A Internal Medicine Specialist in Kings Mountain, NC, USA and has over 24 years of experience in the medical field. He graduated from Maulana Azad Medical College-Delhi in 1996. He is affiliated with medical facilities, such as Atrium Health Cleveland and Atrium Health Kings Mountain.

Love for India: The NRI Perspective

—CA Avinash Nichkawade

Being an Australian Citizen since 1991, my first experience of being an '*outcast*' was graphically brought to reality during cricket matches between India & Australia.

If Australia won, even though I was a major sponsor at SCG with Cricket NSW, my Aussie friends would gleefully say, 'We thrashed you'. Similarly, whenever I wanted to celebrate India's win, my joy was diminished by my Indian friends for being an Australian, saying 'We beat YOU, arrogant Aussies'.

As a school boy in Nagpur, I played national level sports; and I was good.

I however did reel under the self-imposed discomfort of being 'ordinary-hailing from a middle-class family with a doctor mother and an engineer father.' I, therefore, chose to pursue the career of Chartered Accountancy in Mumbai, to simultaneously do my graduation and CA, whilst living in a hostel accommodation.

Attending college in morning, working full-time as part of CA articleship, travelling every day in Mumbai local trains during peak hours from Bandra to Church gate was a thrill, and it prepared me mentally & physically for all the challenges of life to come. The selfless friendship that I experienced whilst doing CA from my room-mate (now a Canadian Citizen), who showed me no mercy when he forced me to study hard for my CA Intermediate exams against my wishes, was endearing in retrospect. I cherish today, with gratitude, his use of very 'flowery' language and his verbal abuse to show his concern for my future. Yes, I did pass my CA intermediate exams in my first attempt whilst studying in 2nd year B.Com.

These life experiences are treasures for those who, like me, have spent their formative years in India and have chosen to adopt a new motherland for their career and business.

It was not easy to adapt to western culture and values when I moved to Australia in 1989. In the initial phase, I compared the prices of essentials in dollars to their rupee value and found them ridiculous. I can blame the extra kilos I put on in Australia to the fact that a slice of my favourite desert-Black Forest Cake was much cheaper there. In fact, it cost only as much as a cup of tea back home.

A strong desire to succeed coupled with my willingness to work hard and take risks, propelled me into starting my own Tax practice in Sydney and Melbourne in 1993, which grew to over 7000 clients including 20 public listed companies within 4 years.

Yes, I do love India from the bottom of my heart and cherish all the life experiences I had whilst living there. These have hence shaped my life and enabled me to face all the challenges that life threw at me, abroad.

In my personal view, there are two key attractions for overseas nationals to visit India:

1. Spirituality

In India, whether we realise or not, from our childhood we were brought up with spiritual values as a subconscious reality. We have been proud of our traditions wherein the kings would offer riches to the 'wandering sage' with no material possessions and would personally wash their feet.

This showed us that historically, our society respected 'spiritual achievements' over financial success. Our culture prides itself on no limit to sacrifice in exchange for selfless love; where spiritual enlightenment is still regarded as the highest goal to achieve in life.

Over the years, I have witnessed personal & family values change with the western influence on Indian society; largely owing to the media, films and the worldwide web for the exchange of knowledge and information in real time.

It saddens me to see how materialism is slowly decaying Indian society at an individual and collective level. Personal greed for money and power resulting in compromised ethics, is affecting the society today around the whole world. Hence the revival of Indian spiritual values, harmony among religions, and pure love and respect amongst each other as family, society and country is of paramount importance for our existence as a well-rounded culture and therefore, society.

The current tragic pandemic which sadly caused so much pain, suffering, deaths and devastation is also forcing humanity to re-evaluate desires, life goals, family values and ambitions.

India after all is the *Yoga Bhumi*; A land of enlightened seers, sages, saints, gurus even in the recent modern times. India can become the guiding light, a source of knowledge and inspiration to the entire world to emit peace, joy and inner happiness.

2. Business Opportunities

India has been an ancient civilisation, the crown of the British Empire and was very advanced in terms of education, science, business and trade. Indian institutions such as IIT, IIM and others have moulded today's top CEOs of many major international corporations.

I have been living in Silicon Valley, California since 2012. I have heard time and again in the business circles, almost like an unwritten law, that for any start-up to attract capital, it is imperative to have at least one 'Indian' in their top 4 management team. Yes, we Indians have done very well overall, whilst living overseas.

Like me, all NRIs are still Indian at heart and crave some real connection with India, which would allow us to 'give back' and benefit Indian society with our new skills, knowledge, contacts and financial resources. The large population with an average Indian speaking minimum of 3 languages including English, India is a desired business destination for every international company in the world.

In the current global socio-political environment, India stands to benefit largely in terms of attracting foreign investment.

What I am stating is not a new revelation, but a well-known fact.

Yes, India can become a magnet in the true sense of the word for future business investment from across the world. Prime Minister Modi since 2014 has been remarkably successful in attracting large interest in India as a capital destination.

Personally, I have a lot of respect for the officers of Niti Aayog-India's premier think-tank. I am sure they can do an intensive analysis on whether we have achieved what we set out for as inward investment goals, what the reasons are if we have not met the targets, what has been the experience of those who responded and invested in India in the last 10 years as well as what incentives and benefits we can further offer, to attract overseas investments into India.

I am certain that ease of doing business and an attractive return on investment will encourage the patriotic NRIs to invest more in India.

Some Ideas & Thoughts on the Education Sector:

A. Indian Education can be a noticeably big attraction for overseas parents/students and can be an excessively big contributor to the Indian Economy. As of today, many top CEO roles of global companies are held by Indians, whose founding studies have been in India.

   This phenomenon has garnered true respect globally for the intellect of Indians and the education that they have received in India during their formative years. As a part of my business undertakings, I did own several International Business Colleges in Australia & New Zealand until 2007. With 200 employees, we almost listed our company on Australian Stock Exchange. I used to travel around the world to enrol students from over 35 countries for our campuses. Based on my personal experience and knowledge of the international students market, I know for a fact that the international education sector has a large revenue potential for India. Education has been the second largest export earner for Australia over the years. We all know how much the USA, UK, AUSTRALIA, CANADA and other countries have benefitted, with the net export dollars they have earned through the education sector.

B. There is an exceptionally large pool of NRIs throughout the world, who, like me want their children who are born and brought up overseas, to have some connection with our Mother India. I am not just saying this to make a point, but I have done it myself.

   All of my three children lived in a full-time residential boarding school in Dharamshala from the age of 5. I was married to an Australian and yes, all the family members thought we were cruel to put them in a boarding school at the age of 5. I truly wanted them to imbibe our Indian culture and respect their roots. My daughter studied in India for 6 years, my older son for 4 and the youngest for 2 years in India. There were many children from around the world, who benefitted from the beautiful setting of the Himalayas, knowledge of meditation, Indian Classical Music & Dance and the Indian welcoming culture.

Today, the three are much older but the cultural exchanges in India, the travel–the overall experience of it all, makes them stronger and more importantly more empathetic as human beings. I couldn't be any prouder.

I, therefore, humbly request the relevant professionals in India to consider my ideas as a proposition, which if done well, can potentially bring in long-term financial prosperity to the Indian Economy. I, for one, would love to contribute.

C. When I looked into the reasons why overseas students coming to the USA were prepared to take financial loans & dive into the unknown, I found that the main reasons were the hope, prospect and desire for better future in terms of financial rewards, career prospects and the possibility of permanent residency or a green card. I feel there can be some serious thought put into 'How to make India an Attractive destination for overseas students'. In my view, overseas students should have a pathway or opportunity with 'visa enabling' and corporate support, to be able to gain valuable work experience and future job opportunities in India. This will need huge willingness from the government policy point of view and the private sector, to treat this with an open mind along with a broader vision of the future.

Good education and the positive work experience of foreign students will foster friendships, bonding and relationships which will result in future trade exchanges, business ventures and other exchanges. While they bring in immediate financial reward and benefit to the economy, there needs to be a huge change in the overall mindset from the private sector as well as government policy makers which will enhance their security, well-being and protect them. We will need to treat overseas students as guests of our country.

D. Having travelled across India over the years, I have noticed that there are many students from African Countries, who come to study in India. Speaking to some of them, I noticed that there is a definite cultural divide and this gap needs to be bridged.

I have also noticed that Indian businesses are either established or trying to establish themselves in African countries in a big way. So in my view, a concerted education campaign to facilitate better communication, understanding, education for the educators, education for the service teams taking care of overseas students and finally, to bring in some regulatory changes to bring in the desired changes can bring in huge benefits to the Indian economy.

There is a definite interest for overseas nationals to travel to India, embrace the culture and they look up to India as a place of learning.

We need to raise the bar on our delivery standards, our residential boarding facilities, quality of food and the resources available to international students to attract them. In return, the fees can be a lot higher as well, thus resulting in improved revenue and a better image of the institutions.

The Pandemic and the New World Order:

a. When I boarded my flight on 8 March, 2020 from New Delhi to New York, little did I know that the India I experienced on this trip is going to be vastly different to the one I visit the next time. No global event in the past has ever had such a powerful effect on the individual, social, state or national level in terms of family life, life goals, economic impact and business directions. As a current resident of USA, I can see the direct impact of complete shutdown, fear in the minds of the people, wrath of nature in the form of fires and the hurricane, compounded with the heat of the upcoming presidential elections. It is as if god is hitting reset in terms of our perspective to life itself and appreciation towards our loved ones.

b. In my view, India as a country and the Indian economy in general is well positioned in the new changing world order. India stands to gain vastly with the relationship between USA & China in terms of trade and manufacturing. Personally, I used to have full-time staff in Beijing and Shanghai. It was enjoyable to travel extensively in China from 2003-2007 and to have a first-hand understanding of China then. Now, it is up to the private sector to stand up and be counted as the trusted manufacturing partner of USA and the world. We have the knowledge, competence, ability and resources to make it happen.

c. As an International Business consultant helping Indian Businesses to expand overseas (USA & Australia) and having particularly good knowledge of the Indian business community, I am fully aware of the current challenges faced by them. The biggest challenge being the liquidity crunch due to the lockdown and non-moving investments in the real estate sector. The Indian government led by the dynamic Prime Minister Mr. Narendra Modi, has taken a positive and active role through its policies to support Indian Businesses during these difficult times. And I am sure, that the resilience of Indians during these uncertain circumstances will prevail and India will reach its true potential glory soon.

Self-reliant India

Globalisation has been the buzz word (until recent times), which provided companies with the wind beneath their wings to fly to various continents and benefit from the advances in technology. As a result, cultural barriers came down and the world became global village in terms of business travel, communications, trade and vacations.

Since 2016, USA government policies have changed their direction, with the aim of reducing the fiscal deficits and have introduced more protectionism for its national economy.

With the unprecedented damage to the world economy with the Corona global epidemic, every nation is aiming largely to look at its national economic interests and self-reliance has become priority over globalisation, as things stand today.

India is faced with a very tough road ahead in the short to medium-term outlook, but I am optimistic about its overall success in being completely self-reliant and prosperous.

I want to take this opportunity to congratulate Mr. Sunil Vashisht, FCA for coming up with this patriotic book 'Self-Reliant India'.

To end, I would like to remind us all of an important aspect of our Indian culture. Vasudhaiva Kutumbakam or 'world is a family' verse of the Maha Upanishad. It is engraved in the entrance hall of the Parliament of India and for good reason. We need to truly believe this. Treat everyone you cross paths with from all over the world with humility and respect, like you would your family, and you will see yourselves reaping the benefits both personally and professionally.

□

A Chartered Accountant, Entreprenuer & International business consultant, currently based in Dallas, Texas, USA. He is an Australian and USA citizen as well as Indian OCI.

Self-reliance in Defence through Indigenisation

—R.C. Bajpayee

Self-reliance particularly in the field of defence is an inescapable necessity in protecting the sovereignty and independence of any nation. After independence in 1947, India met her defence requirement by import, mainly from Russia to augment the resources left over by British raj. India had inherited few defence Public sector units like Ordnance Equipment Board (OEB), Garden Reach Shipbuilders & Engineers (GSRE) Ltd, Mazgaon Dock Shipbuilding (MDL) and Hindustan Aircraft Ltd. A need was felt to manufacture and produce as well as maintain more types of defence equipment. Accordingly, additional PSUs were established. Bharat Electronics Limited (1954), Hindustan Aeronautics Ltd was formed in 1964 by amalgamating Hindustan Aircraft Ltd and Aeronautics India Limited to manufacture aerospace equipment, Bharat Earth Movers Ltd (1964), Bharat Heavy Electricals Ltd (1964), Bharat Dynamics Ltd (1970), Mishra Dhatu Nigam Ltd (1973).

These PSUs have done a commendable job towards building up the defence inventory of three services. Some of the items produced by these PSUs are of dual use, meaning that these are both for defence and civil applications. The basic manufacturing approach has been technology transfer mainly from countries like Russia, UK, France, USA, Israel etc. This approach did not eliminate our dependence on these countries, both for technology update and product support. Cost and time over-run has been a perennial problem. By the time the item is developed, the requirement changes, because the equipment so developed should be at least equal, if not superior to the adversary's equipment.

As mentioned earlier, we have a good mix of defence industries, then how is it that we are still importing about 70% of our defence equipment. How can we reduce this dependence on foreign vendors? How and to what extent we could be self-reliant? Is it because of poor R&D, or lack of technical manpower like Scientists and Engineers or is it lack of funds or the leadership? We will now examine, how we can reduce the dependence on foreign countries and become self-reliant.

Policy

Government policy regarding indigenisation has evolved over the period. Department of defence production was assigned the task of indigenisation because the items required for the old equipment of second world war were not available from the vendors abroad. DGI for the Army and DTD&P(Air) for the Air Force were assigned the task of import substitution. Initially, small components like resistor, capacitor etc. were taken up for indigenisation. This was followed by modules and then to major equipment. Despite our best efforts, big industries were not coming forward to undertake the task due to (a) large capital investment (b) uneconomical, because of small volumes of order and (c) stringent requirement of Quality Control. There were also government restrictions in releasing the items for indigenisation by private sector. Even the X-tal used in communication equipment was classified as secret. The technical knowhow was also not readily available. Due to time and cost over-run by PSUs, services had no option but to resort to import.

The major items like radar, communication equipment, aircraft etc. were produced under license and by transfer of technology from Russia, USA and European countries. This approach continues even today. We should have done one time import, gained the experience, and confidence and then work on the update of technology in-house and start production of the updated equipment. Simultaneously, we should have started in-house Research & Development activity which is not very satisfactory even today.

PSUs, Universities, Private sector and MSMEs need to be encouraged to invest in R&D activity. Financial assistance need to be enhanced for such activity. Lately, Government has started involving Private sector like L&T, Tata, Mahindra & Mahindra etc. This is a very welcome move. FDI in defence sector has also been greatly enhanced. Prime Minister Narendra

Modi, realising the gravity, has already launched Make-in-India and Atmanirbhar programmes. At the same time during any major acquisition from abroad, a clause has been inserted in the contract for 50% offset under which the vendor is required to invest in India 50% of the contract value. According to the recent guidelines by government, limit of FDI has been enhanced to 100% with some restrictions. This will enable us (a) to understand and assimilate the technology (b) will generate a pool of trained manpower and (c) increase the export of defence equipment.

Statement of Requirement

There is a certain amount of commonality in equipment used by 3 defences services. Pooling the requirement will help in indigenisation and production. Certain special features of the particular service can be taken care of. There is a need to start a long-term strategic planning rather than restricting to short-term goals. Well before the life cycle expiry of the equipment, work on the next generation equipment must start. Generally, while planning any procurement, we browse through foreign glossy magazines and choose the equipment incorporating the best features of all such equipment. Instead, we should plan our modernisation and updates in relation to our adversaries. Special attention, apart from the operational requirement, must be paid to (a) life cycle cost (b) product support throughout the life of the equipment (c) Ease of operation and maintenance (d) provision of updates (e) Quality Control during different environments (f) Acceptance Test procedures (g) Mean Time between failure. Association of user right from development stage till final production is must. A dedicated department is already working under MOD.

Infrastructure

While establishing a new unit, there is a need to ensure the availability of land, rail, road, air connectivity, water, electricity, communication, transportation etc. While there may be government priority for equitable development of all regions of the country, these criteria and specially other facilities like school hospital etc., should be given due weightage. Otherwise, workers prefer to stay in the bigger cities and commute for work, as happened in the case of HAL Korwa in UP.

Current procedure for any new acquisition is that the requirement is first vetted by DRDO. If the item/equipment can be developed by the defence laboratories, it is not cleared for import unless there are certain compelling reasons. A caution needs to be exercised that the DRDO units must be able to deliver the product meeting the QRs within the time-frame and cost. Special attention must also be paid to available expertise and technical manpower. There is a need to encourage PPP (Private, Public, Participation) mode for faster development of defence manufacturing sector. We should remember that there is a lot of talent in the private sector. Strict security control can be maintained by the government. MSMEs should be involved in supporting the major projects. This will also generate additional employment. We have already inspection agencies like DGQA and DGAQA under department of defence production in place, to ensure the quality control, which could be augmented by involving the user right from formulation of QR till final production. Peer review must be carried out during development of the product. For this purpose, a committee of eminent experts needs to be constituted.

Participation of Educational Institutions

Educational Institutions are a hub of knowledge. The Ph.D. scholars in these institutions are primarily involved in fundamental research. These institutions must dedicate themselves to project oriented research. Few IITs have established technology development centres. The participants are given some incentive. This practice needs to be encouraged in other institutions of higher education all over India. Wherever necessary, we should import expert scientists, Engineers and Technicians. A large number of our scientists and engineers are working in large organisations like Intel, NASA etc. in USA and in other countries, on major projects. They should be provided the necessary working environment and incentive to come back to India.

Conclusion

The Covid-19 pandemic has adversely affected our economy and manufacturing sector. USA is so angry with China that she has started pulling out her manufacturing units from China and so are other nations. Therefore, we should use this challenge as an opportunity. India is a huge market and everybody realises this. Thus, we should make all efforts including tweaking our policies, if necessary, to invite these industries to India. Our Prime Minister has already sanctioned a package of ₹ 10 lakh crore through which MSMEs can be developed, which can support the major industries which would be set up on a PPP mode. Government may consider providing more financial support to educational institutions for undertaking project oriented research. Industries should be encouraged to invest in R&D activity. Self Reliance through indigenisation is a must for national security.

□

Commissioned in the Air Force in the year 1960. After more than 36 years of distinguished service, he superannuated in 1996 in the rank of Air Marshal as Air Officer Commanding-in-Chief of maintenance command. While in service, he obtained M.Tech in Radar Technology and Ph.D. in Electronic Warfare, both from IIT Delhi. He is also a graduate of National Defence College, New Delhi and has passed Advanced Diploma in Russian language. He has been trained in USA and Italy on Electronic Warfare.

Understanding the Spirit of PM Modi's Swadeshi Challenge

—K.G. Suresh

Many years back, on the last day of one of my hectic tours, I picked up a few garments from a showroom in Oxford for the 'phoren' stuff-crazy relatives, only to realise on reaching home that they had 'Made in India' tags, which obviously I had failed to notice in my tearing hurry to catch the flight.

Since then, I had restrained myself from shopping abroad and confined it to buying some cheap street side souvenirs such as a miniature red double-decker in London or a traditional mask from Bali. Once the state-of-the-art Indira Gandhi International Airport started operations, I started procuring even the customary chocolates and other stuff from Delhi Duty Free, which offered a better bargain than many international airports and the advantage of paying in Indian currency rather than dollars.

Even that stopped, once these chocolates and other imported stuff became easily available in South Delhi shops.

Certainly, the father of the nation, Mahatma Gandhi and leaders such as Dattopant Thengdi were great inspiration in my opting for Indian products but at a very pragmatic level, I found that it was far more easier to buy back home in terms of service availability. Being prudent spenders, Indians are not the ones to junk things once they develop problems particularly electronic items. It's easier to go back to your local shop and get it repaired.

Secondly, with Liberalisation, Privatisation and Globalisation setting in the early 1990s, almost every brand worth its name was available in India and over a period of time, Indian brands offered equally good quality and international experience. That made 'Be Indian, Buy Indian' a great experience in itself.

The Prime Minister's clarion call for Swadeshi and Self-Reliance has triggered a fresh debate on the concept which had ignited our freedom movement in the first place. Seeking a place under the sun for India in the new global order, Narendra Modi did not ask for a boycott of foreign goods but strengthening Indian enterprise, enhancing manufacturing, facilitating greater employment opportunities and consequent liquidity and spending to boost the economy further.

A call for adopting Swadeshi does not mean a return to the era of Ambassadors and Premier Padminis. The call is not confined to the consumers, but also to local manufacturers, to produce world-class products which will make 'Make in India' a brand to reckon with globally. 'Make in India' is intrinsically linked to Brand Incredible India. Locally manufactured products engaging local labour and involving lesser logistical expenses also means they would be reasonably or competitively priced. Indian consumers have always looked for '*Sasta, Sundar* and *Tikau*' (Cheaper, presentable and durable) products. For him or her, the mileage is no less important than the looks of a car.

Much of the foreign products owe their success to aggressive marketing and its here that Indian MSMEs falter. The need is for creating a common branding and distribution platform for these products wherein the consumer is made aware of their quality and availability.

Indians should choose Swadeshi products and services, not to prove their patriotic credentials, but because they offer world-class quality at affordable prices. This indeed is the spirit behind the Prime Minister's Swadeshi Challenge.

(The author is a Senior Journalist and Dean, School of Modern Media, UPES, Dehradun. He was earlier Director General, Indian Institute of Mass Communication)

□

A senior journalist, columnist & Communication Specialist. He is currently serving as Vice Chancellor, Makhanlal Chaturvedi National University of Journalism and Communication, Bhopal.Earlier, he has served as Director General, Indian Institute of Mass Communication–India's premier media training institution; Senior Consulting Editor with DD News, India's public news broadcaster; Editorial Consultant with Asianet News Network; Chief Political Correspondent with Press Trust of India.

Higher Education in India: Role of Private Universities

—Hemant Goel & Suresh Garg

Introduction

Private universities have become a significant contributor to enrolment in many parts of the world including India. Any discussion on their role and relevance has always excited academic attention on both sides of the spectrum. Some feel, and rightly, that private universities present a viable solution to widen access to the burgeoning aspirations of masses particularly in developing and transition economies. But strong critics of privatisation, based on their philosophy, are skeptic of the motives of the providers/state for crass commercialisation of higher education. The first published literature on private universities appeared at the UNESCO World Conference on Higher Education in 1998 wherein the issue of private higher education was raised but all its dimensions could not be addressed. A decade in preparation for its second world higher education conference, UNESCO commissioned a comprehensive report on private higher education as one of the major discussion documents at the conference reflecting the importance of and significant growth that this sector had attained in one decade, a journey that continues at varying levels of acceleration to this day despite criticism for cost and quality.

Public and Private Higher Education in India

With about 1000+ universities and more than 41,000 colleges, 1.6 million teachers and 37.4 million students, India has the third largest higher education system in the world. (It is next only to the US and China.) Yet, as has been reported widely, graduates produced by Indian Higher

Education in majority of subject areas are not employable since they pass their examinations on the strength of rote learning. That is majority of Indian graduates study for the sake of marks rather than enjoying the subject. Moreover, they are not trained to inculcate intellectual creativity needed for problem solving, independent thinking, critical questioning and other skills suited to 21st Century. It is essentially because our HE system has largely remained examination-centric in spite of the advice to the contrary by eminent educationists, committees and commissions (GoI, 1966).

We failed to evolve innovative teaching-learning strategies that promote deep learning. Also, our teachers continue to behave as sage on the stage rather than guide by the side of the learner to navigate them successfully through their respective programmes of study. In fact, the journey of Indian higher education particularly in post-independent India has been incoherent, unplanned and unorganised; it catered largely to public pressure to enhance access to affordable higher education. (This, in spite of the fact that our ancient universities like Nalanda and Takshsila promoted tradition of advanced learning.) Due to over-emphasis on access, by and large our HEIs continue to miss drive for quality, excellence and innovations-led entrepreneurship. Also, our learners are not being trained to enthusiastically go beyond the known and familiar. As a result, we have collectively failed to contribute to the knowledge pool through path breaking ideas/theories/discoveries for international acclaim. For such reasons, our higher education system has been criticised, even ridiculed, by the stakeholders including employer groups. Yet, hermetically conserved forces have surprisingly helped it not only to survive but also to grow, based on the fictitious argument that it has served the purpose it was designed for.

Guided by the success of private secondary school education in India, the private sector was invited to invest in higher education and establish universities to impart quality education, as in US and put the country in the front row of educationally advanced countries. It is now commonly understood that the term private university refers to universities established through a State/Central Act by a sponsoring body, such as a society or a public Trust or a Company registered under Section 25 of the Companies Act, 1956. Though private universities in India are not operated by the Central or State governments, those located in educationally disadvantaged regions do receive tax breaks and flexibility for enrolment and tuition charges. Also, an indirect support may come by way of the provision of making public money via student loans and grants. Moreover, the state also has a stake in helping private provision for expanding access and alternative opportunities to those who may not or do not want to enrol in public universities. In addition, if the land is state property, substantial subsidy in land acquisition is made available as in states like Jharkhand and the NE Region.

But most private universities essentially depend on their fee revenue and contributions in the form of endowments for their major source of funding. (This is in direct contrast to public universities, which are supported by government agencies from the very outset for infrastructure as well as development.) The private universities in India were initially set up by educational philanthropists as 'not for profit' bodies though the situation has now undergone a change of 180 degree. Several universities have been created by non-literate owners who grease the palms of politico-bureaucratic nexus for recognition and other such benefits. This obviously is undesirable and must be stopped by creating awareness against it if quality and innovations are to survive.

Strictly speaking, the basic distinctions between public and private universities--funding and state control--are getting increasingly blurred in the evolving dynamic higher education scenario. In most parts of the world, and India is no exception, state funding for public universities is being sharply cut down and everyone is being advised to become self-sustaining by rationalising fee structures. This is notwithstanding the quest of being entrepreneurial; public universities are being forced to engage in as many revenue generating endeavours as possible to create surplus over their expenditure. (This, however, is not applicable to universities dominated by progressive intellectuals and their disciples in India. They continue to believe in the concept of social welfare state and wish to enjoy highly subsidised education lifelong at the expense of poor and honest tax payers.) In a parallel development emanating from self-sufficiency considerations, public universities are attempting to move towards increasing freedom from state control. Even the GOI is promoting autonomous status (but it is surprising that for some vague reasons, teacher associations oppose the concept). It is pertinent to mention that by enhancing their institutional funding options outside the state funding, public universities can ask for lesser controls. But there is a lurking fear that our bureaucracy will not be favourably inclined to loosen its control.

Having closely seen the system from both sides, we are of the considered view that private universities may be allowed to charge higher fee from the students to (i) meet expenses incurred on various academic and administrative tasks, including payment of salaries and (ii) raise reasonable financial reservoir to meet challenges of expansion and maintenance of infrastructure necessary to undertake research and offer quality education. However, clear guidelines should be put in place to observe financial and administrative prudence. Moreover, national statutory agencies such as UGC and Central/State Governments as also sector agencies like AICTE, BCI, NCTE, PCI, NCI, DCI, etc. should provide academic support as well as recognition to private universities at par with public universities in the offer of futuristic innovative programmes or research. This is also true for harnessing the available expertise and ensuring participation of private sector universities as equal partners in developing capacity in academic initiatives such as development of MOOC courses for SWAYAM portal. (As of now, UGC allows all students to earn up to 20% credits based on SWAYAM courses in a programme.) It is unfortunate that Govt. policy debars more than three hundred private universities to contribute to MOOC courses because of the fear that due to lack of philanthropic values, majority of private providers may view this as 'for profit' opportunity with little concern for quality. Though UGC and MHRD have made sporadic efforts to check undesirable practices of private providers by putting such institutions on check, any substantial tangible outcome is awaited. (It is no secret that such universities have somehow managed to survive. It is well known that most private universities have not been able to implement the Seventh Pay Commission recommendations issued in 2018 due to lack of state support.)

Developments in Higher Education in Post-independent India

Broadly speaking, the growth of higher education in post-independent India took place in three distinct phases: The *Reconstruction and reintegration phase* from 1947-66, *Expansion and consolidation phase* from 1967-90 *and Post-liberalisation phase* from 1990 onwards. The reconstruction phase was guided by the recommendations of Radhakrishnan Commission (GOI, 1949). New institutions were established and existing institutions were supported/ strengthened to improve higher education and promote research. The Kothari Commission (GOI, 1966) provided framework for the expansion and consolidation through integrated changes in the pattern of education from school stage to university level. In a way, these phases had imprint of Gandhian thoughts and philosophy. In spite of very original thoughts and categorical directions, intended targets could not be achieved due to lack of will on the part of the ruling political leadership to implement many new suggestions. The policies in the post-liberalisation phase were guided by POA-1992 based on the New Policy of Education-1986, which reiterated the need to enforce '*the national and integrative character of education to maintain quality and standards* (GOI, 1986, 92).' To keep pace with emerging realities fuelled in part by the surge in the number of aspirants for higher education due to success of the universal primary education programme and inadequacy of public institutions to cater to the growing numbers, inherent barriers and limitations as also guard against the lurking fear of digital divide between haves and have-nots, the National Education Policy approved by the Central Government on 29th July, 2020 (GOI, 2020) has put reasonable emphasis on technology-led innovations, entrepreneurship and inclusion, in addition to several path breaking recommendations. For instance, use of artificial intelligence in education for democratisation of education is a well thought out suggestion though the committee has left details for domain experts to suggest a way forward.

Private Higher Education: Indian Scenario

Introduction of economic liberalisation in early 1990s accelerated the growth of private higher education, as central and state governments showed signs of withdrawal. In fact, the expansion of higher education largely took place through affiliated private colleges and universities. In 2000-01, there were 5507 private aided and 3223 private unaided institutions that enrolled 3134k and 1822k students, respectively (Agarwal, 2013 quoted in Ahmed and Garg, 2015); the private initiative now dominates enrolments over public institutions (3443k) as a viable option. This ratio further tilted in favour of private enterprise following the recommendations of Ambani-Birla Report (2001) which elucidated the shift very clearly in favour of the private sector. It advised the government to 'leave higher and professional education to the private sector', 'support disciplines that have no market orientation', 'progressively reduce funding for universities and make them adopt the route of self-sufficiency', 'promote credit market for private financing of higher education', 'enact a Private University Bill to encourage establishment of new private universities in science and technology and management', 'allow FDI in education' and 'encourage market-oriented education through private investment'.

Acceptance of these recommendations, the growing capacity of parents to pay for education, short supply of government institutions and rising demand for higher education for social empowerment combined to lead the growth of private higher education in the first decade of 21th Century. In fact, during this period, very few universities and colleges were set up by the state and fewer still were brought within the domain of government funding. Yet, due to cumulative (public and private) efforts, we now have 1000+ universities and 41,000 colleges in a vast spectrum of locations ranging from cosmopolitan cities to far-flung towns in remote areas. It may, however, be mentioned here that private universities cater to almost 80% professional education in the country. In fact, the contribution of private sector has started to grow even in liberal education now. Though India is yet to reach the world average in Gross Enrolment Ratio (GER), she aims to increase it to 50 percent by 2030. However, this is very challenging and cannot be achieved without ensuring use of technology. Moreover the UGC and other regulators will have to shed their biases towards private universities for some valid and some not so valid reasons. Instead of putting unnecessary hurdles in the offer of educational provisions, particularly in blended education mode, offer of open and distance learning and online education (which was introduced abruptly in the Covid-19 time), it would be desirable to advise them on adhering to quality benchmarks without relaxing basic conditions on qualifications and number of faculty positions as also infrastructure including ICTs. (When HEIs in the country switched over to online education overnight, the teacher shifted from blackboard to computer screen. But strictly speaking, they did not practice online education.) Ideally speaking, these requirements should be applicable to both, public and private universities. It is pertinent to mention here that growth of private sector is not unique to India; private universities have contributed significantly to enrolment all over the world.

In this context, it is pertinent to mention here that the New Education Policy approved by the GOI recently (GOI, 2020) lays great emphasis on use of technology for universalisation of quality HE. The policy places a lot of confidence in the creativity of tech-savvy teachers and student entrepreneurs to integrate technological developments with education in multiple ways. In paragraph 23.2, the committee visualises that new technologies involving artificial intelligence, machine learning, block chains, smart boards, handheld computing devices, adaptive computer testing for student development and other forms of educational software and hardware will bring about drastic changes in what and how students learn in the classroom and beyond. It also acknowledges in paragraph 23.8 that the NEP is being formulated when disruptive innovation of Artificial Intelligence has emerged with huge capabilities and applications in education at all levels. The Committee recognised the importance of AI as a valuable aid to the education system and hoped that soon, our HEIs would be poised to quickly respond to new challenges and developments. The most important point that NEP emphasises is that to take higher education to the unreached, HEIs should use technology around Artificial Intelligence (AI). But as we know from experience, there are several constraints in implementing even conventional technology supported education in the country (NKC, 2009) and without AI, it may not be possible to democratise higher education.

Higher education needs to be adaptive and evolve continuously. It will be impacted by AI in many ways and one of the major areas is curricula. The strength of AI is its speed, accuracy, and consistency. Artificial Intelligence is making a radical impact on the education system. With the introduction of AI in HEIs, machines will soon handle repetitive tasks such as paper setting and grading, thereby freeing teacher time for more meaningful academic work. Some of the potential benefits of AI through technology in education include personalised learning; free teacher's time through automation of grading for professional development and lecture preparation; identify instructional gaps in course content based on learner's performance; improve efficiency through customised learning interfaces and digital learning guides; help hearing impaired through real-time subtitles and translation; and tutoring. AI-powered platforms can read students' handwriting and auto-grade schoolwork; remove geographical national boundaries and forge cultural synergies by catering to the unreached.

In short, technology in collaboration with teachers would help create a system where students could learn faster and more efficiently. However, there will be paradigm shift in the role of teachers and delivery of education; teachers will be facilitators and help learners to successfully navigate through a programme, while AI lights the way. However, it is important to realise that teachers would continue to be an important ingredient in the teaching-learning process. Moreover, teachers would be required to unlearn existing and relearn new skill sets. This necessitates continuous professional development as absolutely necessary component to be undertaken by public and private providers. For a country of the size, diversity and complexity of India, it would be a huge task, because taking teachers away from their respective places of work for F2F training would cause disruption; it would be prudent to make a beginning in this direction immediately.

China is the world leader in AI-centered education and US is taking steps to put AI in the classroom. European countries are also investing in AI for education in a big way. Although we in India are convinced that AI in education will change the way we learn, a lot of planning would be needed for its implementation; the committee probably thought it more appropriate to leave the details to domain experts in the face of various other challenges. There is a belief that we in India are good in planning but poor in implementation. However, dealing with AI in HE the same way could prove disastrous as the pace of change is too rapid and we may be left far behind the leaders in the field. To conclude, if the country has to achieve 50% GER by 2030, inclusion of AI and association of knowledgeable tech-savvy academic experts to work the way forward, must be given immediate attention.

Conclusion

Private universities today furnish viable solution to bridge the huge gap between the availability of institutions and the number of aspirants for higher education. That is, these are major provider of higher education, even though the quality of education and equity of access offered by them vary widely. There is also no doubt that such a provision should be regulated well so as to ensure that education offered by them meets the standards of fitness for purpose for which it was designed. Every private university would be required to invest heavily in (i) technology to supplement the efforts of GOI and implement AI in education, (ii) encourage continuous professional development of all stakeholders in general and teachers in particular.

□

Founder & Chairperson, Himalayan University. He is (Founder Member; Global Jurix, Advocates & Solicitors), B.Com, L.L.B; associate attorney has been practicing for more than a decade.

An academician and Vice Chancellor of Himalayan University.

Covid-19 and Us... A Different Reaction!!

—Ashis Mehrotra

A different way is to consider the Covid-19 pandemic as a transition rather than an event. It will help us in coping with the uncertainties.

Background

Covid-19 hit India in March 2020. The government quickly responded and took needed actions by executing a nationwide lockdown. This was the largest in the world and lasted for approximately 2 months. During this period, people got oriented to wearing masks, social distancing, quarantine and maintaining personal & neighbourhood hygiene. With focused & well-monitored efforts, it was ensured that all essential services & supplies were constantly available and maintained.

Various arms of the government along with voluntary organisations came to the forefront. The police, health care workers, administrative staff worked tirelessly, even exposing themselves to the risks. They faced not only health threats but were also sometimes ill-treated by the very people whom they were trying to serve. They started with testing of people with symptoms and followed up with contact tracing and isolation to prevent spread of the disease. They were aptly called the 'Corona Warriors'. We owe them all a sincere appreciation & Salute.

The government has lately followed an approach of phased 'unlocking' where people have started getting back to work, subject to precautions.

The government continues to closely monitor the situation. With the increased focus on testing, the number of positive cases is going up as expected, but so are recovered cases. The recovery rate in the country is 77%+ which is much better than most other countries in the world. (now crossing 90 %). India has one of the lowest fatality rates at 1.7 %, half of the 3.4 % rate globally. India also has one of the lowest per million cases in the world at 3,102. Similarly, deaths per million are 53, against 265 each in the USA & Brazil.

One single most enabler of basic activity in this difficult time has been Technology & digital connectivity. Courtesy the internet, we are able to order & receive groceries, medicines to meet our daily needs. We are also able to connect with our loved ones via video bridges and provide the necessary bonding and support. There are many companies where employees are able to work from home thus protecting their economic activity. A lot of schools have started online classes so that studies of children do not suffer.

As anticipated, this had a direct impact on the economy as it forced shutdown of businesses, reduction in demand, loss of livelihood for the vulnerable. The hospitality, aviation & tourism industries are among the worst sufferers. The government announced a fiscal stimulus of approx. 10 % of the GDP and launched many schemes like Atmanirbhar Bharat Abhiyan package etc. Most experts feel that we will bounce back stronger from this phase.

Many companies across the world are intensely engaged in vaccine and drug research & development and are satisfied with progress even as some of them go through trials. The coming months will see commercial launch. Once that happens successfully, it will give the world, the much-needed relief and bring life back to normal.

Till then, our approach, basically, should be to look at opportunities & not threats....it is all about learnings from situations of challenges. Keep the following in mind.

Prepare

Preparation can help reduce feelings of worry. Being diligent is the key.

Healthy food and sufficient physical movement are needed.

Make sure you are well connected via internet.

Keep emergency phone numbers saved & handy.

When going out, we should always wear masks and go out only when needed.

Sanitise always, once you come back.

Report to the nearest medical center in case of any symptoms.

Be Positive

This is not the first time the world is facing a pandemic. Our ancestors went through difficulties which had greater severity & impact. They had far lesser resources & advancements to help them. The world still survived and even became better.

One way to lessen worry is to merge yourself in the present moment. Do not think of solving whole life problems now. Just adhere to the guidelines.

Try to focus on what you are grateful for, not worrying like how long it will last, who will be impacted etc. It's important to revisit the beginning of the outbreak and compare with now....how much more we are confident. Just 2 months back, we had no clue of the future, yet, we are here and seeing the unlocking!!

Be Active

Action is the solution for anxiety and there's a lot that we can do in this time

Try to find ways to improve way of doing things. Perhaps we learn how to stitch at home or something else or pick up a new interest. All of these are skills that will stay with us for long-term.

Help

Lockdown and social distancing measures to prevent spread of the virus causes people to spend long dedicated time inside the confines of their homes. This may cause friction and there may be heightened cases of domestic violence etc., especially in families with a background. Be vigilant in your communities and create awareness about the measures being taken across the world to completely defeat the virus.

Take initiatives to support your society, whether by helping neighbours with household items or by simply staying safe at home.

This will generate hope and happiness resulting in greater resilience and courage to adjust to the changed world.

Remember, there is much more for us, than the Covid-19 virus, even though currently it is what may be dominating our mindspace.

Conclusion

Our Prime Minister, Shri Narendra Modi led the country from the front, addressing the nation multiple times and shared his advice, requests and updates about the pandemic situation in India and the concrete steps being taken to support the entire population of India.

He taught us what we needed the most in these tough times....Courage to come out a winner.

He exhorted us to stay safe by adhering to personal hygiene, washing hands, wearing masks and maintaining social distancing. He personally led us in offering respects to the corona warriors who were the most critical link to human safety. He stayed in constant touch with states to build consensus irrespective of which party was in power in that state.

He directed various ministries of his government to offer support to the public at large by financial packages, extension of due dates, moratorium on loan EMIs, reduction in tax rates and so on. Under his leadership, India has even extended medical and other assistance to more than 150 countries in their fight against Covid-19.

In this time of global calamity, we are a very fortunate lot of Indians to have a Prime Minister like Shri Narendra Modi. We are very confident that under his able guidance, we will overcome the current difficult times at the soonest and emerge stronger.

□

M.Com., L.LB., MBA (HR), Manager, Corporate Affairs, Rockwell Automation India Pvt. Ltd. He is a political and social activist also.

PMJAY: Atmanirbhar Bharat

—**Dr. Tarun Kumar**

Total population in India is 138 million, over 69% of population being rural and 31% urban. In view of Federal nature of the constitution, areas of operations have been divided between Union Govt. and the State Governments. Comprising of three exhaustive list viz.–Union List, State List and Government List.

Health in India is the responsibility of State Govt. under the Constitution.

A self-reliant system can be developed by all the States by following the Policies and guidelines of Centrally Sponsored Health Programmes.

The financial assistance is provided by the Union Ministry of Health & Family Welfare through successive Five Year Plans, National Health Policies, Planning Commission (now Niti Aayog).

India could develop a vibrant self-reliant Health System to cover its vast Rural and Urban population. Selective Primary Health Care has been transformed to comprehensive Primary Health Care.

Role of Primary Health Care Centres

At present 1,50,000 sub-centres, their Primary Health Centres and Urban Health Centres are being transferred to 'Health and Wellness Centres' under the umbrella of AYUSHMAN Bharat. Pradhan Mantri Jan Arogya Yojna (PMJAY), the largest Govt. funded Health Protection Scheme of the World entitles 107 million poor families an insurance cover of ₹ 5 lakh per annum per family for secondary and tertiary care hospitalisation.

Health Services in Urban Slums

Urban slums are highly susceptible to infectious diseases and respiratory problems besides worm infestation due to dense population.

Due to poverty, people in slums live in subhuman conditions which expose them to ill health and outbreaks of diseases and poor access to health facility in spite of availability of health service.

Covid-19 Exposed the Following Vulnerabilities

- Urban health centres which have been set up in slum areas should have sub centres. Each centre with IPD facility should be linked to 4-5 PHCs.
- Though under the Ayushmann Bharat, PHCs have been upgraded as 'Health and Wellness Centres', but their referred linkages are weak.
- Need for convergence of health services with other programmes and local bodies.
- Strengthening the coordination between ASHA, AWWS and ANMS is required to avoid duplication of effort, time and money.

Health Services in Rural areas

Rural health care system is well organised and ensures adequate coverage and quality of Primary health care services on normative bases. Some of the weaknesses which needs to be urgently addressed are:

- Aggressive promotion of People and Community participation.
- Urgent priority should be revival of 5.2 lakh village health sanitisation and nutrition committees, most of which are dormant. Health development plans by Gram Sabha and Panchayat Raj Institutions (PRIs) should be taken up on priority basis.
- Convergence and coordination of different departments and ministries at village level will ensure better results.
- Coordination between service providers of different levels like ASHA, AWWs, ANMS, supervisors, medical officers and development programme officers.

Roles and responsibilities of all health functionaries needs to be redefined in view of launch of package of comprehensive health care services thorough health and wellness centers.

Management of PHCs and Medical education

Medical officers at PHC level should be trained for community interaction, supervision and monitoring of the field activities and coordinating various health programmes apart from OPD clinics.

Public health care programme officers at district/ State level must be actively involved in medical education system.

Undergraduates must be trained in District and CHC the art and science of Primary Health Care system, National health priorities and programme interventions.

Weak Referral System

Linkage between household, community and health facilities needs to be developed.

Most of the illnesses can be treated at lower level of health facility; there should be two-way referred systems among PHCs, CHCs, district hospitals and medical colleges.

Treat more and refer less should be the approach.

District Level Hospital/Organisation

It is a vital organisation to support referral services and for control of health of all, besides running National health programmes and emergency services. District training centre should play vital role in reorientation and continuing education of health function areas.

District Epidemiological Units

These units need to be strengthened by appointing trained epidemiologists and public health laboratory services. These units should play proactive role and make the surveillance system lively and responsive to the needs of local community at district level.

District Hospitals

District hospitals should follow the standard treatment protocols and National guidelines for controlling outbreak-prone diseases, and act as sentinel surveillance stations for early warning outbreaks.

National-policy Level

Policy of appointment: Person from the public health care should be appointed for DGCH direct to justify his role for public health services and spearheading National Health Programmes.

Public Health Cadre: It should be developed at National, State and District levels.

Policy on research: Priority should be given to health-based operational researches and translational researches. Adequate proportion of funding should be given for EMR.

Policy on Medical/Paramedical Education

Senior Public Health Programme Officers should be officers at district and state level and should be involved in training and teaching as faculty at Medical Colleges.

Continuing education system for all cadres should be developed.

□

A Consultant, Community Medicine and Former Deputy Civil Surgeon, Haryana. He is also Former Professor and Head of Deptt. and a Musicologist & Poet.

Naya Kashmir—Towards Atmanirbhar Bharat

—CA R.L. Peer

The novel idea of our beloved PM to reform the strife-torn Kashmir Valley into a dream state as NAYA KASHMIR, stands acclaimed & celebrated by all Indian nationalists who had been raising their voices against self isolation of the state due to existence of Article 35A/370 in the Constitution of India. Just one stroke of well thought out legislation on 05th of August, 2019 paved way for total integration of the State with the Union of India. Though, by virtue of the said amendment, the state has been granted status as a union territory for the time being, we are sure that the complete merger of the State will dawn a new era of growth and development in the State like other States till its final logical conclusion of being at par with other developed and industrialised states of India.

While conveying respectful appreciation to our leader for the historical step taken, we have received some feedback from the people of the State which are being highlighted hereunder with regard to additional measures needed to be initiated, in addition to measures already implemented so that the goal of Naya Kashmir becomes a reality. These issues to our knowledge are as under:

1. That unrelenting determination to eliminate terrorism in the Valley by isolating and destroying the root causes thereof, including stoppage of all cross-border infiltration needs to be continued in future till the valley is free of such rogue elements.
2. That further strengthening of in-house intelligence to ward off any evil designs, either of the members of the previous administration or from members of any other political party or across the border, who

have suffered humiliation at the hands of public after 05th August 2019, needs to be ramped up.

3. That commendable steps by the administration, though initiated lately, to safeguard the properties of migrants including place of worship have not been acclaimed by a sizable portion of majority community in the State. The process of claims and counter-claims with regard to migrant property are seriously fraught with prolonged legal battles in Shrinagar Courts which the migrants cannot afford to follow up for a longer period. As such, the formation of designated courts only to decide such cases within a fixed time period need to be established at Shrinagar and at all District levels, to mitigate the sufferings of the migrants.
4. That the matter of settlement of migrants in clusters, as proposed by the Government, is again perceived to be disadvantageous to the migrant community in the long run since such clusters once established, will always remain an eyesore for the majority community and thus the risk of being subjected to prejudice and discrimination may eventually lead to another migration in foreseeable future of such cluster residents.
5. That in lieu of development of clusters, migrants suggest that such clusters be developed as SMART MINI CITIES, wherein not only the Kashmiri migrants but all other communities like Sikhs, Hindus, Buddhists, retired army, BSF and CRPF personnel from other parts of the country are settled so that development of such clusters helps usher in a new era of community living in the State. Such multinational communities can immensely help the State in maintenance of peace and provide support to the state morally, socially and geographically.
6. That as alternative to above, a separate homeland be carved on southern side of Kashmir which will always remain under direct control of Central Government as a Union Territory, and, thereafter, the statehood of J&K restored back for holding elections and electing their representatives so that such administration does not interfere in the affairs of the matters of such separate homeland and the inhabitants thereof live in peace and tranquility.
7. That persecuted non-muslim communities of Pakistan, Afghanistan, Bangladesh and other specified SAARC countries are granted citizenship in India under the new provisions of CAA provided they

agree to settle down permanently in the Kashmir Valley and for that matter submit a declaration to remain permanently stationed there at least for a decade. The government can seek their livelihood by bestowing them responsibility as eyes and ears of the Government, to safeguard its territorial integrity, since such communities being subjected to successive humiliation by Muslims in their home countries for more than seven decades, definitely continue to carry resentment in their hearts and thus, they are bound to prove true nationalists desperately needed in the State.

8. That to identify throughout India, staunch followers of organisations like RSS, Bajrang Dal and other affiliates, to volunteer and migrate to settle down in the Valley. Such persons need to be made in-charge of safeguarding all Hindu monuments, temples and other places of worship which have been abandoned in the State for the last more than thirty years. They can be provided free education and some assistance & accommodation at the outset as an incentive to have a respected living. Settlement of these people will help in increase in the membership of other communities throughout the State to ensure a healthy mixture of all religions and communities.
9. That to rope in some big Industrial houses in India by allotting them all waste/barren lands for setting up of industries and growing agriculture produce on modern lines which will have an employment ratio of 50% for Muslims and 50% for other communities to usher in a new era of economic development in the State, which besides providing employment opportunities to educated youth, becomes an attractive destination to people from other States to provide expertise in these fields and besides, some of them deciding to settle down in the valley can help generate a new wave of inter-dependence of people from the state and people in India.
10. That the power shortage in the state needs immediate attention and for achieving desired results, efforts are required to completely privatise the power supply in the State of J&K, to ward off rampant power thefts and simultaneously making availability of power 24 × 7 to the state which is essential for development of industry and economic growth on the pattern as is provided in other developed States of India.
11. That the augmentation of railway line from Udhampur to Banihal is under progress but the pace of the development needs to be

accelerated so that with the development of the rail link between Delhi and Shrinagar, the people of the state are bound to come closer to other states by land, rail and air.

12. That repair and renovation of Sharda Temple located in POK needs to be expedited, being birth place of Sharda language, which has been the basic foundation of SHARDA SCRIPT since ancient times. The development of Sharda language will ensure revival of tenets of Hinduism to the world at large which has realised the true teachings of Hinduism in words, deeds and thoughts which no other religion of the world has been able to match uptill now.

Kashmiri migrants are already indebted to the Government of India for the help, assistance and guidance received from time to time since 1990 till now including establishment of migrant camps, providing of cash assistance, admission in schools, colleges and professional courses which have ushered growth of new generation of intellectuals in the country. However, all said and done, every person from Kashmir is searching for his roots which can only be traced to Kashmir and i.e. why the development of Kashmir is essential to very existence of their soul and well-designated crown of India.

□

A practising CA (originally from Kashmir) for the last more than thirty five years. He operates under the same PEER AND CO., having office at Srinagar and Delhi.

Atmanirbhar Bharat: A Simple Road Map

—Anirudha Ray

In my first visit to my friend's newly constructed house, he told in peak summer, rooms are uncomfortably hot in spite of having proper air conditioning. Having a quick look, I noticed big parts of the house are directly exposed to blazing sun from the west side. My friend had few choices like putting more powerful AC systems and imported movable curtain systems covering the buildings; all are having both substantial initial cost and maintenance cost over their lifetime. I suggested him to put a few leafy mango trees along the boundaries, which not only will give shadows but also having joy of home-grown mangoes other than improving the scenic beauty of the house at minimum cost without being dependent on outside agencies to run the system properly. But the trees require regular nurturing and protection till they are grown up at a sustainable level.

I see the same philosophy behind Hon'ble PM Modiji's clarion call for 'Atmanirbahar Bharat (self-reliant India). After Covid-19, which is the biggest disruption in 100 years, there can't be a better time to have a focus on this as every crisis is an opportunity to improve.

Self-reliant does not mean closing the door and be protectionist. It implies much more, it first starts from the mindset, then to be successfully implemented, then our education, governance and also legal system have to be synchronised with this thought and need for a big change.

I was planning to write detailing my recommendation about my suggestions to change the Educational system to a more practical one but before I completed my draft, Modiji has already put the game-changer **New Education Policy.**

So, before other parts of my suggestions get irrelevant by new policies, let me complete this article fast.

For successfully implementing any new ideas, following steps are necessary:

1. Vision
2. Mission
3. Strategy
4. Planning
5. Tactics
6. Trial & Implementation

Modiji has already explained his vision of making India as Economic superpower with 5 trillion USD Economy. To do that, he had shown his mission for Self-Reliant India where India will not only produce goods and services for domestic consumption but also will provide these to the rest of world.

And Strategy to implementation of this noble vision and mission will be combined responsibilities of not only Bureaucracy but also of all sections of society starting from Parliament, Judicial systems, Business houses and last but not the least, the general public.

Let's start with Bureaucracy first. On the administrative side, there should be a separate body for 'Atmanirbhar Bharat' in same line or under Niti Ayog whose main aim should be to identify opportunity from self-reliance, nurturing the probable solutions, giving continuous feedback and ensuring to make the solutions sustainable. Also, it should help entrepreneurs to arrange bank finances, to make this happen. All these requires tremendous efforts, both analytical and dynamic ones, to make it fast among many prevalent obsolete systems. And all these processes, whether internal to administrative systems or with external stakeholders, to be done digitally without wasting time and money for physical presence.

Similarly, all government authorities' interaction processes with public should migrate to digital platforms. This will result in transparency, faster process, thus boosting efficiency.

Parliament needs to look at this with practical point of view and cutting across individual or party line to formulate and pass necessary laws, to expedite the progress of the nation. To give an example, most of the major bills were passed in United States in bipartisan way as both Democrat & Republican senators are unanimous as regards interest of America. Indian Parliament members have to understand that Country and its Citizens need progress and only way to stay relevant to the voters of their constituencies is to fast track the progress and not be a stumbling block. Gone are those days and now Indian voters are matured enough to reject anti-progress and road blockers.

Thirdly, our justice system needs to be fast and uniform. We have a huge backlog of cases from primary to highest courts and sometimes, multiple courts have given diametrically opposite views resulting in confusion and time wastages. To do this, the legal system needs to move on to digital platform. There can be designated secure video conferencing facilities in every district court and high courts and from there, all proceedings even with the highest court can be transacted without wasting time and money to travel. Lawyers can present their cases over video conferencing to the judge and only in rare cases, the judges should call the sides to the court. Due to Covid-19 outbreak, hearing over video has started thus making a default trial run. And now its necessary to improve the system based on those, to make it efficient and glitch-free. This will reduce huge backlog of legal cases, after all, justice delayed is justice denied.

On trade and commerce, each ministry should identify list of imported products, based on total import value and their needs to be sorted with time and efforts required to produce locally. There are many products which may not have high technology requirements but might require infrastructure or scale. Each major product imported should be classified into essential/non-essential but also on feasibility of replacements in short, medium and long time spans.

Last but most important today, is to support the self-reliant initiatives with proper financial and banking supports. After conceptualisation and prototype, any new product and service requires to be launched and this stage requires funding support in terms of banking. Our banking systems should have the push in handholding these initiatives in line with other countries where entrepreneurship is encouraged by banks and financial institutions with many innovative funding, rather than traditional banking asking for huge collaterals. To be 'Atmanirbhar Bharat', this support is essential, as we need to compete with other countries' state-funded organisations for the market.

Once these identification & analysis happens, proper action needs to be taken on each category under specific nodal agency who will in turn coordinate with respective Departments to make it fast, hassle-free and quality systems rather than on ad hoc basis.

For example, in spite of India being a leader of low-cost high volume pharmaceuticals and despite the presence of so many Indian and global pharma companies manufacturing so many drugs in the country, 17.73

billion USD worth of Active Pharmaceutical Ingredients (API) was imported from China in 2019, which in volume terms are 80% of raw materials. More surprising facts are price difference in India and China are negligible and 3 % as highest. So, why then these are imported and the cause is from macroeconomic, environmental and local regulations in India, higher trade financing cost in India in absence of specific market assistance, compared to abundant credits available to Chinese exporters at very low interest rates, which in turn makes their capacity utilisation more efficient (70%) compared to 40% of Indian plants. Sunny side is: All these issues can be rectified with proper focus and goal-oriented change & implementation by Government & Pharma industries together. This will make India undisputed leader in pharma raw materials alongside final products thus not only **Atmanirbhar** for life-saving pharmaceuticals but generating huge employment for our citizens from all walks of life: from a vehicle driver to research scholars. Its heartening to see that Government has already started working in this direction and is on path to create specialised Pharma parks in many parts of the country.

Also with the implementation of new Agricultural policy just passed in Lok Sabha, farmers have the freedom to sell their produce to anybody anywhere, thus breaking them free from the clutches of middle man through whom they were earlier forced to sell in local mandis only. At the same time, farmers have the advantage of availing Minimum Support Price (MSP) from government like an insurance. This will make our farmers 'Atmanirbhar' and they will help prosper themselves and the economy.

The biggest contribution of Modiji-led government in my opinion is the rise of self esteem for Indians, whether inside country or based in outside world, among many other positive changes. And I sincerely believe if we can implement the few basic steps outlined, not only 'Ease of doing Business' in India will have a quantum jump but we will also be 'Atmanirbhar' in a holistic way.

Few years down the line, I visited my friend's house and was over joyed seeing and hearing birds chirping on the grown-up mango trees.

□

Managing Director of ACC India Pvt. Ltd., a renowned global construction and contractors company involved in constructing of high-rise towers. He is handling various prestigious construction projects in various parts of India.

Looking East Towards Self-reliant India

—M.K. Shome
—Uday Sankar Das

Abstract—*Modern-day India is located at the heart of Asia, sandwiched between West Asia and South East Asia. However, the Islamic invasion and the post-colonial division left the western frontier practically locked out and sentimentally hostile to the very idea of India. The transportation bottleneck in reaching North East India and the geographic distance from New Delhi, meant that the east and the particularly North East was naturally neglected by the highly federal bureaucratic structure adopted from the British. The freedom of India came at the cost of retaliatory, whimsical vile intention of the British Empire that forced a cleverly devised partition of the lands re-establishing a never-ending religious hostility. This partition left millions of fellow citizens to be killed in the hands of ones that they once trusted and shared a social construct. The ones that were not killed were left to live a life of pity, landlessness, humiliation and severe precaution based on linguistic barometers back in India. Several waves of human migration were also forced into North East India pertaining to this unrecorded holocaust threatening to ruin the very fabric of the already fragile tribal society. The Ancient polity of India that once influenced Entire Asia from Mongolia to Sumatra and Bamiyan to Goryeo, was systematically reduced through persecution, neglect and narrow intellectualism, into an idea of ruins and apathy. The North East of India is geographically located in Far East Asia, and the narrow bureaucratic vision always confused it with East of India, that has little or no cultural connections with it, whatsoever. Societal construct, food habit, culture, dressing sense and historical leanings of this region are oriented from Far East Asia. This gives India a unique opportunity to open* *up this region for rest of the Far East Asia, to explore and develop strong cultural bond.*

The NER region has plentiful of natural resources, land space and a large number of functional graduates which can easily provide for the factor of production. Strategic leverage is the answer to fulfil the objectives oriented towards capturing the Far East Asian economy in symbiotic win-win situation. This paper is a commentary based on inputs from practical observation, extensive reading, verified web sources, literatures and industry reports, that were presented with focused approach, keeping the concerns and benefits of North East India.

Keywords— *Far East Asia, NER, Strategic Leverage, India*

India's Constant Tryst with Destiny

Our home India sits at the crossroads of the world's all major cultures, religions or languages that did have some influence in its long journey of antiquity. Major historical trade routes and maritime waterways connect us to the rest of the world. We were a powerhouse of knowledge during the golden age of Buddhism that balanced the underlying tragic inequalities of the society. Long before the modern west learned to replicate the structures of a republic propagated by the Romans and ideas of justice idealised by Plato, India was already in its path of becoming a republic with various city states or *'Mahajanapada'*, they being no less than sixteen in number, namely Kasi, Kura, Kosala, Panchala, Anga, Machchlia (Matsya), Magadha, Surasena, Vajji, Assaka, Malla, Avanti, Chetiya, Gandhara, Vamsa and Kamboja. There was a slow but an incessant progress towards democracy.[1] There were reputed learning centers like Taxila, Nalanda, Valabhi, Vikramashila.[2] All this glory and fame subsequently met its fate on the day when Muhammed bin Qasim attacked India for the first time in 715 ADs; rest is a history wrapped in persecution, subjugation and ruthless conversion,[3] Until 14th-15th of August 1947, when the first prime minister of the county addressed the nation at the stroke of midnight and declared India as a free nation dedicated in service of world peace[4] Ironically, the freedom for most of the Indians was attained at the cost of partition that forced millions of Indians homeless, landless and persecuted once again in both the lands. They were persecuted in the new land owing to their religious alignment and once they moved away to the old land, they were persecuted once again owing to their linguistic non-alignment. These issues forced a mass disruption within India amongst its own population and was subsequently utilised by several divisive forces to attain, retain and gain political power at the cost of silent murder of millions of fellow citizens. This reignited a new tussle and tryst with destiny to attain freedom for preserving one's own linguistic, cultural heritage, while defining a new place value at any cost in this great game of democracy.

A Peek into the History of India's Shrinking Cultural Polity

The Pre-Islamic India was heavily influenced by the dictates of Indo-Aryan or Indo-Grecian societal structures. The Vedic texts defined the hierarchy of social structure in a similar setting where the priest or high priest was placed at the top, followed by the martial races and the non-martial races at the very-very bottom. This structure was counter balanced by the revolutionary theological philosophy of Buddhism, Jainism and later, by the materialistic renascence of the Charvaka School of thoughts. This inter-mix of competitive philosophy promoted intense debate in the debacle of Indian polity and attracted scholars, travellers and writers from across the globe to learn, investigate or witness the glory of India.

This exchange of knowledge allowed Indian school of thoughts to penetrate into the polity of most of Asia. For example, Atisha *Dipankara,* a Buddhist monk, played a significant role in cementing the already established Buddhist religion in Tibet.[5] The Tibetan school of Buddhism is actually an extension of Nalanda School of Buddhist traditions.[6] Similarly, towards the far west, Buddhism also flourished in the *Bamiyan* region as accounted in the texts of historic Chinese travellers.[7] The tales of Ram, Ramanya and various interpretations portraying different heroic angles circulated in Far East Asian countries of modern day Thailand, Laos, Cambodia & Myanmar,[8] before a total conversion into Buddhism at later stages.

In this way, India was able to exert influence and include this geographic vastness in the perceived conceptual map of *'Bharatvarsh',* *(Entire India or Entire Earth)* without ever having to set out for a conquest which is contrary to the ideas propagated by imperialists about unifying the country into one single province. Another self-defeating idea of *'Akhand Bharat'* was successfully implanted during the imperial period that portrayed that India is a divided nation and it needs to be reunited, whereas the fact *'Bharatvarsh'* is a complex polity of affiliation to the beautiful idea that stands in consonance with the term of Upanishad *'vasudhaiva kutumbakam' (world is one family),* hence essentially needing no subjection or unification, rather a continuous propagation of brotherhood and unity.

The complex polity of India started shrinking with the invasions from barbaric *'Umayyad Caliphate',* that systematically enforced *'Sharia'* through enslavement, slaughter and creation of bogus principalities in the western frontiers of India. [9] Slowly, this had a ripple effect that transcended into the common masses regarding these own lands of *'Gandhara'(present-day Kabul)*as foreign territories, as the systematic subjection erased even the bleakest of linkages of these people to the heartlands of India. Moreover, whatever little the Brits could conquer and subjugate termed as a nation before intentionally hasting a whimsical division as a last nail in the empire's coffin. Again, ruthless neglect and racial disassociation from our eastern cousins left India as shrunk as a snail in a shell of its own delusion of the golden era of the past.

Looking East & Far East

Indian independence came at a time when most of the world was reduced to ruins by the Second World War. Moreover, the Brits sold out or closed most of their industrial and business ventures before moving out of the country creating a sudden industrial vacuum. The bureaucratic system left by the British was also not designed to significantly benefit Indian business owners resulting in deadlock that taxed capital gains, investment and discouraged any forms of profit-making venture which is still reflected till today. The estimated Hofstede score for India reflects this irony.

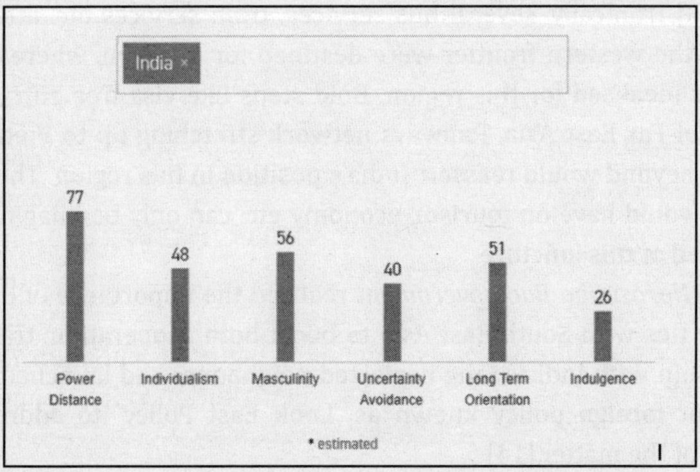

Exhibit: Hofstede Insights Scores for India[10]

India scores (77) in the Power Distance scale, which implies that the social structure is top-down and easily accepts social inequality, imposed by the powerful and the privileged. On the individualism scale, the score is (48) which is moderate in nature and signifies the 'we' aspect of Indian individual is dependent on the societal structure for decision-making process, thus lacking in authoritative decision-making. India scores poorly in Uncertainty Avoidance (56) and indulgence (26) despite having a high score in Masculinity (56), that signifies that despite being a competitive society, there is a tendency for risk avoidance and pessimism.[10]

Eastern India faced the resource curse paradox, while North East India was left to defend, manage its own fate battling nature, infrastructure bottlenecks and persistent neglect of New Delhi since day zero. The fixation over the fascination of improving an ever-deteriorating relation with our western neighbours meant that entire focus was shifted towards mending a broken relation that resulted only in betrayal and war.

Entire South East Asia except for Japan, which is an Island nation, is virtually connected by routes accessible by land. The island nations of the Malaysia, Indonesia had direct maritime connections to the eastern ports of *Kalinga*,[11] an important part of the Silk Road, also known as the Tea Horse Road criss-crossed through the North East of India to transport tea to the European nations through the Bay of Bengal.[12] In fact, even the British Empire built a road and named it *'Stilwell Road'*, that connected the North East of India starting at Ledo in to Kunming in China, that acted as a supply route for the Allied Forces in their struggle against imperial Japan.[13] Ironically, several bus services, train services etc. attempted towards the western frontier were destined for a failure, whereas none was ever idealised for this region. Bold steps like visa free entry to the citizens of Far East Asia, Railways network stretching up to Vietnam or perhaps beyond would reassert India's position in this region. The ripple effect it would have on tourism, economy etc. can only be imagined and speculated at this juncture.

The *Narasimha Rao government* realised the importance of building strategic ties with South East Asia to boost both cooperation, trade and partnership with India's long neglected neighbours and launched a very important foreign policy known as 'Look East Policy' to address the urgency of the matter.[14]

The North Eastern Council (NEC) was the first ever advisory body created to address the problems specific to North East India. Subsequently, it also realised that India needed a holistic approach to fix its problems in the North East of India, with undivided attention, in order to bridge the gap between North East India and New Delhi. To address the issues, the Department of Development of North Eastern Region was set up in 2001 which was later converted to a full-fledged ministry in 2004 and renamed as Ministry of Development of North Eastern Region or DONER Ministry.[15] North East of India is also home to several trans-boundary rivers that flow across the region. It is true that the region is landlocked but is connected by these rivers that flow freely across these nationalities and holds the answer to breaking this bottleneck and allow access to the Bay of Bengal.

Strategic Leverage to Fix issues of Land, Labour, Capital & Entrepreneur

Strategic leverage can be defined as the firm's ability to manoeuver and change the competitive position, in order to align with the terms of competition to accomplish the objectives.[16][17]

In this era of excessive competition and marginal profits, all firms, small or large, need to align their objectives, tactics and strategies as per the industry and the organisation's competitive position, in order to match the terms of market competition and hence obtain strategic leverage to fulfil its objectives. The figure below depicts how any firm can achieve strategic leverage.

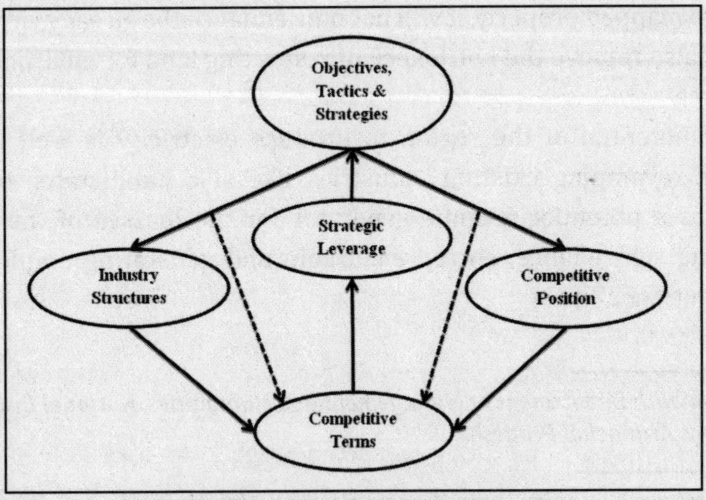

Figure: Strategic Leverage Framework adapted and Modified form [16]

The North East of India has abundant raw forest products, agricultural products, minerals and vast stretches of fertile plain lands particularly in the Brahmaputra Valley. Even if we disregard the monsoon season and the paddy cultivation tenure, much of the land sits idle during the winter months unlike parts of central and western India where agriculture is practiced throughout the year. This gap provides a renewed opportunity to Farmer Producer Organisations to initiate contract farming for Agriculture-based food product companies as there is immense potential for food processing in the region.[18]

The agricultural landscape has the potential to empower the literate but unemployed youth in alternate agricultural marketing, training and consultancy provider in collaboration with the Union or State Government in maximising crop revenues, exploiting technological advances like hydroponics, aeroponics or vertical farming, in explaining farmers' income over a planned period of time.[19]

Land mapping and land planning issues will put to rest the issues of sustainability and free up space for agricultural land without destroying natural ecological habitats for economic activity.[20] North East of India comprises of 8 states, out of which Assam and Arunachal Pradesh constitute around 62% of the total land area; hence, a renewed focus needs to go towards these two areas, followed by Meghalaya, which constitutes around 9%, followed by Manipur and Mizoram 8%, Tripura and Sikkim constitute around 4% and 3% respectively.[21] Once these states are mapped properly, it will not only enhance the already rich forest land but also remove the bottleneck of respecting land for environmental clearances.

The potential of the region to produce electricity is well known, however, revamping existing industries like silk, handicrafts, tourism can act as a potential revenue generator for the masses of the region promoting self-reliance, entrepreneurship and generating employment opportunities.[22][23]

□

A professor with Department of Management and Humanities, National Institute of Technology, Arunachal Pradesh.

A Ph.D. research scholar, with Department of Management and Humanities, National Institute of Technology, Arunachal Pradesh.

Legal System and Atmanirbhar Bharat

—Kamal Jain

Despite the introduction of a new constitution in 1947, the Indian legal system of today is old and orthodox, much reminiscent of the legal system established by the British more than a century ago. With more than 30 million pending cases across all courts, it is clear that the system of filing complaints, legal suits and adjudications is effete and has not been upgraded in accordance with the size of the population and the number of legal cases. The legal system and the pendency in legal cases has failed to keep pace with the modern times, particularly the last three decades, where information technology (IT) has evolved to become an important part of our day-to-day lives. Today's times demand the legal system to be improved with the help of information technology (IT). A good legal system is the backbone of a country, not only important for the feeling of security and peace of mind of residents but also ensures harmonious social and business environments. We need to bring more transparency in the legal system right from lodging police complaints to the announcement of the final judgement.

With the help of IT we can lodge all FIR's (first information reports) on an online system with recording facilities so that it is not manipulated later. The conversations between the police official and the people inquired in connection with the case should be recorded. These recordings should then be produced before a court and the court proceedings should also be recorded. The recordings should be made available to the public in general but restricted by inquiry officials and courts according to the need of cases. Till the judgement reaches finality, all the proceedings of the case should be recorded and litigants should be allowed to participate online so that their time is not wasted in appeals. Also, the recorded proceedings should go along with the written documents. This will not only bring transparency but also help in early disposal of cases.

Law is supreme but the delay in legal justice and the cascading effect of legal proceedings make people lose faith in the law and avoid courts and legal proceedings despite having issues that need legal attention. Throwing light on such issues, we need to encourage and empower the businesses and individuals to seek justice with the help of advanced technology in a more convenient manner. The delay because of backlog of cases in the courts of the country and the heavy costs of legal procedures discourage and disappoint the litigant before judgement. The alternate dispute resolution methods like arbitration, mediation, conciliation and mutual settlement should be encouraged, Experts from different fields should also become a part of the legal system to fasten the decisions. The filing, proceeding and disposal of legal cases should be done online with the help of IT.

If we want an *Atmanirbhar Bharat*, a self dependent India, it is imperative that we immediately upgrade our legal system according to the requirements of Modern India, which is going to be '*Atmanirbhar*' in all aspects of life.

One thing the Covid crisis has taught us is the importance of being *Atmanirbhar* or self reliant, which is not a mere slogan but the need of the hour. As India collectively aspires to achieve a truly *Atmanirbhar Bharat*, the current legal system if not updated will prove to be an obstacle in the path.

Despite the introduction of a new constitution in 1947, the Indian legal system of today is old and orthodox, much reminiscent of the legal system established by the British more than a century ago. If India has to become *Atmanirbhar* it has to firstly have a legal system more original and suited to its modern needs, not just an old rotten system borrowed from the very colonisers of India.

A huge hindrance in achieving an *Atmanirbhar Bharat* is the lack of faith in the system. The loss of faith is a result of the lack of transparency in today's legal system. We need to bring more transparency in the legal system right from lodging police complaints to the announcement of the final judgement. With the help of IT we can lodge all FIR's (first information reports) on an online system with recording facilities so that it is not manipulated later. The conversations between the police official and the people inquired in connection with the case should be recorded. These recordings should then be produced before a court and the court proceedings should also be recorded. The recordings should be made available to the public in general but restricted by inquiry officials and courts according to the need of cases. Also, the recorded proceedings should go along with the written documents. If everything is on the record people would consider the system to be less corrupt or vulnerable to manipulation and would hence, co-operate more.

With more than 30 million pending cases across all courts, it is clear that the system of filing complaints, legal suits and adjudications is effete and has not been upgraded in accordance with the size of the population and the number of legal cases. Many businesses and households avoid courts and legal proceedings despite having issues that need legal attention because of the delay in legal justice and the cascading effect of legal proceedings. A harmonious social and business environment is very important for an *Atmanirbhar Bharat* and can be partly achieved through updating the legal system, making it more efficient. We need to encourage and empower the businesses and individuals to seek justice with the help of advanced technology in a more convenient manner. Digital infrastructure should be created for the filing, proceeding and disposal of legal cases and the litigants should be allowed to participate in court online. This would not only make the legal proceedings more time-saving and convenient for the litigants but also allow the courts to function more effectively by helping easy disposal of cases. The delay because of the backlog of cases in the courts of the country and the heavy costs of legal procedures discourage and disappoint the litigant before judgement. This discouragement and disappointment can also be reduced by adopting alternative dispute resolution methods like arbitration, mediation, conciliation and mutual settlement that would reduce the burden on the country's courts. Experts from different fields should also become a part of the legal system to fasten the decisions.

Currently the Indian legal system has minimal digital infrastructure in place especially considering the poor state of the physical infrastructure. In the last three decades, technology has evolved to become an important part of the lives of many Indians which in the future would become even more significant. To become *Atmanirbhar* right now, we have to be ready for the future and as up to date with modern times as possible in all aspects. Having a good legal system is one very important aspect which not only creates a feeling of security and peace of mind of residents but also ensures harmonious social and business environments.

□

B.Com., FCA who has expertise in real estate and corporate consultancy. Presently he is the member of UP RERA Appellate Tribunal.

How the New Atmanirbhar Bharat will Affect Economy?

—Dr. Ashok Madan

Atmanirbhar Bharat

The world has witnessed one of its major downfalls, the global economy, education sector and healthcare sector have been very adversely impacted. INDIA, being the 2nd largest populated country in the world has seen its own setbacks too.

'ATMANIRBHAR Bano', the recent slogan which was given by our Hon'ble Prime Minister Narendra Modi, who has announced an economic stimulus package of ₹ 20 lakh crore and big-bang systemic reforms under the 'ATMANIRBHAR Bharat Abhiyan (self-reliant India)' to counter the ongoing Covid-19 crisis. There is an urgent need to take action and bring back the derailed economy and reforms back on track.

How the new ATMANIRBHAR Bharat will affect Economy?

Self-Reliance was the stated goal of economic policy in India in the early years after 1947. The architect of this plan was Jawaharlal Nehru, whose record as prime minister–especially economic–intellectuals associated with this government has trashed relentlessly.

The 20 lakh crore stimulus economic package is the government's way to deal with the current situation. This includes:

- These reforms are steps towards the **One Nation One Market** objective and help India to become the **FOOD FACTORY** of the world.
- These would finally help in achieving the goal of a self-sustainable rural economy.
- Also, the MGNREGA infusion of ₹ 40,000 crore may help in alleviating the distress of migrants when they return to their villages.
- Also, as the MSME sector is the second largest employment generating

sector in India, this step will help to sustain the labour-intensive industries and thereby help in leveraging India's comparative advantage.

Also, the newly launched PM e-Vidya, programmed for multi-mode access to digital online education, provides a uniform learning platform for the whole nation which shall enable schools and universities to stream courses online without further loss of teaching hours.

Together, these steps may revive the economic activity, impacted by Covid-19 pandemic and create new opportunities for growth in sectors like agriculture, micro, small and medium enterprises (MSMEs), power, coal and mining, defence and aviation etc.

Moreover, after China, India is the production hub which caters to the manufacturing demands of the global industry. Thus, self-reliance is promoted if India starts producing its own goods rather than to be dependent upon China. On the other hand, the world is blaming China for this Novel Corona Virus spread which has disturbed its relations with other countries to a bitter end. Thus, during the forthcoming period, other countries may invest in India in production and manufacturing sector. This may also result in employment and economic boom which would be highly beneficial for the country.

Why 'Make in India' is Necessary to Counter Security Concerns from Countries Like Pakistan-China-Sri Lanka-South African Countries?

China is now about to replace Kenya's best-selling Mombasa. Beijing has invested heavily in developing the Kenyan rail network, an African country, that is not in a position to pay for it. Besides this, the central depot in Nairobi is also in danger of being taken over by China.

We should remember that the modus operandi is the same as it was in Sri Lanka where Colombo had to give the Hambantota port to China for 99 years of employment due to non-payment of Chinese loans.

China has loaned $ 550 billion to Kenya to build a Ghana Railway project. It did not collect enough money and lost ten billion Kenyans in the first year itself. China will not only get the project but also the port of Mombasa to make up for that shortfall. A Kenyan auditor says that one agreement was reached with Exim Bank of China, and even settlement of this agreement can only be done in China. Essentially, all SGR receipts are still going to the escrow account according to an unequal agreement in favour of China.

The most dangerous clause in the agreement is that the Kenyan government has confirmed that there will be an unusual stay on the rail project to China. This now leads to the state of Kenya losing its important public goods. In fact, if we look closely at it, the entire Belt and Road Initiative (BRI), set up by China is actually proving to be a part of its debt deal.

Significantly, BRI has been called a major infrastructure program, which will improve roads, rail and sea routes, which will make the movement of goods between different countries easier and cheaper thus promoting international trade. China is trying to make the world more receptive to the argument that the BRI project will prove useful to developing countries in expanding bilateral trade, economic relations and communications. While explaining the benefits of the BRI, efforts are being made in public discourse to conceal its political, economic, and environmental consequences.

The success of any program depends on its finances. This is particularly applicable to infrastructure projects. At the launch of the Belt and Road Project, all the money came from the government of China, led by the Asian Infrastructure Investment Bank and other institutions from Beijing. Since investments in BRI and other related infrastructure would come from China, whether the Chinese government itself or the financial institutions under the Chinese government, many countries are caught in a debt trap for different reasons. In most cases, these funds have been at high interest rates or are for projects that don't work or both. Sri Lanka's Hambantota Gate proved to be a shocking example in this regard. In light of this, many countries have begun to opt out of China's infrastructure proposals. Similarly, another port of Djibouti, the largest US military base in Africa, is now about to be taken over by a Chinese company due to heavy debt. The opposition to BRI is increasing because of the increasing debt burden on many countries. In the last two years, not only opposition groups in BRI's partner countries, social organisations have also strongly opposed the project.

China-Pakistan Economic Corridor (CPEC) is said to be the first BRI project. Pakistan's experience should be viewed as a future direction. Four years ago, Pakistan's Prime Minister Nawaz Sharif had said that CPEC would introduce a 'game-changer' in Pakistan and South Asia. But the way Pakistan has been in debt after four years, shows that this is not the case. In addition, that growth has decreased from 5.8% in 2017-18 to 3.4% in 2018 to 3.7% now. With the worsening economic situation in Pakistan, no one in the nation calls CPEC a 'game of change'.

Due to the high cost of infrastructure projects that China is building in Pakistan, the debt burden is growing unbearable and there is pressure on repayment on Pakistan. And the benefits from these infrastructure projects are few and far between. Therefore, Pakistan is not so optimistic about the CPEC.

It must be understood that the World Bank has many fears about the BRI initiative. This has been discussed in detail in several World Bank reports, but so far international financial institutions have not collectively worked to acquire BRI projects. China's all-encompassing contradictions and that country's expansive policy may become an obstacle to addressing these issues. Time will tell if China will come out of its monopoly telephone policy and make extensive efforts to push the BRI through global forums. If China does not correct its ways, it creates obstacles to its own plans. However, the reality is that about 10 countries today are embroiled in China's debt-trapping diplomacy by the BRI.

If you notice closely, China has captured every country surrounding India, which may cause security threats to India in near time economy or trade war. Indian Ocean is dominated by China these days and due to this debt trap, every country is like a puppet for China which may turn against India. Hence to counterfeit the Chinese Debt Trap, India should avoid Chinese software & hardware.

As stated by MP Wangchuk from Ladakh, that we should boycott Chinese software within a week and the hardware by a year. Hence, we will have a 'Wallet Advantage over China', which will weaken its economy in the coming future.

Media and politics are the two equal and opposite sides of the same coin and none can persist without other. With the advent of most recent term 'Globalisation', the crown of Indian Politics has taken a dramatic shift towards its most modern form. Along with maintaining the responsibility of fourth pillar of the Nation, media is performing as the mover and changer from stereotypical type to most modern and most updated form of politics. Media plays a very dominant role in politics while shaping the public opinion towards the Nation as well as parties. In the era of Information Technology, it is quite difficult and too impossible for respective governments to keep centripetal force over its citizens in the midst of Internet, Facebook, Twitter, Satellite channels and radio stations. Starting from Mirat-ul-Akhbar till date, there are crores of print media tools which have spread the policies of respective government for the betterment of its people, but with the passing of time and situation, the demands for most modern technology always rest on the top. Media has unique power in any political system and this power stems both from their main source of information about its culture, people, and events on a regular basis and their multiple functions in politics. Media is a most powerful stem of politics in creating its audience attitude, opinion as also behaviour for the betterment and most prospective nation. In a democratic country like India, there are thousands of complexities starting from societies to nation like flood of new events with most modern concepts and with new and updated form of technologies, media have enormous power to formulate the real understanding of world which also affects the behaviour of its citizens. Media helps to correlate the responses and to face the challenges and opportunities in modern societies, to reach consensus on action of the society to its new members while keeping good relationship among its people and expert policymakers. The footprints of the modern media form are highly pervasive in nature than earlier decades and their roles in politics are becoming the major points of discussion and controversy. The spread and restriction on media and its content can define the concept and understanding of any government. With the understanding and clearance of concept, the respective government will work as the pressure group or pro group to media. Many times it is seen that the media-politics relationship has affected the exact content in numerous scenario, derailing the train to different juncture. Media is the most utilised and most useful tool in the hands of any government as well as citizens to run the country in the most effective and most updated way. The Indian media landscape has changed significantly over the last decade. With the advances in technology, the media industry has been burgeoning like never before and expanded its reach in terms of the number of outlets, whether in television, radio or newspaper. While this has set an impressive trend for market growth, the underlying consequences of this rapidly growing media landscape has thrown up a few challenges as well. The people with access to the corridors of power have been successful in influencing dissemination of information through media houses by partially owning these outlets and tangentially influencing the way news are presented. Clearly, ownership of the media significantly affects the perspectives presented in the reporting and bias becomes inevitable in such circumstances.

Within the sample of this study, as many as ten media owners have direct or indirect links with politics while some of them even represent a political party. There are countless others, however, who have refused to declare their political affiliations but yet own media companies. Between them, media owners with political links control a sizeable share of viewership/readership.

□

B.Tech., M.Tech London, Ph.D. and is currently working as Professor, DTU (Formerly Delhi College of Engineering). Approximately 100 research papers in various national/international journals of very high repute.

Back to Roots: Self-reliant Naya Bharat

—CA Amresh Vashisht

Amidst the pandemic which is hanging with all kinds of uncertainties and speculation, but with a firm hope to come out from this unexpected spell of hitting the world economies, Prime Minister Narendra Modi Ji addressed the nation on 12th May, 2020 and declared to fight the pandemic coupled with the opportunity to be self-reliant. Thus, he has marked the national goal to become self-reliant with a clear intent to speed up the economic development of the country so that the living standard of the people would improve further to create a community of 130 million Indians who appreciate their cultural heritage and would be capable of creating new things with a strong feeling for modern civilisation. The move was set to build a generation that will be self-reliant and participate with their head held high in worldwide affairs. We have to show to the World how well we can cope with and overcome a crisis like the unprecedented one brought on us by the pandemic and lockdown.

The Traditional Self-reliant Bharat

In the golden era of Hindustan, it was Independent, Self-Sufficient and Self-Reliant. The Hindustan was ruled through the villages and all the villages were self-sufficient to its needs. Self-sufficient village economy refers to such kind of situation in which the village is equipped with all sort of facilities required by the people within it. It doesn't depend upon neighbouring villages or other places for its needs. At the time of formation of a village, the representatives of a community were called and offered the basic infrastructure at their disposal to serve the villages. The occupations were Lohar, Barai (carpenter), Dhobi (washerman), Nai (barber), Teli, Kumhar (Potter) Sunar (goldsmith) Mallah (Boatman) Julaha (Weaver) Tarkhans, Bhishti (Waterman), Mochi, Mirasis, Churas, Bajigar, Sansis etc. The self-reliant society was the foundation of the self-reliant village. Throughout the historical ages, Indian village remained a unique and remarkable socio-economic organisation. From time immemorial, it has assumed a stable character of its own with its peculiar but distinct characteristics. Till the introduction of the British rule, the village remained the basis of the rural society and economy (Desai, 1948). Interrelating with economic sense, the village has been termed the village community of its sources and resources. The villages enjoyed a self-contained and self-sufficing existence. Our villages were little republics having nearly everything they want within themselves. "The activities of the villages were regulated, as far as possible, as a self-propelled and self-dependent economic unit (Moreland, 1968)."

Hence, the needs of the village community were satisfied either within the village or by the neighbouring villages. The necessities were Food, Clothing, Vaidh, Tools, Carpentry etc. The majority of members of the typical village community were, therefore apparently cultivators and weavers. The additional needs such as farming implements and utensils were provided by the smith. The potter made pots, and the goldsmith, ornaments. These craftsmen or merchants could meet the simple needs of the villager. The small trader supplied the other goods which the village did not produce. Economic transactions within the village were conducted smoothly and logically. Traditionally, the cultivator purchased his cloth, oil or pot by paying in grain. Other professional groups of the society were also paid a fixed annual share of grain. This procedure of mutual exchange has been termed as a barter system. Even the salary to the local village school teacher was paid in goods at a particular festival like Dashhera. None of the jobs was there where the residents were required to see outside from their village window. Thus the people of the village in such type of economy consume food made from the crops grown in their village land and wear clothes that are spun in the mills of local areas.

It was only in the British era that money generally began to replace the barter system. But in the traditional village economy, money served the purpose of wealth, either in the shape of gold and silver (Bose, 1993; Charles worth, 1982). Whatever any particular village community could not produce, the adjacent village or villages could supply and thus, the villages remained interdependent to meet mutual needs. If the needs could not be satisfied within the immediate vicinity, there was a periodical or weekly market of various neighbouring villages where the required commodities could be available. These markets were arranged at regular intervals.

Moreover, there was the annual fair to which the inhabitants of several villages eagerly looked forward to buying commodities of a specialised nature or technique. It is remarkable that in the traditional village community, the moneylender had an important socio-economic character to perform. The community lived on the principle of self-adjustment. The members shared their prosperity as well as adversity according to prevailing conditions. Their wants being limited to bare necessities, the villagers worked intensely to produce them. Self-sufficiency was, more or less, a universal feature except in times of natural calamities. Against such merits, the demerits were equally weighty. The isolated existence of the village and the still and quiet village life made the economic activities stereotyped. The incentive for material prosperity was lost in quietist attitudes of self-contentment. The immobile peasant, after his seasonal fieldwork, had much time to spare. The craftsman and the artisan, with all his gift and talent, did not try to create a higher demand for his goods. The small traders had no transport facilities to carry village products to distant markets. The wealthy people of the village may donate money for infrastructure facilities with the help of which all needs are satisfied within the village. It may have schools, hospital, banks and even the police station too. Now, it is time to look towards our past for our glorified self-reliant society, and further to look into the future with more open eyes from now onwords.

The Gandhian Dream of Self-Reliant India

In between the self-reliant Bharat and the present concept of Modi's Atamnirbhar India, there was a Gandhi philosophy which always stood for the self-reliant villages of India. There is only a hairline difference among the old days of Self-Reliant Bharat, the Gandhian economy of self-sufficiency and today's thought of Modi's Atamnirbhar India.

Gandhi highlighted the necessity of self-reliance to achieve equity and sustainability in economic growth. "Swadeshi is the outward, practical manifestation of patriotism. Their pleas for national self-reliance are not incompatible with international co-operation, provided that latter is on equal footing-with due regard to the national respect of every country." He stressed that a person could learn from camp life to stay together with mutual co-operation, work together, live a disciplined daily life, follow the rules, respect religious beliefs and be self-reliant. Dattopant Thengadi, an ideological stalwart of the Rashtriya Swayamsevak Sangh (RSS) in his book" Third Way", had propounded Swadeshi economics in a series of essays in the 1990s. They detailed the conceptual framework of a 'self-reliant' India. Both studies spell out the finer details of the Swadeshi School of economics and the model of 'self-reliant' India. Gandhi had promoted this alternative British technology in the textile sector with the Khadi movement that was affordable to people. The vision behind the movement was to make people self-reliant which ultimately led to fearlessness. The underlying philosophy behind the movement was to empower people with technology so that they became fearless. Three years were spent in acclimatising people in the production of alternate clothing.

It was an economic philosophy and was an essential part of the national movement as well. This philosophy is relevant in the present day as well, because people should be economically self-reliant. Detailed mathematical simulation studies carried out at IIT, Delhi by Alit Kumar (1991) have shown that it is possible to design village republics using the currently available decentralised rural technologies which are not only self-sufficient in so far as their basic needs are concerned but can also generate appreciable surplus produce for the cities.

Gandhi Ji has rightly mentioned that there is nothing to prevent us from profiting by the light that may come from the West. Only we must take care that we are not overpowered by the glamour of the West. We must not mistake the glamour for true light. When Gandhiji endorsed the self-sufficiency and self-reliant villages, his vision was clear that the self-reliant villages mean a self-reliant India. If we are to increase the scope on a bigger scale and look at the World as a unified country and countries as villages, the relevance is clear. Gandhi visualised the problems associated with industrialisation and modernisation. He believed that unless villages are developed and made self-sufficient, it will lead to mass migration, overcrowded cities, and the vicious circle of poverty and under-development cannot be extinguished. Along with the freedom struggle, vigorous efforts were made by Gandhi for the development of villages by making them financially independent through the establishment of small and cottage industries. He believed that political independence without economic independence was hollow.

He was sure that the progress of the country lies in the development of the majority of its rural villages. Gandhi said that the only way of bringing the hope of good living to the rural people was by making the village the central place in the economic programme. To Gandhi, the qualities of the village and rural life far surpassed that of the city. Still, he recognised that the playing field had to be levelled, with both landscapes providing opportunities for personal growth and lifelong learning. Dhiru Thadani (2011). The technology that enabled this exploitation, therefore, needs to be eschewed. In 1934, he created All-India Village Industries Association (AIVIA) to work towards the development of a model of non-exploitative rural industrialisation. It is not that he was opposed to all heavy industries. He was not against science and technology but wanted them to be used judiciously so that the inequity in the society was reduced. But the real development could not be achieved by following the western model of industrialisation, mentioning it as the exploitation of Indian tiny Industries. Such two patterns of development were the need of the hour. India can't ignore the substantial and new technical advancements. The question is to take a path where a Gandhian thought of economy, which was an extension of his love and care for the rural areas, can be merged with the modern thought of development through the present Modi regime.

Though, in some way, this indication was made by the 2014 declaration of 'Make in India'. That was surely an extension of old Bharat culture, clubbed with the Gandhian thought of self-sufficiency at ground level but keeping a bird's eye on the development of other nations, innovation of technology and requirements of the rest of India. Hence, the present declaration of Atamnirbhar India by Modi is aimed at clubbing all the previous versions on this front with a bright path for the future.

Modi's Declaration of Self-reliant Naya Bharat

With the taking over the reigns of our nation, Prime Minister Narendra Modi has launched an initiative of 'Make in India'. The concept of making in India was that technology is a powerful tool when it is given in the hands of people. Hence, Make-in-India initiative was to encourage self-reliance in the country on seeds which were sown several decades ago by the Father of the Nation, Mahatma Gandhi.

During the past few months, we are facing an unprecedented emergency of Covid-19 which disrupted most channels of national and international trade. The declaration by Prime Minister, under Atamnirbhar declaration, gave a clarion call for the country to become self-reliant. This is an official move to come out from the mess of Covid-19 with confidence. Atamnirbhar is a type of sustainable living in which nothing is consumed other than what is produced by self-sufficient individuals. So, Self-sufficiency or say self-containment is the state of not requiring any aid, support, or interaction for survival; it is a type of personal or collective autonomy. On a national scale, a self-sufficient economy that does not trade with the outside World is called an autarky. Here Atamnirbhar is different from autarky. The Prime Minister himself clarified that the current idea of self-reliance is not about a return to import substitution or autarkic isolationism, instead aimed at a quantum jump to the economic potential of the country by strengthening infrastructure, using modern technologies, enriching human resources, and creating robust supply chains. We need to give the fullest support to Modi Ji's Declaration. The leadership has a vital role in injecting greater self-confidence in the people by reducing the country's dependence on other nations.

At ground level, people are having their fullest support for the move. The support from the public can be enumerated in the following way.

House of an older man collapsed in the heavy rain.

The opposition leader asked the older man, are you worried?

Older man: Not at all.

Opposition Leader: Your house has fallen.

Older man: Right. But instead, my spiritual mainstay has become more robust.

Opposition Leader: What do you mean by that?

Older man: As long as we are led by our PM Narendra Modi, we have nothing to worry about. Wait and see. We'll be leading a much happier life.

To become Atamnirbhar, Modi Ji has a vision and commitment to make it. The first key factor is to spend more money and investment in infrastructure. The increase in public spending will undoubtedly boost demand and generate employment in the short term and add to infrastructure capacity in the medium term. For those measures, the

Government has already taken up the stimulators to the tune of ₹ Twenty Lac crore. This shows the commitment of the political leadership and the capability of the administration to deliver. Few policy reforms were in the pipeline and the same have been activated. A recent change in the agriculture sector where the sale proceeds of agriculture have been opened up, and the farmers made free to sell their produce at any place or at any rate of their choice.

Further, such changes in land, labour and other policies could yield results in the medium term. The time will tell about the results of such measures, but the challenge with the Government is to implement quickly and efficiently. But for now, investors will wait and watch to test the sincerity and efficiency of governments at the centre and in the states.

This industry is ever-changing with the development of technological advancement, so this sector will always be there at the forefront. It will be ever multiplying because of the sensitivity of the products. For example, one product is the drone manufacturing. The World is changing; there is a need to have the combat drones and a squadron in the Air Force, a brigade in the Army and also in the Navy. This can also be used in agriculture. Tremendous probabilities may be generated through one such activity. The oil-exporting jobs are another field where we account for a bulk of imports. Whatever new sources of energy India may tap in the foreseeable future, it will scrap our import-dependent status. The sky is the limit on this front also. The other sectors which are open and much can be done, are solar energy plates, electronics, pharmaceuticals etc.

Recently, we have faced the border dispute with China. China is a manufacturing hub. However, the spread of Corona has opened up the eyes of the World and now they are realising the wrongdoing with their dependence on China. Now the companies are shifting their base and India can be a potential place to invest. We have to come out with a high authority which can be helpful to those industries which are willing to shift to India. The local laws also require to be exempted for few years on their inception. This exercise requires a close watch over the activities from industry to industry and the primary job in the hands of the Government to attract such industries here. Japan has already announced its subsidy plan to their companies, shifting their base from China. Our nation should not miss this opportunity and if we analyse, such shifting will also be a part of broader Atmanirbhar Naya Bharat of 2020. India will surely achieve self-reliance and be globalised at the same time. We are hopeful that multinational companies existing in China will relocate to India and make India more export-dependent, since these MNCs aim to sell globally.

Being 'vocal for local' is a crucial complement of Atmanirbhar Bharat. We have to value our local products. We should have the government policies out of the clutches of the babus sitting in the air-conditioned chambers and red tape. The favourable policies alone can give a remarkable boost to our dreams of self-reliance. Thus, policies should enhance domestic competition and eschew crony capitalism. We cannot become self-reliant until we have control over domestic and global supply chains. Thus, there is a need to ensure greater control over certain parts of the global value chain to protect strategic interests especially in healthcare, agriculture and defence.

After Atmanirbhar success, we can survive even if the World turns upside down. It is because we have our territory, our people, our system and our leader. We lived in difficulties in the past as well. Thanks to the leadership of Modiji, this noble spirit is cherished by his cultured, spiritual approach and has fully displayed his calibre in the building of a thriving India. There is no nation more reliable and more excellent than the Indian people who regard the collectivist outlook on value as a criterion of life, imbue the whole country with human fragrance and work today for a better tomorrow.

'Live in the future.' We live in the present and head for the future. An important problem for everyone is how to approach the past and the future with the present, as the centre. The present is the continuation and accumulation of the past and simultaneously the starting and turning point of the future. 'Let us live not merely for today but tomorrow!'—this is a view of life cherished by Modi Ji. Those who believe in their strength, those filled with the hope that tomorrow will be better than today will surely come and those who wish for the coming generation's happiness rather than theirs, can live for tomorrow. 'Love the future' and 'For posterity'—this is a fighting slogan.

□

A qualified Chartered Accountant since 1986. Law in 1998, DISA (ICAI) in 2010, Certification Course of Concurrent Auditors in 2014 and Arbitration in 2015. He has authored a book Peering Footprints—An untold mapping of Saraswati & Rig Veda with Mohenjodaro. He is a regular writer on professional issues at Tax Guru.

Conquering Digital Divide: A Road to Self-reliance

—Kavya Vohra

Inevitably, life in the post-Covid era will not be the same. The aftermath of the pandemic is expected to have a deep-rooted impact on every aspect of the nation's economy and peoples' livelihoods. In this situation, the rural population has had to take in a considerable hit as its means of sustenance is mostly agriculture and allied sectors that are the backbone to maintaining the supply and demand of the urban market. As pandemic-enforced lockdowns bruised economies, affected livelihoods across different industries and rattled global import-export, Honourable Prime Minister Narendra Modi came up with the inspiring message of 'Atmanirbhar Bharat' to make India self-reliant.

In the age of digital transformation, it is the need of the hour to stress upon the inclusion of technological developments for the advancement of rural areas for realising a 'Self-Reliant' India. The vision of 'Atmanirbhar Bharat' would not be possible without self-reliant villages. The rural sector of the nation is the key example of 'Digital Divide'; in the urban set-up-India has approximately 104.25 subscriptions per 100 population, whereas in rural areas, it languished at 27.57. Such numbers confirm the extent of India's rural-urban digital divide. The divide is a result of both-either feeble connections or unavailability of internet services in various regions and the incompetence of individuals to adopt those services. Discriminators such as locale, gender, income, education level, age and language influence the access to these services.

The financial aid provided by the government for the upliftment of the rural sector through various policies including the Atmanirbhar Bharat Abhiyan seems promising. However, a more data-driven and holistic approach is required to ensure not just 'Rural Development' but specifically 'Inclusive Rural Development'.

At the most basic level, it is essential to acknowledge the vast span of digital illiteracy which can be overcome only by promoting a better understanding of how ICTs and internet are assets for socio-economic development. An integrated approach to digital skill development by the inclusion of IT skills in the school curricula, as proposed in the recently announced National Education Policy, seems reassuring. Access to the internet ensures access to a global digital market which nullifies the need for intermediaries and hence a better income leading to a finer quality of life. This would avoid underuse of publicly available infrastructure and aid in the overall economic development of the country. The digital tutelage must be aided by proper availability of services. It is crucial to ensure public access to internet-enabled services. Hence, it is imperative to build-up on the idea of administering high-speed internet hotspots such as Common Service Centres, Post Offices, Cyber Cafes, Public Wi-Fi Hotspots, Schools etc. This would involve suitable incentives for private sector investors. Investment in broadband infrastructure is of vital importance to ensure that the 'last mile' reaches even the most under-connected demographics.

Hence, digital skills must be delivered alongside digital infrastructure to enable people to benefit from it.

This extent of development seems reassuring; however, it can only be accomplished if it does not succumb to the deep-rooted social biases present in these areas. By ensuring wage parity between men and women and including programs such as 'Internet Saathi' (which would ultimately require more gender-specific data collection and research), a more skill-driven development can be brought about.

Conclusion

Hence, overcoming the digital divide is critical for attaining self-reliance in the rural sector. The several aspects which need to be addressed by policymakers are:

1. Acquiring better access to devices and technologies
2. Providing the necessary training and skill development to make better use of the available infrastructure
3. Fostering a culture of innovation and upgradation
4. Overcoming social biases that are ingrained deeply in the mindsets

The ultimate aim is to make different policies work together to attain more resourceful ways to promote a more inclusive aspect of rural development. This can only be achieved by implanting rigorous data-driven decisions to assess which factors are hurdles and derive the reasons behind it. Once we get a multidimensional insight of India's digital divide, only then we would be equipped enough to combat it.

Self-reliance can only be achieved by harnessing existing and emerging technologies and social innovations that add value to the lives of the citizens and make them skilled enough to innovate and upgrade.

□

A research scholar with Indian Institute of Technology, Delhi.

Making Economic Sense of Religious Tourism

—**Manish Kapoor**

India, being one of the ancient civilisations of the world, has been the birthplace to many religions, and religions other than those have also flourished here. From time immemorial, Teerthasthal (Teertha Yatras) & Bharat Darshan have remained one of the basic tenets of religions in India. These Teerth yatras have also played a positive role in promoting cultural and national integration.

Religious tourism (RT) is an important part of tourism industry. Tourism like any other commercial activity is affected by economic ups and downs, but religious tourism is more resilient in nature, due to stronger urge to travel for personal or traditional reasons. RT is often addressed as heritage tourism or cultural tourism despite slight difference.

India's travel and tourism sector ranks 7th in the world, in terms of its total contribution to the country's GDP and was almost equal to 9.6% of GDP in 2016. It is forecasted to rise by 6.7% per annum, to almost 10% of GDP by 2027. Majority of tourists in India are domestic and as per estimates, roughly 60% of domestic tourists are religious tourists. Tourism sector created 40.3 million jobs in 2016 which ranks India 2nd in the world in terms of total employment generated. The sector accounts for 9.3% of the country's total jobs. India's travel & tourism sector was also the fastest growing amongst G 20 countries in 2016. The sector unfortunately has badly been hit by Covid-19 worldwide.

Uttar Pradesh Perspective

Area-wise, UP is the fourth largest state in India. UP is 2nd state in terms of total tourist arrivals, 2nd in terms of the domestic tourist arrivals. The tourism industry in UP has significant contribution to the state's economy. UP has also been fortunate to have major RT destinations for Hindus, Buddhists and Jains. UP is the proud birthplace of Rama & Krishna, abode of Shiva, Sarnath, Shrawasti, Kushinagar, Prayag and the list goes on.

The Govt. of UP understands the importance of the tourism sector and especially its religious component. In order to tap the infinite possibilities offered by the sector, strategic and organised initiatives were required to be made and the present Yogi govt was swift to grasp this. In 2017 itself, just after assuming office, CM Yogi instructed the officials of the tourism department to launch an advertising campaign to make people aware of historical & religious places in UP. CM had his vision & priorities set very clear and encouragement & guidance of PM Modi also helped. On the occasion of launch of portal of tourism department 'One Stop Travel Solution', CM said: RT can be the state's mainstay. UP has enough potential for RT and state needs to tap the resources and promote it.

Special emphasis was given to RT through ambitious Ramayana, Krishna, Ganga and Buddhist tourist circuits. He announced that after Jewar airport in Noida, the state would get another international airport in Kaushambi, a world famous tourist destination for Buddhist pilgrims.

New Tourism Policy

The state came out with its new Tourism policy in 2018. The benchmarks were set. State primarily aimed to achieve the following:

1. To become the most preferred tourist destination in the country by 2023.
2. To attract investments with a target of INR 5000 crore every year.
3. To promote city-wise events and festivals with a predefined calendar and promoting the same nationally & internationally.

This policy was to help UP in creating a sustainable, pro-growth and pro-poor ecosystem. Policy also envisaged a dynamic & long-term approach to achieve the true growth potential of the tourism sector in the state.

Divya Bhavya Kumbh

Yogi Govt. took hosting of Divya & Bhavya Kumbha in Prayagraj during winters of 18-19 as a challenge and achieved objectives remarkably well. It was an unforgettable Kumbha Mela. It was for the first time that representatives of 172 countries have participated. This time, the Mela was spread over 3200 hectares as compared to 1600 hectares earlier. It was also a Swachha Kumbha with 11000 Safai Mitras pressed into service. A record 24.01 crore people visited the Kumbha Mela 2019, more than total tourists in UP during 2014-2017. Out of 24.01 crore visitors, approx 0.18 crore were foreign nationals.

Varanasi

Meanwhile, Varanasi being PM Modi's constituency was undergoing metamorphosis in infrastructure and tourism eco system since 2014. Yogi govt in 2017 hastened its pace of development. As per AAI data, Varanasi airport saw passenger growth of 23.4% in FY 2015, 35.7% in FY 2016 & 46.4% in FY 2017, much above the national average of 20%.

In 2015, PM Modi alongwith his Japanese counterpart Shinzo Abe attended Ganga Aarti. In March 2018, the French President Immanuel Macron visited Varanasi accompanied by PM Modi and took a boat ride in the Ganga. Both these events helped showcase Varanasi on the world tourism map. Varanasi hosted 17th Pravasi Bhartiya Divas in 2019 successfully under PM's guidance. Now his dream project Shri Kashi Vishwanath Dham, when complete, is expected to double the number of devotees.

Ayodhya

In 2019, the young tourism & culture minister, Neelkanth Tiwari took the agenda further and celebration of Deepotsav was organised on the banks of Saryu River in Ayodhya. Diwali was celebrated with 4.01 lakh Diyas in 2019 improving upon its own Guinness world record of 3.51 lakh diyas in 2018. This event turned out to be a huge success for RT in UP. During the last five years, tourists in Ayodhya have multiplied 2.5 times. Ramayan Circuit would encompass places related to Shri Rama like Shringverpur, Chitrakoot as a complete RT package. Once Ram Janmabhoomi Temple is complete, Ayodhya would emerge as major RT hub with expected 3.6 crore footfalls every year i.e 1 lakh per day.

UP govt in its budget 2020-21, has set aside ₹ 500 crore for an airport in Ayodhya and ₹ 200 crore for the beautification of Varanasi's Kashi Vishwanath Dham. The focus is to develop Ayodhya and Varanasi as tourist hubs.

Brij

Krishna circuit in Brij Bhumi encompassing all significant places like Mathura, Vrindavan, Barsana, Govardhan Parvat would be major RT attraction near NCR.

Challenges

The projected influx of tourists in UP would throw up some challenges for the ecosystem. The state would have to gear up to ensure that tourists get world-class experience for repeat visit. Safety of tourists, maintenance of Law & Order, adequate infrastructure for travel and stay and training of guides would be very crucial.

UP tourism is all upbeat with its new taglines 'Milega Yahan Sara Desh–Yahi Hai Uttar Pradesh' & 'Uttar Pradesh Paryatan–*Uttar Apke Har Prashn Ka*'. An entire ecosystem projecting an 'Eager to Welcome' brand 'Uttar Pradesh' would help the state to achieve great economic leverage.

□

A qualified CA and at present an entrepreneur and industrialist. He is presently state treasurer in BJP, UP.

Indian Travel Industry & Atmanirbhar Bharat

—Varun Chandna

Atmanirbhar Bharat (*Self-reliant India*) is the vision of the Prime Minister of India, Narendra Modi of making India a self-reliant nation. Travel and Tourism contributes very significantly towards the economy, the industry contributes over 9 percent to India's GDP and generates employment for more than 12 percent of the total workforce. Apart from a strong growth trajectory on its side, the travel and tourism industry offers immense opportunities for both organised and unorganised segments within the sector.

Tourism in India can play an important role in creating alternate livelihoods through sustainable development. As of 2019, 4.2 crore jobs were created in the tourism sector in India which was 8.1 percent of the total employment in the country. For the longest time, however, India's tourism policies have focused on creating destinations that pander to tourist demands.

According to 2018 report of the World Travel and Tourism Council (WTTC), India was ranked third in the tourism sector. Total earning from the sector in India stood at US$ 28.6 billion in 2018, and it is targeted to reach US$ 50 billion by 2022. During 2019, foreign tourist arrivals (FTAs) in India stood at 10.89 million achieving a growth rate of 3.20 percent y-o-y.

India has a diverse portfolio of niche tourism products—cruises, adventure, medical, wellness, sports, MICE, eco-tourism, film, rural & religious tourism. India offers geographical diversity, attractive beaches, 30 World Heritage SBPM and 25 bio-geographic zones. The country's big coastline is dotted with several attractive beaches. India was ranked 34 in the Travel & Tourism Competitiveness Report 2019 published by the World Economic Forum.

However, tourism needs to evolve in the new normal to create better places to live first, and host second. When tourism development focuses on the needs of the local community, incentivising the preservation of their traditional way of life but also facilitating access to urban conveniences, it automatically creates destinations worth visiting. In turn, it helps pave the way for long-term sustainability and resilience.

The Covid-19 outbreak is expected to make travel within the country more attractive for Indian tourists, experts believe. "The local holiday market will boom this year, as the majority of the people feel safer travelling to nearby destinations close to their homes,"

International tourists arrival is expected to reach 30.5 billion by 2028. Electronic tourist authorisations, known as e-Tourist Visa, launched by the Government of India, has resulted in increase in number of tourist visa issued in the country. The facility was extended to citizens of 169 countries as of December 2019. During 2019, a total of 29,28,303 tourists arrived on e-Tourist Visa registering a growth of 23.6 percent.

Tourism is an important source of foreign exchange in India, similar to many other countries. During 2019, India earned foreign exchange of US$ 29.96 billion from tourism recording a y-o-y growth of 4.80 percent. Foreign exchange earnings (FEEs) from tourism in India, witnessed growth at a CAGR of 8.96 percent during 2007-2019. The tourism & hospitality sector's direct contribution to GDP is expected to reach ₹ 12.68 trillion (US$ 194.69 billion) in 2028.

Ministry of Tourism launched **Dekho Apna Desh** webinar in April 2020 to provide information on the many destinations and the sheer depth and expanse of the culture and heritage of Incredible India. Till 20 July 2020, 42 webinars were conducted under the series. Ministry of Tourism is promoting Buddhist Circuit to increase India's share in global tourism market. Prime Minister Narendra Modi urged people to visit 15 domestic tourist destinations in India by 2022.

Medical Tourism: Tourists seek specialised medical treatments, mainly ayurvedic, spa & other therapies, the primary purpose is achieving, promoting or maintaining good health & a sense of well-being. The widespread practice of Ayurveda, Yoga, Siddha and Naturopathy complemented with nation's spiritual philosophy makes India a famous wellness destination. Indian Government has also released a fresh category of visa, the medical visa or M-visa, to encourage medical tourism in India.

Medical tourism is growing by 30% each year. Chennai is named as the 'Health Capital of India', as it attracts 45% of medical tourists due to number of multi and super-speciality hospitals.

India provides the highest quality healthcare at the lowest price and treatment of high quality using the latest technology and technique. India has 28 JCI accredited hospitals. In developed countries like US, UK and Canada, patients have to wait for major surgeries. India has no waiting time or very less waiting time for surgeries. Despite linguistic diversity in India, English is considered as an official language due to which communication becomes easy with foreign patients, as it is an international language.

Heritage Tourism: Tourists visit India for its cultural heritage. In various cities, the country's rich heritage is amply reflected in the various temples, majestic forts, pleasure gardens, religious monuments, museums, art galleries, urban & rural sBPM.

The Taj Mahal of Agra in India is one of the 7 wonders of the world and one of the most famous buildings in India, also known for its beautiful Mughal gardens, great gates and symbol of India's rich history. Agra district of Uttar Pradesh is also known as the historical city of India for its number of historical tourist attractions such as Taj Mahal, Fatehpur Sikri and the famous sister monument, Agra Fort.

Qutub Minar is the second tallest minar in India after Fateh Burj and a World Heritage Site. The Qutub Minar is surrounded by several historically significant monuments including the Iron Pillar of Delhi.

The Red Fort is located in the centre of Delhi and houses a number of museums, named for its massive enclosing walls of red sandstone. The most important surviving structures of India has number of big gates known as Lahori Gate, Delhi Gate, Water Gate and Khas Mahal, Rang Mahal and Mumtaz Mahal in the complex.

The Charminar is a famous monument and mosque located in Hyderabad, Telangana and the landmark is a global icon for Hyderabad. Charminar is one of the top 20 major attractions in the new state of Telangana.

The Palace of Winds (Hawa Mahal) is one of the prominent tourist attractions in Jaipur city. This beautiful five-storey palace was built by Maharaja Sawai Pratap Singh and now adopted as the historical monuments of Jaipur by the Unit Trust of India.

Jama Masjid of Delhi is the largest mosque in India and one of the 10 most popular Jama masjids in India. The mosque has three great gates, constructed of strips of red sandstone and white marble and is one of the most famous landmarks of Delhi.

Adventure Tourism: A wide range of adventure sports are covered under this category with specialised packages. The activities include mountaineering, trekking, bungee jumping, mountain biking, river rafting & rock climbing.

Adventure trips can be taken to a number of destinations in the country with each one being famous for a particular activity.

- **Ladakh:** The rough terrain and natural beauty of Ladakh have made it an admirable destination for adventure lovers. With an average elevation of over 10000 feet above sea level, Ladakh has a cold arid climate.
- **Rishikesh:** This sacred place is located in the state of Uttarakhand, and is a well-known spot to indulge in thrill-inducing sports like rafting, rock climbing, rappelling and more.
- **Lonavla:** It is about 65 km from Pune and is a popular hill town. With a moderate altitude of approximately 2050 feet, Hot Air Ballooning is popular here.
- **Kolad:** Another amazing place to relish thrilling sport of rafting, this little village lies on the banks of the Kundalika River. Away from urban centres and immersed in tranquility.
- **Goa:** It is a perfect place to indulge in some fabulous and exciting water sports.

Adventure Activities in India:

- **Treks**: Can trek at a number of destinations like Ladakh, Uttarakhand, Sikkim, Himachal Pradesh and Kashmir.
- **Motor Bike Expeditions**: Biking trips on the Leh-Manali highway and through South and West India are hosted by many travel agencies as they are highly admired.
- **River Rafting**: The state of Uttarakhand and the village of Kolad are two prime destinations for rafting.
- **Hot Air Ballooning**: Jaipur in Rajasthan and Lonavla near Mumbai are the two most sought after places for hot air ballooning.

- **Scuba Diving**: Travel to Andaman and Nicobar Islands, the state of Goa or the town of Murudeshwar in Karnataka.
- **Wildlife Safari**: The country has many protected areas like Corbett, Bandhavgarh, Kanha and Pench national parks where wildlife safaris can be availed.
- **Camping**: There are many places in Uttarakhand, West Bengal, Rajasthan, Karnataka and Himachal Pradesh, which you can pick.

Pilgrimage Tourism: India has been recognised as a destination for spiritual tourism for domestic and international tourists. It is one of the biggest contributor to tourism industry. India being a religious hub for different cultures, attract many tourists every year. India has long been known as the seat of spiritualism and India's cosmopolitan nature is best reflected across its pilgrim centres.

Tourism of India has carefully crafted **pilgrimage tours in India** to Haridwar, Jyotirlinga destinations, Amarnath, Kailash Mansarovar, Mathura, Char Dham destinations, viz. Badrinath, Kedarnath, Gangotri, Yamunotri, Buddhist destinations, Vaishno Devi, Shirdi, Sikh destinations viz. Golden Temple, Hemkunt Sahib, Dwarka, Varanasi, Ujjain, Puri and several other religious destinations so that you can seek the blessings of your Lord.

Luxury Tourism: The luxury travel market in India is expected to grow at a rate of 12.8 percent during 2015-25, the highest in comparison with any other BRIC country

India is known throughout the world for its amazing luxury experiences and unforgettable destinations. There is a huge spectrum of breathtaking places, spellbinding sites and locations with remarkable and astonishing stories pervading the length and breadth of this vast and incredible country.

- **A Night in the Floating Palace—The Lake Palace in Udaipur**
- **A Ride on the Maharajas' Express**
- **Spa in the Himalayas**
- **Houseboat Tour to Explore**
- **Backwaters of Kerala**
- **A Private Yacht in Goa**
- **A Romantic Night at a Desert Camp of Thar**
- **A Unique Stay at the Treehouse**

Need of Immediate Attention of Government

Finance Minister, Nirmala Sitharaman ended the fifth and last part of relief and reform package to revive and build an 'Atmanirbhar Bharat' but the **Travel, Tourism, Aviation and Hospitality** sector remained totally ignored. All these four sectors have been badly affected since the coronavirus pandemic hit and lockdown was imposed in India.

Travel, Tourism, Aviation, and Hospitality sectors companies have completely shut for around four months and expecting some relief and bailout in 'Atmanirbhar Bharat' Package. Some common demands of these sectors are tax holiday, GST (Goods and Services Tax) holiday and payment of salaries to the employees by the government.

The Federation of Associations in Indian Tourism & Hospitality Sectors, the policy federation of all the national associations representing the complete tourism, travel, and hospitality industry of India (ADTOI, ATOAI, FHRAI, HAI, IATO, ICPB, IHHA, ITTA, TAAI, TAFI) in a statement said...

"Indian tourism industry has gone into a state of disbelief and shock. It was looking forward to a deep set of survival measures for tourism from the ₹ 20 lakh crore package announced over 5 days, which however were not addressed,"

So, any support on loans with easy terms for mid to long-term, would be of immense help. Loans could be extended looking at the track record of the companies and their potential paying capacity etc., but with a long-term view, rather than taking a conventional, super conservative, and collateral-based lending approach.

□

BBA & MBA and consultant in travel and foreign tours.

Tourism Industry *VS.* India's Development

—Vishnu Goyal

The tourism industry of India is economically important and grows rapidly. The World Travel & Tourism Council calculated that tourism generated INR 6.4 trillion or 6.6% of the nation's GDP in 2012. It supported 39.5 million jobs, 7.7% of the country's total employment. The sector is predicted to grow at an average annual rate of 7.9% from 2013 to 2023. This gives India the third rank among countries with the fastest growing tourism industries over the next decade.

There is no doubt that the social distancing pandemic has most affected the tourism sector. By now, it is also established that the revival of tourism sector will take longer than expected. The pandemic offers us an opportunity to hit the reset button to make the tourism sector a sustainable engine for economic growth and development.

It is widely accepted that the hospitality and tourism sector is a key driver of employment and growth the world over. In the Indian context, Narendra Modi government has identified this sector as key to generating jobs for the millions of youngsters who join the workforce every year– with sound reason.

Tourism Industry has emerged as one of the fastest growing industries in the world and is economically important for rapid growth for India. There are various types of tourism branches in India. The Ministry of Tourism identified 10 niche products for development and promotion to attract tourists with specific interest and India as a 365-Days tourist destination.

1. Cruise Tourism: Cruises are one of the most dynamic and the fastest growing components of the leisure industry in India. Cruise tourism is the new marketable product for India to explore beautiful coastline, undisturbed idyllic islands and virgin forests.

2. Adventure Tourism: Adventure tourism includes mountaineering, trekking, hand gliding, paragliding, bungee jumping and white water river rafting. The Ministry of Tourism has identified list of places in India for thrilling and extremely adventures sports, mostly in Gulmarg, Jammu & Kashmir, Rishikesh Uttarakhand, Goa and Maharashtra.

3. Medical Tourism: Medical Tourism or medical travel is used for the procedures of complex specialised surgeries of human parts such as joint replacement, cardiac surgery, dental surgery and cosmetic surgeries.

4. Wellness Tourism: Wellness Tourism includes a travel for less stressful lifestyle, to promote a healthier and finding balance in one's life. Ayurveda, Yoga, meditation, Panchakarma, Rejuvenation Therapy are among the most ancient systems of medical treatment in India and best way to promote Wellness Tourism.

5. Golf Tourism: India has several golf courses of international standards and as sports tourism in India is gaining interest, Ministry of Tourism is creating a comprehensive and coordinated framework for promoting golf tourism in India.

6. Polo Tourism: The game of Polo originated in India and still preserved and practiced in Kolkata Polo Club, the oldest Polo club in the world. Polo can be listed as Heritage Sports of India.

7. Eco Tourism: Eco Tourism also known as ecological tourism is travel to fragile, pristine and usually protected areas. It will include regulated tourism in protected areas of the country.

8. Film Tourism: In an endeavour to establish India as a filming destination, Ministry of Tourism will promote Cinema of India as a sub brand of Incredible India. International Film Festivals like IFFI Goa, European Film Market, Cannes Film festival will be held in India in future.

9. Sustainable Tourism: Sustainable Tourism includes approval and classification of hotels to the expected standards for different classes of tourists. This system will rate hotels from one star to five star and Heritage and Classic etc.

10. Meetings, Incentives, Conferencing, Exhibitions (MICE): Conventions and Conferences are the segment of the tourism industry. In order to promote India more effectively as a convention destination for travel industry, Ministry of Tourism set up the India Convention Promotion Bureau.

Government Initiatives

The Indian Government has realised the country's potential in the tourism industry and has taken several steps to make India a global tourism hub.

Some of the major initiatives planned by the Government of India to boost the tourism and hospitality sectors of India are as follows:

- Ministry of Tourism launched Dekho Apna Desh webinar series to provide information on many destinations and sheer depth and expanse on the culture and heritage of India.
- Ministry of Tourism launched Audio Guide facility App called Audio Odigos for 12 sites in India (including iconic sites).
- Prime Minister, Mr. Narendra Modi urged people to visit 15 domestic tourist destinations in India by 2022.
- Statue of Sardar Vallabhbhai Patel, also known as 'Statue of Unity', was inaugurated in October 2018. It is the highest standing statue in the world at a height of 182 metre. It is expected to boost the tourism sector in the country and put it on the world tourism map.
- Government of India is working to achieve one percent share in world's international tourist arrivals by 2020 and 2 percent share by 2025.
- Under Budget 2020-21, the Government of India has allotted ₹ 1,200 crore (US$ 171.70 million) for development of tourist circuits under Swadesh Darshan for eight Northeast states.
- Under Budget 2020-21, the Government of India has allotted ₹ 207.55 crore (US$ 29.70 million) for development of tourist circuits under PRASHAD scheme.
- In 2019, Government reduced GST on hotel rooms with tariffs of ₹ 1,001 (US$ 14.32) to ₹ 7,500 (US$ 107.31) per night to 12 percent, and those above ₹ 7,501 (US$ 107.32) to 18 percent, to increase India's competitiveness as a tourism destination.
- In September 2019, Japan joined a band of Asian countries including Taiwan and Korea among others, to enter India's tourism market.

Road Ahead

India's travel and tourism industry has huge growth potential. The tourism industry is also looking forward to the expansion of the e-Visa scheme which is expected to double the tourist inflow to India.

The future looks bright. The tourism sector will be among the early beneficiaries of continued growth with most analysts agreeing that the Indian economy will expand at or about 8 percent per annum over the medium term.

□

A qualified CA and a corporate consultant specialising in tourism and real estate industry.

Domestic Tourism: The Game Changer

—Amit Joshi

There's something about India that not only makes it an exotic, exciting and incredible tourist destination but also offers enchanting, mysterious, exhilarating and humbling experiences not only to the International tourists but even to the domestic tourists from different parts of the country.

Being the land of myriad experiences and exotic locales, it is a world of resplendent colours and rich cultural locales, be it magnificent monuments, heritage temples or tombs. The country's ancient cultural heritage inextricably linked with its technology-driven present existence, along with the co-existence of a number of religions, cultures, an awe-inspiring topography makes it one of the perfect tourism locations on the globe.

Despite the fact that though a very little has been done in the past to tap its potential, tourism is still the largest service industry in India contributing 6.23% to the national GDP and 8.78% to the total employment in India. According to UNWTO, India witnessed 17.42 million annual foreign tourist arrivals in 2018 and the domestic tourist numbers grew up to 1.82 billion in 2018-2019. According to the World Travel and Tourism Council, tourism generated ₹ 16.91 lakh crore (US$240 billion) or 9.2% of India's GDP in 2018 and supported 42.673 million jobs, 8.1% of its total employment. We will have to admit that despite all this growth wherein India welcomed close to ten million international visitors in the first 11 months of 2019, the numbers are much lesser and almost one-third the number that visited Thailand, and far fewer even than Vietnam in the same period. Something is just not right. It has been forecasted that India will become the world's third largest economy by 2025, but our status as a tourism destination does not reflect this.

As we enter a new decade, India's tourism industry is standing at a crossroads: in one direction we can see, on the not-too-distant horizon, the many benefits associated with being one of the world's most popular international visitor destinations. In the other direction, a tourist economy, which has already started paying dividends and is primarily focused on domestic growth.

Beyond any doubts, India has all the ingredients to become one of the world's premier tourism destinations, as it is blessed with abundance of positive assets that any other country can only dream of. Geographically, we are perfectly positioned between the emerging east and wealthy west. We have a large, friendly and largely English-speaking population. We have a deep and diverse heritage with almost 40 UNESCO-listed sites, an attractive climate, rich and unique wildlife, and a famously popular national cuisine. We have jungles, mountains, beaches, deserts and vibrant mega-cities. Despite all these positives, the governments in the past have not been too focused on tourism sector ever. Though time to time, there have been some great campaigns like Incredible India and *Atithi Devo Bhava* on National level and God's Own Country, *Khushboo Gujarat Ki, Sau Rang, Devbhoomi, Jane Kya Dikh Jaye* etc. etc. on the state levels but all these have been more focused on Inbound Tourism. Our approach towards the tourism sector generally revolves around inbound and outbound tourist numbers and so is true with the studies, researches, policies and actions taken. On the contrary, we have hardly given any importance to the Domestic Tourism. We, being one of the world's growing economies, have immense possibilities including huge domestic tourism. For most of the years, the total domestic tourism numbers are grossly underestimated. We probably have never been able to acknowledge and appreciate the innumerable advantages we possess in the form of our diversity, demographics, varied climatic conditions and many others, which if tapped properly, can take our Domestic Tourism to altogether a new spectrum, where it can not only be a great contributor to the country's GDP but can surge the growth in employment and therefore contribute to the overall socio-economic growth of the country. No matter the spending of a foreign tourist may be more when compared with that of a domestic tourist, but the massive volume of the domestic tourists makes it up for the lesser spending. The multiplier effect in domestic tourism is evident from the fact that the foreign tourists increased by only a quarter from 20 million to 25 million during 2011-2016, the number of domestic tourists almost doubled from 865 million to 1.61 billion.

Many countries in the world have realised the potential of domestic tourism and have reaped great results. We can always learn from some of the major domestic tourism generators such as USA and China, who have contributed to the promotion of tourism by locking the leakage of money through outbound tourism activities. According to the statistics by WTTC in 2006, the number of domestic tourists within China has exceeded all of the international inbound tourists.

Let's try to understand logically as why and how promoting Domestic Tourism can result in the exponential growth of the tourism industry in a more methodical manner. Domestic tourism, when compared with the international tourism, drives on some intrinsic characteristics which in turn provides it an edge over international tourism. Few of these characteristics are as under: 1. In contrast to international tourists, domestic tourists know the destination, its language, its customs, its laws, its climate, its cultural context. 2. Domestic destinations are nearer: Land transport is predominantly used: 88%, compared to 51% for international tourism; as the destination is nearer and land transport is used more, the cost of trips is lower. 3. Given that the barrier represented by trip cost is brought down, domestic travellers seek the best price-quality ratio or often the lowest possible price in all segments of the tourism value chain: accommodation, food services, tourism activities, shopping, etc. The amalgamation of all the three discussed advantages of Low cost of Transportation, Knowledge and proximity of the destination consequentially facilitates in (a) Broadening the social composition of the tourists; involving the entire social strata from the richest to population with modest but stable incomes. (b) Certain social categories which are predominantly represented in domestic tourism, when compared to international tourism are • Families • Children and teenagers • Senior Citizens • Disabled persons • Households with modest but stable incomes. Such social diversity of tourists results in a large diversity in the demand, in terms of accommodation and tourism products as well as activities and destinations. (c) Domestic Tourism, being less geographically concentrated, is relatively better distributed throughout the national territory with a strong presence in the region of provenance of families. (d) Average expenditure is markedly lower than in international tourism especially interregional tourism, but because of the huge volume of tourists, the overall expenditure is markedly higher.

For many countries, domestic tourism has been a major growth driver and often accounts for over 70% of travel and tourism's contribution to GDP. With respect to India, the figure shoots way higher to an exceptional 90%. It is forecasted that domestic travel, tourism and hospitality spending will expand by 7.3 percent this year to 12.9 trillion rupees and grow by 7.4 percent a year to 26.4 trillion rupees in 2028.The expansion of the domestic tourism sector, as a result, directly stimulates the job market by creating more opportunities.

Having been neglected for decades, one can see a ray of hope as the present Government seems to have understood the promising potential of domestic tourism and is leveraging its ability to generate employment, eliminate poverty, upgrade infrastructure, and increase economic growth. This was evident in the Prime Minister's Independence Day speech where he asked people to travel to at least 15 tourist destinations within India by 2022, in a bid to energize domestic tourism. Apart from this, in the last five years, the government of the day has taken a lot of initiatives towards the promotion of Domestic Tourism. 'Ek Bharat Shresht Bharat' is one of them involving a lot of ministries to showcase India's culture. PM also launched 'Bharat Parv' wherein all the states showcased themselves. 'Paryatan Parv' is yet another initiative launched in 2017 with around 3000 to 4000 events organised all across the country to commemorate the festival. Also, very recently 'Dekho Bharat' webinar has been organised by the Ministry of Tourism.

It's difficult to recall any time in history when the Govt. of India and specially the Prime minister himself have taken such keen interest and been so significantly speaking about domestic tourism.

It is beyond any doubt that Domestic Tourism can act as a game changer by propelling the growth of India's Tourism sector and overall socio-economic development of the country.

Domestic Tourism is indeed the need of the hour as it is much less sensitive to crises, whether economic, natural, health or political and may act as an excellent crisis shock-absorber especially in the case of economic crises. More so, apart from being an excellent instrument for easing social tensions by allowing social categories of modest income to gain access to holidays, it also facilitates income redistribution (from tourists to local populations), combined with various multiplier effects all throughout the value chain thus acting as an effective tool for territorial development.

All said and done, it is important to understand that all the forms of tourism are important and have their own relevance to the growth of the country. While inbound tourism contributes to country's growth by earnings in foreign exchange and acts as a window to showcase our rich heritage and culture to the world, the domestic tourism has a great multiplier effect that boost up the earnings exponentially and serves a great deal in the socio-economic development of the country. Our country has immense possibilities as far as the Tourism sector is concerned and an unbiased proactive approach in promoting the various forms of tourism in a manner that they complement each other, can do wonders in the growth of Tourism and achieving the larger objective of overall growth of the country.

□

Promoter of Kyari Exp-Leisure Destinations Pvt. Ltd. A seasoned entrepreneur with experience in varied fields, specially experiential tourism.

Self-reliant India

—P.K. Sharma

अपि शाकं पचानस्य सुखं वै मघवन् गृहे।
अर्जितं स्वेन वीर्येण न व्यपाश्रित्य कञ्चन॥

Mahabharat–Vana Parva

***Meaning**: O Maghvan (Indra), even he is happy who cooks only little leaves (for his food), earned by his own efforts without having to depend on others.*

Prime Minister Shri Modi, while addressing the nation on Covid-19 pandemic, stressed the need of a 'Self-Reliant India: Atmanirbhar Bharat'. He said the need was brought home by the absence of domestic production of personal protective equipment (PPE) when the pandemic struck but India started and quickly stepped up PPE production. He emphasised that it is time to become vocal for our local products and make them global. He envisaged for a Self-Reliant India broadly founding on five pillars, they are:

1. Economy: Quantum jumps, not incremental changes
2. Infrastructure: That represents modern India
3. System: Technology driven
4. Demography: Vibrant demography of the largest democracy
5. Demand: Full utilisation of power of demand and supply

In 1991, for the first time, India opened itself to the global market through the policies of liberalisation, privatisation and globalisation but could not make the desired headway as it remained cautious and skirted around the whirlwind of FDI in the next decades. This indecisive approach of India often led to hue and cry from various quarters and demand for faster and deeper opening of its economy but this relative insulation several times turned out to be protective against disruptive global headwinds in these decades.

At the same time, the pandemic brought to the fore the limitations and inevitability of globalisation. Many countries including the United States that relied on others for the supply of essential medicines and medical equipment, quickly and unexpectedly became vulnerable.

On the other hand, China's incomparable mechanical power and capacity to manufacture/produce in bulk and strategic advantage in global supply chains that it may weaponise trade, have propelled and regenerated global discourse on the issues of national security, and how to guard themselves and compete with the Chinese aggressive trade practices.

At once, this unprecedented pandemic continues to demonstrate how inseparable is the future of human beings across the national boundaries. P.M. Shri Modi essayed this dynamic of global politics and very thoughtfully attempted to bring forward India's interest within the emerging framework. He did not renounce the significance of globalisation, rather suggested a new syntax for India which is human-centric as against the existing profiteering model. And therefore, he places India at world's centre by adhering to our ancient ethos of '*वसुधैवकुटुंबकम'.*

Need for making Indian Industries which are Globally Competitive

Self-reliance in state-run heavy industries and strategic sectors in the decades after independence had placed India ahead of most developing countries. However, in the 1970s and 80s, India did not modernise these industries to climb higher up the technological ladder. The private sector too, which had backed the state-run core sector approach in its Bombay Plan, stayed content with near-monopoly conditions in non-core sectors in a protected market. Little effort was made to modernise light industries or develop contemporary consumer products. India's industrial ecosystem was thus characterised by low productivity, poor quality and low technology and was globally uncompetitive.

India completely missed out on the third industrial revolution comprising electronic goods, micro-processors, personal computers, mobile phones and decentralised manufacturing and global value chains during these lost decades. Today, India is the world's largest smartphone market. However, it does not make any of these phones itself and manufactures only a small fraction of solar photovoltaic cells and modules currently used, with ambitious future targets.

At the turn of the millennium, when India embarked on liberalisation, privatisation and globalisation, the very concept of self-reliance was rubbished in the belief that it was tantamount to reinventing the wheel when advanced technologies could simply be bought from anywhere at lower costs.

Two related ideas have not delivered the desired results. The first was that Public Sector Undertakings (PSUs) are, by definition, inefficient and sluggish for the competitive globalised scenario. No effort was made to engender either real autonomy or a transition to new technological directions. Instead, PSUs with capability and scale for the task were undermined or abandoned, along with many nascent research and development (R&D) efforts (for instance, in photovoltaics, semiconductors and advanced materials). On the other hand, the private sector displayed little interest in these heavy industries and showed no appetite for technology upgradation. Further, with entry of foreign corporations, most Indian private companies retreated into technology imports or collaborations.

Even today, most R&D in India is conducted by PSUs and much of the smaller but rising proportion of private sector R&D is by foreign corporations in information technology and biotechnology/pharma. Given the disinclination of most of the private sector towards R&D and high-tech manufacturing, significant government reinvestment in PSUs and R&D is essential for self-reliance.

The second idea was that inviting foreign direct investment and manufacturing by foreign majors would bring new technologies into India's industrial ecosystem obviating the need for indigenous efforts towards self-reliance. However, mere setting up of manufacturing facilities in India is no guarantee of absorption of technologies (the ability to independently take them to higher levels).There is no evidence from any sector that this has taken place or has even been attempted. The fact is, foreign majors jealously guard commercially significant or strategic technologies in off-shore manufacturing bases. The key problem of self-reliance is therefore neither external finance nor domestic off-shore manufacturing but resolute indigenous endeavour including R&D.

Vocal about Local, but no snub to globalisation: Experience and achievements in other countries in Asia endorse to this and also contradict the notion that self-reliance is a hangover from Nehruvian 'socialism'.Learning from Japan's post-war success, countries like South Korea, Taiwan, Singapore and Hong Kong took huge technological and industrial strides in the 1970s and 80s. South Korea, in particular, climbed determinedly up the technology ladder and value chains in electronic goods, consumer durables, automobiles, micro-processors, personal computers and heavy machinery. It emerged as a global powerhouse not only in manufacturing but also in indigenously developed technologies. Taiwan developed technologies and manufacturing capacities in robotics and micro-processors while Singapore and Hong Kong adapted advanced technologies in niche areas. These self-reliant capabilities were enabled, among other factors, by planned state investments in R&D including basic research (3-5% of GDP), technology and policy support to private corporations, infrastructure and, importantly, education and skill development (4-6% of GDP).

On the contrary, countries like Thailand, Malaysia, Indonesia and Vietnam have focused on off-shore manufacturing, lower down the value chain and without the thrust on self-reliance. This is useful for job creation but is an unsuitable model for a country of India's size and aspirations. China is, of course, unique in scale and in its determination to become a superpower, not just geopolitically but also in self-reliant S&T and industrial capability. China advanced purposefully from low-end mass manufacturing to a dominant role in global supply chains. It has now decided on shifting to advanced manufacturing and has set itself a target of becoming a *world leader by 2035 in 5G, supercomputing, internet of things, artificial intelligence (AI), autonomous vehicles, biotech/pharma and other technologies of the 'fourth industrial revolution'*.

The way forward for India: No doubt, India may well have missed the opportunity in many of these technologies in which the U.S., European countries and China have established perhaps insurmountable leads. Yet self-reliant capabilities in electric and fuel cell vehicles, electricity storage systems, solar cells and modules, aircraft including UAVs, AI, robotics and automation, biotech/pharma and others are well within reach. Large-scale concerted endeavours would, however, be required, since self-reliance will not happen by itself. State-funded R&D, including in basic research, by PSUs and research institutions and universities, needs to be scaled up significantly well above the dismal 1% of GDP currently. Upgraded and reoriented PSUs would also be crucial, given their distinctive place in the ecosystem. Private sector delivery-oriented R&D could also be supported, linked to meaningful participation in manufacturing at appropriate levels of the supply chain.

India's meagre public expenditure on education needs to be substantially ramped up (as against current trends of privatisation, which would only shrink access) including in skill development. No country has achieved self-reliance without mass quality public education. And no country has developed without a much stronger public health system than what we have in India.

A special economic package worth ₹ 21 lakh crore has been announced for all sections of people. This package is to help and assist the people who had given up all hopes. P.M. Shri Modi in his address to the nation, also assured that his government will give full support and said that it is not that difficult to get the growth back. Many major reforms have recently been brought in by the government in various sectors such as labour reforms, agriculture reforms, allowing private companies in strategic sectors, commercial mining of coals, etc. With these measures, the government is hopeful that the fundamentals of India's economy will be more inclined towards growth and a leap towards a Self-Reliant India.

□

FCA, LLb., has served as Director in Indian Bank and was also Non Executive Director in Oil India Limited. He was member of the National Committee for Promotion of Social economic Welfare.

Self-reliant India: Strategic Roadmap to Growth and Glory

—Dr. Rajeev Kumar

Reliance on its own resources is very important for a country. Good life through lifestyle changes, better quality of life, self-respect and happiness quotient comes to our mind when we talk about self-reliant India. Independence is not merely the freedom from the clutches of an external power but in real sense, independence, as Mahatma Gandhi has idolised, is the freedom from poverty, freedom from the wide gap between the rich and the poor, and the freedom from the mindset that stops us from spreading our wings towards better growth, prosperity, joyful life and positive development. The idea of self-reliance is 'Economic Independence' in real sense.

Following the Gandhian principles, our honourable Prime Minister, Shri Narendra Modi is working passionately with the purpose of self-reliant India-Atmanirbhar Bharat, a road leading to ultimate growth and glory. As most people confuse self-reliance with isolation, it is imperative to make it clear that self-reliance is not at all isolation from the world, instead it means being a bigger and more important part of the world economy because India very well realises that the world is interdependent and real growth without globalisation is merely a dream. Being self-reliant is indispensable because when you have it with yourself and you are floating in abundance, then only you can help others as well. In simple words, self-reliant India means more valuable and more resourceful India.

So, some of the tremendously amazing initiatives by the Indian government like Make in India movement where Indian goods are produced keeping in mind all the international quality standards, promotion of Khadi and other indigenous products, encouraging the local artists, handicraft products, cottage industries, MSMEs and being enthusiastically 'Vocal for Local' are a real elixir for the attainment of the desired goal of self-reliance. India has jumped to 63rd position in World Banks's Ease of Doing Business 2020 report. Its rank in 2014 was 142nd.

At present, only large companies are coming to India. There is an urgent need that we should attract even medium and small industries from overseas. Following measures may play an important role towards ease of doing business and attracting investments.

- Power connection should not be delayed and must be given within 30 to 40 days from the application.
- Bank loan should be sanctioned within 30 to 40 days from the application.
- District Collectors should be made responsible to increase investment in their districts. Their appraisals should be linked with this parameter also.
- Land acquisition is a lengthy process and takes lot of time. There is an urgent need to change land acquisition law.
- All State Industrial Development Corporations must allot land to the applicant within 30 to 40 days. At present, it takes about 180 days to get land allotted.
- Government should introduce one comprehensive all-inclusive application form incorporating all approvals & sanctions.
- Revision of Minimum wages is required to attract foreign investment in case of India. Countries like Indonesia, Taiwan, Thailand and Vietnam have been gaining significance as a destination of export manufacturing because of the availability of cheap labour. The fact is that out of 56 companies which exited China, only 3 have come to India. Others have gone and established in other ASEAN countries.
- Focus on skill development; India is lagging behind many countries like Vietnam, Thailand, Russia and Indonesia in the skill set desired by the foreign investors and the salary structure of the labour. Skill development programs and capacity building workshops are the need of the hour and should be started at school and college levels to fulfil the dream of self-reliant India.

International trade and investment specialists have raised concerns over the world's over-reliance on China and predicted a shift in both global supply chain and investment. New investors are doubtful about making investment decisions at this time particularly in China. There is an excellent opportunity for India to attract many foreign businesses and investments because of changing global investment patterns and supply chain strategies. India's big consumer base is also another factor for attracting foreign investment.

India has a long history of great civilisations and was considered as 'Vishwa Guru'. Lord Buddha, Swami Vivekananda and Rabindranath Tagore have been the global personalities and driving force for a peaceful India. As a strategy, we have to work in a well-planned and constructive way and promote indigenous goods and services which will definitely empower India. We should not look at 'Quick-Fix' or cheap methods as we have to be more scientific and more innovative and must be prepared to work much harder in a systematic manner to achieve our objectives.

It's a fact that you cannot fill anything from an empty bucket. So if India wishes to contribute in the world economy with the power of its potential resources, strengthening the channel of self-reliance is indispensable. Today, in the testing times of Covid-19, the world is looking up to India in terms of medical sector specifically. India has been in the advisory of WHO to provide inputs to tackle the situation. Also, India has helped other nations by supplying 'hydroxychloroquine' to fight the virus. With the team of best medical professionals, India is relentlessly working on designing its own vaccines to fight this virus. National Institute of Virology, Pune has been the nodal agency for testing. Not only this, best quality masks are also being manufactured in our country and exported all over the world which is serving as an employment generation method as well for us.

Covid-19 has triggered a deeper recession in major economies of the world during the last few months. Because of global economic deceleration, many countries have engaged in protectionist action eg. USA, China and EU etc. The Covid crises have hit the global markets many of which have been competing suppliers for India. The major challenge for India is how to protect Indian industry and boost economic prosperity of Indians in this critical situation.

Many of our businesses have suffered because of inefficient supply chains, lack of sustainable production in our manufacturing units and declining exports to regularly importing global countries. The export sector is facing big cancellation of orders.

When it comes to growth, the idea should always be fewer imports and more exports. Our focus should be to look at the opportunities available to us in the ever-changing global scenario. Identifying markets and products where India gets competitive advantage, should be our priority now. We have to also see as to who all are our competitors, apart from China? Of course, Vietnam, Thailand, South Korea, Indonesia etc. are few names which come to our mind immediately.

To compete with the above mentioned countries, India must have competitive advantage in manufacturing sector vis-a–vis these ASEAN economies. We must also learn as how to gain competitive advantage through logistics and efficient supply chain management.

Our policy makers and industry experts must pay attention and focus on Productivity Advantage, Value Advantage, Cost Advantage and Technology Advantage in terms of competing with ASEAN countries. Better capacity utilisation, inventory reduction and closer integration with suppliers at planning level, is desired. Our manufacturing industries must learn to create Value at each level of upstream and downstream linkages.

Once the gap between rich and the poor is eliminated, growth will automatically happen. For that, we should always make a point not to bargain with the low-income groups like small artisans, vegetable sellers etc., rather encourage and uplift them. You definitely don't get hurt while paying to big brands. So why to exploit the needy?

Education is real empowerment and e-learning and technological advancement is the real need of the hour, to walk with rest of the world and accelerate the journey to self-reliance. Now, we can think of Pre-Covid era and Post-Covid era. Rapid change is taking place in all spheres of day to day and lifestyle patterns. Are we ready for this change? Our 60% population is young and this is the right time to plan and think about their opportunities or threats after Covid goes. Skill-based education will be the key differentiator in near future.

The ban on 267 Chinese applications that were a deterrent for the nation, is really a commendable step by the Indian government and takes us a step forward in this journey of self-reliance. It is of paramount importance for India to think of import substitution as a short-term plan and try to become self-sufficient promoting 'Make in India'.

Unleashing the potential of organic farming can be proved very significant to being self-reliant. There are tremendous benefits that organic farming hold, like reduced production cost for farmers, manufacture of healthy products that do not have any chemicals and pesticides; it's an environment friendly initiative that slows down global warming and encourages biodiversity and of course, would play a major role in employment generation for the youth.

India has to focus into newer product category segments in terms of consumer behaviour. As already mentioned earlier, consumers preference is also shifting and emphasis on digital education and technology platforms is expected to increase. Individuals and families' orientation is tilting towards healthy lifestyle giving rise in consumer demand for natural, fresh, organic and healthy foods, organic clothing and home décor, mental well-being through spiritualism, yoga and boom in e-commerce transactions.

This is a very good growth area and big opportunity for India. Indian expatriates settled abroad, should be targeted through different marketing strategies. India needs to focus on promoting organic agro product exports particularly organic tea, spices, rice and fruits and vegetables. Efforts should be made to boost and new technologies should be explored in the area of 'waste to wealth concept' and for extending possibilities of secondary income and contribution to vision of 'Doubling Farmers Income' by 2022. Production base and quality of KHADI fabrics and Ayurvedic medicines and supplements have to be increased through closer integration of gram panchayats and knowledge sharing in these important areas of value addition. Indian MSMEs should be provided special support through consortiums to boost cross-border trade via e-commerce.

Conclusion

Immediate attention should be given to the following industries which have suffered very badly:

i. Tourism
ii. Agriculture
iii. Education
iv. Logistics & Supply Chain
v. Food & Beverages

We must focus on opportunities in less Covid effected countries like Latin America, CIS, Africa, Middle East etc. in place of traditional destinations like USA and EU. India should sign free trade agreement in such potential countries also. India should play a proactive role and this is a very good opportunity for India to gear up and capture growing demand of selected importing countries.

Indian embassies/missions abroad should be instructed to work wholeheartedly to attract FDI, promote trade and also to explore technology transfers from developed countries to India. Group Exchange Programs of technical experts from industry and academics might play a significant role to share knowledge. China learnt a lot from Germany and other developed countries through such methods.

In order to encourage employment generation, entrepreneurship and to promote MSME sector in tier 2, tier 3, hilly and rural areas, special incentives and subsidiaries should be given to cottage industry sector like handlooms, silk, jute, carpets, agro–based products, handicrafts etc. Special monitoring should be done by financial institutions like banks etc., so that they recover their money in due course of time. Giving loans to MSME on discounted rates has to be encouraged but these loans should also be recovered to boost our financial sector and our economy.

Animal husbandry is a very important area which has to be focused, as it creates great value in each household of rural economy. Farmer skilling in dairy farming is required at grass root level. Indian milk products are now also being exported to USA. There is a need to further strengthen milk co-operatives. Milktech start up like MooFarm should be supported and encouraged (We are also cooperating and supporting this initiative of MooFarm as General Secretary of Social Action Foundation). Good hygienic packaging has brought about revolutionary change in this industry. Agri business systems have to be changed and improved to boost rural economy. The focus has to be Agri business from Agriculture. Investment in green supply chains and sustainable supply chains is required at village and town levels. This strategy will stop the migration of rural youth from villages to cities who leave villages for want of employment at a very low salary or wages.

Special strategies should be made for focusing and developing industrial clusters. Sectors should be identified for cluster development keeping in mind the proximity to raw material. Special discount should be given to these cluster areas in electricity rates and no power cuts should be ensured in these areas. I would like to cite few examples here. Ferozabad and Sardhana (Distt. Meerut) in Uttar Pradesh are suffering because of frequent power cuts and irregular power supply. Both are famous for glass work and handlooms and powerloom industry respectively.

Government also has to work on revenue model for MSME sectors. There should not be a one way traffic. This sector can pay back to Government in the form of taxes only, if they are made profitable and self-sufficient. Special provisions and support should be provided to this sector in terms of Quality and Processes as we have to go global using our strength of this sector. Associations and formations of Consortiums in this sector are very necessary to boost Indian economy. Collaborations of MSME Industries and Institutions like IITs should be encouraged to improve systems and technology in this sector so that we can beat China and enter global markets where a big vacuum has been created particularly in the area of consumer products. District Commissioners and Industrial Development Commissioners should be made responsible and answerable to implement this task and they should be given targets to fulfil this challenging initiative.

Pan India redistribution of resources is required to boost overall development in all sectors of Indian economy. The principle of rethink, redesign and redistribute should be implemented. If India wishes to achieve increased GDP, generate more employment, wish to build a good position in the international markets and wishes for no more brain drain, then being self-reliant is the way out. Let's join hands to boost Indian economy by channelising and integrating potential resources and developing rural areas along with metropolitan cities.

□

PGD (IIFT), Ph.D. (JNU) and visiting professor in IIFT (under Ministry of Commerce and Industry). His areas of expertise are domestic and international marketing/ business, funding, capacity building, skill development etc.

'Atmanirbhar Bharat' w.r.t. Jammu-Kashmir & Ladakh

—Anil Kumar Goyal

A call for 'Atmanirbhar Bharat' has been given by our Hon'ble PM, Sh. Narendra Modi, after the unfortunate Galwan valley incident by China. This aggression was not the sole or the first such incident but a continuous affair after Independence. It is a bitter truth that the previous Governments, specially those led by First PM, JL Nehru and later under the UPA regime, either ignored or indirectly encouraged such aggression. Under the Nehru regime, we lost almost 1/3rd of Ladakh and under UPA, apart from land, the interests of Indian Economy and the Industry were also 'sold out' to China and instead of 'ATMANIRBHAR', the economy was made wholly and solely 'China Nirbhar'. The trade with China grew one side and imports from China multiplied by more than 33 times during the UPA tenure. Due to this, local production was badly affected and every one started using Chinese goods either for production or for consumption.

However, the unfortunate Galwan incident was taken as a challenge by the present Modi Govt. Every cloud has a silver lining also and taking this incident as a blessing in disguise, our H'ble PM gave a call for **'ATMANIRBHAR BHARAT'.** In this process, the Govt also took a bold step to ban 267 Chinese Apps, which were considered dangerous for the National Security.

In this article, we would be discussing the relevance and importance of erstwhile State of J&K i.e. State of J&K and UT of Ladakh in today's times, for achieving the target of **'ATMANIRBHAR BHARAT'.**

'Atmanirbhar Bharat Abhiyan' is to revive and strengthen the National economy from every sphere of demand, production, manufacturing and to make India Self-Sustaining in any kind of situation in future. As per the focal points of this Programme, the main purpose is to focus on such sectors, where the local manufacturers will get benefit for their production and manufacturing of the local goods and items, as per the requirements. Recently, the Government of India had announced an economic package of 20 Lakh Crore for systematic reforms and to focus on 'Make in India' (Self-Reliant) under this Nation-wide ATMANIRBHAR push.

Now it is also the right time to understand the difference between two important terms i.e. 'Made in India' & 'Make in India'. The PM has very clearly given call for 'Make in India'. For 'Made in India', the manufacturing process carried out within or outside India is not relevant. In case, manufacturing process is carried out outside India by an Indian Company, that country stands to gain in terms of employment & local taxes etc., in which the process is carried out.

However, 'Make in India' is there when the goods are produced in India, whether the Manufacturer is a Local or a Foreign Company. 'Make in India' ensures two things. First of all, it ensures Job Opportunities in India, and secondly, the Revenue for the Govt both in the form of Direct & Indirect Taxation is also ensured. For a country like India, which is short of Capital, but where availability of raw material, industrial inputs, land and manpower, both skilled and unskilled is ensured, 'Make' is win-win situation for all stakeholders and it is the best option for the growth from grass route level to the State as well as to the Country.

It might be a co-incidence that the call of ATMANIRBHAR Bharat Abhiyan was given after the unfortunate incident at Galwan which is located in Ladakh. Ladakh is the largest part not even of the erstwhile State of Jammu & Kashmir but also of whole of India. Erstwhile State of J&K is known for the Diversity of Scripts, Languages, Culture, Food, Plantation & Herbs, Climate etc. It has world's highest snow-clad mountains, world's largest Plateau, Glaciers & Rivers, Forests, world's top seven mountains, natural resources, minerals & even gold & uranium are found here. The Ancient Silk route, the only way to reach the Central Asia & Russia etc. also lies here.

Today's UT of Jammu and Kashmir is having many sectors which contribute in a great way to the process of self-reliance at micro level. Abundance of untapped natural resources & forest produce like medicinal plants, horticulture, floriculture, fruits and vegetables, anti-ageing water, minerals, religious & other tourism, adventure sports and handicrafts etc.

provide a great advantage to the erstwhile State of J&K in self-reliance which is essential to achieve the target of 'Atmanirbhar Bharat'.

Various sectors in J&K and Ladakh for Employment Generation and Economy Building

Protection of Wild Life and Forests: Forest areas have its own importance in J&K. The major forest products for timber are deodar, chir, kail, fir, Bhoj (commonly used for writing manuscripts in Ancient India), walnut and lot of other wood. The natural beauty is found in every dense forest area and much wider scope is there for wild life sanctuary.

Tourism: In Rural areas of the UT of Jammu and Kashmir, there is great untapped potential of tourism. There are numerous tourist spots, hill stations, world famous as well as little known religious & other tourist places which are capable to attract tourists from worldwide to enjoy untapped Natural beauty, Snow Clad hills, Greenery, Mountaineering, Border Posts etc.

Livestock Rearing: Despite having availability of fodder in abundance in Jammu and Kashmir, livestock farming is yet to be tapped. At micro level, it is undoubtedly a money-making business, both on large as well as small-scale basis. Even though it has always been a good source of income for the poor population residing in far-flung areas of J&K, it has great commercial potential. Major advantage of livestock rearing is that a very small capital and a little space is required for great earnings in such small-scale business.

Crops: Wheat, maize, rice, barley, jawar and bajra, saffron, sugarcane, oil seeds, pulses-all these crops are grown in different parts of UT of Jammu and Kashmir. These are mostly cultivated by the local residents and skilled labourers. World famed spices and handicrafts etc. which are having great export potential, are available in abundance in every part of J&K & Ladakh.

Fruits: Local fruits of Jammu and Kashmir like mangoes, plum, peccanut, peach, apricot, pear, walnuts, apple, citrus etc. are very delicious and famous worldwide. Due to 370, the food processing always remained untapped and it resulted in wastage of very considerable quantities of valuable fruits. Apart from this, there is a great potential for fresh horticulture also in rural as well as urban areas.

Handloom & Art Work: J&K has always remained famous for kashidakari embroidery works on handloom products i.e weaving by hand.

Basohli was always famous for its Unique Premium Paschmina Shawls. Other unique items famous for weaving by hand in specialised fabrics are kani shawls, ladies' suits, pashmina and raffal shawls, cotton bed sheets, Lois, mufflers, wood carving, blankets etc. Thousands of families are engaged in these kinds of small-scale home industries for their livelihood. There is great export potential worldwide for such spectacular art work. Spectacular Hand Painting made from natural colours at Basohli are always in great demand.

Medicinal Plants for Ayurvedic: There are numerous commonly known Medicinal Plants for Ayurvedic purposes which are found in forest and hilly areas of Jammu and Kashmir. These Ayurvedic plants are very commonly used for treatment of many typical diseases and are immunity boosters. These plants are Amla, Neem, Hrithki, Saptparn, Nirgundi, Tulsi, Vasa, Gilloy, Gudduchi, Mahanimb, Palash, Kuth, Ashwagandha, Aloevera, Babbul, Darim, Brahmi-Booti, Kattha, Kikar Singhi, Aconitum and much more, which are found in different forest areas of J&K.

Craft items: Small-scale manufacturing units in different parts of Jammu and Kashmir for making utensils of copper and aluminium and other essential items made of clay (earthenware), for daily use for different purposes.

Sericulture: A large number of families are engaged in extraction of the Silk fibre. Kashmir Silk is always in great demand but in recent past, the silk industry witnessed declining trend due to lack of equipment and problems in the expansion of mulberry trees. The production of raw silk has potential to multiply many times.

Sports Items Manufacturing Units: There is a huge demand of cricket bats being made of willow wood not only in different parts of the country, but worldwide also. Small units can be setup at various locations in J&K for this. There is great potential for the production of Badminton Rackets, TT bats, Football etc.

Adventure Sports: J&K & Ladakh have great potential for adventure sports like water sports, winter sports, mountaineering, trekking, camping etc.

Mineral Resources: Many of the important mineral resources like Limestone, Coal, Copper, Lead, Zinc, Bauxite, Chromium, Gold, Arsenic, Marble, Granite, Slate Gypsum, Dolomite, Quartzite besides Building Stones etc., are found in J&K and Ladakh.

Important steps required in J&K & Ladakh to achieve 'ATMANIRBHAR Bharat':

Preservation of Vegetable and Fruits: Earlier, the local fruit growers were facing several issues and difficulties due to the non-availability of essential services such as Cold Storage facilities etc. for storing and processing of fruits and vegetables in far-flung areas. Old methods for preservation such as drying, refrigeration, and fermentation etc. are very time consuming and suitable for small quantities only, due to which a large portion was wasted. Now after abrogation of Article 370, there is no such problem in establishing of modern facilities at local levels for preservation of fruits and vegetables by using modern methods for preservation like canning, pasteurisation, freezing, irradiation etc.

Vocational training Institutes: It is an important aspect for providing training to all skilled and unskilled farmers, labourers and workers who are actively involved in all such activities of growing fruits, vegetables, handlooms, farming, sericulture, horticulture, craft and handicrafts etc. Such training programs and workshops for these people would certainly increase the potential and coupled with other modern facilities and techniques, would fecilitate the increase in production at macro level.

Religious Tourism: There are numerous ancient well-known as well as little known religious places spread over every region of the erstwhile State of Jammu and Kashmir. But due to lack of transportation and accommodation facilities and also due to lack of information, these places, despite having great potential, could not be developed as Pilgrim Tourists Spots. The development of these Sacred Holy Shrines would certainly help to achieve 'Atmanirbhar Bharat' through "Make in India' in a great way in the long term.

In the nutshell, The State of J&K and UT of Ladakh are undoubtedly the best suitable to 'Make in India' a great success. Just a small push in the form of simplified Industrial Policy coupled with Training & easy finance would make "Atmanirbhar Bharat' a reality. Availability of all three essential elements i.e. Man-Power (Highly Skilled as well as semi-skilled & unskilled), Raw Material (both for Production as well as for rendering of Services) and availability of vast land which is suitable for all types of industries, is capable for the success of 'Atmanirbhar Bharat' not at the local, but at the National as well as at International level also.

□

B.Com., MSW, FCA, DISA, FAFD, was government nominee director in RITES Ltd. and is also a member of GST grievance redressal committee, Delhi Government. He is founder trustee of Jammu Kashmir Adhyayan Kendra.

Towards Self-reliant India

—Parmod Kr. Gupta

"Not I, nor anyone else can travel that road for you.
You must travel it by yourself.
It is not far. It is within reach.
Perhaps you have been on it since you were born, and did not know.
Perhaps it is everywhere-on water and land."

What the famous American Poet Walt Whitman once said is the defining part of the theme of this publication viz., 'The **Self-reliant** India'.

The crux of pronouncement of our Prime Minister Hon'ble Narendra Modi is summed up in most fascinating words, 'the current idea of self-reliance is not about a return to import substitution or autarkic isolationism, rather aimed at a quantum jump to the economic potential of the country by strengthening infrastructure, using modern technologies, enriching human resources, and creating robust supply chains.' It amply attempts to define the macro, the Nation as a whole and not blocks, since the macro can be developed when all enjoining micro-states, its people, resources are best contributing their true potential in making an enviable and proud India, in her reincarnated role.

Essence and Importance

Gandhiji envisioned India as a nation of self-sufficient villages. This enlightened the minds of Indian policymakers post-independence.

The vagaries and distress of partition that was a consequence of Independence embedded with British strategy endowed the Nation with three acute problems–the influx of refugees, a severe shortage of food, and also surmounting inflation.

At the time of independence, rural population with its main dependence on agriculture was around 80%, and successively reduced to 65.53 % in 2019, as was reported according to the World Bank collection of development indicators. Urbanisation is happening at faster pace with consequent challenges too. Rudimentary economic planning deriving from the sovereign authority of the state, was first initiated in India in 1938 by the Congress President and Indian National Army supreme leader Netaji Subhash Chandra Bose who had been persuaded by Meghnad Saha to set up a National Planning Committee. After independence, a formal model of planning was adopted and the Planning Commission, reporting directly to the Prime Minister of India, was established on 15 March, 1950. Authority for creation of the Planning Commission was not derived from the Constitution of India or statute; it is an arm of the Central Government of India.

The first Five-Year Plan was launched in 1951 focusing mainly on development of the agricultural sector. Though many economists like Professor P.C. Mahalanobis were of the view that agriculture needed continued impetus, but the second Five-Year Plan centered on a shift towards developing capital goods and heavy industry for long-term economic benefit. Large funds were allocated for large and medium-sized businesses while the rest lay with mineral development and village and small industries. However, lack of investment in agriculture and a period marked by food shortages and drought, led to inflation. The wholesale price index rose at 6.2 percent per annum between 1956 and 1961.

The debate on 'urban–rural divide' dented the direction of growth and slowed down development.

Indian Perspective—The Contrast

'To be great is to be misunderstood.' Thus said Ralph Waldo Emerson, in his book Self-Reliance and Other Essays.

'The future of India lies in its villages.' This famous statement by Mahatma Gandhi is being challenged by urbanists today who see a shining future for India in its cities. India shares 16% of the world population while its land is only 2% of the total geographical area of the world. Even 67 years after independence, 60% of our rural population (100 million households) lives in conditions of poverty. The rural people lack the basic amenities of life that we take for granted.

According to the latest World Bank report, 33% of the world's poorest people live in India.

We are living in what is often described as the 'urban century'—Urbanisation spreading at an aggressive pace. It is laced with enormous problems-Poor quality, overcrowded housing, Risk of forceful eviction; Lack of safe, readily available water supplies, poor provision for sanitation, drainage and solid waste collection, lack of access to healthcare, emergency services and policing, difficulty accessing government schools, and locations at high risk of disasters and with risk levels increasing because of climate change.

In contrast, there is another India which has an ambitious space program, globally dominating information technology (IT) sector and joining the top five economies in the world. The pressing quest is–can we be proud of our achievements unless and until this 60% of the rural population is brought into mainstream development. It is the real agenda of a self-reliant India.

India's diversities-geographic, regional, ethnic, economic are another dimension that has to be integrated in development efforts.

The Contemporary Challenge: (Covid-19 Pandemic)

Though the spread of (Covid-19 pandemic) is global, the risks extend beyond mortality as the economic consequences of the current pandemic are likely to be frightening.

A key element of the pandemic control strategy everywhere has been to shut down economic and social activity and to impose social distancing with varying degrees of strictness. India's lockdown, imposed in the last week of March 2020, was among the most stringent. The first month of the severe lockdown, April 2020, witnessed a sharp rise in unemployment. A substantial slowdown of economic activities and its effect on India's GDP is shivering, with future fallout in terms of health related issues, mortality, regeneration of urban employment, aggressive pressure on already burdened agricultural land due to return of urban labour to their native habitat necessitating providing alternative employment and vocations to these returnees in rural areas.

In an effective response to an unprecedented emergency (Covid-19 pandemic) that disrupted most channels of national and international trade, Indian Prime Minister, under **Atmanirbhar Abhiyan**, gave a clarion call for the country to become self-reliant.

Future-challenges and opportunities–conflicts, their management, coherence and direction is calling for an unprecedented concerted effort at all levels.

The Approach

The dream of making India self-reliant can't be accomplished in a sporadic manner but by concerted efforts of all stakeholders-The Federal governance-Centre and State, Corporates, Professionals, and other Non-Government players.

It reminds of two case studies aimed and working as change agent.

Launched in June 2000, **ITC 'e-Choupal',** the Value Chain-Farm to Factory Gate-

Aimed at unshackling the potential of Indian farmer has already become the largest initiative among all Internet-based interventions in rural India. 'e-Choupal' services today reach out to over 4 million farmers growing a range of crops-soyabean, coffee, wheat, rice, pulses, shrimp-in over 35000 villages through 6100 kiosks across 10 states (Madhya Pradesh, Haryana, Uttarakhand, Uttar Pradesh, Rajasthan, Karnataka, Kerala, Maharashtra, Andhra Pradesh and Tamil Nadu). Such a market-led business model can enhance the competitiveness of Indian agriculture and trigger a virtuous cycle of higher productivity, higher incomes, and enlarged capacity for farmer risk management, larger investments and higher quality and productivity. Further, a growth in rural incomes will also unleash the latent demand for industrial goods so necessary for the continued growth of the Indian economy. This will create another virtuous cycle propelling the economy into a higher growth trajectory.

Another case study **'Rural Shores'**-Bringing jobs to rural India', founded in 2008, is a business process outsourcing (BPO) company started by a group of like-minded and senior executives from organisations including Ernst & Young, Hewlett Packard (HP), HDFC Bank, Mastek and Wipro Technologies, focused on generating rural employment. The Bangalore, India-based firm hopes to provide employment to more than 100,000 rural youth by setting up centers in each of India's 500 rural districts. To help stem the tide of rural young people who migrate to cities in search of jobs, Rural Shores creates employment opportunities in small villages, giving NSDC Mission a gigantic push.

CSR initiatives have opened more vistas for larger private participation in National reincarnation.

Prime Minister Narendra Modi recently made out the agenda of development through **five 'I's** to make India a self-reliant economy. He envisaged-

The Intent, Inclusion, Investment, Infrastructure and Innovation

...are of utmost importance to make a self-reliant India.

A massive stimulus package to revive Indian economy-PM Modi pins hopes on ₹ 110 lakh crore National Infra Pipeline to ease Covid-hit economy. The Govt. has already identified about 7,000 projects in different sectors that will be part of the National Infrastructure Pipeline.

PM said that the government has made decisions to make India's economy and sectors future-ready and the latest reforms are not scattered, rather, they are planned and futuristic. With the new policies and measures, India will embrace the world with even more strength and a self-reliant India will be more integrated with the global ecosystem. PM Modi aimed at synching national agenda of sustainable development through CSS-Central Sector Schemes mapping with UN Sustainable Goals set out in declaration of 2015 enjoining and furthering MDG (Millennium Development Goals) set in 2000 by UN aimed at eradicating extreme poverty and hunger; achieving universal primary education; promoting gender equality and empowering women; reducing child mortality; improving maternal health; combating HIV/AIDS, malaria, and other diseases; ensuring environmental sustainability; and Developing a global partnership for development.

Conclusion

To conclude, the case of urban and rural development is not a case of versus but a vision of mutually exclusive coexistence emphasizing the two parallel futures of India, the city and the agrarian landscape. As Nehru wished to eradicate poverty through industrialisation and urban commerce, whereas Gandhi idealised diverse self-governing communities in both the rural and urban landscapes. A vigorous community life is essential in the rural village, as it is in any urban neighbourhood, the building block of a successful city. An enviable India-the largest democracy, a vibrant self-reliant nation as the World is looking towards India as a leading player at Global political and economic landscapes' with proper skill empowerment of our youngsters, we can really show the World, we have the largest skilfully employable people, worthy entrepreneurs with Indian MNCs behind them and professionals.

□

Chartered Accountant with career spanning 4 decades. He is a proficient speaker and his views on contemporary issues have been widely published in various journals in India and abroad.

Self-Reliant India

—**Dr. J.P. Bhartiya**

India is a great country rich in its youth, manpower & natural resources.

It is very surprising that even after 73 years of independence, most of our population is living in abject misery and below the poverty line.

We are almost completely dependent on other countries even for essential items such as edible oils, pharmaceuticals, health care equipment's & military hardware. In times of crisis like pandemic, natural calamities or warlike situation, we find ourselves in a very hopeless position looking for immediate assistance from other countries. This precarious situation propels us towards SELF-RELIANCE or atmanirbharta i.e. producing and manufacturing all the required things in our own country.

Atmanirbharta is the best way to prove the self-worthiness of those who are ultimately going to build our nation. It means livelihood for millions of people. Atmanirbharta also means आत्मविश्वास ie SELF-CONFIDENCE as well.

Self-reliance is not only MAKE IN INDIA or MAKE FOR INDIA but it also includes MAKE FOR WORLD.

We are supposed to develop an industrial ecosystem within which all industries can flourish.

Atmanirbharta is today's NEED, today's STRENGTH & it means Freedom from dependence. This freedom comes from Power (power of wealth & manpower), development, education & scientific research. The think-tank, intellectuals, administrators all have a role to play. Our thinking should be more realistic & result-oriented. Emphasis must be on modernisation. The mindset and actions of the individuals & entrepreneurs will make all the difference.

Even as the Government is trying to revive businesses and industry, much more is desired in this direction. It requires a host of policy changes at the Centre and State level. Ease of doing business needs friendly policies, easy loans and helpful laws concerning labour and land and commerce etc. Licence Raj, Red Tapism should not come in the way. New Start-ups should be given all the facilities and encouragement to attract new blood.

Excellence can not be obtained in one stroke. It is multi-pronged, which is based on Govt. Efficiency, (reforms) Infrastructure, Will of Entrepreneurs & Public demand.

To be self-reliant, non-essential imports should be stopped forthwith replacing them with local products. Initially, the imported items can be assembled here with their collaboration and the issue of indigenisation can be left to the local vendors under strict cost & quality control. The local workforce can be trained by their foreign counterparts or can be sent abroad for advanced training and knowledge.

It is also equally important to provide support to the local entrepreneurs giving them a level field to thrive. This will generate jobs and create wealth.

India has lot of opportunities in so many fields such as Entertainment, Tourism, Games, Toys, Automobiles, Electronics, Electric goods, Health & Wellness and Agriculture. Cottage industry, SMS Industries should be promoted keeping in mind the slogan:

'Vocal for Local.'

The start-ups need a push, a helping hand in the form of financial aid & technical support. This present crisis should be dealt effectively with discipline, self-confidence and innovation. Industrial Clusters can be created. Agriculture sector has tremendous scope which can be further expanded by modernisation and bringing latest equipments.

Our PM, Shri Modiji has announced "when the world is in crisis, we must pledge-a pledge which is bigger than the crisis itself. We must strive to make the 21st century India's century and the path is Self-reliance." People should be made conscious of local products made in India with a little dose of nationalism. 'VOCAL FOR LOCAL' should be our mission. The people should be urged to use only the indigenous goods.

The challenge is to keep pace with global developments for the end-user needs. Collaboration with technical giants is imperative for the latest technology to come to India, for developing our infrastructure and for nurturing our Indian companies.

Our doctors, engineers, scientists and researchers are among the best in the world. The biggest advantage which India has is its young population which is confident, skilled and has unique ideas to start their own ventures. Our land is full of natural resources, raw material and minerals. We only need innovation, upgradation and technology to come to our aid. Always remember "कोशिश करने वालों की कभी हार नहीं होती"

Spiritually also, we have to be more awakened so that our lives can be more meaningful, Self-reliant & peaceful. Let us keep our goals growing and the momentum continue.

Our cultural heritage should be preserved at all costs. Nationalism & social harmony would come along. Educating ourselves in every field is a must. Nelson Mandela had said "Education is the most powerful weapon by which you can change the world. Just believe in yourself, learn from your own mistakes."

"वसुधैव कुटुंबकम, बंधुत्व, विश्वास, सबका साथ सबका विकास" are the basis of our nationalism and a vibrant, Self-reliant nation. JAI HIND.

□

A doctor by profession and is past district governor in Lions Clubs International. He is a religious and spiritual person and serves the poor and needy.

Abrogation of Article 370: A Step Towards Atmanirbhar Bharat

—C.L. Shah

A Historic Decision

There is no denying this fact that 5 August, 2019 will be considered as a 'Red letter day' in the history of erstwhile Jammu & Kashmir state. A new era of normalcy dawned in Jammu and Kashmir with the historic decision of Indian Parliament to Abrogate Article 370 from the erstwhile J&K state and its subsequent bifurcation into two Union Territories i.e. J&K and Ladakh. The decision has definitely paved the way towards overall development of all the three regions viz-Jammu, Kashmir and Ladakh.

The Article 370 and Article 35A were like a blot on heaven called Jammu and Kashmir but thanks to Prime Minister Narendra Modi who eradicated this blot from our heaven. After the abrogation of article 370, J&K has been transforming from a 'separate state' to a 'super state'.

The End of Mustafa Hegemony

With the rise of pan-Islamisation of insurgency which still has scriptural belief of 'Ghazwa-e-Hind', whereby Islamic forces led by them will break up and subjugate India, a dream to establish 'Nizam-e-Mustafa' in the state of Jammu & Kashmir was shattered on 5th August 2019, when Government of India revoked the special status or limited autonomy granted under Article 370 of the Indian Constitution to Jammu & Kashmir. The President of India under the power of Article 370, overriding the prevailing 1954 Presidential Order, issued an order to nullify all the provisions of autonomy granted to the state. On the same day, the Hon'ble Home Minister, Mr. Amit Shah, introduced the Jammu and Kashmir Reorganisation Bill, 2019 along with the resolution seeking revocation of the special status under Article 370 in the Upper House of Parliament to divide the state into two union territories to be governed by a lieutenant governor and a unicameral legislature which was debated and passed by the Rajya Sabha. On 6th August 2019, the said reorganisation bill along with the resolution recommending the revocation of Article 370 was discussed, debated, and passed in the Lok Sabha, India's lower house of parliament.

As per legal procedure, the Law Ministry came out with a gazette notification saying President Ram Nath Kovind has notified the revocation after the resolution to revoke Article 370 was passed by Lok Sabha a day after it was passed by the Rajya Sabha.

The declaration by the President states, "In exercise of the powers conferred by clause (3) of article 370 read with clause (1) of article 370 of the Constitution of India, the President, on the recommendation of Parliament, is pleased to declare that, as from the 6th August 2019, all clauses of the said article 370 shall cease to be operative except the following which shall read as under:

"All provisions of this Constitution, as amended from time to time, without any modifications or exceptions, shall apply to the State of Jammu and Kashmir notwithstanding anything contrary contained in article 152 or article 308 or any other article of this Constitution or any other provision of the Constitution of Jammu and Kashmir or any law, document, judgement, ordinance, order, by-law, rule, regulation, notification, custom or usage having the force of law in the territory of India, or any other instrument, treaty or agreement as envisaged under article 363 or otherwise."

Further, the Jammu and Kashmir Reorganisation Bill, 2019 also received the assent of the President of India on 9th August 2019, subsequent to which it was published in The Gazette of India. A notification published on the same day provides for the union territories to come into effect from 31st October, 2019.

The Conception and Birth of Article 370

In 1949, the then Prime Minister of India, Jawaharlal Nehru directed Kashmiri leader, Sheikh Muhammad Abdullah who took oath as Prime

Minister of Jammu and Kashmir on 17th March, 1948, to consult Dr. B.R Ambedkar to prepare a draft suitable for Jammu and Kashmir. But Dr. B.R Ambedkar, who was the first Law Minister of India and also the chairman of the Constitution drafting committee, refused to draft Article 370 because he was strictly opposed to get such dirt inserted in the Indian Constitution. Sheikh Mohammad Abdullah also wanted it should not be placed in Indian Constitution as a temporary provision, but wanted permanent autonomy for the state of Jammu and Kashmir.

Dr. Ambedkar thought that by inserting that Article and making limited application of laws made by Parliament for the state of Jammu and Kashmir would create lots of problem in the years to come and therefore, Dr. B.R Ambedkar had refused to draft Article 370 of Indian Constitution by saying, "You wish India should protect your border, she should build roads in your areas, she should supply you foodgrains and Kashmir should get equal status as India. But government of India should have only limited powers and Indian people should have no right in Kashmir. To give consent to your proposal would be treacherous thing against the interest of India and I, as a Law Minister of India, will never do".

When Dr. B.R Ambedkar refused to draft Article 370 as part of Indian Constitution, Sheikh Muhammad Abdullah approached Pt. Nehru again. And on the direction of Pt. Nehru, Gopalaswami Ayyangar, the man trusted by Nehru, drafted Article 370 after Dr. Ambedkar's refusal.

Thereafter, Article 370 was made a temporary provision of the Indian Constitution which gave special status to the State of Jammu and Kashmir. Under this Article, all the provisions of Indian Constitution were not applicable to the state of Jammu & Kashmir.

Article 370 Gave Idea of Separatism

According to Article 370, the Parliament needs the state's concurrence to apply any laws in Jammu & Kashmir except defence, foreign affairs, finance, and communications. The citizens of Jammu & Kashmir live with separate laws as compared to other states of India. The laws relating to citizenship, transfer of property even their fundamental rights are also different from other states. Under this Article, the Central Government have no power to declare financial emergency in the state. The Central government can only declare emergency in case of war or external disturbances. A citizen from other states is not permitted to purchase land in Jammu & Kashmir. Under this Article, Parliament has no power to increase or reduce the border of the state.

Under Article 370, the residents of Jammu & Kashmir had separate laws including citizenship, fundamental rights, and ownership of property. Top of all, the Directive Principles of State Policy and Fundamental Duties, as mentioned in the Constitution of India, were not applicable to Jammu & Kashmir, thereby it had autonomous state power.

Article 370 Cause of Corruption & Terrorism

Due to Article 370, the state of Jammu and Kashmir was a 'broken state' and there was 'no system' in place, due to years of misgovernance, corruption and unbelievable levels of fraud committed by the leaders of mainstream political parties and separatist organisations. Therefore, not a 'single soul had cried' over the detention of political and separatist leaders in August last year when the Centre announced its decision to revoke Jammu and Kashmir's special status under Article 370 of the Constitution and introduce the Jammu and Kashmir Reorganisation Bill, 2019.

There were scores of incomplete projects, land acquisition scams and dozens of instances pertaining to doctors working in the Middle East, who continued to draw salaries from the Jammu and Kashmir treasuries as there was no system to monitor and trace these financial transactions. The laws were made fragile to enable the menace of corruption get unnoticed in back door appointments. The interview system was abolished in Government recruitments with the result that deserving and meritorious candidates were left out to get their deserved right as there was no fair selection process in place.

Even the Jammu and Kashmir High Court has recently hauled up the authorities for decades of delay caused by investigative agencies in filing charge sheets against government servants in corruption cases. Data gathered from anti-corruption court in Jammu have shown that charge sheets had not been filed in a large number of cases, some of which were more than 22 years old. In Jammu alone, no charge sheets have been filed in as many as 226 cases registered from 1996 to 2008.

The Jammu and Kashmir High Court also observed that cases wherein charge sheets had not been filed, pertained to cases of forgery, bribery, misuse of government money, fictitious withdrawals from treasury, embezzlement of government money, disbursement of loans without proper documents, allotment of public works without tendering process, possession of assets disproportionate to known sources of income, fabrication of fictitious bills for purchase of goods and services, etc.

People in Jammu and Kashmir will have to keep patience to enjoy a whole lot of benefits of the Centre's move to nullify Article 370 as many positive initiatives have not been rolled out fully yet. Maintaining that there will be zero tolerance for corruption and terrorism under Narendra Modi Government, the administration is working sincerely to create a robust, transparent and institutional framework, which is free of corruption.

Integration of Whole of Jammu & Kashmir Not Yet Complete

Pakistan-occupied Kashmir (PoK) historically belonged to Maharaja Hari Singh, the erstwhile ruler of the princely state of Jammu and Kashmir. On 21st October, 1947, several thousand Pashtun tribesmen from the North-West Frontier Province (NWFP) supported by the Pakistan army infiltrated into Jammu and Kashmir in order to liberate it from the Maharaja's rule. The soldiers of Maharaja tried to avert this invasion, but the pro-Pakistan rebellions were armed with modern armaments and gained control of almost the entire region called Pakistan occupied Kashmir (PoK) which includes Gilgit-Baltistan. But on 24 October, 1947, the Maharaja requested for the military assistance of India, which provided the assistance on the condition that Maharaja Hari Singh has to sign an 'Instrument of Accession'. On 26 October, 1947, Maharaja Hari Singh signed the Instrument of Accession and agreed to accede to the Dominion of India. Hence, PoK is legitimately an inherent part of India but under Pakistan's unlawful control ever since the Pakistan army orchestrated the tribal invasion of the territory in 1947.

A part of Pakistan-occupied Kashmir's Hunza-Gilgit, the Shaksgam Valley, region of Raksam and Baltistan was handed over to China by Pakistan in 1963. This area is called a ceded area or Trans-Karakoram Tract.

Aksai Chin is a disputed border area between China and India since 1950. India claims that China has occupied approximately 37,244 sq. km. area of Jammu and Kashmir by constructing a road connecting Tibet and Xinjiang in the year 1957. This development led to Indo-China war of 1962. India further claims that this invaded area being part of the Ladakh region, has been administratively made a part of the Kargilic district of Xinjiang Province.

India has always maintained that the PoK is part of the whole of Jammu and Kashmir. On 22 February, 1994, both Houses of Indian Parliament adopted a resolution that J&K is an integral part of India and therefore, Pakistan & China must vacate portions of the state that is under their illegal occupation.

While abolishing Jammu and Kashmir's Constitution in August 2019, the bill declaring J&K a Union Territory in its clause 14 sub-section 4 (a) states, "Until the area of the Union Territory of Jammu and Kashmir under the occupation of Pakistan ceases to be so occupied and the people residing in that area elect their representatives, 24 seats in the legislative assembly of Union Territory of Jammu and Kashmir shall remain vacant and shall not be taken into account for reckoning the total membership of the assembly. Interestingly, the Lok Sabha does not provide for a Parliament seat in PoK, despite India declaring PoK an integral part.

During the discussion over the abrogation of Article 370 and Jammu and Kashmir Reorganisation Bill, 2019 in Parliament, the Home Minister, Amit Shah, asserted that PoK and Aksai Chin are part of India and BJP leaders would sacrifice their lives for the region. Speaking on how the government plans to take back PoK, Shah had said that PoK and Aksai Chin would be integrated and when it happens, people will come to know as they did in case of Article 370.

Under the Modi 2.0 regime, India can proactively pursue its claim on PoK and Aksai Chin, in order to alter the discourse in her favour. India should develop a blueprint to recalibrate its approach on this long pending issue.

Development Mantra after Abrogation of Article 370

After abrogation of Article 370 and bifurcation of the state of Jammu and Kashmir into the Union Territories of Jammu and Kashmir and Ladakh, a special developmental plan for the UTs has been worked out which includes the setting up of industries, state-of-the-art educational institutes, healthcare facilities etc.

The government believes that the change in Jammu & Kashmir's status will encourage private sector investment in the new Union territory. Till now, the provisions of Articles 370 and 35A have prevented business houses from purchasing land and hiring skilled manpower in the state. The change in administrative status, the government believes, will have a positive impact on the ease of doing business, as it would give industry ownership of establishments and will encourage hiring.

The potential growth areas have been identified as tourism, hydropower, horticulture, floriculture, bio-medicinal plants, food processing, handicrafts and handlooms. With the change in local laws, it has made it possible for industrialists from anywhere in the country, to set up enterprises to spur industrialisation, growth and multiply enormous job opportunities for local youth.

In the past one year, the local administration of UTs of Jammu & Kashmir and Ladakh have been proactive to promote trade-related activities and infrastructure and have successfully levelled the field for these UTs to integrate in the country's growth journey. It is indeed the next destination for investment with progressive and competitive investors and friendly policies.

Delimitation

Delimitation is the process of fixing limits or boundaries of territorial constituencies in a country or a province, with a legislative body.

The Government of India vide notification issued on 6th March, 2020 constituted a Delimitation Commission to redraw Lok Sabha and Assembly Constituencies of the Union Territory of Jammu and Kashmir and the North-Eastern States of Assam, Arunachal Pradesh, Manipur and Nagaland.

The last delimitation across the country was conducted in 2002, but these states were left out due to various reasons. In the four states of North-East India, delimitation could not be carried out along with other Indian states due to prevailing security reasons. But now, the government thinks the situation has changed.

The delimitation in the Union Territory of Jammu and Kashmir comes seven months after the controversial Article 370 was scrapped and the state was divided into two Union Territories. The Jammu and Kashmir Reorganisation Act 2019, which was cleared in Parliament in August 2019, mentioned new delimitation to redraw the constituencies of Jammu and Kashmir according to section 62 of the Act.

The setting up of Delimitation Commission for the Union Territory of Jammu & Kashmir is a welcome step. However, to base it on 2011 census will be a faulty exercise. Even a child in street knows that census data of 2011 pertaining to Jammu and Kashmir was fudged and using it for delimiting new constituencies will be a mistake and injustice to the people of the state.

Under the new domicile law, the communities like Valmikis, West Pakistan refugees and Gurkhas, who were deprived of equal rights for years in Jammu & Kashmir, are now being granted domicile certificates, therefore, their headcount should also be included in the delimitation process.

As 2021 census is on the anvil, we, therefore, urge Government of India to review its decision. Otherwise, the Delimitation process based on the 2011 fudged census and exclusion of new domicile certificate holders, will again help Kashmiri Mustafa leaders to re-establish Islamic rule in Jammu & Kashmir.

Political Process

With the Delimitation Commission in place and election to the UT Legislative Assembly slated post the delimitation, UT of Jammu and Kashmir will soon return into the new hands of political leadership. The appointment of Manoj Sinha as J&K's Lieutenant Governor is considered as a move meant to resume the political process in J&K. Known for his political acumen and administrative ability, Manoj Sinha will be the second politician to occupy Raj Bhawan in Jammu and Kashmir to shape the new journey of progress, prosperity and development of Naya Kashmir. The duly elected peoples' representatives will soon lead the destiny of Jammu and Kashmir.

A Comparative Chart Showing Changes in the Union Territories of Jammu & Kashmir and Ladakh before and after Abrogation of Article 370 and Article 35A

Before	After
Article 370 of Indian Constitution accorded special status to the state, allowing it to have its own constitution.	Jammu & Kashmir and Ladakh will be like any other Indian state or union territory.
Most of the laws except defence, foreign affairs, finance and communication, passed by Indian Parliament, need to be approved by the State Government before they are made applicable in the State.	Centre responsible for administrative and local regulations also.

Under Article 370, the Indian Parliament cannot increase or reduce the borders of the State.	Abrogation of Article 370 facilitated to carve out a separate UT of Ladakh.
The state of Jammu & Kashmir has two flags; a separate State Flag along with the National Flag.	Only Indian Tricolour National Flag will fly high.
Insulting of national symbols is not cognizable offence in the State of Jammu & Kashmir.	The Prevention of Insults to National Honour Act, 1971 is now applicable.
Unlike other State legislative Assemblies, J&K legislature has a six-year term.	It will have 5-year term.
The Jammu & Kashmir Constitution provided separate posts for Sadar-e-Riyasat(President) and Wazir-e-Azam (Prime Minister), that gave birth to the idea of separatism in the State.	All such posts are abolished.
The Centre has no power to declare financial emergency under Article 360 in the State.	Article 360 made applicable.
Majority of Indian laws including RTE, RTI and powers granted to statutory authorities like CAT, CIC, CVC etc. are not applicable in the State of J&K.	All these laws will be now applicable.
The citizens of J&K are governed by State-specific laws, which come under the Constitution of Jammu and Kashmir.	All citizens of Union Territories of Jammu & Kashmir and Ladakh will be governed by the Indian Constitution.
State assembly defined 'Permanent residents' of the State.	Section 3A & Section 5A of the Jammu and Kashmir Reorganisation (Adaptation of State Laws) Order, 2020 defines domicile and his special rights.
The residents of J&K enjoy dual citizenship of Jammu & Kashmir and India.	J&K and Ladakh residents will have single citizenship of India
If a woman marries a man in other Indian States, she loses her citizenship of Jammu & Kashmir. Whereas if she marries a person from Pakistan, then Pakistani man gets citizenship of Jammu & Kashmir.	All these rights & privileges stand cancelled.
The Article 370 gives Pakistan's citizens entitlement to Indian citizenship, if he marries a Kashmiri girl.	All these rights are revoked.
Non-residents of J&K could not permanently settle in the State.	Any Indian can settle in J&K

Non-residents could not buy immovable property or acquire land in the State.	Non-residents having domicile certificates can buy land but Industrial units can buy land on 90 years' lease only.
Any J&K resident woman married to a non-resident could not inherit property	Resident woman married to a non-resident can inherit property.
Directive Principles of State Policy (DPSP) as mentioned in Part 4 of the Indian Constitution are not applicable in the State	DPSP applicable.
Panchayats did not have any rights in the State	Panchayats will have the same rights as in other states and union territories.
The Scheduled Tribe (ST) community comprising of Gujjars, Bakarwals & others did not have any political reservation in the State.	The Scheduled Tribes & Other Traditional Forest Dwellers (Recognition of Forest Rights) Act,2006 has been made applicable.
SC, OBC and Safai Karamcharis were not getting benefits of reservation in the State.	All these categories will get full benefits of reservation, like in the rest of the country.
Over 20,000 West Pakistan refugees living in Jammu since 1947 are denied democratic rights as well as citizenship and property rights in the State.	They will enjoy all democratic and other rights as citizens of the country.
Over 600 Valmiki Dalit families (Safai Karamcharis) living in Jammu since 1947 were denied Permanent Residency Certificate in the State.	They will enjoy all democratic and other rights as citizens of the country.
No reservation for minorities such as Hindus and Sikhs.	Minorities will be eligible for 16% reservation.

Conclusion

The people of Jammu and Kashmir will benefit immensely from the abrogation of Article 370 and its bifurcation into two Union Territories. These two historic legislations will enable the people to access and enjoy the same rights, same privileges and same facilities as their fellow citizens enjoy in the rest of the country.

□

B.Sc., FCA, FCS, FCMA and is a financial and corporate consultant. He is also a migrant Kashmiri Pandit.

Towards Making India Self-reliant

—N.K. Upadhyay

Background

India has attained a distinct position in the global emerging economies. It has taken a lead in many frontiers, and set an example for developing countries to follow, be it sufficiency of food, dairy etc. through its green revolution and white revolution. It was the need of the time and we proved that it can be done and achieved. We have excelled in space science and many more frontiers of science. The proactive industry initiatives especially software and pharmaceuticals, has placed India as a source of reliable, competitive and innovative products. India has not only fulfilled its own requirements, but sectors like above became a source of foreign currency also. There are many more examples. However, if we introspect, we will find that we have missed to create sufficient base for manufacturing consumer durables like mobile phones, electronics, solar photovoltaic, telecom etc.

In the past, there have been efforts to create and take a lead in solar photovoltaic and for that purpose, facilities were created to develop solar photovoltaic cells, panels to tap renewal energy which is abundantly available in India but the scale and push to achieve was marred by more competitive and aggressive approach in this area by China. Perhaps, the priorities were misplaced or misinterpreted when there was need to create efficient, sustainable and robust system to develop.

Present Situation

We have a huge trade deficit. What is needed is to curtail imports, and at the same time boost exports. These two areas require lots of brain storming. However with the good governance and direction, this can be achieved.

There is an urgent need to take a quantum jump. We can't afford to move at a snail's pace. So what is needed is to create a clear, determined and achievable roadmap for short term and long term. We need to specify the priority areas.

Optimisation

The situation demands introspection, firstly at the individual level "whether I need this article/product without which I can't lead my normal life" and then at nation's level. Everyone has to align with nation's priorities. A cumulative effect will bring change in people's thinking, thus reducing imports of non-essentials.

There is also a need to inculcate in people's mind the saying that "one drop saved is one drop produced", thereby suggesting not to waste even a drop or grain thereby maximising utility of available resources.

Imports Revisit

Categorisation of imports–Segregate the essential imports, not so essential imports and non-essential imports. What is meant here for non-essential import is the goods and services for luxury, entertainment etc. for example, toys and consumable articles like items related to our festivals and high-end gadgets, be it luxury mobiles, watches etc.

How to control imports of non-essential items. First of all, we all admit that the precious foreign exchange can not be drained for non-essential imports especially when the country is passing through a difficult phase. Creating a list of such items and permission mechanism to be introduced. Secondly, measures like imposing import duty on e.g. luxury goods, which will discourage such imports. May be, no institutional loan facility for import and distribution of items under such category to importers and distributors.

Another suggestion is on import of low-end mobile and other gadgets, if can't be supplied indigenously for the time being such imports to be allowed in bulk by a few importers, who should assure the nation that such phones etc. will be manufactured in India within a time-frame. This will ensure self-sufficiency and at the same time, create employment opportunities.

Priority Areas

Sectors like lifesaving drugs/devices, industry and defence, essential electronics, telecommunication, raw material and intermediates for pharmaceutical industry etc. are few of the items that need attention.

Secondly, developing technologies, goods and services for infrastructure, and newer frontiers which will give edge to India in the strategic areas like robotics, artificial intelligence, clean energy etc. These need long-term planning and policy for financial and advisory support.

Funding

The resources like trained and qualified manpower, technologies and funds for the essential strategic areas are to be selectively drawn and used. Funds are scarce.

It is suggested that about 10% of Corporate Social Responsibility fund from industry to be pooled under one **Self reliant Fund, SRF**. This SRF would be a huge amount to begin with, to fund at least one of the focus areas.

Capacity Building

Another activity is to develop export capabilities of indigenous industry–this is one of the potential areas which may turn out to be a big export revenue generator. There are no dearth of examples where exotic fruits, vegetables, floriculture have successfully been grown at individual level thus proved that these can be grown in India. A few of such growers have also manufactured value added products and exported. But many of the enthusiasts are left alone, and without proper technological and advisory inputs, they lurch and end up in low profit margins and discouraged lot. These people need handholding.

Suggestion: There are number of exporters, who are well experienced about the market needs, processing and procedures and at the same time, technical expertise is available at institutional and/or individual level who can guide such growers on how to convert their produce to high value, long life and competitive products as per international standards. For the purpose as a **Guru Shisjya parampara** the existing exporters, preferably in the same area should be encouraged to handhold one or two such enthusiastic growers and guide them technically and on how to export. The existing exporters may be asked/ incentivised to personally involve in the process. Once the grower is versed with and equipped with the knowledge, he himself becomes a guide for others.

The model can be replicated for other sectors like agriculture and herbals etc.

Reinforce Strength

India has strength in basic pharmaceuticals but there is a need to develop and manufacture intermediates and inventing/ innovating new molecules for life-saving areas which not only save foreign currency but by exporting them, the country can earn huge foreign currency.

One of the promising areas could be the raw materials like rare earths Minerals extraction which can be converted to value added product. This is not only of commercial advantage but will give India strategic lead in semiconductors, electronics etc. Likewise, support for other ores and minerals available in India.

Highly skilled manpower in the area of IT, pharma, research and development, space science etc. is yet another strength. Ways and means to be devised for the individual sector to tap further potential.

Health sector, whether it is Ayurveda, Yogi, modern hospital services, procedure and health care; these are other promising areas for earning foreign currency.

Create Common Facility Centers, CFC

Create CFC at and around large clusters of producers of agriculture, dairy, herbs etc. The growers can bring their produce to these CFCs and under expert guidance and available state-of-the-art equipment and machinery, convert their produce to high value products. Further, if industries are also involved at this level, they can buy the products and transport, store, package and market. There will be a win-win situation for growers, common facility centers and industry.

These CFC's can be created by government and industry partnership on PPP model. A colossal wastage can be avoided. It is estimated that around 40 % is wasted annually and situation has not improved since decades.

To sum up:

1. Self-commitment, do I really need this product, can I do away with this. This self-discipline will save a lot without compromising essential needs. The message should percolate down the line through advertisements, counseling etc.
2. No to wastage-one drop saved is one drop produced.
3. Identify core areas and create targeted time-bound plan.
4. Developing funding mechanism for the core areas, redirecting

available funds like corporate social responsibility funds, may be 50%, which otherwise are used by industry of their own. Time demands that all efforts should merge with nation priorities.

5. Creating pool of experts for novice and potential growers/ manufacturers of industrial goods to make them successful exporters.
6. Creating Common Facility Centers under PPP model.
7. Developing and converting available resources e.g natural sources and skilled manpower etc.
8. Devise ways and means to control recurring calamities like flood, drought.

□

M.Sc. (AIC), MBA (United Kingdom) with around 40 years dedicated service to the nation in fields of science and technology.

Industrial Development & Atmanirbhar Bharat

—Ram Prakash

Under the dynamic leadership of Hon. Prime Minister Shri Narendra Modiji, India is attaining New Heights. He is not an ordinary Manav. In my opinion, He is Maha Manav, who is dedicated and committed--a leader with Clear-cut Vision with Priorities all set. He is a leader who owns responsibility and leads from the front.

He has understood the role of MSME and taken good steps to encourage the same.

Some of his achievements on ground level are as under:

(A) Availability of Bank Credit and Affordability:
Reduction in rates of Interest.
There has been a marked improvement in the above two important Fiscal matters in the last few years.

(B) 'Vocal for Local' and 'Make Local Sell Global' are some of the important steps initiated by the Present Govt in achieving Atmanirbhar Bharat. Continuous dialogue with the Industry and taking steps to improve business environment are again typical of this Government which are proving to be a shot in the arm for the Atmanirbhar Bharat.
Imposing Anti Dumping Duties, Discouraging Imports and Requesting large corporates to encourage 'Make in India' are having an impact.
Today, Maruti has started preferring local manufacturers over imports—is because of Government push only.
We have moved ahead; however, there are still some areas which are a stumbling block towards growth of Atmanirbhar Bharat.

For Growth of Industry, I can identify the following factors which need Govt push:

(C) Availability and Quality of Electric power:

Although many improvements have been carried out, still some power reforms are required:

There is no answerability of the Discoms about the loss of business, when electricity fails.

Discoms be held responsible for any electricity related loss to MSMEs.

Although Solar power is slowly catching up and is a great source of alternate cheap energy. Govt has done a good job in promoting Solar energy across the Country.

(D) Another area which needs atrention is the availability of Skilled Manpower. Although much has been attempted in this direction, we are still far from Reality.

Although many schemes on Skilling and Reskilling have started, we still find that the availability of the skilled manpower is scarce, and because of this big factor, most of the Industries are not able to run at optimum level.

We need workers. We have enough of Supervisors and Managers but ground level workers are not available.

Another reason is our social fabric. No person wants his son to become a worker. Everyone wants his son/daughter to be a Manager.

In this process, even the National Education Policy needs amendment to give more focus on Vocational Studies.

(E) Now that a new Educational policy is under implementation, we hope it will make a headway soon.

We are sure under the Dynamic Leadership of Hon Prime Minister Narendra Modiji, India will surely regain its historic '*Sone ki Chidiya*' status soon.

Bhiwadi—Gateway to a New Rajasthan. Gateway to an Industrialised Rajasthan-A new Rajasthan more than just Camels and Hand Weavers. A new Emerging Rajasthan full of Industrial Possibilities.

Bhiwadi was planned by RIICO (Rajasthan Investment and Industrial Development Corporation)—way back in 1980.

Since then, it has emerged as the Highest Contributor to the State Exchequer as well as a significant Contributor to National Exchequer too. Today, it houses more than 5000 Tiny, Small, Medium and Large Industries including well-known Multinational Brands such as HONDA, SAINT GOBAIN, CHAMPION, BAUSCH AND LOMB and many others.

It is on the edge of National Capital Delhi and Gurugram which is full of entrepreneurial talent.

The Rajasthan Government has been doing its bit in the field of Infrastructure Development. However, the State Government has its own limitations and now the time has come for the Central Government leadership under Hon'ble Prime Minister Sh Narendra Modi to pitch in directly.

The time demands him to play a Steller role (As he played during his leadership in Gujarat).

Bhiwadi has the potential to invite a lot of FDI in the region.

I have a few suggestions worthy of his precious time and Energy:

(A) Provision of a Halting Station for Bhiwadi and adjoining Industrial Area in the Rapid Transit Delhi-Alwar corridor. This will not only help in providing job opportunities to youth of the nearby rural population but will also help the industries tap this young population to train and adopt for exponential growth.

(B) DMRC is passing through Bhiwadi Region. It does not help the region if there is no Loading/ Unloading Station. With potential to Export a sizable quantity, connectivity of Bhiwadi Region to the Seaport is of utmost Importance.

The second request is to create a Multi Modal connectivity to the Seaport.

(C) I understand Central Government is planning a 'Cargo only Airport' in the vicinity. I welcome this step. However, the need is to develop a Passenger Airport as well. I see a lot of possibility of Air Passenger traffic. So if it is planned right away, it will prove to be a good step towards increasing the share of export business from India from this region.

(D) Creation of Good International Level Universities and Educational Facilities in and around the Region. With not even a Single degree college in the Region, we lack in providing Quality Education to our youth in the rural areas. We have to depend on nearby States for Education beyond High Schools.

Boys somehow manage to stay in Hostels of nearby States, Girls are denied the opportunity of higher Education. We all know your love for Girl Child Education and request your attention towards this.

Bhiwadi Industrial Area is a Mini India and can truly represent India's stride forward.

It houses the most diverse Industries in all sectors—right from Kutir Udyog to a Large Multinational Conglomerate such as HONDA.

It has working population from all parts of not only India but from the whole World. We can find experts from East and the West and from North to the South of India.

We have Expats from Korea, Japan, Germany, France and USA, working for this Mini India.

Being close to New Delhi, it is only an hour away from the seat of power.

Under the Dynamic leadership, very bold decisions have been taken in the past such as Demonetisation, Introduction of GST, Merger of Banks, thereby improving the business scenario and the Ease of Doing business ranking for the country.

Other bold political decisions of Article 370, CAA and other matters have shown the iron will of the Hon Prime Minister Sh Narendra Modiji.

Handling of the Covid Pandemic is again an example of Great Governance.

Government push for Atmanirbhar Bharat and Swadeshi, will usher in a new Era for the Young India.

The whole world has recognised India's strength and command in IT Sector.

Now with 'Make In India' and 'Vocal for Local', we will see India Emerge as a Global Manufacturing Hub for the World.

India today is the highest recipient of FDI worldwide and certainly these reforms will bring a boost to local manufacturing. These steps will certainly create many new jobs for the Indian Youth--be it manufacturing, or even the Service Industry.

India is moving fast towards not only in the direction of self-reliance but also towards Export. 'Make Local Sell Global' is the latest mantra.

Who could think India could start planning towards Exports of Defence items hitherto reserved for highly developed Countries like

USA, GERMANY, FRANCE, JAPAN etc.

India is moving fast in this very strategic direction of Exports of Defence Equipments for the World.

We are in safe hands of the Present Government under Sh. Narendra Modi as Prime Minister.

Natural Calamities such as present flood-like situations do dampen our march towards self-reliance. However, India is known for bouncing back to normalcy sooner than the World after such natural calamities.

I am sure India would certainly find long-term solutions to such natural calamities.

We are not far from our old '*Sone ki Chidiya*' and this time, it will be '*Sone ka Baaz*' in place of '*Chidiya*'.

Long live India.

GOD BLESS US ALL.

JAI HIND

JAI BHARAT

□

Mechanical engineer from IIT Delhi and Ex President, Bhiwadi Manufacturers' Association.

Atmanirbhar Bharat

—Arvind Singh

Recently, we experienced a sudden crisis that we had never thought of, and it affected the globally dependent economies in a hazardous way and of course, our economy also felt a widespread slowdown. This was the time when every country of the world was working hard to revive their economy, there our nation was looking for a new opportunity.

It was much anticipated that Corona would affect our economy in a very harsh manner and now the official data is proving that. At this juncture, the visionary Prime Minister of India, honourable Mr. Narendra Modi initiated 'Atmanirbhar Bharat', to make India a self-reliant nation. Our Prime minister always thinks that crisis brings opportunity, therefore, this ongoing crisis also brought opportunity to be self-reliant. These days not only we are fighting with Corona but also on border a deceit from expansionist China. So in this situation, it is very much necessary to be self-reliant.

First of all, we have to know, what is a self-reliant nation, because after announcement of this initiative, many people were confronted with different set of queries like, we don't have technology and factors of production, how shall we become self-reliant? But all these queries are absolutely confusing; however, self-reliance implies "to have that much of capacity so that we can manufacture product from available factors by learning new technology." If we do achieve self-reliance, then we shall be able to reduce our dependence on other countries.

Atmanirbhar Bharat

Now the question is, why do we need a self-reliant India and when can any country be self-reliant? Self-reliance depends on availability and abundance of resources in any country. Our India is a big and resource-abundant country. In India, every resource is available in enough quantity and we can produce every product in our country and for this, we don't have to rely on any other country. For this thing, youth must have a strong will-power and efficiency in work. It is not like we don't have those types of people. In our country, we have such types of people who can do anything for our country.

If we take a glance of the world data, then we see that almost all of IT sector of the world is dependent on Indians. In 2017, Nasscom's Chairman Raman Roy told that even credit cards and insurance policies can not be sold without Indian talent, so we are solution to their problem. He also said that US do not have talented employees, that's why they are employing approx. 60 thousand workers under H1B Visa.

Therefore, we can say, India has enough of human resources and natural resources as well. Natural resources are the resources which are obtained directly from the nature.

In India, we have plenty of natural resources. According to GSI, we have 400 places in 50 mineral fields, in spite of all these, we are dependent on the world for everything from pin to aircraft, that's the tragedy with us.

Our legendary PM started this initiative to fulfil the dream of Mahatma. Mr. Deendayal Upadhyaya also suggested that deterioration of national Identity is also the reason for ongoing problems. Earlier we had boycotted the English goods, but now this looks very surprising that now when the Britishers are gone, Westernisation had become the synonym of development.

Keeping these things in mind to re-energise the spirit of India, our PM put forward Atmanirbhar Bharat programme in front of us.

Benefits:

- Reduction in dependence on any nation.
- Growth of industry and prospering of local market.
- Rise in employment and efficiency.
- Free from unemployment as well as poverty.
- Growth in National income.
- Increase in export and reduction in import.
- Food security.
- Empowerment of nation on every front.

According to Prime minister "Atmanirbhar Bharat means creation of a self-reliant nation, not a self-centered nation."

We always followed the principle of '*Vasudhaiv Kutumbakam*' meaning the whole world is our family, so If India will develop, it will contribute to the development of the whole world.

Therefore, India has banned many Chinese apps and games; in this field Indian app developers have immense opportunities.

In Annual CII meeting, Prime Minister Modi suggested that to increase the growth of India and to be self-reliant, five I's are necessary, which are the following:

- Intent
- Inclusion
- Investment
- Infrastructure
- Innovation

For this programme, government has announced a package of 20 lakh crore, which is equal to 10 percent of GDP. Package will be focused on four L's (Land, Labour, Liquidity and Laws).

This will be divided into two steps; first step would be concentrated to enhance growth of these sectors viz. Health, Textiles, Electronics, Plastic and toys, and this will lead to production in local market and export in Global markets. Second step would be to ensure growth of Gems and jewelleries, Pharma and steel industries.

Under this programme, several steps have been taken for Agriculture and farmers, in which some important ones are the following:

- Allocation of 11lakh crore for the establishment of agriculture infrastructure.
- Allocation of 10 thousand crore for formalisation of micro food units.
- Allocation of 2000 crore for fishermen under Pradhan Mantri Matsya Sampada Yojana.
- Allocation of 15000 crore for setting up founding stone for Animal husbandry.
- Allocation of 4000 crore for Herbal farming.
- Allocation of 500 crore for bee-keeping.
- Allocation of 500 crore for fruits and vegetables and expansion of Operation Green.
- Some Amendment would be brought in necessary food items (Cereals, oils, pulses, onion and potato).

- Improvements in Inter-state Agriculture marketing would be made through new laws.
- Price and Quality assurance would be given to farmers through facilitating agriculture produce.

Beneficiary:

- Poor citizen of India
- Labour
- Migrant labour
- Animal keeper
- Fishermen
- Farmers
- Persons of organised and unorganised sector
- Tenant
- Cottage industries
- Small industries
- Medium industries

This can be said that this programme will help our nation grow in a balanced and quicker way, will create employment and will provide opportunities in industry and agriculture. This programme will take India to its Golden age for which India was known.

□

M.Com and Managing Editor in 'Manthan' Magazine and a social and political activist.

Self-reliant India: Today's Necessity

—R.C. Naithani

Atmanirbhar Bharat or Self-reliant India—is a great idea. But is broadly misinterpreted purely due to selfish interests/lack of communication & poor understanding, in general public.

The Prime Minister's call for 'Atmanirbhar Bharat' or 'Self-Reliant India' has resonated in the minds of young India & given tremendous rise to the spirit of nationalism urging the country to go for 'Make in India' mantra. One can term the later i.e. 'Make in India', in larger sense, an integral part of former. The whole idea is to make the country self sufficient, self independent & powerful, and not dependent on external forces. It is not that PM has spoken about 'Atmanirbhar Bharat' or 'Self-Reliant India' only now, but also in 2014, the PM did the same by coining the 'Make in India' mantra.

The biggest reason for failure, was at the door of the initiators of that time who could not do their job well by giving head start to the 'Make in India" campaign, by creating and turning it into a social tornado by running door-to-door awareness program, motivational classes at urban and rural, village level and by bringing it as government-funded scheme at panchayat level and turning it into a national priority for everyone everywhere.

We should introspect as to why, in spite of the right vision, given by our great ancestors & Hon'ble Prime Minister, its implementation had gone wrong and where?

We should learn from our past mistakes and do not repeat the same lest we again fall apart.

Once again, the call for a self-reliant India has been fueled by recent incidents such as the ongoing Covid-19 pandemic and the external threats to the country by its biggest neighbour, China.

To know the truth, we should examine, India's initial lack of domestic production of personal protective equipment (PPE) at the onset of the pandemic and the realisation of our heavy dependence on imports from other countries.

The Vision

'Make in India' was launched just after PM Modi came to power in 2014 and the 'Self-Reliant India' package of ₹ 20 lakh crore was announced for the economy's revival in the midst of the pandemic Covid-19 in the year 2020.

The 'self-reliant' program was launched with dual objectives of resurrecting the Indian economy through fiscal measures and to make the economy self-reliant, which by itself takes care of fledgeling manufacturing sector by spurring the growth of productivity and employment generation, thus creating a business-friendly environment that will help in increase of private investments and foreign capital whereas, earlier in 2014, the vision was to promote foreign investment in India by making it a favoured destination through improvements in its ease of doing business.

Now the question before us comes, what is the correct vision we should adopt in terms of objectives and goals for achieving the 'self-reliant India' target.

There are enough risks and temptations today in the 'Self-reliant India' slogan such as attempts to insulate the economy from the external world and thereby going back to the 'import substitution' in the Nehruvian era, as it means adopting tariff and non-tariff barriers to protect a nascent domestic industry. In May 2020, Hon'ble Minister Shri Nitin Gadkari although mentioned that the Centre is mulling over the idea of import substitution in the wake of the pandemic but the same types of tariff barriers cannot be thought of, in today's world.

The idea of third way propagated by Sangh Pracharak, Late Shri Dattopant Thengadi, who saw society as a whole and sought to maintain a balance between material and non-material needs while rejecting both the extremes of individual values (capitalism) and enforced collectivism (communism).

Today, it has so inter-woven the country's economy with the global one that it is hard to abandon the current version of Euro-centric economic model which is devoid of a sense of proportion, and thus necessitates a new phase of brainstorming... a new framework, new terms of reference, a new scale of values which would facilitate the globalisation, based on the Hindu principle of *dharma* which is the best guide to a new way of looking at the economy model based on 'Self-reliant India' mantra.

Scheme like Mudra loans to promote small, local entrepreneurship to vegetable vendor or local Chai wala, many of these ideas were first propogated in detail in The Third Way. For instance, the idea about the self-employed and small industries. The idea of self-employment was so embedded in Hindu culture that there was even a god for the craftsmen and self-employed, Vishwakarma. Today also, the Trade Unions celebrate the day of the Vishwakarma Puja as National Labour Day.

While the rural economists of that time were convinced in noting, that polluting countries shall never join hands with poorer nations to control ecological damage, and today we are seeing the catastrophic effects in term of 'Pandemic Covid-19'. Even as America has walked out of the global alliance called the 'Paris Accord"to fight climate change, it is interesting to read that Thengadi wrote, "... some of the advanced countries... do not want to co-operate with the efforts for ecological balance but... only dump their pollution in the courtyard of the developing countries. But this strategy cannot put off for long the global environmental catastrophe which would not spare the northern countries themselves. This is One World and adversity anywhere would, in the long run, destroy prosperity everywhere which would focus on collective happiness and not just on a relentless, competitive process of individual race to material prosperity.

Today, his spoken words a decade earlier, are coming true.

Sir, It is happening today, in the form of "Pandemic Covid-19". The whole world is reeling under the damaging effects of it. Millions of people in every country are duking it out today.

Need for self-reliance has to be inculcated at micro level and at the level of each and every household in the country if we really are serious and want to succeed in it in the near future.

Inequality of Wealth is a Major Irritant to the Road for 'Self-reliant India'

Further, while we are championing the cause of caste and creed *samrasta,* even in our many *anusangik sanghathan's* platforms, we are shying away from dicussing about *arthik samarasta* or equality of wealth among each and every creed, caste and household in the country.

From the ancient times, Hindus were divided and enticed to convert to other religions because they were cursed to live in abject poverty while the 'Kuleens' were having access to good food, living, wining and dining.

It is happening even today.

There is a rampant inequal distribution of wealth in society which requires no introduction and it is a major irritant for achieving 'the Self-Reliant India" tag to the country in near future. Policy makers must take this serpent head-on and through ordinance and law, it must be tackled.

Until the wealth is not equally distributed in real terms, the country cannot progress and our self-reliant India dreams will remain hollow.

Ancient India—A Self-Reliant India—THE GOLDEN SPARROW

Ancient India was called a Golden Sparrow, because it was wealthy, prosperous and had established Socio-economic systems. India has a long and successful history of trade with many different forms of business organisations including the *Sreni*. The *sreni* can be dated from a period much older than many would expect for the development of the corporate form–from around 800 B.C. This predates, by centuries, the earliest Roman proto-corporations. The details of *sreni's* formation, governance and regulation tell that its development corresponds well to more modern theories about the development of the corporate form. First Evidence of usage of Coins and replacement of barter system:

Around 600 BC, the Mahajanapadas minted punch-marked silver coins. The period was marked by intensive trade activity and urban development. India was one of the first countries in the world to transition from barter system to money-based trade system along with the Greeks. Around 350 BCE, Chanakya laid down the foundation of classical economics. He also laid down the foundation of Maurya Empire, which provided political unity and military security providing the basis for common economic structure in India.

Historical Facts Supporting the Logic of—The Golden Sparrow

India's Economic Status after 1 AD

1. Pre Mughal Rule (1 AD–1500 AD): India was the world's largest economy during the years 1 AD and 1000 AD. In 1500 AD, India's economy had a 24.5% share of world income, the second largest in the world after China which had a 25% share.
2. Mughal Rule (1570-1793): Momentum of India continues. In 1600 AD, India's income of £17.5 million was greater than the entire treasury of Great Britain in 1800 which totalled £16 million. Perceptible decline starts after 1700.
3. East India Company era (1793-1857): India's GDP becomes 40% of China's GDP. India missed industrial revolution and it slipped further.
4. The British Raj (1860-1947): India's economy had a 3.8% share of world income in 1952.

India was a global powerhouse with an evolved business system thriving with good administration. It just subsequently lost its position. The declining wealth of India owing to countless invasions, leads one to think that the 'Golden Bird or Golden Sparrow' could have been a sarcastic coinage. India was a land of wealth, but also a nation that was divided and weak. The vulnerability to attack could have led to the coinage of '*Sone ki Chidiya*' or 'Golden Sparrow', sparrow being a weak bird.

India can be 'Self-Reliant' if Technology is its New 'Mantra'

The pandemic Covid-19 has brought a unique opportunity for humankind to reinvent itself and whosoever grabs the opportunity, will be racing ahead in the next generation. India, too, can do so, but only if the country adopts it as 'Morning Mantra' *jaap*. If the government of India thinks for the people and not just the next election then we can win the war. We need to compete with the world outside and not with ourselves, politically and economically. India is blessed with the best talent, and supportive climatic conditions.

The first step is to recognise our core strength which is knowledge and wisdom. Vedas and Upanishads came out of hundreds of years of research by several *rishis*, right from the days of Aryabhata.

We have been good with numbers—a basic ingredient needed for technological advancement including artificial intelligence. Our other major strength is agriculture. The Green and White revolutions prove the hard work and capabilities of our farmers.

During the lockdown, GOI, announced the big structural reforms & stimulus package of ₹ 21 lakh crore, which was a blueprint for '*atmanirbhar Bharat.*'

To answer how long it will take for India to become '*atmanirbhar*', we need to look at US & China, two countries that are self-reliant.

Politically, the US is the oldest democracy with strongest institutions, fearless media and fearless private sector with minimum government interference and above all, the best and some of the oldest universities in the world. China is maximum government and not democratic. But whatever the system, it works well for them. China is racing ahead of India now even though the two countries started their journey to development almost together. India is stuck between the US and China, neither a fully established democracy nor authoritarian. The bureaucracy seems more committed to their political masters rather than the people. So, rule of law takes a back seat and mediocracy gets promoted.

We have—Satya Nadella of Microsoft, Shiv Nadar of HCL, and Sundar Pichai of Google. Unless we set our house in order and attract our talent back and give chances, irrespective of caste, creed, religion, colour or party affiliations, '*Self-Reliant India"* may remain a pipe dream.

We need to start the process of adding to IITs and IIMs and make our higher education free and independent. Higher education needs to be more research-based and must be rid of political party-based student unions.

R & D, Innovation in Tech

A nation becomes a superpower with its military, energy and technology.

As long as we are dependent on defence imports, we cannot become a superpower. Today, apart from the US, China and Israel are also self-reliant because they are net arms exporters whereas India is dependent on imports, about 70 percent of its defence equipments are imported. India's biggest advantage is its information technology power and its young talent but it is busy building a new world order in foreign borders. India's core competence is knowledge and agriculture. India's new 'Morning Mantra' should be technology.

We have to reverse the order of government policy & technological innovation. In the US, technological innovations and public policy come from universities because governments and the private sector have invested in them and not interfered. We need to concentrate on the country's technological capabilities and increase exports in agriculture/food sector. Let rural India become our food processing zones and let the farmers and farm labourers become partners in the country's progress.

□

A political and social activist.

Atmabal Se Atmanirbhar

—Manoj Kumar Gulati

'*Atmabal se Atmanirbhar*' that means Self-Confidence for Self-reliant but it should not be merely a catchy short term slogan but this MANTRA has to become our way of life and work culture. We have to change the work ethics and values. Zero tolerance policy on quality control mass production for cost effectiveness; upgraded machinery and equipment installation and world class infrastructure and it's maintenance facilities with no scope for *jugaad* mentality. This will lead us to the golden path of a Self-Reliant Confident India. Pollution, Peace and Protected Environment, to sustain the concept of Self-Reliant India—these four issues must be addressed on priority basis in a systematic approach. All the possible positive gains of intended progress on economical and social upliftment will be nullified if we do not envisage a comprehensive policy to regulate the fast growing demon of population. We are the second largest populated country in the world after China but its total land area is almost three times more than ours.

India's density of population is the maximum as compared to Russia, Canada, USA, Brazil, Australia etc. Hence, if this population growth is not streamlined our country will face a very grim situation as our natural resources may shrink and the problem of unemployment and poverty will surely surge ahead of the graph of progress and the dream of a Self-reliant Confident India will get a setback. The compared analysis of some vibrant and healthy economic powers of the world shows that they have large lands with controlled populace and hence better opportunities for growth in general.

To add further impetus to the new National Population Control Act (NPCA) the first time violators shall be disfranchised with a bar to contest any elections. The second time habitual violation should result in a specific jail sentence. India is a young country with approx. 65% of the population below the age of 45 years and we can afford to adopt this two child norm policy without any adverse effects. Pollution is also an area of major concern in our path to Self-reliant Confident India. Clean drinking water, acid and arsenic free river and water bodies are actually the basics of a developed country. This is the treasure of our future generations and their survival. Polluted city breeds polluted mind and culture. Development cannot be sustained for long time in polluted surroundings Peace. It shall not be out of place to emphasise that progress lies in peaceful society only and yes of course for peace and tranquillity in the society the people shall be convinced and confident that they will not be discriminated on the basis of their respective caste, creed, class, gender or religious beliefs by the government. This is the ultimate essential essence of true democracy in letter and spirit '*Sabka Saath-Sabka Vikas*'.

As a matter of fact if India has to sustain the economic development and growth then the NPCA should be enacted by the government and implementation of this should be perused as NATION MISSION without any exceptions on grounds of caste, faith, religion, region or economical status etc. Of course this is not an easy task for such a vast country but it has to be honestly done and done at the top most priority. The mission of smaller family—two child norms can not and should not be enforced by duress as it was done during Emergency days with disastrous results. People should be sensitised through awareness programme involving community leaders and social activism. Law enacted should be based on the principles of dissuading and discourage. Those not adhering to the norms of the welfare law should not be able to get any benefits under the government scheduled schemes and subsidiaries etc. including government jobs.

The world is looking at India with curious anxiety and exciting expectations and India must not let go this opportunity off. Tourism industry can go a long way in strengthening the muscles of Reliant India by generating foreign exchange besides localised generation of employment and revenue. A few instances of general dissatisfaction and social acrimony is bound to crop up now and then in a vast democracy like India but the inherent perception and identity of our NATION shall always be that of a peaceful and peace loving country. The onus lies on the government and the public both. As a matter of fact, in a democratic republic we are not chasing the mirage of utopian dream of idealistic society as such but an endeavour to develop a society that is aware of its rights, responsibilities and duties. A country that is free of injustice, discrimination and hatred is definitely bound to feel privileged and protected and hence confident. A country oozing with confidence and trust in itself like Japan and Vietnam have changed the norms of the game by rising from the ashes. The *Mool-Mantra* is Nation First and Nation First only. Protection plans for Environment last but not surely the least important issue to write about is the protection of the Mother Nature. A lot is being done by the Central/State governments/NGOs, social workers and even by individuals but a lot more needs to be done. Ecological imbalance shall not be allowed to hamper our mission of making a Reliant India. Industrialisation and urbanisation is interconnected with each other. Urbanisation has to be done scientifically keeping focus on the ecological equilibrium otherwise often occurring floods, droughts and landslides shall not only result in human loss and tragedies bur adversely affect the economic growth and stability. These man-made calamities put a lot of pressure on general health facilities.

The global economic arena is very vast but full of enormous challenges, opportunities and competition too. Though our immediate task for Reliant Confident India has to be NEED based but it we WANT to be a giant global economic power than PEACE at home is a pre-requisite. An atmosphere of total security & safety and business friendly environment will not only strengthen bilateral relations in economic arena but will also change the scenario of tourism industry in India. Now India is not perceived as a country of snake charmers and steer jugglers but a vibrant, colourful and exciting destination which is full of enormous potential for experience and exploration. A country full of astounding heritage sites that the world would have never ever seen or dreamt.

The vast greenery, the dense forests, the flowing rivers, the beautiful flora and fauna, the towering trees and cycle of the changing weather is a natural property of the Nation and its protection should be a priority of each citizen to realise the cherished dream of a New-reliant India.

*'Agar Neeyat mein **SATYAM** aur Neeti mein **SHIVAM** ho to Niyati **SUNDARAM** avashya hoti hai'.*

Under a strong & visionary leadership, we resolve to succeed—'*Aaj Raat Bhale Ho Andheri Par Naya Bhaskar Nikal Raha Hai. PHIR SUBAH HOGI*'.

□

Social worker and entrepreneur.

Research & Development is Key to Self-reliant India

—Shriyans Jain

An Overview

When we talk of 'vocal for local', we keep an eye on the vision of our worthy leaders of the nation. Self-Reliant India mission is a key to turn the crisis into opportunities. The Covid-19 pandemic has generated a crisis of worldwide recession. The industrial activities were put under a lockdown condition all over the world and the economic slowdown has hit the biggest crisis of unemployment and degrowth in income & opportunities. The Government of India has taken a wise step by stimulus packages of ₹ 20 lac crore to stimulate the growth in all sectors to make our country self-reliant under the Self-Reliant India Mission.

Importance of Research & Development (R & D)

The economic growth and productivity largely depend on Research & Development. It is observed that two-third of economic growth in Europe between 1995-2007 was attributed to R & D which accounted for 15% of all productivity gains for this period. An increase of 10% in R & D expenditure leads to 1.5 % increase in productivity & growth. During the last decade, U.S, China & Japan were the leading countries in R & D. India's share was around 2.8%. Government of India is continuously focusing and emphasizing on science & technology to increase its efforts and make improvements in R & D. The contribution of R & D to socio economic well-being is phenomenal. The quality of life of our citizens has been improved by R & D. The challenges are still there like energy efficiency, security, climate change and health hazards after Covid-19 are being faced by Indian Society, and R & D can help overcome all these challenges. R & D has played a crucial role to anticipate and respond to these needs. The impact of R & D is felt across all sections of society and it is a well established fact that investing in R & D is fundamental to India's national Security and to address the multiple uncertainties of climate change and global meltdown.

Our Defence Minister, Rajnath Singh has launched 'Atmanirbhar Bharat Saptah' in keeping with the Prime Minister's vision for a self-reliant India with increased local manufacturing. Mr. Rajnath Singh has announced to stop import of 101weapons and military platforms like transport aircraft, light combat helicopters, conventional submarines, cruise missiles among others, on a staggered basis till 2024.

The indigenous production of all these defence products need a lot of R & D support without which we can not even think to be Self-Reliant.

Our honourable Prime Minister Narendra Modi Ji mentioned about his vision for an 'Atmanirbhar Bharat' in his address to the nation on 12th May, 2020 while announcing a ₹ 20 lakh crore economic stimulus package to boost the economy hit by the Covid-19 pandemic. Since then, various ministries & departments have announced several measures to encourage domestic manufacturing in key sectors.

Our main emphasis is centred on R & D to improve the quality of life in every walk of life. Whether it is agriculture, education, social relations, health, trade or industrial production, we need good quality of Research in every sector.

R&D is the Heart of New Self-reliant India Mission

Recently, the Institute of Statistics of United Nations Educational, Scientific and Cultural Organisation (UNESCO) has reported that India is amongst the top ten R&D spenders in the world, i.e. $48.1 Bn R&D spending (adjusted for PPP) constituting 2.7% of the global share. India improved its ranking in the Global Innovation Index by five places to 52nd in 2019 and is likely to get into the list of the top 25 nations by 2027.

With growing globalisation, engineering and R&D market in India is estimated to grow at a CAGR of 14 percent to reach $ 42 Bn by 2020. In 2019, India had close to 7000 R&D institutions. The maximum number of R&D institutions i.e. 1392 (20.3 percent) are in the state of Maharashtra, followed by Karnataka, Tamil Nadu, Andhra

Pradesh and Gujarat with 685 (10.0 percent), 672 (9.8 percent), 570 (9.7 percent) and 547 (8.3 percent) respectively.

India accounted for 40 percent ($ 13.4 Bn) of the total $ 34 Bn of globalised engineering and R&D in 2016. India adds 6000 PhDs, 200 thousand engineers, 300 thousand non-engineer postgraduates, and 2100 thousand other graduates to its workforce annually. In 2016, India produced the maximum number of graduates worldwide with 78 million fresh graduates, of which 2.6 millions were from Science, Technology, Engineering and Maths (STEM). India is fast becoming a top R&D outsourcing destination with 60 percent of new MNCs having established global in-house R&D centres. This is likely to accelerate as new MNCs eye India to set up their bases. As per a study by Confederation of Indian Industry (CII) published in 2017, from among the top 100 global R&D spenders, around 83 of them have a presence in India in some shape or form. The total patents in India have doubled (from 30,822 in 2008 to 60,777 in 2017) Companies like Microsoft, Oracle, Motorola, Intel, IBM and GE have set up their R&D or design centres in India. Companies like GE and Bosch have their largest and second largest R&D facilities respectively in India.

The Covid-19 pandemic has forced the world into a recession. However, India is one of the only two countries in the world to witness a positive growth rate with further projections of India's faster recovered growth trajectory. This growth rate is predicted to be one of the highest in the world.

The Covid-19 pandemic also brings with it a unique opportunity for India to attract FDI especially from large companies seeking to diversify their investments into new geographies with the aim to mitigate risks and to ramp up production. Government of India has already taken active steps in this direction by setting up of an Empowered Group of Secretaries, headed by the Cabinet Secretary, to make India a more 'investor-friendly destination'.

Trends of Segment-wise R & D Expenditure in India

- The expenditure on R&D is undertaken almost entirely by the Central Government.
- Within the Central Scientific Ministries/Departments, the top three spenders in 2017-18 were Department of Atomic Energy, Department of Space and Department of Science and Technology.

- Private investments in research have severely lagged behind the public investments in India. The top three companies which have contributed to R&D in private sector in 2017 were SAP Labs India Pvt Ltd, Mphasis Ltd and Olympia Tech Park Pvt Ltd.
- Out of 257 profit-making Central Public Sector Enterprises (CPSE) in 2017-18, only 25 percent contributed to R&D. The top three companies which have contributed to R&D in 2017-18 were: Hindustan Aeronautics Ltd, Bharat Electronics Ltd and Bharat Heavy Electricals Ltd.
- State governments also spend on R&D. The top three R&D spenders on agriculture, research and education in 2018-19 were Maharashtra, Tamil Nadu and Karnataka.

Brief Analysis of Segment-wise Investment in R & D

- Public expenditure is the dominant driving force of R&D expenditure in the country. This is in sharp contrast to the pattern in most advanced countries where the private sector is a dominant force. However, the share of public expenditure in total R&D spend, has come down from three-fourth of all expenditures to about three-fifth since the last few years. Further, the government is not only the primary source of R&D funding but also the primary user of these funds.
- The major player in the R&D expenditure ecosystem is the Central Government.
- Other public authorities like CPSE, state governments and universities are also key players in the ecosystem though their combined contribution to overall R&D spend is less as compared to the Central Government.
- The private sector which is an important player in other countries, is not a potent source of R&D spend in India.
- The R&D spend, as a percentage of GDP, has remained stagnant over the last decade even though R&D expenditure in total and in absolute terms, has been increasing over the last couple of years.

Promising Sectors for R & D Expenditure In India

- **Healthcare:** The healthcare industry spent $ 782 Bn on R&D in 2018 and is poised to have the highest R&D expenditure by 2020. The healthcare market in India is expected to be among the top three in the world by 2020 and therefore, presents a tremendous opportunity to investors within the sector.

- **Automotive:** In 2018, the automotive industry spent $ 130 Bn on R&D marking a growth of 6-7 percent from 2017. A key sub-sector driving the investments in R&D is electric mobility.
- **Software and IT:** In 2018, the Software and IT sector accounted for $ 117 Bn of the R&D spend, registering a growth of 18-19 percent over 2017. In India, this is reflected by the fact that $ 1.6 Bn is spent annually on training workforce and growing R&D.
- **Semiconductors:** With a 7-8 percent growth rate, the semiconductor sub-sector is among the top five industry spenders on R&D with an investment of $ 61 Bn. The sector is characterised by rapid technological changes, which demand high levels of spending on R&D.

Our Goals in the Path of Strengthening R&D Segment in India

- More than double the expenditure on R&D to about two percent of GDP by 2022.
- Target 50 percent of the global R&D market.
- Double exports of R&D from $ 3 Bn to $ 6 Bn.
- Create 30 dedicated R&D export hubs.
- Target FDI investment of $ 500 Mn by 2022.
- Aspire to be having one of the top ten global R&D institutions in emerging technologies.

How to Achieve our Goals

The Government of India has designed a programme to incentivise the growth of R & D segment in our economy and for this purpose, the following fiscal and other incentives and programmes have been chalked out:

Fiscal Initiatives

To encourage investments in R&D, Government of India offers various tax incentives. Some of these incentives are given below:

- The corporate tax rate for existing companies has been reduced to 22 percent plus surcharge under section 115 BAA. This has certain implications for scientific research, not only affecting companies but IITs, government-run research labs, deemed universities and private technology institutes as well. The implication for companies availing reduced corporate tax rate with respect to scientific research is as follows:

- Section 35 (2AB): will not be able to claim weighted tax deduction at 150 percent for capital and operating expenditure for scientific research carried out in DSIR approved research laboratories but will be able to claim 100 percent deduction on operating expenditure u/s 35 (1)(i) and capital expenditure u/s 35(1)(iv) along with 35(1)(2ia).
- Section 35 (2AA): tax deduction of 175-200 percent provided for research funding to Indian Institute of Technology, government-run research labs and universities.
- Section 35 (ii): tax deduction of 175 percent for carrying out scientific research at research association, universities and colleges.
- Section 35 (iia): tax deduction of 125 percent for carrying out scientific research with companies.
- Section 35 (1)(iii): tax deduction of 125 percent for carrying out social or statistical research with research association, universities or colleges.
- Section 35 (2AB): weighted tax deduction of 200 percent on R&D expenditure to companies.

Other Incentives Include

- Accelerated depreciation allowance at 40 percent for investment on plant and machinery and on indigenous technology as against 15 percent for normal depreciation as per rule 5(2) of IT rules.
- Customs and central excise duty exemption to in-house R&D units of industry.
- Excise duty waiver for three years on goods designed and developed by a wholly owned Indian company and patented in any two countries out of India: USA and Japan; and any one country under the European Union (to be viewed in relation with the GST regime).
- Exemption from customs duty on imports made for R&D projects, funded by the government in industry.
- The Case for FDI in Research and Development in India
- Specified goods for use in pharmaceutical and biotechnology sectors are allowed to be imported duty-free by an importer registered with DSIR.

- Sector-specific stimulus like a INR 100 Bn nano-mission project has been initiated by the government to develop R&D infrastructure around nanotechnology in India.
- The Indian Institute of Technology, Delhi (IIT-D) is targeting external R&D funding of $ 72.83 Mn this year, up from $ 52.97 Mn last year. In addition, the institute will also get a grant of $ 132.42 Mn from the government over the next five years after it bagged the coveted Institute of Eminence (IoE) tag.

International Collaboration

Presently, India has bilateral S&T cooperation agreements with 83 countries and active cooperation with 44 countries. During the recent years, the cooperation has strengthened significantly with Australia, Canada, EU, France, Germany, Israel, Japan, Russia, UK and USA. Cooperation with African countries has also been strengthened through India-Africa S&T Initiative.

Recommendations

There is a need for an enabling ecosystem with policy support, innovative solutions, risk mitigation to make R&D in India attractive. The following focus areas may be considered:

- More participation by states.
- Tracking of MNC's R&D activity.
- Developing human capital for R&D work.
- Improving contract enforcement.
- Foster linkages between MNCs and local entities.
- Improving land and infrastructure.
- Providing incentives based on expectations of MNCs.
- Formulate long-term government priorities for R&D ecosystem to enable industry alignment.
- Develop forward looking policy measures benchmarked to global best practices to help innovations.
- Engage young generations in R&D for a strong foundation for a career in research. Industries should collaborate with professors for research-based activities.
- To allow more tax concessions to MSME in partnership firms, Hindu undivided families and association of persons. Presently the tax

concessions are available to only corporate sector but the small partnership firms, professional firms and association of persons are still being taxed at maximum marginal rate. The tax rebate under section 87A must be allowed to Hindu undivided families, association of persons, trusts and other body of individuals, and the rate of tax must also be reduced for partnership firms from 30 percent to 22 percent, in parity with corporate sector. The remuneration of partners in professional firms must also be allowed in full upto ₹ 12 lakh and then 90 percent of the remaining profit of the partnership firms. The professional partnership firms must be allowed exemption from GST and other indirect taxes so as to motivate the professional persons to come in the field of research and development in partnership with other processionals and they may form association of persons to establish R&D labs in the country.

- To strengthen the Biotechnology sector. The potential of the sector is well recognised by the central government. The Department of Biotechnology (DBT) has introduced several initiatives to promote development of biotechnology in the country, across sectors like agriculture, affordable healthcare and medical technology, food and nutritional security, animal biotechnology, environmental safety, clean energy and bio-fuel, bio-manufacturing etc. India is among the top 12 biotech destinations in the world and the (USFDA)–approved plants, outside of the US and has three percent share in the global biotechnology industry. The country is also a leading supplier of the DPT, BCG and measles vaccines and supplies them across 150 countries. India already has 2600+ start-ups and a biotech workforce of a million.
- To strengthen the electric vehicle manufacturing industry to promote the use of electric vehicle to save the environment.
- To strengthen the Electronic system development and monitoring enterprises so as to motivate further research in the electronic sector.
- To provide good governance in tax monitoring system through honouring the honest tax payers and reducing the tax burden on professionals who are involved in Research and Development sector and who are associated with consultancy services to industrial organisations.

□

B.Com., FCA and a gold medalist. A leading CA in the field of finance, taxation and consultancy. He is also socially involved with various organisations of repute.

Atmanirbhar Bharat

—**Rajesh Kumar Khattar**

'Atmanirbhar Bharat Abhiyan (Self-dependent India Mission)' is PM Modi's vision of making India a self-reliant nation in every aspect of fulfilling the needs of every Indian citizen, to the extent possible and practical, whether these are items of material needs or otherwise.

The Self-Reliant India Mission points towards chopping down import reliance by focusing on replacement while improving well-being, consistence and quality merchandise to increase worldwide piece of the pie.

Self-Reliance neither means any exclusionary or non-interventionist methodologies, however, it includes formation of some assistance to the entire world.

The Mission centers on the significance of advancing "nearby" items.

The Mission will be done in two stages:

Stage 1: It will consider divisions like clinical materials, hardware, plastics and toys where neighbourhood assembling and fares can be advanced.

Stage 2: It will consider items like pearls and gems, pharmaceutical items and steel, and so on.

The Five pillars of Atmanirbhar Bharat focus on:

- Economy
- Infrastructure
- System
- Vibrant Demography and
- Demand

The Five phases of Atmanirbhar Bharat are:

- **Phase-I**: Businesses including MSMEs
- **Phase-II**: Poor including migrants and farmers
- **Phase-III**: Agriculture
- **Phase-IV**: New Horizons of Growth
- **Phase-V**: Government Reforms and Enablers

The Mission is likewise expected to supplement 'Make in India Initiative', which plans to energise fabricating in India.

The intended objective of this mission is two-fold. First, interim measures such as liquidity infusion and direct cash transfers for the poor will work as shock absorbers for those in acute stress.

The second, long-term reforms in growth-critical sectors to make them globally competitive and attractive.

Together, these steps may revive the economic activity impacted by Covid-19 pandemic and create new opportunities for growth in sectors like agriculture, micro, small and medium enterprises (MSMEs), power, coal and mining, defence and aviation, etc.

However, there are several challenges that are needed to be addressed in order to fulfil the vision of this plan.

Impact of this Stimulus Package

- **Primary Sector:** The measures announced for the agricultural and allied sectors are aimed at strengthening infrastructure, logistics and capacity building at farm gate and this package is of an astounding sum of ₹ 1.63 lac crore.
  - These reforms are steps towards the **One Nation One Market** objective and help India become the **food factory of the world.**
  - These would finally help in achieving the goal of a self-sustainable rural economy.
  - Also, the MGNREGA infusion of ₹ 40,000 crore may help in alleviating the distress of migrants when they return to their villages.
- **Secondary Sector:** Given the importance of MSMEs for Indian economy, the ₹ 3 lakh crore collateral-free loan facility for MSMEs under the package will help this finance-starved sector and thereby provide a kick-start to the dismal state of the economy.

- Also, as the MSME sector is the second largest employment generating sector in India, this step will help to sustain the labour intensive industries and thereby help in **leveraging India's comparative advantage.**
- Additionally, limiting imports of weapons and increasing the limit of foreign direct investment in Defence from 49% to 74% will give a much-needed boost to the production in the Ordnance Factory Board while reducing India's huge defence import bill.

- **Tertiary Sector:** The government has adopted a balanced approach in addressing concerns across various sectors. For example:
  - The newly launched **PM e-Vidya programme** for multi-mode access to digital online education provides a uniform learning platform for the whole nation which shall enable schools and universities to stream courses online without further loss of teaching hours.
  - Public expenditure on health will be increased by investing in grass root health institutions and ramping up health and wellness centres in rural and urban areas.

Associated Challenges

- **Issues Related to Liquidity:** The package of ₹ 20 lakh crore comprises both fiscal and monetary measures, the latter being in the nature of credit guarantees and liquidity infusions into banks and other financial sector institutions rather than the economy per se.
  - Majority of the package are liquidity measures that are supposed to be transmitted by RBI to Banks and Banks to Citizens. This transmission wouldn't be as smooth owing to inefficient transmission of monetary policy.
- **Lack of Demand:** The lockdown has lowered aggregate demand and a fiscal stimulus is needed. However, the package, by relying overwhelmingly on credit infusion to boost the economy, has failed to recognise that investment will pick up only when people across income segments have money to spend.
- **Lack of Backward and Forward Linkages:** Unless the rest of the domestic economy is revived, the MSME sector may face a shortage of demand and its production may soon sputter to a close.

- **Burgeoning Fiscal Deficit:** Government claims that the stimulus package is around 10% of India's GDP. However, financing it would be difficult as the government is worried about containing the fiscal deficit.
- **Difficulty in Mobilising Finances:** The government also seeks to take up disinvestment route to mobilise the finances for the plan. However, the problem is that:
  - Majority of Indian industries are already a bit debt-laden and have no surplus funds to take up the stake in PSUs.
  - Further, it is difficult to borrow in the foreign markets due to the overall economic crisis feared in India in the minds of the foreign lenders and fear of rupee falling with respect to dollar to an all-time low.

Corrective Steps to be Taken

- **Enhancing Demand:** The economic package for the country emerging out of the lockdown requires a stimulus enhancing demand across the economy.
  - The best way for this is to spend on Greenfield infrastructure.
  - Infrastructure spending uniquely creates structures that raise productivity and extends spending power to the section of the population most affected by the lockdown, namely daily wage labourers.
- **Mobilising Finances:** For financing of the stimulus package, India's foreign reserves stand at an all-time high, could be strategically used to finance its needs.
  - The rest may have to come from disinvestments, privatisation, taxation, borrowings and more loans and investments from overseas sources.
- **Holistic Reforms:** Any stimulus package will fail to reflect the trickle-down effect until and unless it is backed by reforms in various sectors.
  - Thus, Atmanirbhar plan also encompasses the unfinished agenda of holistic reforms which may include reforms in Civil services, Education, Skill Development and Labour, etc.

Key Takeaways

The Abhiyan shall include:

- **new economic package** (earlier announced by the Finance Minister)

- **earlier** government **announcements** during Covid crisis
- decisions taken by RBI to give stimulus to banks of ₹ 6 lac crores

This is equivalent to almost **10% of India's GDP**.

India's self-reliance will be based on **five pillars**–

- Economy
- Infrastructure
- Technology-driven system
- Vibrant demography
- Demand

Government of India has been taking several steps to ensure that we are well prepared to face the challenges and threats posed by Covid-19. But only with the active support of citizens of India, we can be able to mitigate the spread of the virus. One of the most important factors in the fight with the virus is to empower the citizens with accurate information and enable them to take precautions, as per the advisories being issued by different Ministries. The Covid-19 Inter-Ministerial Notifications website serves this purpose efficiently by providing Covid-19 related notifications from various Ministries in a format, that is accessible, built using the Secure, Scalable and Sugamya Website as a service (S3WaaS framework) which is secure & scalable.

As they say "Every adversity gives birth to new opportunities". The Prime Minister has in his recent utterances repeatedly stated that building a self-reliant India was an absolutely essential requirement during the continuance of and subsequently in a post-Covid-19 world. Even now, so many months after the announcement was made, the eradication of the virus is nowhere in sight and looks like it has become part of our life in the sense that maintenance of social distancing has become the way of life jeopardising the movement of a large portion of the Indian population and forcing them to stay indoors fearing that they may catch the deadly disease, if they move out and consequently, the already precarious unemployment situation caused by recent manifold increase in computerisation, use of ultra automatic machines and unhindered imports of cheap products from China, has been further aggravated by the Covid-19 pandemic. In fact, although most of the manufacturing activities have restarted albeit at lower capacity levels, at the same time, demand of luxury and non-essential items has contracted which is a great concern for the employment scenario. Therefore, the need for 'Atmanirbhar Bharat' is absolutely critical for the very survival of heavily overpopulated India where the numbers are increasing unhindered on day-to-day basis and the level of unemployment needs to be checked.

Earlier, the WTO norms prevented the Government of India from doing anything concrete on this count and had to accept the bitter fact that in spite of having a large number of population capable of delivering the goods, the advent of free import regime meant that 'cheaper in prices goods' had to be imported from China, no matter, even if it meant that millions of Indian workforce became unemployed as a consequence thereof. With due and highest respect to the 20 Indian martyrs who lost their lives in the skirmishes with China and with due respect to the nears and dears of these martyrs, for whom in particular and for the entire nation in general, their lives were priceless indeed, but then, it gave rise to a situation which allowed the Indian Government to make an 'official' call to stay away from the Chinese products which not only has opened opportunities for millions of Indian workforce to get employment and lacs of small and medium enterprises to get a lease of life, and even many of the large-scale companies too, to expand their manufacturing base and provide gainful employment to our own Indian brothers and sisters. This will be rooted in the pillars of culture, heritage and knowledge for becoming a global force. In addition, the dependence on self-reliance will also reduce the outflow of Indian talent from migrating abroad like it has been happening in the past and causing huge losses to India in terms of human capital outflow which is a matter of great concern especially in terms of losing doctors, scientists, top level management graduates, engineers and other highly skilled professionals who leave India for better careers abroad.

60 years ago, India was a nation of 45 crore. The average family size was 6 to 8 members, what with every normal family being led by a working husband plus non-employed housewife having four to five children plus in many cases, their children's grandparents forming part of and constituting one family. The only earning member used to be just one male member or in some rare cases, only two members. All said and done, to feed a population of 60 crore, only about 7-8 crore of jobs were required, whether in self-employment or dependent employment. And

even in those days, there was large-scale unemployment. Imports were literally banned or at least were exorbitantly taxed at the point of entry, as custom duties and word smuggling was a word of common parlance in those days. Except for import of crude oil, armaments, aircrafts, critical types of plant & machinery, patented technology items and a few other items, which necessitated huge capital expenditure in setting up their manufacturing capacities, every other import or attempt to import was considered a sin!! We never could imagine that in future, Indians would be freely importing toys, Deepawali lightings, rakhis, Idols of Lord Rama, Lord Ganesha and even items as common as textiles, shoes, utensils, textile items, ordinary stationary items and what not!! Today, India is a nation of nearly 138 crore and with the advancement of our women force being more educated and ambitious, being a housewife for every woman born during the past 40 years is literally considered a matter of shame, at least in the ever-increasing urban areas. Today, with the increased desire for luxury items and services, coupled with availability of higher number of educated, skilled and highly qualified women work force in almost every field, the number of employment seeking Indians has increased to at least 50 crore, a sevenfold increase in 60 years, whereas the population has increased only by slightly more than three times!! The only way to cater to this requirement of higher job seeking population is to become self-reliant than to depend on imports.

The Prime Minister declared the **'Atmanirbhar Bharat Abhiyan'** along with a monetary improvement package—worth ₹ 20 lakh crore towards accomplishing the mission. It is linked with the advent of Covid-19 to overcome the difficulties associated with the virus which is causing lockdowns/partial lockdowns adversely pushing India as well as the entire world towards negative GDP growth and unprecedented unemployment in many sectors of the economy in particular, and in the overall economy of the nation in general.

- The declared financial package happens to be worth 10% of India's Gross Domestic Product (GDP) in 2019-20.
- The sum incorporates package previously reported towards the start of the lockdown, fusing measures from the RBI and the payouts under the Pradhan Mantri Garib Kalyan Yojana.
- The package is relied upon to concentrate ashore, work, liquidity and laws.

From all possible angles, self-reliance is the biggest virtue in every human being. It gives him pride, it saves him from seeking mercy from others and it gives him strength to fight and ward off all kinds of adversities. Similarly, these virtues should be there in the general characteristics of every nation too. In addition self-reliance brings prosperity too to the nation and obviously to its inhabitants also. Every country through its rulers needs to stand true to the aspiration of its own population in terms of fulfilment of their day-to-day requirements of essentials as well as not so essential requirements and even of luxuries to the extent possible. The unprecedented technical advancements which the mankind is making during the past one century or so, has transformed the aspiration of the human beings of today to such an extent that what was considered a luxury in the past has become an absolutely essential necessity today.

India is a country enriched with almost all kinds of natural resources barring crude oil. The manpower whether unskilled, semi-skilled, skilled, highly skilled and technically skilled, are all available in abundance and any kind of imports into India of any item which its own manpower can produce, is highly unpatriotic and idiotic act. In fact, it is a sin which deprives our own Indian workforce from earning its livelihood and on the contrary, provides employment to a foreign national and in the recent few decades even to the nationals of an enemy nation!! The fact of the matter is that barring manufacturing of commercial/passenger aircrafts, advanced versions of fighter aircrafts and armaments and a few other items for which a patent or copyright is lacking with us, Indians are capable of producing each and every item of its requirements even today, not only for captive consumption but also for exports. This will also improve India's foreign exchange reserves and her capacity and capability to meet all the natural and unnatural calamities that may arise in future too, apart from the prevailing calamity she is facing in the guise of Covid-19, the end of which nobody can even predict, rather, it is nowhere in sight !!

The call for Atmanirbhar India is also in a way India's tacit or rather direct rebuttal to China politically, apart from what the Indian brave armed forces are giving to the Chinese army. As already stated elsewhere above, Indians have been importing in very large numbers, items and services, even apps, and that too from China, items as ordinary as toys,

Deepawali lightings, rakhis, Idols of Hindu Gods, Lord Buddha, and even items as common as textiles, shoes, utensils, textile items, ordinary stationary items, and the reduction and eventually elimination in imports of above items from China has a dual advantage effect for India, improving employment opportunities for Indians and breaking the backbone of Chinese economy at least to some extent, and giving them a stern message and warning that India will not take any nonsense from them at the Line of Actual Control.

India is facing the Covid-19 situation with fortitude and a spirit of self-reliance that is evident in the fact that from zero production of Personal Protection Equipment (PPE) before March 2020, India today has created a capacity of producing more than 3 lakh PPE kits daily which is also growing steadily.

Additionally, India has demonstrated how it rises up to challenges and uncovers opportunities therein, as manifested in the re-purposing of various automobile sector industries to collaborate in the making of life-saving ventilators. The clarion call given by the Hon'ble PM to use these trying times to become Atmanirbhar (self-reliant) has been very well received, to enable the resurgence of the Indian economy. Unlock 1 to Unlock 4 Guidelines have been issued to enable resumption of economic activities while maintaining abundant caution, thus allowing graded easing of restrictions.

Conclusion

The economic crisis triggered by Covid-19 pandemic is much like the 1991 economic crisis which was a harbinger of a paradigm shift via liberalisation, privatisation and globalisation. The post-Covid-19 era may usher in unprecedented opportunities provided the implementation deficit is adequately addressed.

In fine, self-reliance will prepare the country for tough competition in the global supply chain and it is important that the country wins this competition. The package will also focus on empowering the poor, labourers, migrants, etc., both from organised and unorganised sectors.

□

B.Com., FCA and a gold medalist. A leading CA in the field of finance, taxation and consultancy. He is also socially involved with various organisations of repute.

Rohingyas: Problem/Disease Transplantation, An ISI Conspiracy

—Binay Singh

What is the Rohingya issue? Is it a case of a persecuted minority of Myanmar? Or, it is merely transplantation of the problem from Myanmar to India which India does already have enough of it?

The History of Rohingyas: The truth is that Myanmar's Jihadi scourge is decades old, a legacy of British colonialism. After all, it was the British who, more than a century ago, moved large numbers of Rohingya from East Bengal to work on rubber and tea plantations in then-Burma which was administered as a province of India until 1937. In the years before India gained independence from Britain in 1947, Rohingya militants joined the campaign to establish Pakistan as the first Islamic republic of the post-colonial era.

When the British, who had mastered the art of "divide and rule", decided to establish two separate flanks of Pakistan on either side of India, the Rohingyas launched a campaign to drive out Buddhists from Muslim-dominated Mayu peninsula in northern Rakhine. They wanted the Mayu peninsula to secede and be annexed by East Pakistan (later Bangladesh).

Subsequently, the Gambit to secede Mayu peninsula failed, and gave rise to a self-declared jihad by Rohingyas. Local mujahideen began to organise attacks on government troops and seize control of large areas in northern Rakhine, establishing a sort of Islamic caliphate. However, just after months of gaining independence in 1948, martial law was declared in Myanmar and government forces regained control of lost territories by early 1950s.

Rohingya Islamist militancy continued to thrive with mujahideen attacks occurring intermittently. In 2012, fierce clashes broke out between the Rohingyas and the ethnic Rakhines who feared becoming a minority in their home state. The rape and murder of a young Buddhist woman sparked a chain of events. The sectarian violence that followed aided the Rohingya militancy to mushroom into a full-blown insurgency with rebels launching guerrilla attacks on security forces.

Rohingya's Activities in India: Seeking refuge is not the only motto of Rohingyas in India. There are several incidents which make the presence of Rohingyas in India questionable.

The terror attack on Mahabodhi Temple in Bodh Gaya on 7 July, 2013, was directed at international Buddhist tourists to avenge the so-called atrocities on Rohingya Muslims in Myanmar according to arrested SIMI and Indian Mujahideen terrorists, Umair Siddiqui and Haider Ali. It also was the same group that had planned the assassination of Narendra Modi, the then Chief Minister of Gujrat at a rally in Gandhi Maidan, Patna. On, 27 October, 2013, six died and hundreds were injured as a result of the cowardly attempt.

In April 2018, Samiun Rahman, a 28-year-old British Rohingya terror suspect serving Al-Qaeda in Syria, was sent to India to recruit and mobilise youths to fight for the Rohingyas. The NIA, in its charge sheet against Rahman, mentions that it was a plot by the Al-Qaeda against India. Rahman was found to have connections in West Bengal, Jharkhand, Delhi and many other states. In September 2017, Delhi police received information that a person named Raju Bhai was planning terror activities. Later, it was disclosed that Raju Bhai was none other than Rahman and was attached with the Al-Nusra-Front in Syria. Rahman had received arms training, was in touch with Al-Qaeda and fought against the Syrian Army.

In August 2019, police picked up three members from Rohingya Muslim community for questioning after ₹ 30 lac was recovered from them. The cash was found at a Jhuggi in the Channi Himmat area of Jammu city. Investigations have shown that the money belonged to two Bangladeshi nationals named Ismail and Noor Alam. Both were living in Jammu for the past six years without any valid documents. It was also revealed during the investigation that the money was parked for some treacherous activities.

There is an organic link between the Rohingya and Jihadist terror groups in Pakistan that go back a few decades, allowing the Rohingyas, a run of the place in India which will constitute a severe threat to the National security.

Many Rohingya were part of the 'Jihad' against the erstwhile Soviet Union in Afghanistan and had later participated in jihadist action in Kashmir. A large number of them also went back to Bangladesh. It formed the nucleus of the jihadist organisations that struck roots in Bangladesh during the regime of General Ershad and later Begum Khaleda Zia. Using Bangladesh as a base, they have established links with Indian jihadists and also carried out actions inside Myanmar.

Bertil Lintner, a Swedish journalist, who has been covering Myanmar and Asia for more than three decades, in his report on Rohingyas' Muslim militant group in Myanmar, called the Arakan Rohingya Salvation Army (ARSA), previously known as Harakah-al-Yaqin (Faith Movement) responsible for attacks on 30 police posts and an Army base in northern Rakhine State in August 2017, stated that the ARSA was having connections with foreign extremist groups despite their blanket denial of such accusations.

This dreaded terrorist group in Myanmar claims to be fighting for self-determination like the other terrorist groups who were killing people for the same self-determination logic in Kashmir for decades. The format of Kashmir insurgency and the Myanmar terrorist group has much in common including a standard back-up like ISI, and handlers like Hafiz Sayed. There were instances of Rohingya terrorists fighting in Kashmir and later killed in action by the Indian Forces.

The Arakan Rohingya Salvation Army (ARSA) has claimed its attacks were part of a campaign to achieve fundamental human rights for self-identifying Rohingya Muslims living in Rakhine.

In "The truth behind Myanmar's Rohingya insurgency" published in Asia Times, dated 20 September 2017, Bertil Lintner cited intelligence analysts declaring the group's mentor to be one Karachi-based Abdus Qadoos Burmi, a Pakistani of Rohingya descent. He has appeared in videos broadcast on social media calling for 'jihad' in Myanmar. According to the article:

"Abdus Qadoos has well-documented links to Lashkar-e-Taiba, or the Army of the Righteous, one of South Asia's largest Islamic terrorist organisations that operate out of Pakistan. The group was founded in 1987 in Afghanistan, with funding from now deceased Al-Qaeda founder, Osama bin Laden. Abdus Qadoos has even appeared in meetings together with Lashkar-e-Taiba supremo, Hafiz Mohammed Syed," writes Lintner.

The article describes the group's leader as Ataullah Abu Ammar Junjuni, also known as Hafiz Tohar, who was born in Karachi and received madrassa education in Saudi Arabia. Lintner highlights ARSA's second-ranking leader, *"a shadowy man known only as 'Sharif' who comes from Chittagong in southwestern Bangladesh and does not appear in any of the group's propaganda videos."* He reportedly speaks with an Urdu language accent, the official language of Pakistan. Security analysts note 150 foreigners in the ARSA ranks, according to the story, *"angry and desperate young men. Most of them are from Bangladesh, eight to ten come from Pakistan with smaller groups from Indonesia, Malaysia and southern Thailand. Two are reportedly from Uzbekistan. Training held in the Myanmar-Bangladesh border areas have been carried out in part by older veterans of the Afghan wars, the security analysts say."* (Asia Times, 2017)

Massacre of Hindus in Myanmar

In a report published by Amnesty International in January 2020, it mentions a brutal massacre by the ARSA of around 100 Hindus in Myanmar's Rakhine State in 2017. The report provides first-hand accounts of the survivors from a Hindu village called **"Ah Nauk Kha Maung Seik."**

On 25 August, 2017, at around 8 am, armed men dressed in black and local Rohingya villagers in plain clothes rounded up dozens of Hindu women, men and children in the village. They robbed, bound, and blindfolded them before marching them to the outskirts of the town where they separated the men from the women and young children.

A few hours later, ARSA fighters executed 53 Hindu villagers starting with the men. Eight Hindu women and eight of their children were spared after ARSA fighters forced them to convert to Islam and flee with the militants to Bangladesh. Raj Kumari, an 18-year-old girl, who survived the massacre, says:

'They slaughtered the men. We were told not to look at them ... They had knives. They also had some spades and iron rods. ... We hid ourselves in the shrubs there and were able to see a little ... My uncle, my father, my brother–they were all slaughtered.'

Another survivor named Formila, a 20-year-old girl told that as she and the other seven abducted women were being marched away, she turned back and saw ARSA fighters kill the other women and children. The same day, all of the 46 Hindu men, women, and children in the neighbouring village of **"Ye Bauk Kyar"** disappeared, presumed killed by the same ARSA fighters.

The bodies of 45 people from Ah Nauk Kha Maung Seik were unearthed in four mass graves in late September 2017. The remains of the rest of the victims from that village, as well as all 47 from Ye Bauk Kyar, have not been found.

On 26 August, 2017, ARSA members killed six more Hindus, including three children, and injured another woman on the outskirts of Maungdaw town, near **"Myo Thu Gyi village."**

Kor Mor La, a 25-year-old girl who survived the attack while her husband and five-year-old daughter were both killed, says:

'The people who shot us were dressed in black. ... I couldn't see their faces, only their eyes. ... They had long guns and swords; my husband was shot next to me. I was shot [in the chest]. After that, I was barely conscious.' However, Amnesty in its report criticises the Myanmar Army for a brutal response to these killings.

Rakhine State, where most of Myanmar's Rohingyas reside, is attracting jihadists from far and wide. Local militants are suspected of having ties with the Islamic State (ISIS), Al-Qaeda, and other terrorist organisations. Moreover, they increasingly receive aid from militant-linked organisations in Saudi Arabia and Pakistan. The leading insurgent group, ARSA, is led by a Saudi-based committee of Rohingya émigrés. The external forces fomenting insurgent attacks in Rakhine bear considerable responsibility for the Rohingyas' current plight. It is the link between Rohingya militants and such external forces especially terrorist organisations like ISIS, that have driven concerned governments to declare that their entry poses a severe security threat. Even Bangladesh acknowledges Rohingya militants' external jihadi connections.

The Rohingyas as a community along the eastern border pose a severe security threat not only to the state of Assam and other northeastern states but also has considerable security implications for neighbouring Bangladesh as well. The security agencies have warned the Union government that Pakistan's intelligence agencies may try "to exploit Rohingyas to support jihad" and thereby, Rohingyas can create trouble in the sensitive areas of Assam which had faced violent clashes a few years back due to large-scale illegal immigration. (Amnesty International UK, 2020)

Ataullah abu Ammar Jununi, leader of the Arakan Rohingya Salvation Army (ARSA) © Private

Photo courtesy: www.amnesty.org.uk

Reports published in The Economic Times by Dipanjan Roy Chaudhury dated 12 July 2018, provided a clear picture of the direct lineage and linkage of the Rohingya Terror outfits with Pakistan-based ISI and other terror groups and explain the Rohingyas' international connections in very detail:

Rohingya's ISI Connection

A little known Rohingya terror group named "**Aqa-Mul-Mujahideen (AMM)**" blamed for attacks on Myanmar border outposts in the year 2015, not only maintained links with Hafiz Saeed's Lashkar-e-Taiba (LET) but also developed a connection with the Jaish-e-Mohammed (JEM) cell in Jammu and Kashmir.

Aqa-Mul-Mujahideen (AMM) leaders were trained in Pakistan and later recruited Rohingya youth in Rakhine region of Myanmar, claimed persons familiar with the group and its activities. AMM is a new armed group that originated from the Harkat-ul-Jihad Islami-Arakan (HUJI-A).

There are reports of Rohingya terrorists fighting alongside Pakistani extremists in Kashmir. One of their top leaders, Chotta Burmi, was killed in Kashmir along with JeM commander Adil Pathan last year. Earlier, Burmi allegedly shared the dais with Hafiz Saeed in Pakistan.

It is understood that security agencies of India, Bangladesh and

Myanmar are coordinating their actions against Rohingya terror groups.

The current HUJI-A chief—Abdus Qadoos Burmi, a Pakistani national of Rohingya origin, who, it is claimed recruited one Hafiz Tohar from Maungdaw in Myanmar. Tohar is now said to be heading the AMM and Qadoos Burmi is reported to be close to Saeed. Saeed's other terror group, Jamat ud Dawa (JuDD)'s humanitarian arm, Falah-e-Insaniat (FiF), was active in Rohingya relief camps in Rakhine State after the 2012 riots.

Qadoos Burmi also developed the HUJI-A network in Bangladesh using the remote hills along its border with Myanmar, according to government sources in Dhaka. It may be recalled that JuD launched Difa-e-Musalman-e-Arakan conference in Pakistan to highlight the Rohingya cause in 2012. Subsequently, two senior JuD operatives, Shahid Mahmood and Nadeem Awan, allegedly established direct contacts with Rohingya extremists based in camps along the Bangladesh-Myanmar border.

Earlier, the Bangladesh authorities arrested Maulana Shabeer Ahmed, a Pakistan-based Rohingya operative in 2012, who revealed that he was coordinating with Rohingya terrorists in Bangladesh on behalf of JeM. Bangladesh authorities are not ruling out the fact that Rohingya armed groups may have close links with Bangladesh's home-grown terrorists and could share hideouts, finances and sources of weapons supply. Pakistan-linked Rohingya terror groups have also allegedly been noticed in Mae Sot area on the Thai side of the Thai-Myanmar border. (The Economic Times, 2018)

Bangladesh's history is replete with HUJI-B's violent campaigns against the pro-democratic and secular Awami-League (AL) political party and other civil society members. The leaders who have spearheaded the Sunni (Hanafi-Deobandi) militant movement in Bangladesh such as Mufti Hannan, Sheikh Farid and Maulana Abdus Salam, guided both covert and overt actions of the group in Bangladesh and beyond especially in neighbouring Myanmar where both HUJI-A and HUJI-B were active.

We have discussed earlier regarding SIMI, NDF and PFI; these radical organisations have mastered in disguising themselves. HUJI-B, much before it was banned in Bangladesh, morphed into Islami-Dawat-E-Khalifa in March 1999 to evade scrutiny. Again in 2004, HUJI-B changed its name into Islami-Gan-Andolan Bangladesh(IGA-B). Finally, HUJI-B in all its formations was banned by the US-State Department in February 2008.

When the Indian Prime Minister, Narendra Modi and Myanmar State Counsellor, Aung San Suu Kyi decided to broaden the bilateral security and counter-terrorism partnership, the drivers were New Delhi's concerns over ISI infiltration into the ranks of Rohingyas and Yangon's fight against the Rakhine terrorists.

India and Bangladesh, through their joint counter-terror cooperation, have recently discovered that the ISI had allegedly played a key role in masterminding a terror attack in Myanmar's Rakhine state, ahead of Prime Minister Modi's visit. India-Bangladesh-Myanmar may now move toward trilateral info-sharing mechanism to counter this threat in the region.

India and Bangladesh recently discovered that Hafiz Tohar, the military chief of Arakan Rohingya Salvation Army (ARSA), has been maintaining close links with Pakistan's ISI and the spy agency may have played a vital role in the terror attacks that killed several members of Myanmar's Army.

Phone calls between Tohar and ISI discussing detailed attack plans have been intercepted in the last week of August, indicated people familiar with the issue. Hafiz Tohar set up the Aqa Mul Mujahideen (AMM) and was trained in Pakistan by the Lashkar-e-Taiaba (LeT) also named in the just-concluded BRICS Summit declaration. Tohar is widely believed to be behind the deadly attacks on Myanmar security forces in October 2016 and on 25 August, 2017.

After the training of a few initial AMM recruits in Pakistan, new cadre members were recruited from among the Rohingya youth in Rakhine State and at refugee camps in Bangladesh's Cox's Bazar. They were then trained in camps set up on the Bangladesh-Myanmar border especially one at the Chittagong Hill Tracts of Bangladesh, according to experts, who have followed this development closely.

"Brigadier Ashfaq" and "Major Salamat", two alleged ISI operatives, have been mentoring AMM and assisting this group in developing close links with JMB in Bangladesh, according to one of the experts cited above. The ISI Brigadier also allegedly maintains close relationships with Bangladesh's Opposition BNP. In this context, India and Myanmar have decided to step up counter-terror cooperation and information sharing. The joint statement issued after Modi-Suu Kyi dialogue said: "Both sides... agreed that the fight against terrorism should...hold accountable and take active measures against States and entities that encourage support or finance terrorism.

The 'Quadriga' Facilitating Rohingyas in India

The Civil Society and Human Rights NGOs, gang of so-called activists and Urban Naxals who ran helter-shelter for rescuing a terrorist, are trying to put forward a very human and persecuted type of image for Rohingyas in India. The 'Quadriga' gang propagated that deportation of Rohingyas from India is contrary to the Constitutional protections of Article 14, Article 21 and Article 51(c) of the Constitution of India which provides equal rights and liberty to every 'person'. And this would also be in contradiction with the principle of 'Non-Refoulement', which has been widely recognised as a principle of Customary International Law. They also said that India has ratified and is a signatory to various Conventions that understand the Principle of 'Non-Refoulement' which prohibits the deportation of refugees to a country where they face a threat to their life.

In reality, each of the above premises was factually wrong and baseless. The first premise that around 40,000 Rohingyas or more like them have taken refuge in India. This by itself is a false statement because none of them have entered the Indian Territory by law. Each one of them has entered clandestinely dodging the eyes of the law and are now seeking equity. They have entered India through human trafficking networks that operate in tandem with all negative forces. It emanates a conspiracy at the highest levels.

The UNHCR in India in 2016 have granted refugee I-cards. The Quadriga tries to convince that the Identity cards do not in any manner supersede the Indian laws. It is, however, outrageous that on Indian soil, it is not the Indian Government but an outside agency that is seeking to determine the status of illegal immigrants. Sovereignty to this extent has never been ceded by India to empower any outside agency to determine who our refugees are and who not. The sole discretion lies with the Central Government. Parliament has not enacted any law about refugees from Myanmar.

It was also said that the deportation "would also be in contradiction with the principle of 'Non-Refoulement', which has been widely recognised as a principle of Customary International Law" is also absolutely wrong. It must also be noticed that the policy of "Non-Refoulement" is not part of customary international law.

The logic that "India has ratified and is a signatory to various Conventions that recognise the Principle of 'Non-Refoulement', that prohibits the deportation of refugees to a country where they face a threat to their life" was also wrong and incorrect. Principle of Non-Refoulment is rooted in the 1951 Treaty that has not been signed by India or ratified by it.

Lord Denning in his book **"The Due Process of Law"** has written an "Introduction" to Part Five—"Entrances and Exits" (p. 155) and the opening paragraph thereof reads as under:

"In recent times, England has been invaded—not by enemies—nor by friends—but by those who seek England as a heaven. In their own countries, there are poverty, disease and no homes. In England, there is social security—a national health service and guaranteed housing—all to be had for the asking without payment and without working for it. Once here, each seeks to bring his relatives to join him. So they multiply exceedingly."

Article 370 of the Constitution till very recently imposed many restrictions on non-domiciled people from staying in the state of Jammu & Kashmir. While the rest of India was not allowed to stay in the State of Jammu & Kashmir, the illegally immigrated Rohingya community were permitted to settle near the sensitive Pakistan border.

The situation posed before India by the Rohingyas, is one by invaders, by those who deliberately chose to pay no respect to the authorities or the laws, and clandestinely entered Indian soil and now seek protection under the same Indian constitution.

The European nations have recently suffered the results of this kind of entry like France, Germany, Belgium, and Britain and also due to the Bangladeshi Muslims in India where attacks by refugees have become the order of the day. The fact remains that illegal Rohingyas are not refugees; they must be seen as aggressors/invaders. And without doubt, all of them settled in the most strategic locations of the country like Jammu and Kashmir, Hyderabad, Delhi must be a matter of great concern.

The Quadriga's effort to colour the Rohingyas issue with the Chakma refugees was also ill-conceived. There are a great many distinctions in both cases. While the Chakmas never jeopardised India's relations with any friendly country, Rohingyas do. While Chakmas never ran a terrorist organisation, Rohingyas do run ARSA. While the Chakmas were relatively peaceful people, Rohingyas are not. Rohingyas are an indigenous ethnic group belonging to the state of Myanmar unlike the Chakma refugees, who were found to be persons of Indian origin. The lack of any discernible connection to the Union of India on the part of the Rohingyas makes this case completely different from that of the Chakma refugees.

The connection of Rohingyas with ISI, facilitation by radical Islamist group PFI and PFI's coordination with the Communist groups, the Communists' cordiality with the Christian missionaries, and overall, the back-up and cover-up by a particular set of journalists with Human rights organisations, makes it a perfect recipe of the Quadriga Gang.

□

A writer, columnist, researcher and writes on national security and policy issues.

Atmanirbhar Bharat

—Dharmendra Madaan

Today, world's environment is changing rapidly which gives rise to lots of challenges before Indian economy and Indians as a whole. We all need to work on 3S viz. speed, scale & skills. We are facing lots of challenges such as communal disputes, disputes from China, Nepal & Pakistan, high unemployment rate, low economic growth rate, coronavirus threat, corporate frauds and lack of defence goods and others.

To handle all these challenges, we need economic re-engineering and new and innovative thinking on all fronts such as to develop new innovative products, own search engines, have chat forums and other social websites owned and controlled by Indians.

New structures are required to be established for children, youth and women of our country, such as work from home for women who cannot join office due to family responsibilities, developing coding and other skills in children by establishing skill development schools for this purpose and also need to work on sports skills of students who after a time, could not get enough opportunities to compete at the global level.

For youth who are ready to work, enough job opportunities should be generated. Youth should be encouraged & supported (financially, technically and in all other ways) to run their own start-ups and develop them. Funding & legal regulations should be relaxed for this purpose. No official visit and notices-free system should be developed.

If India has to become superpower, it first has to become the largest manufacturing hub of the world. For this purpose, government has to closely monitor the ground level implementation of its financial and other schemes and stop corruption and favouritism.

Secondly, although the government has taken lots of steps towards deregularisation, still further major steps need to be taken in this direction. Delicensing is also important to push up the manufacturing sector. Government should make business persons hands free of legal formalities.

Out of a total population of 130 crore people, only 1.5 crore pay income tax. Government needs to simplify GST and club the corporate and individual income tax into it because imposing tax on income after charging GST leads to double taxation on single individual. Single Tax system should be implemented. Government should think over increasing the tax payers by giving direct benefits to middle income groups as well. Government needs to give 5-10 year tax exemptions to those starting manufacturing units and development projects.

Government needs to trust the finance professionals who are contributing towards the economic growth by helping their clients in depositing income tax & GST. Government needs to vest strong powers in the hands of professionals, combined with liabilities of misuse. Since finance professionals are acting as agents of government as far as the tax collection matters are concerned, a certain percentage of tax collected through a professional should be credited to his account as reward. It will enhance the tax collection in the country.

Judicial system of the country should also be upgraded for expeditious resolution of cases. For this purpose, fast-track courts, 24X7 system and e-adalats should be given priority. Indian Judicial system should be kept free from financial and political corruption.

As far as our education system is concerned, we need to develop double shift system and online systems in all government schools and colleges. We also need to develop skills in the students, which are important for the practical world. Education system should include practical trainings to students from time to time, which are next to nil right now. More public & private universities and schools need to be opened.

Government needs to start business support Centres for financial, technical, legal and other help to entrepreneurs. Government further needs to reduce GST on Diesel and other essential goods and services so that the demand for goods and services could be increased in the country.

Government should develop its own business Centres and corporates on PPPP (Public Private People Partnership) model. Those corporates should be supported in which large public has financial or other interests. Family-oriented business houses should be left at their own standing.

As far as debts becoming NPAs are concerned, government should come up with new loan settlement scheme and restructure the debts due upon business persons and allow them further time to repay their debts. Partial or full interest waiver would also be a great step to assist entrepreneurs.

To save the cost and time of the country, election reforms are required to be done. One time election system should be implemented. Prevention of Horse Trading Act should be passed by Parliament to ensure stable government in Centre and States.

Government should open more IITs, IIMs & AIIMS in the country. Government should club ICAI, ICSI and ICMAI and form a single largest Financial Body namely Indian Accountants Federation (IAF) in the world, with all professionals (CA, CS, CMA) working within their respective jurisdictions.

I would end up saying that although the government has taken major steps to win the trust of people of the nation, but lots of expectations are still waiting for response...

□

B.Com. (H), FCA, LL.B. and is a Visiting Faculty of ICAI & ICMAI for Law & Audit.

'Make in India' and 'Vocal for Local' is the Only Path for Economic Growth

—**Shankar Lal Agarwal**

Recently, the Prime Minister, Shri Narendra Modi, gave out the slogan-BE VOCAL FOR LOCAL. This is not a new concept. He has respected 'SWADESHI' from the very start. In his previous office, Prime Minister Modiji had given out the slogan: 'Make in India', thereby promoting local production by advancing loans to many start-ups. At one point of time, there were only one or two mobile manufacturing companies in India and consumers were mostly dependent on foreign companies. The effect of 'Make in India' campaign on 25 September, 2014 resulted in establishing more than 200 mobile operational production units pan India. In the automobile sector, there has been a revolutionary innovation. However, the target of boosting the GDP from 15% to 25% by manufacturing sector was not achieved due to various reasons. It was evident that this program gave full freedom for foreign investment. This resulted in many foreign investors starting production by setting up their industries here. This meant that we were now producing what we were earlier importing, with the help of foreign investments. Consequently, employment opportunities grew and various regions witnessed considerable growth. This was the singular thought behind the Prime Minister's initiative.

By announcing the relief package during the recent Covid-19 pandemic that brought about distress in the economic segment, the Prime Minister has not only voiced his perspective of SWADESHI, but has also propounded the slogan: 'Vocal for Local'.

The feeling behind announcing relief packages for micro and small scale industries has been *Swadeshi* and self-dependence. We have not to take the sentiments behind *Swadeshi* lightly. We must look back into history. The year 1991 witnessed the government attaining cheap popularity when Late Prime Minister, Chandra Shekhar mortgaged 46.91 tons of gold. Late Shri Narasimha Rao's government invited multinational companies to run their businesses to ameliorate the imbalanced economic scenario. This has caused us to deviate grossly from the path of *Swadeshi* and self-dependence-the basic formula that was given to us by the architects of India and by Mahatma Gandhi, who pioneered the same. Sprouted from the same soils of Gujarat, our Prime Misnister, Narendra Bhai Modi envisions India's prosperity through the path of *Swadeshi*. Looking at the current Indian scenario, we must not overlook that we have with us the world's largest fertile land, highest youth population and the most number of micro and small scale industries. All that is required is to encourage them and provide them with adequate government support. Soon India will attain its lost glory and will be re-titled the 'Golden Bird'. Looking at India's big market and countless consumers, many foreign multinational companies are inclined to do business with India. If *Swadeshi* products are promoted, then nothing can stop India from becoming economically self-dependent.

As a mark to oppose the atomic blast during the time when Late Shri Atal Bihari Vajpayee was the Prime Minister, many countries put an economic ban on India but the government did not get destabilised. As a result, the countries that banned trading with India got segregated from the market and faced heavy economic losses. Eventually, all the refraining countries withdrew their economic ban on India unanimously.

Japan is a unique model of Swadeshi. Even though Japan's population holds a mere 1.6% share in world population, it has retained its hold of 7 to 12 % of world production for the past three decades, purely because of its self-dependence model. The Japanese market sells 4% foreign cars as compared to 96% locally manufactured Japanese cars. The same is with other electronic items, wherein Japanese products have a huge demand in the international market. It is ironical to note that in India, 13% cars are manufactured by Indian companies, while 87% cars are manufactured by foreign car making companies.

Indo-China Import–Export Tabulation

(₹ in crore)

Year	Import	Export
2016&17	379126.00	64134.00
2017&18	492236.00	85999.00
2018&19	492070.00	117275.00
2019&20	440091.00	111270.00

Today, many of our products have 'MADE IN INDIA' printed on them. The ownership of nearly 70 to 100 % production capacity of cold drinks, soaps, paste, washing powder, shoe polish, mobile phones, TV, refrigerators etc., is reserved with foreign companies. 'Made in India' is written on these commodities whereas they are only assembled here under the name of 'Make in India'. Most of the employment and costing related to the major components is done in foreign countries.

In the 90s, before the policies related to import and foreign investment were initiated, 100 % of TV, fridge, cold drinks, cement, self–driven vehicles etc., were categorised under the segment, 'Poorn Swadeshi' or 'Made by Bharat'. With the onset of globalisation, liberalisation of imports and fostering foreign investments, Indian industries gradually became sluggishly sick or were shut down. Some of them were taken over by foreign companies. For example, the Indian refrigerator company, Kelvinator was taken over by an American firm, Whirlpool. Alwyn of the Birla Group and Maharaj International were taken over by the Swedish Company, Electrolux. Before this, all refrigerators were *Swadeshi*. Cement units of Tata Group, ACC, cement units of Raymond, Juari cement, Gujarat Ambuja, etc., were taken over by European companies like Lafarge and Hillsome etc. Earlier cement was manufactured by Indian companies. For the past 29 years, production of bottled water, cold drinks, ice creams, soaps, cosmetic items, production of cement and fridges has gone into the hands of foreign ownership thereby raising the question: who will have full control over the country's import-export-commercial and agricultural prospects?

Today, China is glaring at India. I believe that this is quite natural. We have to blame ourselves for it. It can easily be predicted that in coming days, many other countries would also be casting a snare at us, because like China, we have handed over our ability to be self-dependent to them. Today, we are importing raw materials for industries as well as finished products mainly from China. The result of importing goods equal to 5 times of our export to China has already come up before us. Today, China is becoming the world's economic powerhouse.

Owing to global business associations and various other agreements, India is not in a position to ban trade with any particular country. This task needs to be fulfilled by the people of India. The one and only way out is to boycott Chinese products as well as all other imported items and to incorporate *Swadeshi* into our lifestyle. Indian citizens are criticising China and holding it responsible for its sour relationship with India as they hold China solely responsible for slaying of Indian soldiers at the Indo-China border. The people of India have also started voicing their opinion about boycotting Chinese products. The need of the hour is to foster this flame in the minds of the Indian public. Only then we shall begin to tread upon the road to self-reliance. There is a strong need for 'Make in India' and 'Made by Bharat' products. There has already been an investment income deficit of 40 billion dollars because of exceeding the limit of foreign Direct investment causing a decrease in outbound domestic investment. The rupee has drastically fallen because of a heavy business loss of approximately 160 billion dollars, in addition to more than 40 billion dollar losses owing to excessive FDI, as already stated. At the beginning of economic reforms in 1991, a dollar was equivalent to ₹ 18, which has now reached almost ₹ 75. Hence, promoting domestic investment along with government assistance will bring about monetary liquidity.

Prime Minister Narendra Modi on 12 May 2020, talked about India being self-dependent so as to offer stern competition to global chains. He emphasised that local production should be supported and current challenges should be seen as rising opportunities. With 'Make in India' and 'Made by Bharat' or 'Vocal for Local' and its sentiments of being self-reliant through Swadeshi production, we need to steer our nation towards economic freedom. And this will only be possible when every Indian will adopt SWADESHI and say an emphatic NO to imported products.

□

B.Com., FCA, is presently independent Director in Hindustan Salt Ltd., a public sector undertaking. He was a member of State Public Grievance Committee, Member Finance, Govt. of Rajasthan.

Self-Depend, Self-Sufficient and Prosperous New India

—Raman Tandon

India was called a 'Golden Bird' in ancient times and not without a reason. In olden times, till the 18th century when industrial revolution started in Europe, India's share of global GDP was more than 25 %. So India was the largest economy of the world. But in olden times, Indian subcontinent accounted for 1/4th of world population also; therefore, the GDP per person was meagre and was stagnant. So it was famously said that India was a rich country inhabited by poor people.

In 1947, one Indian rupee was almost equal to one USD in value. Today, the world is dominated by western countries' currencies like USD, EURO and POUND so that their exuberant lifestyle can be maintained cheaply. The calculation of GDP is done in US dollars which are valued 75 times Indian rupees, and therefore, in USD terms, India is placed at much lower position than the so-called developed economies. But in terms of absolute & real production, India would probably stand second to none in the world.

Indian rupee has traditionally been under pressure due to previous government's absolute neglect of Defence production capabilities and therefore ever-increasing Defence Budget, burgeoning oil and gold imports and large-scale shifting of manufacturing base from India to China. Lowering Indian rupee valuation had traditionally been the Congress government policy to benefit the exporters, which along with large budget deficit policy, induced large-scale inflation in our country which touched annual rate of 10 % and above under the Congress government rule. The real effect of the big inflation numbers was borne by the middle economic class of the country and to some extent, the lower economic class.

Things have changed a lot under the present BJP government in India which has adopted the policy of lower budget deficit, lower gold imports, increase in indigenous defence capabilities and lower Chinese imports.

The present government has, however, had to face the global recessionary trends from the year 2014 onwards and the current unfortunate conditions caused by the China-created Corona virus for which there is no parallel in recent history. Large-scale disruption has been caused in the economic activities which has resulted in almost 75% reduction in demand and the supply of industrial output and also in the service sector output. India is hampered further by the fact that still in the 21st century; a large part of workforce has remained unskilled and suited for agricultural activities only. Further, most of the skilled workforce is also employed in activities not related to its skills. Putting the economy back on the track again and provision of jobs to those displaced is the highest priority for the government of India and the Hon'ble Prime Minister has candidly declared that Self-sufficiency and self-dependence are the key words in the economic policy of new India. A lot has been done already and a lot more needs to be done in right earnest, to bring prosperity back to each and every household of India. Tougher situations need tougher solutions and having a 'KARMATH' Prime Minister at the helm, will definitely help.

India has a unique problem related to its population. The education system introduced by Britishers and still followed by us, is deficient and is aimed at creating clerical talent at the most. Moreover, the education system is very stressful, right from the beginning level and by the age of 18 years, a student learns hardly anything worth its name to be able to engage in self-employment or be worthy of a meaningful job. Time has come to self-introspect, and take a hard look into the systems to do a meaningful overhaul.

A few humble suggestions are listed here which are not part of the traditional monetary tools employed by the RBI, but which are untraditional steps which, if taken promptly, will put the economy back on the rails. The aim of the proposed steps is to change the basic mindset of masses and ensure availability of jobs in abundance and also to promote self-employment among masses.

1. Create a parallel education system in which the students can opt out of standard education system after 5th or 8th standard and learn

specific profession, art, talent, sport, trade. Those aiming for general higher education system can remain in the present system.

2. Stop insisting on English medium education system in the parallel education system which restricts the growth of intelligence in the masses and fills them with a sense of inferiority to others.
3. The present crises related to Covid-19 is a good opportunity for reversing the labour and talent migration flow into the cities. The Central Government could develop schemes for all the states to follow wherein it should be made mandatory to acquire certain amount of land near all smaller towns, break it into very small plots of 20 to 30 square yards, do very basic development of providing drainage, shade, water and electricity. These plots, the number of which should be in lakhs near every small town, could be provided at a nominal rent to people looking for self-employment.
4. The states could further be told to provide land and economic stimulus to encourage small and medium industries located near the big cities, to shift to the smaller towns in multiple numbers of states where the labour live. This step would ensure decongestion of four big metros and ensure provision of jobs and self employment opportunities in the smaller towns near the homes of the unemployed talent and labour and ensure all-round development of all the states. The economic stimulus to encourage mass level shifting of industries, could be in the shape of income tax, GST rebates, exemption from Factory Act provisions, elimination of Inspector Raj laws, etc.
5. India has a unique problem of substantially big number of uneducated people, who are employable into the very basic jobs of physical labour only, into either the construction industry or the factories. The present Governments in the centre as well in the states have a huge responsibility to provide employment opportunities to them. An immediate solution could be to develop housing for the poor, near all the smaller towns, all over India. The way to go is to identify parcels of land all over India, and develop them into housing projects with Government and the poor people as the main beneficiaries and also the main contributors of resources and labour. For example, in a plot of two to three acres, 500 families could be enlisted, who would provide 2 members per family for labour to develop that plot as a 1000 flats multi-storey housing project. The Government could provide the land,

infrastructure and materials to the project as a major partner. All the 500 families, at the end, would get a flat each and the remaining 500 flats would be sold to others to recover the cost to the government. This step has the potential to ensure employment to crores of displaced migrant labourers and other people.

6. All housing societies with 50 to 60 years' old two to three storey construction in the four metros, could be compulsorily asked to redevelop the housing societies, with multi-level modern construction with proper underground parking facility for all and with water and energy conservation systems in place. There would be huge employment generation with this step and the problem of congestion of parking would be sorted out to a great extent.
7. It is a common knowledge that Indian police is overburdened and overstretched. The time has come to decentralise the policing duties, with a purpose to reduce the burden on the police and also to ensure more efficiency and more employment. For example, the police are routinely entrusted with the job of solving white collar crime puzzles for which they have no expertise and time. The result is that the investigations drag on for years and the litigants suffer enormously with multiple trips to police stations and courts etc. The government could make it compulsory to refer the white collar cases to professionals like Chartered Accountants who understand the system better than unqualified police personnel. The litigants could be made to pay nominal fees for the services of the professionals. This way, the police investigations would become more transparent and professional and most of them would be completed in a few days.
8. The Indian courts have crores of pending cases which linger on for years. The government could look at providing professional support to the courts. The Chartered Accountants, company secretaries, Engineers, senior lawyers could be hired by the courts to provide help to the courts, to solve cases on priority basis and with more professional accuracy. The government could reduce the number of pending cases drastically in one year and bring more efficiency to the court system by reducing the time taken to deliver the judicial order.
9. One dominating reason why our exports could not pick up at a good pace while the Dragon outpaced us smartly, is the lack of sector-wise government effort and incentives. While there are multiple number

of Chambers of Commerce, which get huge funds for promoting knowledge, the system hardly works. There is an urgent need to hire professionals by the government at each level, to form teams for each and every product and service which has the potential for exports. The specific team should cater to one specific product or service and should continuously monitor the internal and external developments, to keep the industry stable and keep the country export-efficient related to each and every field.

10. The Start-Ups have been given utmost importance by our respected Prime Minister, and lots of funding schemes have been initiated at the behest of the government. Our experience has revealed that most of the Start-Ups are failing because of lack of Management skills, Marketing and Financial support without which the Start-Ups find the sailing tough. India would do well to bring up Management, Marketing and Personnel Management, as special status industries, and provide financial incentives to professionals to form teams and provide independent management services to millions of small and medium scale industries and business. In the absence of these efforts, our Engineers and MBAs would remain unemployable which would be a shame on our country.
11. It is a common knowledge that our youth is scaling newer heights in USA, Canada and other developed countries. It is time to request those Indians living abroad to come back and create employment in the field of their expertise. India would need to offer them huge benefits in terms of land and protection from Inspector Raj, so that they think of doing the country a favour. But this is possible and hardly needs any emphasis here to realise that this is the need of the time.

I am very hopeful that our country, under the leadership of our visionary Prime Minister, will sail through this period of crises and put hundred steps forward in making our country prosperous, self-sufficient and self-reliant and become a financial power, which the world will salute.

□

FCA (ICAI), ACA (New Zealand), is a social activist and also a member of PHD Chamber of Commerce and Industry.

Village Entrepreneurship

—Rajeev Kumar

Heart of India lies in its villages. If heart is strong and healthy, then naturally, the whole body will be so. According to census 2011, out of the total population of India 1210854977, 833 million (68.84%) live in rural areas. Predominantly, India being an agricultural country, farming is its main occupation with an estimate of 61.5% dependent on agriculture.

Rural Development is the development of rural people aimed towards their economic and social strata. The pathetic condition of rural India would be a major hindrance to a developing country like India. The core issues in the backwardness of rural India are the poverty level, illiteracy, lack of awareness, techniques and technology and natural disaster like floods, etc. Illiteracy makes the poor vulnerable to political and economic exploitation. Although many provisions have been made by the government of India to enhance rural development, the fruits of development have not percolated down to them. It is important to make villages self-dependent so that they can make products by themselves. This issue can be addressed by enlightening the masses through formal and non-formal education. They should be able to make small technology which can help to eradicate unemployment. This may give rise to many small industries in village itself. This is indeed a herculean task and it requires strong financial support from government.

Innovative Ideas for Rural Development in India:

1. **Establishment of Rural Industries:** All the village industries come under the following categories:
   - **Agro Based Industries:** Includes cultivation under controlled conditions of horticultural and agricultural crops which includes floriculture and cultivation of vegetables, also post-harvest

operation on all fruits and vegetables such as Dairy products, Fruit juice, Pickles, Sugar industries, Jaggery, Oil processing from oil seeds, Spices, etc.

- **Forest Based Industries:** includes products which are obtained from **forest** like wood products, sports goods, plywood timber **industries**, gum, tobacco, match-box, Bamboo products, Honey, Coir industry, etc.
- **Mineral based industry:** use raw materials like Manufacturing **industries**. It includes the iron and steel **industry which** is the basic **industry** on which all other **industries** depend upon–Wall coating powders, red oxide making, stone crushing, Cement industries etc.
- **Textile Industry:** For the generation of employment for both skilled and unskilled people especially in villages, textile industry is a great source of income which is the second-largest employment generating sector in India. In the present scenario, it is offering direct employment to over 35 million people in the country. For example-Spinning, Weaving, Colouring and Bleaching.
- **Engineering and Services:** Mining, Power and energy, building construction, technical application in designing of products are sources and products of engineering services. It also includes Small and medium-sized industries that produce agricultural equipment and machinery for usage in rural areas.
- **Handicrafts:** Handicraft plays a great role in promoting the heritage and tradition of a country because it includes the use of indigenous substances and is very important because it represents our culture and tradition through the preservation of traditional comprehension, recognition and talents. For example-local traditional wooden or bamboo handicrafts and decorative products, toys etc.

2. **Start-ups:** A Start-up is a young company, entrepreneurial venture, to develop a unique product or service, newly emerged business, which aims to meet need, want or problem of market places by developing a viable business model around products, services, processes or platforms. Many village people are still deprived of electricity, clean drinking water, medical facility. Therefore, the social start-ups are trying to bring about a change in villages through them. For example:

Nirmai, Gaatha, Rozgar Dhaba, Maatritva, Rural Health-Rural Primary Health Care and Rural Education, Supply Chain, Trading in Agricultural produce, Processing Agricultural produces, Fisheries-Both Culture and Trading, Rural Micro Finance etc.

3. **Computer & Internet Services:** For today's Generation, **Internet** is the vital system that interconnects the different **computer** systems across the world. The **Internet** system carries an ample amount of data and information resources and services like World Wide Web (WWW), electronic mail, etc. It also Provides Application facilities like E-Commerce, Rail & Bus Ticket booking, Digital Marketing Agency etc.

Encourage Rural Entrepreneurship: They may be of the following types:

1. Individual Entrepreneurship-single ownership of the enterprise.
2. Group Entrepreneurship–Includes partnership, private limited company and public limited company
3. Cluster Formation Entrepreneurship–It comprises of NGOs, CBOs, SHGs, VOs etc. and also include formal and non-formal association of a group of individuals on the basis of caste, occupation, income, etc.
4. Cooperative Entrepreneurship-It is an autonomous association of persons united for a common purpose.

Government Schemes for Rural Entrepreneurship in India

- **Entrepreneurship Development Institution Scheme-** An autonomous and non-profit institute, Entrepreneurship Development Institute of India (EDII), was set up in 1983 and is sponsored by financial institutions-the IDBI Bank Ltd., IFCI Ltd., ICICI Bank Ltd. and the State Bank of India (SBI). The Government of Gujarat pledged twenty-three acres of land on which stands the EDII campus. In order to achieve its mission, EDII has helped set up twelve state-level exclusive entrepreneurship development centres and institutes. One of the prominent achievements, however, was taking entrepreneurship to a large number of schools, colleges, science and technology institutions and management schools in many states by including entrepreneurship inputs in their curricula. According to EDII's expertise in Entrepreneurship, the University Grants

Commission (UGC) had also assigned EDII the task of developing curriculum on Entrepreneurship and the Gujarat Textbook Board assigned to it the task of developing textbooks on Entrepreneurship for 11th & 12th standards.

- **Rajiv Gandhi Udyami Mitra Yojana (RGUMY):** A Scheme of "Promotion and Handholding of Micro and Small Enterprises. World over, micro and small enterprises (MSEs) are significant part of the national economies thus increasing employment and decreasing poverty level. Recognising the importance of micro and small enterprises which constitute an important segment of Indian economy in terms of their contribution to country's industrial production, exports, employment and creation of entrepreneurial base, the Central and State Governments have been implementing several schemes and programmes for promotion and development of these enterprises.
- **Performance and Credit Rating Scheme (Implemented through NSIC): NSIC** is the nodal agency for **implementing** the **scheme** of **performance and credit rating** for Micro & Small Enterprises **through** its various branches/offices located in the country. The unit's **rating** is a combination of **performance and credit worthiness** of the unit.
- **Marketing Assistance Scheme:** Marketing is a tool for business development and is critical for the growth and survival of micro, small & medium enterprises. It is the paramount factor for the success of any enterprise. Large enterprises having sufficient resources at their command can hire manpower to take care of marketing of their products and services. But MSME sector lacks in these resources at their command and thus needs institutional support for providing these inputs in the field of marketing. Ministry of Micro, Small & Medium Enterprises, inter-alia, through National Small Industries Corporation (NSIC), a Public Sector Enterprise of the Ministry, has been providing marketing support to Micro & Small Enterprises (MSEs) under Marketing Assistance Scheme.

□

Banker and Corporate Consultant

Atmanirbhar Bharat through Technology Innovation & Entrepreneurship

—**Ketan Jain**

An ongoing pandemic of unprecedented proportions, Covid-19 has impacted lives and livelihoods across the globe. Even as the best minds in the world race towards finding preventive and curative solutions to combat and curb the spread of the novel coronavirus, the current crisis has been an eye-opener to several opportunities that have presented themselves during this time.

To this end, Hon'ble Prime Minister, Shri Narendra Modi made a clarion call for an Atmanirbhar Bharat, or a self-reliant India, that would be a source of local ingenuity creating global impact. He exhorted fellow citizens to utilise this time of crisis to be vocal for local and be self-reliant.

He identified Technology as one of the pillars on which Atmanirbhar Bharat would stand and to make these pillars incredibly powerful and resilient and design them to withstand any onslaughts of potential new crises, it is imperative to strengthen them through the creation of an underlying ecosystem of institutionalised skills development, advanced research, and technology-driven innovations. This would incentivise a massive upsurge of world-class start-ups and entrepreneurs, that would create new livelihoods across the length and breadth of the country.

Creating a nation of job-creators and not just job-seekers is the key. And central to this, is the need for an extensive collaboration between corporate industry, academia, and governments at the village, district, state, and central levels. Such synergies have indeed gained momentum with the Covid-19 crisis and need to be further capitalised on.

The important pillars on which Atmanirbhar Bharat would stand and create more Entrepreneurs are involving Technology and young Talented population towards nation-building activities by focusing on developing vocational, technical, and managerial skills and fostering the most significant innovation since the internet. Interestingly, **Blockchain Technology** has disrupted every industry, be it retail, healthcare, or manufacturing, and it is expected to transform the lives of almost every entity or individuals in large number. This presents a glorious opportunity for young creative entrepreneurs to tap into and create growing organisations with global impact.

What is Blockchain?

A blockchain is a time-stamped series of immutable records of data that is managed by a cluster of computers not owned by any single entity, while keeping a log of information safe. Each of these blocks of data (i.e. block) is secured and bound to each other using cryptographic principles (i.e. chain).With the use of an immutable distributed ledger, all the participants of a blockchain network can have access to the same information. Additional information can be added, but the original data cannot be altered. Transactions are recorded on the distributed ledger with the consent of most of the blockchain network participants.

For Example, think of a railway company. When we buy tickets on an app or the web, the credit card company takes a cut for processing the transaction. In blockchains, not only can the railway operator save on credit card processing fees, it can move the entire ticketing process to the blockchain. The two parties in the transaction are the railway company and the passenger. The ticket is a block, which will be added to a ticket blockchain. Just as a monetary transaction on the blockchain is a unique, independently verifiable, and unfalsifiable record (like Bitcoin), so can your ticket be. Incidentally, the final ticket blockchain is also a record of all transactions for, say, a certain train route, or even the entire train network, comprising every ticket ever sold, every journey ever taken.

Blockchain In India

According to Blockchain Report 2019 by NASSCOM, the adoption of blockchain technology in India is experiencing rapid growth and investments in blockchain-based projects have touched over $20 billion across various industries. The report further states that many Indian state governments such as those of Telangana, Kerala, Karnataka, Andhra Pradesh, and Maharashtra are supporting blockchain start-ups and projects and organising conferences and hackathons on the topic.

As per data from the World Intellectual Property Organisation, India stands sixth on the list of patents and trends in the blockchain space with a total of 67 patents approval in 2018. A wave of digital payments has swept in ever since demonetisation impacted the Indian citizens in 2016. There has been a huge shift from transacting in physical currency to digital payments through platforms such as Paytm, Google Pay, PhonePe etc.

Indians are gradually realising the importance of digital money and leveraging seamless transactions and a cashless approach that digital money offers. With the large-scale successful adoption of digital payments, India is now keen on moving towards adopting blockchain. **Blockchain technology** is emerging as one of the key innovations that will define the future of digital transactions in India and transform the FinTech landscape.

Role of Blockchain in FinTech in Banking and Insurance

FinTech and Blockchain is the combination with which the technology made an entry within the world. The first time Blockchain was mentioned, it was in the context of changing the banking and finance industry and since then, the industry has been waiting to be decentralised.

Banks in India were quick to realise the opportunities of blockchain for efficient banking operations and are efficiently using the KYC procedures offered by the technology with faster transaction, minimal to zero hacks and lowered transactional costs.

SBI leads as the first bank to use KYC and facilitate remittances based on blockchain followed by banks like Axis, HDFC, ICICI that are implementing blockchain for its KYC and trade finance procedures. Apart from this, the DLT also enables AML, the validation of land records and asset inventory audits.

Inherent inefficiencies in the claim management system of the Insurance Industry lead to losses of about ₹ 10,000 crore per year. Implementing blockchain for claim management is the ultimate solution to mitigate these issues. For the same, Cognizant has partnered with insurance providers such as ICICI Prudential Life Insurance, SBI Life

Insurance, HDFC Life, Kotak Life and more to develop a secure data-sharing solution built on Corda blockchain platform.

Role of Blockchain in Enterprise

It is generally believed that it is difficult to incorporate any new technology in an established business or company that has survived the thick and thins and has emerged as the leaders. One reason behind this difficulty is identified as an inclusion of a new technology that is still in its nascent stage in the legacy systems that have brought a business so far.

But the time has now come for Enterprises to shed the doubts while being safe and incorporate Enterprise Blockchain Solutions in a portion of their process and only scale when they confirm that the technology is working for them.

Using the different platforms-Ethereum, Hyperledger Fabric, Ripple, and Quorum, even everyone can join the list of enterprises who have incorporated and are now benefitting from the decentralised technology. It's time to know the exact process to Introduce Blockchain in Enterprise.

Role of Blockchain in a Start-up

For Start-ups, they are at an advantage in terms of emerging as an industry disruptor by adding the technology that solves almost every problem that cripples a business from offering real value to its customers and internal stakeholders alike. Inclusion of Blockchain technology in a start-up ecosystem is a process that can go untouched with decentralisation-an event that is a blessing for start-ups which are looking to establish themselves as innovators in the market and even for those who are looking to raise funds.

Role of Blockchain in Healthcare

Following are some industrial challenges that the Blockchain technology in Healthcare can solve-

1. Fragmented Data: One of the biggest reasons for EMR frauds or data theft can be traced back to one server where all the medical data coming in from all the different platforms, merged. When every data is stored in a common place, the moment the system is hacked, data gets compromised.

With the combination of Blockchain and Healthcare, your healthcare app gets to store the patients' data across a number of different nodes eliminating the risk of central server getting hacked or crashed.

2. Timely Access of Data: The distributed ledger that comes as a package with Blockchain and Healthcare mix enables distributed and secure access to the patient's health data and the updates that are made to the patient's shared data are also done in real time.

3. System Interoperability: Blockchain offers a decentralised form of computer network and internet across boundaries. So, when a health organisation seeks information about the patient from another healthcare organisation, they no more have to wait for the data to travel several miles.

4. Data Security: Blockchain has become a synonym to Security. Being completely decentralised and immutable, the patient data is A. Only accessible to those, who have the need to interact with it and B. Any change when made to it, is visible to everyone in the Blockchain making it impossible for someone to fetch the data without others knowing.

5. Patient Generated Data: While it is still possible (although difficult) to get consolidated patient data from across different healthcare organisations, combining the data that the users generate through their personal healthcare device–wearables–with the ones generated by healthcare organisations, is not easy.

Role of Blockchain in Real Estate

The Indian Real Estate Industry faces challenges in maintaining, searching, and verifying title deeds, making ownership susceptible to fraud, time-consuming process in transferring property and an over-reliance on brokers, banks, registration officers, etc. Blockchain solves these issues by digitising land titles, therefore, each land would have a digital address stored on the blockchain with details of occupancy, ownership records, finance, specifications of the property and associated legal disputes, if any. Further, the decentralised nature of the technology eliminates the dependence on middlemen and enable instant transfer of property, while the blockchain-based smart contracts solve the issue of repetitive transactions or contracts.

Seeing the acceptance that the technology has received from the Real Estate world, it is safe to say that it is the Property Market from where maximum use cases would emerge very soon.

Role of Blockchain in Transactions

Here are the different ways Blockchain for Transactions can have an impact, no matter which industry is under the microscope–

1. Increased Transparency and Security of Data: The way in which businesses and organisations store data will undergo drastic changes using blockchain technology. Presently, record-keeping is a cumbersome task, that requires dedicated staff and incurs huge overheads. It is also prone to human errors and physical hazards such as fires and thefts. Blockchains are virtual distributed ledgers, free from all these shortcomings. Transactions are encrypted, immutable, and stored in an orderly fashion. They are accessible to all nodes, but cannot be altered.

2. Elimination of Intermediaries: Blockchain in transactions are not mediated by third-party intermediaries. They are verified by miners, who work round-the-clock in solving mathematical puzzles. As soon as these computations are done, the transaction is verified and added to the distributed ledger. The change is reflected throughout the blockchain. There is no need for lengthy documentation or hefty verification charges. The reward for miners is nominal and isn't a burden on parties involved in a transaction. Elimination of intermediaries reduces transaction costs and speeds up the process.

3. Efficiency in Settlements: Traditionally, it took days or weeks for settlement of transactions. For example, you might purchase a two-wheeler, but registration of its ownership can take months. In blockchain technology, settlements are done instantly, and this is perhaps its biggest advantage. As there are no intermediaries and all verification are logic-based, human involvement is minimal and so are processing delays.

Blockchain and Mobile App

The next prominent industry we are going to look at is the mobile app economy.

I will highlight on how Blockchain technology applications would solve these persistent mobile app industry issues.

1. App Approval Process: The decision on which app would get approved and which will not work as a monopoly started and was managed by Google Play Store and Apple App Store, with them not giving the developers any clear guidelines related to app rejection or approval.

Inclusion of Blockchain in App development brings both-approval guidelines and applications-on a public ledger which is open for others to review as well, thus ending the monopoly created by Play Store and App Store.

2. In-App Purchase: What happens in case of in-app purchases is that first, the app store charges an amount for enabling in-app purchases from their platform, and then the debit/credit purchase that users make, charge them in name of transaction fees, processing charges, and several other extra charges.

All these cuts that happen in the amount of in-app purchase that a user makes usually amount to over 30%-something that can easily be avoided by no transaction fees cryptocurrency payments.

3. High Advertisement Cost: The advertisement industry is full of the unclear and non-transparent mode of expenses. Blockchain, by making the advertisement platforms decentralised, not just removes the middlemen from the picture but also brings down the transaction cost by making the whole process more transparent. These are simply a few examples of how Blockchain can be integrated in the mobile app industry to streamline it further.

Role of Blockchain in Future Audits

Blockchain And the Building Blocks of The Future Audit-The technological advantages only multiply, when blockchain is aligned with artificial intelligence (AI) and robotic process automation (RPA), the latter being designed to handle the sorts of routine tasks that used to take up valuable time for audit teams.

In Blockchain, it becomes a Triple entry system, which is Debit, Credit & Confirmations, all together, that happens almost Instantaneously. Blockchain technology can change the age-old auditing process. It can contribute to Auditing profession by means of

- Automation
- Instant verification
- Cost savings
- Efficiencies

Artificial intelligence (AI) techniques-most prominently machine learning—allow us to look at data using advanced pattern recognition and harness this functionality to digitally assist our auditors by:

Analysing and extracting data from unstructured data, such as contracts, invoices, and images to gain further audit evidence.

Analysing large sets of data to help identify, assess and respond to the risks of material misstatement due to fraud.

Potential Roadblocks in its Adoption

The Indian government is yet to implement clearly defined regulations on blockchain technology. The adoption would accelerate when the regulations are well-defined by the government.

RBI and tax authorities in India are not in favour of cryptocurrencies and ICOs, due to the issues related to tax evasion and lack of control of the regulators over the digital currencies. Start-ups and projects based on blockchain technologies are sceptical about going forward due to the battle between Indian authorities and cryptocurrencies.

Many supply chain vendors are not keen on adopting the technology due to the lack of awareness and trust issues in technology. Therefore, accelerated adoption of blockchain requires more digitisation and awareness.

Opportunity for India: Although blockchain is in its infancy, India is pacing towards its adoption and inclusion. Implementing this technology across all spheres of business will certainly prove to be a game-changer despite the roadblocks in its adoption. Combined efforts of the government and diverse industries will aid the policymakers in designing and implementing policies that will shape the future of the disruptive technology in India in Rural and Semi Urban areas

Note: The views and opinions expressed are solely those of the author and looking at the future opportunity in India for Young Population in diversified fields.

□

A Chartered Accountant, MBA, DISA, Cost Accountant, Certified ERP Implementation Specialist from Oracle in JD Edwards Enterprise One 9.1 and leadership in Managing Global Businesses.

Getting to Know Our Senior Citizens

—**Muni Shankar Pandey**

Introduction

As the country draws up lockdown exit strategies and learns to live with the virus, a segment of population which stands at a high-risk, requires even more attention and care, is the senior citizens. While the young will need to get to work so that engines of the economy can be fired up, the elderly in the country face a challenging time ahead both from a physical as well as mental health perspective. The emerging scenario, where the senior citizens with their underlying health conditions and an even more enhanced risk of contracting the deadly virus, necessitates a holistic approach towards their safety and well-being where each stakeholder, from the administration to their families, is prepared, equipped and fully committed to do their part. The Covid-19 pandemic has been like a wakeup call for the country, it has made us realise our ignorance towards the conditions of the senior citizens.

In this chapter we will try to get to know all about the senior citizens in contemporary times. We will try to understand all the challenges they face, the common diseases they suffer from, the coping mechanisms they adopt etc.

Current Population of Senior Citizens in India as well as the World

A thorough knowledge about our elderly is important, because they form a very important section of our society. Currently, there are 18 crore senior citizens in India and the number is only increasing. And globally, every 1 in 10 senior citizens is from India, therefore, understanding them is very urgent. According to studies, the population of senior citizens would double from 900 million (worldwide) to 2 billion in the coming future.

Now is the time for change and we should all come together to bring it. India has a young population, which is a good thing economically but in future, the population of the older people would overtake the population of the younger people which will bring all sorts of problems. According to some studies, India is ageing at a much faster rate than predicted, therefore, the solution for the betterment of the elderlies has to be now and immediate.

Problems that the Senior Citizens Face on a Daily Basis

Senior citizens face many problems on a daily basis regardless of a global pandemic, therefore, first we will try to understand that. The term senescence refers to the process of ageing encompassing all the biological, social, spiritual, intellectual and other changes that a person goes through. These changes though gradual, are life changing and can lead to various kinds of problems, therefore, coping and managing them is very important.

Physical Problems

As the human body grows older, many physical problems are experienced by an individual like slow metabolism, joint pains, menopause in women, loss of stamina and physical strength. These changes can be hard to accept by the senior citizens. Day-to-day activities become difficult for them, as they are not as physically strong as they were before.

Weakening of the senses like eyesight, hearing etc. also become a hindrance for them. Trivial things like cleaning the house, or even reading the daily newspaper becomes a task which has an underlying negative effect on their mental health. Many older people suffer from several physical ailments which have an adverse effect on their daily lives. The following physical ailments and diseases are some of the most common in senior citizens.

1. Diabetes: Diabetes is a chronic disease in which either the pancreas overproduces or underproduces insulin. Diabetes in senior citizens is very prevalent in India, it has been predicted that by 2050, there would be 33 million patients of diabetes in India. To manage diabetes properly, senior citizens should eat a healthy diet consisting of leafy vegetables and fruits.

2. Arthritis: In arthritis, there is inflammation in one or more joints. Common symptoms include joint pain and stiffness. Osteoarthritis is the second most common rheumatologic problem, and it affects about 22% to 39% senior citizens in India. It is more common in women than men. Nearly, 45% of women over the age of 65 years have symptoms, whereas 70% of those over 65 years show radiological evidence of Osteoarthritis.

Conditions like obesity and sedentary lifestyle can cause this kind of arthritis. To manage this disease, regular exercise along with proper intake of medication and a healthy diet should be taken.

3. Hypertension and Hypotension: Blood pressure refers to the pressure of the blood circulating on the walls of the blood vessels. The ideal blood pressure is 120/80 (systolic/diastolic)

Hypertension

It is characterised by increased systolic blood pressure with normal or low diastolic Blood pressure, caused by age-associated stiffening of the large arteries. According to some studies, 9 out of 10 individuals will have high blood pressure over a lifetime. It also makes one vulnerable to heart diseases and stroke. Treatment of hypertension could also help in preventing diseases like dementia.

Hypotension

Hypotension refers to low blood pressure in an individual; many elderly worldwide suffer from it. Low blood pressure without any other symptoms is not that serious and treatment is not required. But in the elderly, low blood pressure can be a sign of a more serious underlying problem. It can cause inadequate blood flow to the heart, brain, and other vital organs, which can be very dangerous.

Both hypertension and hypotension can be managed by regular exercise, a healthy diet consisting of less salt and living a less stressful lifestyle.

4. Heart Disease: Heart disease is very common in the elderly and is one of the top causes of death in them. Heart attack, heart failure, blockage etc. are some of the conditions that the elderly suffer from. Heart disease is also a major cause for disability and limited physical activity. The most common change that is caused by ageing is increased stiffness of the large arteries, called arteriosclerosis, or hardening of the arteries. This leads to high blood pressure, or hypertension which as mentioned before, is also common in elderly.

Heart disease can be managed by taking proper medication and controlling one's blood pressure along with a healthy diet.

5. Alzheimer's: Alzheimer's is a progressive disease that leads to destruction of memory and other mental functions which are very important.

It leads to degeneration of brain cells and their connection which eventually destroys memory.

Currently, there is no cure for the disease but proper management and medication can help a patient.

In India, almost 4 million people, generally senior citizens suffer from the disease, making India the third largest caseload in the world. It has been estimated that by 2030, the number of patients would be 7.5 million in India.

Constant support from family members has a lot of benefits for the patient.

6. Respiratory Disease: There are also various respiratory diseases that the senior citizens suffer from.

The top four respiratory diseases in elderly are lower respiratory tract infections, chronic obstructive pulmonary disease (COPD), tuberculosis, and lung cancer. They are among the ten leading causes of death worldwide. The causes for these diseases can be aged lungs, smoking, etc.

Mental Problems

The older people are just as prone to mental disorders like any other age group, if not more. According to the World Health Organisation, over 20% of older adults suffer from mental disorders. Mental problems of the elderly are generally overlooked, ignored and confused by their loved ones.

The following are some common mental disorders, the elderly suffer from:

Dementia

It affects almost 5-7% of the world population of people over the age of 60 years.

It is a neurodegenerative disease of multifactorial causation, heterogeneous presentation, and variable prognosis. Decline in performance and cognitive impairment in multiple domains are characteristics of it. It affects a person's independence in doing activities of daily living. It is also financially draining for the family of the patients as there are significant health-care costs and caregiver burden.

Depression

According to the World Health Organisation, depression is one of the top causes of disability in a senior citizen. The depression in senior citizens has witnessed an increase in the current scenario of the coronavirus pandemic. Imposed lockdown throughout the country has become one of the causes of depression among the elderly. Especially, senior citizens who live alone become depressed, as they feel alone and helpless.

And senior citizens who live with their families feel like a burden on their family, therefore, we need to start the conversation about the mental disorder in elderly and look for ways to protect them and make them feel safe.

Anxiety Disorders

Senior citizens are vulnerable to anxiety disorders too, they might feel anxious while meeting new people or going in a new social setting. Anxiety disorders are not taken seriously in elderly and the they are left alone to manage it which can have adverse effects on them. Panic and anxiety attacks can disrupt the daily life of an elderly and cause them a lot of difficulty.

It won't be wrong to say that mental disorders are not taken seriously in India as people are not aware about a lot of mental disorders an individual can suffer from. And mental disorders in the elderly are even more ignored. It is assumed that a senior citizen should be able to keep himself emotionally healthy without the help of others because of his/her age, but that is not true as the number of anxiety and depression cases are constantly rising.

Emotional health of the senior citizens should be given extra attention in case of a disaster, as every disaster has more negative effects on them than the rest; this is evident in the case of the corona pandemic.

Social Problems in Contemporary Times

In contemporary times, the senior citizens suffer from a lot of social and sociological problems.

The statistics say that approximately 18 Crore of the population is aged above 60 yrs. in India and, therefore, need attention. Out of them,

2.8 Crore are above 80, who require urgent medical assistance, and 0.18 Crore are homeless or deserted by the families. There are a number of sociological problems that they suffer from, some of them are mentioned below:

1. Generation gap: There is an obvious generational gap between the elderly and the new generation, in contemporary times this is evident through the medium of social media. The older generation are not as digitally active as the new generation. This might be the reason behind why the lockdown hit them a little harder than the new generation. The generational gap can make them feel left out and helpless, therefore, this time (during lockdown) should be used to encourage them to safely use social media and the internet. Another problem for senior citizens is the unsafe use of social media, a lot of senior citizens fall victim of cybercrime, therefore safe use of social media should be encouraged.

2. Bad social environment: The social environment of senior citizens also has an effect on their mental and physical health. Many senior citizens fall victim to an unhealthy social environment which has an adverse effect on their emotional and physical health.

3. Abuse and mistreatment: One in six older persons is a victim of abuse according to a study. Many elders fall victim to abuse and mistreatment by their own caregivers. Elder abuse can be of many forms like financial, emotional, physical and self. The elders should be provided with hygienic diet and a safe environment.

4. Ageism: Discrimination in the workplace because of age is something that many working senior citizens experience. One of the examples can be seen in the work opportunities given to older actors in the film industry especially older women who are not given good roles in films. Ageism is a very serious problem that many people turn a blind eye to.

5. Role of family values: The family values instilled in the families also play a very important role in the treatment of the elderly in the family. A family of poor financial background plays an important role in the treatment of elderly in a family. The interpersonal relations of the elderly within the family also contribute to the social environment which has an effect on the physical and emotional health of an individual.

Therefore, the young members of the family should be taught to respect their elders and not see them as a burden or not notice them at all.

6. Remedies for the senior citizens: As mentioned before, the current pandemic has made us realise our ignorance towards the senior citizens of the society. The government of our country is responsible for the welfare of the senior citizens. The government can help in the betterment of the senior citizens by making schemes and laws while keeping the directive principles in mind. The directive principles which should be the guiding frameworks, legislative act and governmental schemes are explained below.

Provisions by Constitution of India

Directive Principles

The Constitution of India also has provisions for the equal treatment of the elderly of the country in the Part IV i.e directive principles of state policy. The directive principles are not enforceable like the fundamental rights, but the government has to keep them in mind while making laws etc. The following articles in Section IV aim at protection of the elderly.

1. Article 41

According to article 41,"The State shall, within the limits of its economic capacity and development, make effective provision for securing the right to work, to education and to public assistance in cases of unemployment, old age, sickness and disablement, and in other cases of undeserved want." in simpler terms, it is the state's duty to provide jobs and other necessary help to the elderly, so that they can be independent and live a respectful life.

2. Article 38(1)

This article states that the State shall strive to promote the welfare of the people by securing and protecting as effectively as it may, a social order in which justice-social, economic and political, shall prevail over all the institutions of national life. This directive encourages the State to make laws that would be beneficial for the elderly as well as other citizens of the country.

3. Article 39(e)

That the health and strength of workers, men and women, and the tender age of children are not abused and that citizens are not forced by economic necessity to enter a vocation unsuited to their age or strength. According to this article, the health and strength should be protected and no one should be abused which includes elderly too.

Laws by the Legislation

Maintenance and Welfare of Parents and Senior Citizens Act, 2007

The Maintenance and Welfare of Senior Citizens Act was passed by legislation to provide support to elderly parents. The aim of this was to reduce the abuse of the senior citizens. According to this act, a maintenance tribunal was established to provide relief and support to the elderly effectively and taking relatively less time.

The Section 19 of this Act also mandated the establishment of an old age home in every district. The act defines "children" as sons, daughters, grandsons and granddaughters and parents include biological, adoptive and step-parents.

This act is for the welfare of senior citizens who are not able to take care of themselves and require financial support from their children. And in case of childless senior citizens, the relatives are supposed to take their responsibility. The Parents can opt to claim maintenance either under Section 125 of the Criminal Procedure Code, 1973 or under this Act but they cannot opt for both.

Governmental Schemes and Programmes

The government of India has established many schemes and Programmes for the betterment of our senior citizens. The following are the schemes that every senior citizen should know:

1. Integrated Programme for Older Persons (IPOP): This programme is run and managed by the Ministry of Social Justice and Empowerment. The main aim of this scheme is to improve the quality of life of the elderly by providing them basic things like shelter, food, a voice to represent themselves and medical care. Panchayati raj institutions/ local bodies, non-governmental voluntary organisations, etc. are eligible for assistance under the scheme as Implementing agencies. Under this programme, several grants are given to old age homes, day care centres and mobile medicare units, multi-facility care centres for older widows.

2. Rashtriya Vayoshri Yojana (RVY): This scheme too is run by the Ministry of the Social Justice and Empowerment. This is funded from the Senior Citizens' Welfare Fund. The fund was made in the year 2016. The scheme aims to provide aids and assistive living devices to the senior citizens who are financially too weak to afford them. Older people suffer from geriatric syndrome which encompasses all the age-related difficulties. They provide help by giving them walking sticks, elbow crutches, wheelchairs etc.

3. Indira Gandhi National Old Age Pension Scheme (IGNOAPS): This scheme is maintained by The Ministry of Rural Development. Social assistance is extended to poor households for the elderly, widows, disabled, and in cases of death where the sole earning member has passed away, it is provided by The National Social Assistance Programme (NSAP).

This scheme also provides financial assistance to older people aged above 60 years and are below the poverty line. Central assistance of ₹ 200 per month is provided to older persons aged between 60-79 years and ₹ 500 per month to persons aged 80 years and above.

4. Varishtha Pension Bima Yojana (VPBY): This scheme is maintained by The Ministry of Finance. It was launched in 2003 and then relaunched in 2014. They are both social security schemes for senior citizens, aiming to give an assured minimum pension on a guaranteed minimum return on the subscription amount. Life Insurance Corporation (LIC) of India implements this scheme.

5. The Pradhan Mantri Vaya Vandana Yojana: This scheme was launched in May 2017. It aims at providing social security during old age.

Under the scheme, a minimum pension of ₹ 1000 per month is paid for the initial lump sum amount of ₹ 1,50,000 and a maximum pension of ₹ 5000 is provided per month for lump sum amount of ₹ 7,50,000.

Subscribers of this scheme are assured of pension based on a guaranteed rate of return of 8% per annum, payable monthly/quarterly/half-yearly/annually.

The duration of this scheme is a period of ten years.

6. National Programme for the Health Care of Elderly (NPHCE): This scheme(NPHCE) was launched by The Ministry of Health & Family

Welfare during 2010-11 to provide help with various health-related problems of elderly people. The major objectives of this scheme at the district level is to provide dedicated health facilities in district hospitals, community health centres (CHC), sub-centres (SC) along with primary health centres (PHC) levels through State Health Society. The healthcare facilities provided are either free or subsidised.

The following are some facilities provided by this programme.

- Geriatric OPD along with 10-bedded geriatric ward at district hospitals.
- Weekly geriatric clinic at primary health centres (PHC)
- Provision of aids and appliances at sub-centres

7. The pandemic: With their backs already against the wall, the global pandemic has not helped their situation. It has led to many problems for the senior citizens. The following are some of them

Lockdown Blues

Being in lockdown and being cut off from their friends and families, is challenging for them. Many senior citizens used to go to temples and for evening walks with friends but because of the lockdown they have to stay at home.

Self-isolation

Many elderlies had to stay in self-isolation or quarantine in case of getting infected. As 60% of the infected patients are elderly and people with comorbidities, the number of elderly to stay in self-isolation is also large. Self-isolation though for their own safety, affects the mental and emotional health of the senior citizens.

Abuse

The number of cases of abuse has increased in the coronavirus pandemic. As many people had to stay in, the elderly became more vulnerable to physical abuse. But contrary to common belief, the senior citizens are stronger than they look and have managed their situation to the best of their capabilities.

The coronavirus pandemic has also witnessed the rise of **Telehealth/Telemedicine** i.e use of technology to attend to the patients. The technology includes video calling, voice call etc. The information is given to the patients digitally so that both the doctors and the patients remain safe. The pandemic has promoted the use of telehealth facilities provided by a number of hospitals to their patients. The global pandemic has resulted in new ways to reach and help our senior citizens; one of the best examples is telemedicines. By using telemedicines, the senior citizens can consult their doctors through them.

References

1. https://www.betterhealth.vic.gov.au/health/ConditionsAndTreatments/kidneys-age-related-problems
2. https://www.kidneynews.org/kidney-news/special-sections/geriatric-nephrology/caring-for-elderly-patients-with-kidney-disease-the-geriatrician%E2%80%93nephrologist-collaboration
3. https://www.nia.nih.gov/health/heart-health-and-aging
4. https://www.webmd.com/heart/understanding-low-blood-pressure-basics#1
5. https://www.ncbi.nlm.nih.gov/pmc/articles/PMC4292097/
6. https://www.ncbi.nlm.nih.gov/pmc/articles/PMC3503373/#:~:text=However%2C%20a%20study%20in%20rural,areas%20reported%20prevalence%20of%2053.5%25.
7. https://www.nhp.gov.in/disease/musculo-skeletal-bone-joints-/osteoarthritis#:~:text=Osteoarthritis%20is%20the%20second%20most,show%20radiological%20evidence%20of%20OA.
8. https://www.who.int/news-room/fact-sheets/detail/diabetes#:~:text=Key%20facts,in%20premature%20mortality%20from%20diabetes.
9. https://www.aging.com/seniors-and-diabetes-a-complete-guide/
10. https://www.who.int/news-room/fact-sheets/detail/mental-health-of-older-adults
11. https://www.google.com/url?sa=t&source=web&rct=j&url=https://www.news18.com/amp/news/india/memorys-last-breath-living-with-alzheimers-in-india-1827271.html&ved = 2ahUKEwiZhI6lwJ_qAhUBlEsFHfqgDzwQFjANegQICxA0& usg = AOvVaw2s1UhOBUvQn29ML8kUz1ph&ampcf=1
12. https://www.mayoclinic.org/diseases-conditions/parkinsons-disease/symptoms-causes/syc-20376055
13. https://www.thequint.com/news/india/government-schemes-for-senior-citizens
14. https://www.clearias.com/constitution-of-india/

15. https://nhrc.nic.in/sites/default/files/Project%20Report%20on%20the%20Rights%20of%20the%20Elderly_NUALS.pdf
16. https://indiankanoon.org/doc/129471/#:~:text=Article%2039%20%28e%29%20in%20The%20Constitution%20Of%20India,enter%20avocations%20unsuited%20to%20their%20age%20or%20strength%3B
17. http://www.indianjpsychiatry.org/article.asp?issn=0019-5545;year=2018;volume=60;issue=2;spage=165;epage=167;aulast=Sathianathan

□

Director Dadi-Dada Foundation, is a diligent and empathetic social worker with a vibrant experience of working with various reputed organisations such as Centre For Economic Policy Research, Tata Institute of Social Science, Heritage Foundation, Global education promotion council, India Today, to name a few. Under his guidance and supervision, the Dadi-Dada foundation has achieved global recognition as a member of Global Alliance for the Rights of Older People (GAROP).

Self-reliance in Information Technology

—**Kunal Bagal**

Atmanirbhar Bharat is a holistic idea and Information Technology is indispensable discipline of this concept. India has made huge strides in IT sector increasing from 1.2 % of GDP in 1998 to 7.7% in 2017. Self-reliance in IT sector will produce a multiplier effect in Five pillars of Atmanirbhar Bharat-economy, demography, technologically-driven system, infrastructure and demand. This will take us closer to the realisation of our dream of Atmanirbhar Bharat.

Data being the 'new oil', must be generated, consumed and monetised within the country. All the current internet and other key platforms are foreign-owned. India's contribution to the global telecom supply chain is miniscule while being the 2nd largest telecom market in the world. The focus should shift towards the supply side from the demand side. India imports electronics worth 400B$, and this needs to change.

Microsoft or Google were not built in a day. There might be thousand failure stories behind a Microsoft's success story. If we build an environment to nurture multiple start-ups, we can build a company like Google or Microsoft, so the idea is not to build google, idea is to create environment so that thousands of start-ups with aim to be best in their area evolve, and at the end, we will have one like Google. Environment for 'thousands of innovations', 'expectation of failures' and 'determination to continue' will lead to 'an Indian google'. Govt. can set up a PSU like DRDO to promote and support technological initiatives. ISRO is run by a scientist and government representative reports to him rather than a telecom ministry where a person from any background can run the show. A professional should run such PSU. India has to create the right environment to build world-class companies.

Bhartnet-world's largest rural broadband project-The ultimate aim should have been connecting a world-class doctor's service to a patient in rural India, universities to students, or taking technology to help farmers but it was merely limited to laying fiber optics to each nook and corner of India. The last leg (the ultimate connectivity and services to user's mobile phone) was not worked upon with the same zeal as the project itself. Time has come to think holistically, have a broader picture and do not do things for the sake of doing it, rather achieve an ultimate goal.

If India wants to be self-reliant in IT sector, then, apart from creating world-class software applications, making India a hub for hardware and focusing on how to increase internal demand and consumption for IT services, there is a need to seriously look at the new technologies such as 5G, Artificial Intelligence, Quantum computing, as they are going to play a vital role in future. Advancements in such technologies can improve the quality of agricultural products, climate intelligence, forecasting solutions, machine learning to identify crop stages, artificial intelligence to reduce crop wastage, soil health monitoring, plant image recognition and geospatial tracking. NITI Ayog estimates that adopting AI means a 15% boost for the gross value added (GVA) for the economy by 2035 and can create millions of jobs.

After security concerns around the world w.r.t Huawei, India can fill that gap before Taiwan can do but Manufacturing and Innovation is key here. Govt. has announced fresh investments worth at least ₹ 50,000 crore in the electronics sector. The 26 GHz band spectrum is widely seen by telecom operators worldwide as amongst the most efficient airwaves for delivery of affordable 5G services. These airwaves are also ideal for industrial applications. The approval processes and price discovery mechanism should be Govt. priority and there should not be any delay in making decisions. Speaking at the Annual General Meeting (AGM) of RIL, Ambani said that the "Made-in-India" technology can be deployed and launched in a year's time, once spectrum is available. Rising adoption of 'Internet of Things (IoT)' devices will continue to drive the demand for 5G.

India should not end up having to rely on Western nations for the latest computing technologies in the future. In a bid to be self-reliant in quantum computing and other related technologies, India plans to invest ₹ 8,000 crore over the next five years in the National Mission on

Quantum Technology or the Quantum-Enabled Science & Technology (QuEST) programme. It also called for greater thrust on experimental research and an increase in the pool of researchers in the area of quantum technologies. Developing quantum computational capacity should be India's "top national priority", simply because acquiring such technologies from outside the country will be too difficult and expensive. The use of quantum computing can lead to many fundamental scientific breakthroughs and new technologies with wide-ranging societal and commercial applications such as data encryption, new drug discovery, and weather prediction. Few simple steps that can be performed by Govt. is to- Identify the strengths and weaknesses of major research groups working in the area of quantum computing and set appropriate milestones with sufficient funding. Have regular workshops and conferences among such groups. Establish national level high value fellowships to encourage doctoral and postdoctoral researchers to work in this area.

As of 2020, India's IT workforce accounts for 4.36 million employees. According to NASSCOM, the sector generated revenue standing at US$ 180 billion in 2019, with export revenue at US$ 99 billion and domestic revenue at US$ 48 billion. There is a huge potential for IT sector in Indian domestic base. With tremendous strides in internet connectivity, there is huge demand for IT services, and a lot of this space has been used by foreign players. Recently the Govt. banned Chinese apps on account of security, so there is a need for atmanirbhar bharat to achieve national security and digital sovereignty.

□

A bachelor of Engineering in Information Technology with 15 years of experience in building software and application solutions for various investment banks, Asset management firms and hedge funds around the globe.

Ancient India to Modern India

—CA Rajanikant Sharma

Bharat was a country of Rishis and Saints who had started their lives on the banks of rivers and on mountains. They had limited needs and were always thinking about the welfare of all human beings and creatures residing with them. They were connected to each other internally and discovered the existence of nature and Supreme power. Whatever we are rediscovering and researching, had already been written and described in our Vedas and Sutras. As the time passed, we lost our values and learning. Lord Krishna narrated in Holy Gita, whenever Adharma prevails on this holy land, I will appear in some form for the rescue of humanity. Our county never invaded any country, but our Saints spread their knowledge of wisdom in the whole of Asia. Our Country was self-dependent and was rich in culture and natural resources. It was invaded and ruled by number of Kings and religions, but either they merged with the large hearted people of this country or left the country with our wealth, but still we never had any enmity with those invaders. We have forgotten our values and strength but the present Government thought about again making this country self-dependent. Covid-19, though a pandemic, has provided an opportunity to think and work towards being self-dependent country. If we travel back to our past memories, we can realise how our villages were self-dependent with our limited requirements of basic needs. We were happy, peaceful, contented and full of love to each other, without any differences of caste, creed and religion. We used to celebrate all festivals of all religions, and a marriage in the village used to give a festive look with lunch & dinner for full village. On the other side, a death in the village was sorrow for all and no one would have taken meals before the finishing of last rites. For a pot of water, our family used to walk 4 to 5 Kms, no electricity in our village and used to study either in day time only or on examination days under the light of chimney made by our mothers and grandmothers. Lanterns were the luxury for rich families, but still we never felt any scarcity. For calls of nature, every member of village has to walk away from the village with a small pot of water in hand because water was in scarcity and there was no latrine in houses. We must appreciate the drive of our beloved Prime Minister to provide support to construct a washroom for each house and to provide electricity and water to all houses in villages. Today, our villages have turned into towns, towns turned into cities and cities have become Metros and under this turnaround, we lost the values of humanity. It's the time now to think about our lost values and to take the lead in different types of development, with our important resource of huge population. Always we were taught and said that huge population was the reason for our backwardness and shackle on development. Our mind was tuned to blame the population for all causes of backwardness in comparison to developed countries. But under the present leadership, we understood the strength of population when our Prime Minister says proudly on international platforms that I am the representative of 130 crore Indians. Truly speaking, our country has been blessed with plenty of natural resources, not properly tapped and utilised by our past leadership; now under the present leadership, we have seen the light of hope. Self-dependent India means development on all fronts and sectors of economy. Agricultural sector was ignored by past Governments, and we were dependent on other countries for food. We can remember the days of our childhood when poor quality of wheat got imported from Australia and America at the time of drought in the country. Agriculture-dependent economy can sustain all sorts of ups and downs, which was neglected all along the years. Agricultural sector must be the limelight of any development. We must appreciate the efforts of present Government, where agri cultivation to marketing of products were properly financed and channelised and where farmers could get proper price for their hard work. Secondly, young generation will not run away from the villages to cities, as all their needs were properly attended in villages. Our land is fertile and water resources by way of various rivers, should be managed in such a way that there will not be drought in one area and flood in other part of country. The connectivity of rivers was the dream of our leaders but it remained only in books and records. It is the right time for present leadership to take initiative to start this dream project.

Education is the second most important sector where ancient India had University like Nalanda University, but today, not even one University comes in top 100 universities of the world. Our students, who are capable and rich enough, would like to go abroad for higher studies and would never come back to their own country. We are on seven clouds, when we see most of the big multinational companies are headed by emigrant Indians, who left India for studies or opportunity for better life abroad. Covid-19 has shown us the shortage of doctors and nursing staff in ratio with our population, because our country has limited medical colleges with limited seats where the children of rich family can get admission and manage to continue their education. It is time to change the rules and regulations of the Medical Council and the sector can be opened to small and affordable medical colleges in rural areas.

Third most important sector is health, which is fully dependent on agriculture and medical sectors. Proper nutritious meals at village and town level, will bring competitive sports persons and good health to the people of country.

For the last two decades, our service sector is in limelight which shows our capability and strength of education; we are the leader in software and service providers where the whole world is looking towards us for our competitive and best services but we still have some scope of development for hardware sector where our hardware sector can match with software sector.

We are far behind in industrial development, as wealth is stored in limited hands of society. Number of restrictive laws stopped our development which were removed by our new leadership but still bureaucracy and some laws and licenses come as hurdles in putting up the industry. Present government initiatives to have single window clearance will certainly attract investors to invest in India.

Self-dependent India does not mean we restrict our imports and exports but export will be in surplus and there will be development of all sectors of economy. We are now discussing about the theory of "Global Village", where all countries will support each other without interfering in their sovereignty.

We are the firm believer of 'Vasudevam Kudumbakkam' and also believe in the Theory of Karma. We never intruded on any country and would not like any attack or intervention on our country. We are the strict follower of 'Maryada of Ram', but are also guided by the principles of Lord Krishna to take out 'Sudarshanam Chakra' on demand of situation and win the battle by any means of Dharam, Arth, Kama and Moksha.

Self-reliant India is a dream of the present Leadership and we must support our leaders with all means in hands wherever we live and make the dream come true of 'SELF-RELIANT POWERFUL INDIA.'

A small story which I read few months back will motivate all Indians to work towards self-reliant India,

A wealthy man was enjoying sunshine with his coffee when a little ant caught his eyes, which was going from one side to other side of balcony carrying a big leaf several times bigger than her. The man watched it for more than an hour. He saw that the ant faced many obstacles but paused, and took diversion and continued towards her destination. At one point, ant came across a big crack on the floor. She paused for a little, analyzed and then put the huge leaf over the crack and walked over the leaf, picked the leaf from other side, then continued its journey. The incident left the man in awe and forced him to contemplate over the miracle of Creation. When a tiny creation of Creator can overcome all obstacles and reach her destination, why can't we join the hands with the present leadership and make our country SELF-RELIANT.

----* JAI HIND *----* JAI HIND *----* JAI HIND *----

□

B.Com., FCA and a corporate consultant. He is a spiritual personality.

Self-reliant India

—**D.K. Upadhyay & Ashish Sharma**

In mid-May, Prime Minister Narendra Modi gave a call for *self-reliance* while announcing the phasing out of the corona virus-induced lockdown and amid border tension with China, prompting the government to impose curbs on Chinese imports, investments and mobile applications. India has been heavily dependent on China for mobile phones, electronic goods and pharmaceuticals, resulting in a massive trade deficit. The call for self-reliance has been envisioned to boost the domestic economy while reducing dependence on foreign counterparts. It is a reminder as well as an extension of the earlier *Make in India* campaign launched in 2020, focused on boosting domestic production and increasing the share of the manufacturing sector in the economy.

While the Covid-19 outbreak poses several challenges to the global economic system, it has also opened up the possible ways in which countries can display their capabilities. Indian, through their resilience, have locally tried to overcome challenges of N95 masks and PPE kits in innovative ways, drawing inspiration from the Prime Minister's *Atmanirbhar Bharat* slogan. The Prime Minister, drawing upon his earlier slogan of manufacturing in the country with 'zero defects' while ensuring 'zero effect' on the environment has suggested that policies, processes and products must be 'par excellence' in the globalised competitive world. This *Atmanirbhar Bharat* strategy is not just limited to limiting imports. According to the Prime Minister, "when we talk about becoming self-reliant, we do not merely refer to decreasing the import demands. When we talk of self-reliance, it is about our skills, our human resources. When we start sourcing things from abroad, our capabilities start depleting and consequently, it gets completely destroyed over generations. We need to preserve it and enhance that caliber of ours. We need to accentuate our skills, our creativity and with that we need to touch new heights. We need to strengthen skill development for a self-reliant India for improving our competency." Far from suggesting a centralised, top-down model directed from the 'commanding heights' of the Planning Commission, the Prime Minister suggests freeing Indian entrepreneurship and innovation from bureaucratic hurdles. This is about decentralised localism that takes pride in local brands, emphasizes resilience and flexibility and encourages local capacity-building and indigenisation.

While *Make in India* was launched just after PM Modi came to power in 2014, the *Self-Reliant India* package of Rs. 20 lakh crore has been announced for reviving an ailing economy in the post-lockdown scenario amidst the siege by Covid-19. Similar on several grounds, the timing and purpose of both campaigns is dependent on different circumstances. *Make in India* was launched to spur up productivity and employment generation capacity of manufacturing sector by creating a business-friendly environment that would help private investments and foreign capital. On the other hand, *Self-Reliant India* makes clear the dual objectives that the package will serve: to restore the stagnant Indian economy through fiscal measures, and to make the economy self-reliant. In particular, to achieve this goal of *self-reliance*, the special economic package worth Rs. 20 lakh crore or 10% of India's GDP in 2019-20 is motivated by an approach of boosting the supply-side through the easing of loans and short-term fiscal incentives. The special economic package will focus on land, labour, liquidity and laws. It will cater to various sections including cottage industry, MSMEs, labour, middle class industries, among others. The package will also focus on empowering the poor, labour, migrants etc., both from organised and unorganised sectors. As a result, the aim is to create a robust domestic economic system through investment and consumption demand. This does not preclude foreign investment for which congenial business environment is desirable. This is why the Prime Minister's speech while reiterating the ambition of the 5-trillion-dollar economy, talks of the package's focus on land, labour, liquidity and laws. The *Atmanirbhar* campaign is very much a boost to the already in place *Make in India* strategy.

An even more laudable addition to the self-reliance campaign was given through the Prime Minister in his seventieth Independence Day address. PM Modi pitched the nation as a manufacturing hub, with 'Make for World' as the mantra so that local value additions help the country make the switch from a supplier of natural resources and raw materials and importer of finished products. While our country has plenty of natural resources, it is the need of the hour that we start the value addition to these natural resources and human resources; and take the country to new heights. The PM stressed on the importance of promoting 'local' products. For this purpose, the central government also intends to integrate rural industry and the farm sector into the overall strategy and promising to set up Special Economic Zones in rural areas. A web of agriculture and non-agriculture industries will be created and we shall be trying to create Farmer Product Associations which will go a long way in their economic empowerment.

The *Atmanirbhar* campaign is a circle back to the philosophies of great thinkers like Swami Vivekananda. Diverging from the socialist era thinking, it is about resilience, leveraging internal strengths, personal responsibility and a sense of national mission. The recently announced liberalization of the agriculture sector is a good illustration of this world view and its economic implications. Since the 1950s, Indian agriculture policy has been driven by two sets of laws i.e. the Essential Commodities Act (ECA) and the state-level Agricultural Produce Marketing Committee (APMC) Acts. Together, these draconian laws gave government officials the power to tell farmers where to sell their produce, restrict transportation, fix prices, confiscate stocks and even imprison so-called 'hoarders'. The scrapping of the ECA-APMC system enables localised decision-making by farmers even as they can participate in a national common market or export to the global market. Similarly, traders can now invest in supply-chains and agri-businesses without the fear of being arbitrarily labelled a hoarder by an inspector. The government still has a role but it is as an enabler, providing soft and hard infrastructure. The same economic philosophy is reflected in several other supply-side measures announced recently. *Self-Reliance* implies that product and factor markets are made flexible in order to allow the Indian economy to adapt to the problems and opportunities of an emerging post—Covid world. Thus, there is an unapologetic commitment to privatization of non-strategic public sector entities, opening up of new sectors like space to private investment, decriminalisation of most aspects of corporate law, greater flexibility in labour laws and so on. Self-reliant India should stand on 5 pillars of Economy, Infrastructure, System, Demography and Demand, says the Prime Minister, essential in a post Covid-19 world.

Self-reliance also means a commitment to resilience at multiple levels i.e. at a national level, an industry level, and at an individual level. The incentive structure of defense procurement has been changed to encourage indigenisation even as foreigners are encouraged to manufacture in India.

The same idea of resilience, when applied to individuals and vulnerable social groups, calls for the creation of safety nets. This explains the effort to create a health insurance system through *Ayushman Bharat* and the direct benefit transfer mechanism based on *Jan Dhan-Aadhar-Mobile*. An intellectual framework of *self-reliance* leads to health insurance and direct benefit transfer. A decentralised system, where economic entities are expected to be self-reliant, requires a generalised system of social trust and the ability to enforce contracts. In turn, it implies a need to carry out administrative reforms and, more specifically, reform of the legal system. As argued repeatedly in recent Economic Surveys, the inefficiencies and delays of the legal system are now the single biggest hurdle to economic development. This is not just about the judicial process but the wider ecosystem of rules, regulations, policing, investigation and so on. It is not a coincidence that Prime Minister Modi had clearly mentioned 'Law' as one of the pillars of his vision.

In addition, the Prime Minister has outlined the contours of this new *Self-Reliant* India across all spheres i.e. education, health, agriculture, manufacturing, infrastructure, trade, defense, foreign policy, environment, digital connectivity; for all segments of society—the poor, the middle class, women, young, entrepreneurs, labour; and in all regions—from Kashmir to the North-east, from urban to rural areas. Prime Minister Modi's call for an *Atmanirbhar Bharat* is not just a slogan but a vision with deep roots in India's intellectual tradition, one that will push our country to the forefront of the globalised world.

□□□

An academician by profession and President awardee. He is a social and political activist.

MBA Finance and corporate consultant and specialises in finance and banking.